Angels of Mercy
or Development Diplomats?

NGOs & Foreign Aid

D1382374

**Other titles on Aid, NGOs & Development
from James Currey, Africa World Press & Red Sea Press**

A Blighted Harvest
The World Bank
& African Agriculture in the 1980s
PETER GIBBON, KJELL J. HAVNEVIK
& KENNETH HERMELE

Beyond Conflict in the Horn
The Prospects for Peace, Recovery & Development
in Ethiopia, Somalia, Eritrea & Sudan
MARTIN DOORNBOS, LIONEL CLIFFE,
ABDEL GHAFFAR M. AHMED & JOHN MARKAKIS

*Frontline Nationalism
in Angola & Mozambique*
DAVID BIRMINGHAM

When Refugees Go Home
African Experiences
TIM ALLEN & HUBERT MORSINK (editors)

In Search of Cool Ground
War, Flight & Homecoming in Northeast Africa
TIM ALLEN (editor)

The People on the Edge in the Horn
Displacement, Land Use & the Environment
in Gedaref Region, Sudan
GAIM KIBREAB

Angels of Mercy
or Development Diplomats?

NGOs & Foreign Aid

TERJE TVEDT
Centre for Development Studies
University of Bergen

AFRICA WORLD PRESS
TRENTON

JAMES CURREY
OXFORD

James Currey Ltd
73 Botley Road
Oxford
OX2 0BS

Africa World Press, Inc.
P.O. Box 1892
Trenton
NJ 08607-1892

© Terje Tvedt 1998

First published 1998

1 2 3 4 5 02 01 00 99 98

British Library Cataloguing in Publication Data
Tvedt, Terje
    Angels of mercy or development diplomats? : NGOs & foreign aid
    1. Non-governmental organizations 2. Economic development
    3. Economic assistance
    I. Title
    338.9

ISBN 0–85255–817–1 (James Currey cased)
ISBN 0–85255–818–X (James Currey paper)

ISBN 0–86543–675–4 (Africa World Press, cloth)
ISBN 0–86543–676–2 (Africa World Press, paper)

Typeset in 10¼/11 Bembo and Optima display by
Long House Publishing Services, Cumbria, England

Printed and bound in the United States of America

Contents

List of Tables

List of Figures

List of Acronyms

ACROSS	Africa Committee for Refugees from the Southern Sudan
ADAB	Association of Development Agencies in Bangladesh
AGO	Anti-Governmental Organization
ANC	African National Congress
AO	Associational Organization
BNELC	Bangladesh Northern Evangelical Lutheran Church
BRAC	Bangladesh Rural Advancement Committee
CADEC	Catholic Development Commission
CARE	Committee for Assistance and Relief Everywhere
CBO	Community-based Organization
CIA	Central Intelligence Agency
CIDA	Canadian International Development Agency
CEPAD	Consejo de Iglesis Evangelicas Pro-Alianza Denominacional
CO	Charitable Organization
CRDA	Christian Relief and Development Association
CSO	Civil Society Organization
DAC	Development Assistance Committee, OECD
DANIDA	Danish International Development Agency
DM	Dainik Millat
DONGO	Donor Governmental Organization
DS	Daily Sangram
DUH	The Royal Norwegian Ministry of Development Co-operation
EEC	European Economic Community
EECMY	The Ethiopian Evangelical Church Mekane Yesus
ELF	Eritrean Liberation Front
EOC	Ethiopian Orthodox Church
EPLF	Eritrean People's Liberation Front
EPRDF	Ethiopian People's Revolutionary Democratic Front
ERA	Ertitrean Relief Association
ERCCS	Eritrean Red Cross and Red Crescent Society
ERD	Eritrean Relief Desk
ERRA	Eritrean Relief and Rehabilitation Association
ESAP	Economic Structural Adjustment Programme
FACS	Fundacion Augusto Cesar Sandina

FINNIDA	Finnish International Development Agency
FORUT	Campaign for Development and Solidarity
GANGO	Gap-filling Organization
GO	Grassroots Organization
GONGO	Governmental Non-governmental Organization
GSS	Gonoshahajjo Sangstha
ICNPO	International Classification of Non-profit Organization
IDENGO	International Classification of Development NGOs
INGO	International Non-governmental Organization
IO	Independent Organization
ISIC	International Standard Industrial Classification
JRP	Joint Relief Programme
Ksh	Kenya shillings
LWF	Lutheran World Federation
LWR	Lutheran World Relief
MEEC	Ministry of Economic and External Co-operation, Ethiopia
MFA	Ministry of Foreign Affairs, Norway
NACE	European Community's General Industrial Classification of Economic Activities
NANGO	National Association of Non-governmental Organizations (Zimbabwe)
NCA	Norwegian Church Aid
NCA/SP	Norwegian Church Aid/Sudan Programme
NCR/SP	Norwegian Church Relief/Sudan Programme
NCDPZ	The National Council of Disabled Persons of Zimbabwe
NGO	Non-governmental Organization
NLM	Norwegian Lutheran Mission
NMS	Norwegian Missionary Society
NOK	Norwegian Kroner
NORAD	Norwegian Agency for International Development
NOU	Norwegian Public Reports
NOVIB	Netherlands Organization for International Development Co-operation
NPA	Norwegian People's Aid
NTEE	National Taxonomy of Exempt Entities
OCCZIM	Organization of Collective Co-operatives in Zimbabwe
ODA	Official Development Assistance
ODI	Overseas Development Institute
OECD	Organization for Economic Co-operation and Development
ORA	Oromo Relief Association
ORAP	Organization of Rural Associations for Progress
PCS	Public Service Contractors
PFP	Partnership for Productivity Service Foundation, Kenya
PGE	Provisional Government, Ethiopia
PRIV	Office of Private Organization, NORAD
PSO	Public Service Organization
PVDO	Private Voluntary Development Organization
PVO	Private Voluntary Organization
QUANGO	Quasi-non-governmental Organization
RDC	Rural Development Council

REST	Relief Society of Tigray
RRC	Relief and Rehabilitation Commission, Ethiopia
SADCC	Southern African Development Community (prev. Co-ordination Conference)
SAIH	Norwegian Students' and Academics' International Assistance Fund
SCC	Sudan Council of Churches
SCR	Swedish Church Relief
SEBA	Society for Economic and Basic Advancement, Bangladesh
SIDA	Swedish International Development Authority
SPLA	Sudan People's Liberation Army
SSU	Sudanese Socialist Union
SRRA	Sudan Relief and Rehabilitation Association
TPLF	Tigrayan People's Liberation Front
UNDP	United Nations Development Programme
USAID	United States Agency for International Development
VASS	Voluntary Agency Support Scheme
VO	Voluntary Organization
WB	World Bank
WCC	World Council of Churches
YMCA	Zimbabwe National Council of Young Men's Christian Association
ZANU(PF)	Zimbabwe African National Union (Patriotic Front)
ZERO	Zimbabwe Energy Research Organization

Introduction

Is the world witnessing a global associational revolution spearheaded by development non-governmental organizations (NGOs)? Is the relationship between states and societies being fundamentally redefined, even in remote, rural corners of the world? What role does the mushrooming of development NGOs play in this political-ideological process? And what about the NGO staff? Are they angels of mercy, government-paid development diplomats, propagandists for a triumphant West, instruments in a coming clash between civilizations, or what? This book will try to shed new light on these large complex questions. It aims in particular, to make studies and discussions of these topics more fruitful and better informed, and less influenced by the political rhetoric of the day and untenable myths about NGO achievements. It puts forward a strong critique of central theories and concepts which have dominated research and discourse on development NGOs. It also proposes and demonstrates some rather different analytical approaches.

One question is obvious: how is one to describe and interpret the way the aid landscape has been fundamentally changed during the last 15 years or so? In the 1960s and 1970s there were very few NGOs engaged in aid, and in many developing countries only a handful were working as part of the development aid system. The 1980s has been named 'the NGO decade' in development aid. It was, obviously, very important in exporting the growth in NGOs from Western welfare states to the world at large. The total funds transferred by and through 'Northern' NGOs (those from industial countries) increased at twice the rate for international aid as a whole (UNDP, 1993a:88). About 4,000 development NGOs in OECD member countries,[1] dispersing billions of dollars a year, were working with about 10,000 to 20,000 'Southern' NGOs (from developing countries) who assisted, it has been estimated, between 100 and 250 million people.[2] The so-called NGO decade is over, but their heyday does not, apparently, belong to the past. High-placed advisers to the US Government talk about an enlarged role of the NGOs in the future of politics. The Clinton Administration has given more and more support to NGOs in aid; during President Clinton's first term in the White House the support to NGOs was due to increase from 13 to 50 per cent of the USAID budget in 1996, according to Vice-President Al Gore at the 1995 Social Summit in Copenhagen. As public spending on international affairs and overseas aid is gradually and sometimes radically being reduced in most donor countries, the relative importance of NGOs within the aid system will continue to grow. How can this growth be explained? How can NGOs be analysed and understood? Or even more fundamentally, what really is an NGO? And what is the relationship between states and NGOs, and between NGOs and what is now called 'civil society'? Do NGOs really represent the political future, or are most of them irrelevant when it comes to actual development processes? Should the proliferation of NGOs worldwide be hailed as an associational revolution that challenges global power relations? Or is the most important impact of the NGO system perhaps the fact that NGOs have played a very important role in bringing Western concepts of development and democracy to new elites in urban centres and to remote rural parts of the world? This book discusses these issues on the assumption that they are of interest both as an important aspect of modern global history and, more specifically, as central questions in the development aid field.

NGOs in aid are, of course, an aspect of the history of the country or region in which they work, but they are also an important but often neglected part of the donor country's modern history. The NGO decade has played an important role in recent Western ideological history. The line taken by humanitarian organizations in emergencies (the refugee exodus from Vietnam and the Boat-people in Indo-China in the 1970s, crises like those in the Horn of Africa in the 1970s and 1980s, the Rwanda horror stories of the 1990s) and in media coverage has been important in forming and reproducing fundamental development concepts and in shaping images and attitudes. The NGOs have organized altruism and symbolized the 'good act' in a 'post-modern' world, elsewhere characterized by moral fragmentation. They have emerged as symbols of societal responsibility and global morality. The NGO channel has thus been important for Western images of 'the other' and 'us' because the reality of the poor and the relationship between donor and receiver are often filtered through it. This interesting aspect of the impact of NGOs would require a separate analysis, and is not dealt with in this study.[3] The competition and co-operation among NGOs, their different relationships to the state, the amount of public funds transmitted through the NGO channel as compared with other institutions in society are focused on here, and have obviously affected the organizational landscape of donor countries in both institutional and political ways. This book therefore analyses NGOs not only in development aid in the narrow sense, but also as reflecting and impacting on the donor countries' history, because it is thought useful to try to understand the role of the NGO channel as a whole.

The rapid growth of NGOs has been enmeshed in different but powerful ideological currents. Particularly during the last decade or so a definite NGO-speak or NGO language has developed as a means for donors, NGO actors and researchers to communicate about NGOs' role in development ('comparative advantage', 'flexibility', 'empowering', 'grassrooting', 'representing democracy and pluralism', a 'response to state and market failures', etc.) and about development and 'the other' at large. This language has had an impact on the way the aid relationship has become structured and apprehended, and has influenced analytical approaches and theories of social development and supported a research tradition which can aptly be described as NGO-activism by other means. Without some clarification and a more rigorous use of concepts and approaches it is thought impossible to analyse and discuss the channel in a rational way. It is necessary to try to get beneath the political-ideological slogans not only to analyse the past, but also to understand the present and the future. This book takes as a starting point the fact that researchers, politicians, administrators and NGO professionals have been strongly influenced by products (whether true or false) of scientific theory and speculation:

> the ideas of economists and political philosophers ... are more powerful than is commonly understood. Indeed the world is ruled by little else. Practical men, who believe themselves to be quite exempt from any intellectual influences, are usually the slaves of some defunct economist. Madmen in authority, who hear voices in the air, are distilling their frenzy from some academic scribbler of a few years back.(Keynes, 1936, 1946 quoted in Gellner, 1988:12.)

The first four chapters of the book deal with central conceptual and analytical challenges in understanding NGOs. First they put forward a critique of influential concepts and approaches, because science must be criticism before it can be anything else. They also advance alternative approaches, concepts and classifications, so as to help establish a new way in which NGOs may be studied.

Chapter 1 deals with the problem of how to define and identify the organizations working in development aid. There is, and has been, widespread conceptual confusion about what an NGO is, expressed in a proliferation of acronyms. Different studies (and donors and NGOs) employ different concepts or conflicting definitions of the same concepts, without explaining why some are chosen and others implicitly rejected. Definitions have tended to be normative and ideological or so broad as to make discussion and comparison difficult. The chapter discusses definitional practices and argues that a definition should be sought that is universal, descriptive and not normative, and which acknowledges and focuses attention on how NGOs in development aid affect and interact with those parts of a society's organizational landscape which are not directly linked to or a part of this particular channel's resource transfer.

It also deals with the problem of the classification of development NGOs. How NGOs are classified expresses policy orientations and ideological concerns. The way they have generally been classified has tended to create more confusion than clarity. The chapter demonstrates how classifications developed for understanding their role in Western welfare states are not particularly helpful. Classifications employed within the development field are also found to be too vague or too ideological.

In aid, classification systems have been proposed that appear to be neutral, although, as shown, they are often based on untenable assumptions about the characteristics of development NGOs. The need for classification systems that reflect different cultural and political traditions and contexts is discussed, and a new general classification system is put forward in order to encourage more systematic thinking and allow for better planning.

Chapter 2 deals with a question which has important analytical and policy implications: why do NGOs exist? It examines the dominant functional explanations, and argues that these theories cannot explain the historical evolution and position of NGOs in development aid in different countries. Rather, it maintains that they have contributed to a research tradition in which the concrete historical background and actual societal role of development NGOs have been of marginal interest. The tradition has, moreover, helped to create a justification for NGOs in development which is untenable.

The chapter concludes that development NGOs should be regarded as a product of deliberate state policies rather than as the natural outcome of state and market failures. This policy originated in the OECD countries as a result of US and UN initiatives and pressures in the early 1960s. In many countries the state was instrumental in creating the NGO channel in order to broaden the basis, support and financial input for aid. During the 1980s NGOs were promoted internationally by the 'right' as part of the 'new political agenda', but were also supported by the populist 'left' as an answer to the problem of the state. The chapter focuses here on the importance of studying the historical development of donor government initiatives behind the growth of the NGO community.

Chapter 3 discusses a related problem: how should an NGO scene in a particular country be analysed or understood? Functionalist analysis is shown to be insufficient. The growth and strong position of non-governmental organizations have often been conceived of as necessary or historically natural. But merely by comparing countries like Norway, France, Great Britain and Japan, it can be indicated that alternative explanations must be sought. In 1988 the NGOs in these countries received 15, 0.3, 0.4 and 0.7 per cent respectively from the official aid budgets, while in Switzerland the figure was more than 17 per cent of ordinary aid appropriations (OECD, 1990:16). Generalizations built on the perception that 'the state needs private aid organizations', or that the growth of NGOs can be explained by general economic laws about the higher costs of other ways of organizing these activities, cannot be sustained. In trying to understand the position and function of the NGO field, general statements of this kind are of little value.

An alternative, the 'national-style approach' which focuses on the importance of national political and cultural traditions for existing organizational landscapes and relationships with the state and market, is discussed. It is argued that this approach might be useful in a Western welfare state context. It is not so fruitful in a development aid context, however. The NGO scene in countries like Zimbabwe and Bangladesh and the development NGOs' role in Norway are shown to express national traditions and national historical developments. But because of the importance of the NGO channel and the way it functions, it needs to be placed in a concrete historical context, as an intermediary between national tradition and history and different kinds of international influences. Likewise it is necessary to analyse the NGOs working in developing countries in a historical context. In much of aid literature, the NGO scene has been analysed in an ahistorical manner, not only influenced by the jargon of the present, but also determined by it.

This book argues that development NGOs must be analysed not only, or perhaps even primarily, within a national, third-sector perspective, but rather as an outcome of complicated processes where factors like international ideological trends, donor policies and NGO agendas interact with national historical and cultural conditions in complex ways. This perspective allows emphasis on how an NGO scene in a developing country *might* be more a reflection of donor interventions than an outcome of internal, national development processes. It thus underlines that the NGO channel is a new type of international social system which is framed by a particular relationship between internal socio-economic and political mechanisms and external donor interests. A focus on the channel as an international donor-driven system also enables a more realistic analysis of the theory of a global associational revolution, and the processes and distribution of power within it. This approach pays attention to the role of donor money and donor policies in shaping organizational landscapes in other countries, the dilemma between organizations' external dependency and their roots in society and the fact that aid NGOs from donor countries do not necessarily reflect the national traditions in those same countries.

Chapter 4 analyses NGOs as an international social system, building on the definitional discussions, the critical assessment of functional theories and the national-style approach of the previous chapters. It discusses how system structures have brought about the ideal-typical project cycle of the NGO channel: assessment of needs, implementation and evaluation. It brings to the fore mechanisms which show that the NGO channel functions in ways other than the conventional wisdom asserts, at the same time as it highlights the processes of organizational homogenization on a global scale. It analyses the channel within perspectives external to the NGO community itself in order to establish conceptual distance from prevailing role-understanding and -language, and tries to demonstrate the fruitfulness of this approach.

The complexity of the international NGO channel, the ideological popularity of the field and its fast-changing history make it necessary to search for manageable areas where accurate data are available. It is therefore seen as useful to analyse the history and character of a particular sub-system of the global NGO channel.

Chapter 5 therefore presents a description and analysis of a national NGO system, namely the Norwegian NGO channel, how the actors have related to each other and the process of integration between the state and the NGOs and what kinds of contradiction have affected the development field. It focuses on a variant of the so-called Scandinavian model. The aim is to try to show the need for historical analysis to understand the context within which present donor systems have emerged and the constraints and possibilities such histories can create for NGO policies. The Norwegian model has some distinctive characteristics which makes it of general interest and which may demonstrate the fruitfulness of analysing the NGO field as a distinct organizational field in society.

The chapter also deals with a donor state's support to NGOs in other countries, and analyses this state–NGO relationship within a foreign policy perspective. Attention is directed to structural issues of power and institutional culture, and not to 'comparative assessment' of whether the NGOs or the state have been 'best' at this co-operation.

Chapter 6 tests the validity of certain assertions about NGOs' 'comparative advantage', 'efficiency' and 'flexibility', and tries to describe and analyse how NGOs function. It is argued that the NGO 'articles of faith' are untenable, firstly because of the heterogeneity of the organizations involved; they differ in so many respects that they do not warrant assumptions of this kind of commonality. Secondly, it is impossible to measure such advantages, partly because of methodological problems and partly because such a characterization presupposes that states, markets and NGOs have more or less identical objectives. The chapter demonstrates, on the one hand, that NGOs are not in general more flexible or more efficient than governments. On the contrary, they may be less efficient and less flexible in certain cases, not least because they do not have the sanctions available to governments, nor the 'universalistic' approach that governments generally adopt. The very fact that organizations might be strongly value-driven or are organized around shared values may make them inflexible in some contexts and highly flexible in others. On the other hand the chapter shows that under certain conditions NGOs may be flexible, cost-efficient and grassroots-oriented, but that this depends on the relevant tasks, contexts and organizations. NGOs are no 'quick fixes' to problems of development, but they might act in accordance with the prescriptions of the articles of faith in development, in work for democracy and in advocacy. Another section analyses NGOs and the accountability problem, showing that this is a systemic characteristic that the channel has to live with and learn to manage as a permanent dilemma.

The chapter raises problems of urgency for the NGO system. Compared with the NGO articles of faith, there is a great gap between images of the channel and what the organizations are in fact able to achieve. Critics argue that, rather than alleviating poverty and promoting equity, NGOs perform a maintenance function, that they help preserve differences among classes and nations at least in the short run, and reduce the pressure for more radical reforms, partly by harnessing the energy of radical middle-class activists. The study was unable to substantiate the claims of the NGO propagandists or the arguments of their critics. Instead it discusses how NGO potentials may be studied and realized.

Chapter 7 discusses the role of NGOs in furthering democracy and pluralism and assesses their role as conceived in what is often called the 'new policy paradigm', a concept which is being propagated internationally as a new development theory in important NGO circles. It describes this theory, which gives a prominent role to NGOs, and compares it with competing state-centred development theories and theories about future world politics as dominated by the clash of civilizations. The argument is that it is crucial to understand these theories, and to address them consciously in analyses of concrete state-society relationships in different countries. This is also necessary if a useful strategy for NGO activities is to be formulated, both at the general level and for each individual NGO. Lack of clarity and reflection on this issue might lead, and has indeed led, to a practice whereby NGOs have sold out to autocratic governments and increased the fragmentation and disintegration of already weak societies. The chapter shows how a combination of myths about NGO advantages and their micro-perspective and narrow project focus have reduced the channel's potential role and hindered paying attention to and reaching an understanding of the context in which it has operated.

Finally, Chapter 8 discusses the theories of institutional isomorphism within the channel and how some Northern NGOs' search for a new strategy (value-sharing organizations, partnership, advocacy, dialogue, operationality, etc.) may affect the integration process between public donors and NGOs and encourage pluralism in an international network of a new type. It concludes that because of changes in the NGO channel's external environment, NGOs and donors may be forced to redefine the role and potential of NGOs.

Methodology and data

Most of the empirical data forming the basis of this book have been collected in connection with a study of Norwegian support to NGOs, directed by the author and commissioned by the Norwegian Ministry of Foreign Affairs. The study started in 1991 and about 25 researchers from six countries have taken part in it. There was very little data to build on, both internationally and in Norway, and especially in the four developing countries chosen for study (Bangladesh, Ethiopia, Nicaragua and Zimbabwe). An empirical and historical analysis of NGO history in Southern Sudan was added, based on the author's field work there in 1985–6. Almost all previous evaluation reports on NGOs had focused on the effects of projects or impact assessments in developing countries. They seldom dealt with macro-level issues in the recipient countries and even less with the overall historical context and social development which is influenced by and in turn influences the NGO channel in the donor countries. To understand the character of this field, it was considered necessary to study its historical development – in particular the relationship between organizations and the state. In addition to collecting much new data on development NGOs the study also drew on research carried out on NGOs or the voluntary sector in Western welfare states.

It was considered important to acquire a large amount of concrete data on selected and central policy areas and how these policies changed over time. This has been vital in a field of this kind; development aid and NGOs form an arena where grand ideologies and simple theories have competed and replaced each other. From the evidence of interviews, press cuttings and public documents, it is obvious that many participants have definite opinions about NGOs, their influence on 'civil society', their independence, their professionalism, efficiency, etc. But these opinions are often poorly founded, or founded on personal experiences, which, of course, will always be narrow and limited. This study emphasizes the need for the reconstruction and documentation of changes in public policies and the justifications presented by the central actors. Thus a concrete historical background can be outlined – one which may be useful in trying to reach an understanding of current dilemmas and possible solutions. Not because history provides 'lessons' on what organizations and government may accomplish in years to come, nor primarily because it provides a structural framework for participants' future choices in the field of aid (although it certainly does do this), but first and foremost because knowledge about the past may free both researchers and decision-makers from the burden of the past: existing institutional, administrative and political arrangements are not 'natural' or necessary results of general processes in the field of aid policies and aid administration.

NGOs have gained increased popularity internationally during the past decade, when it comes to attracting research activity. In OECD countries research on development aid tends to be kept separate from other forms of social research. Studies of NGOs have largely been limited to project assessments and evaluations of their role in developing countries, at the micro level. Several such evaluations have been carried out in recent years. The data are somewhat patchy and tend to be rather soft, often based on interviews and the researchers' own impressions. Wherever possible, the present analysis has tried to make use of the most reliable data with comparative value.

Two main types of data have been used: written sources on public financial and administrative systems within the aid sector and interviews. Different sources have been used, such as government documents, evaluation reports and scientific articles. Comparative studies encounter serious measuring problems, as regards both the validity and the comparability of the data, not least because the field has been defined differently in different countries. Comparisons made here must therefore be seen as attempts to draw rough outlines. In addition, a number of interviews with NGO leaders and government officials in the above-mentioned study countries have been undertaken (for a list, see Keen, 1994; Tvedt, 1992).

As described below, the study also attempts a comparison between NGOs working in different countries. Based on different criteria, Bangladesh, Ethiopia, Nicaragua and Zimbabwe were chosen, because they are all important countries for Norwegian NGO assistance as regards both the number of Norwegian NGOs working there and annual expenditure. In addition, the Norwegian Agency for International Development (NORAD) has had different roles there with regard to both Norwegian and national NGOs, so that they highlight the heterogeneity of the NGO channel. They were also selected because of the different recent histories of state/society relations, which have had important impacts on the NGO scene. In Nicaragua the Sandinista Government had close contacts with and encouraged strongly pro-government NGOs to co-operate with Northern NGOs. After the Sandinistas lost the election, the former pro-government NGOs became anti-government at the same time as the new government reduced the role of the state and supported the establishment of new NGOs, but this time as social service agents in a society aiming at a rolled-back state. In Ethiopia the history of NGO-state relations is very different. The emergencies in the Horn of Africa in the 1970s and 1980s brought an influx of Northern NGOs, while the Mengistu Government restricted the growth of national NGOs. The transitional government that took power after the fall of the Mengistu regime in 1991, encouraged the establishment of NGOs, on both religious and ethnic grounds, while at the same time attempting to tighten up the control of foreign NGOs. In Zimbabwe NGO-government relations have generally been amicable, and most of the foreign and national NGOs attached to the aid channel have been pro-government. Partly as a result of the restructuring programme, this is about to change. Bangladesh is a country where NGOs are very visible in public life, and the past decade has witnessed a proliferation of national NGOs. The conflicts between the state and NGOs have been related not so much to political issues as to questions of legitimacy and foreign influence. The four countries thus provide different types of state-NGO relations in the period studied, and also different types of Norwegian NGO channel. In its analysis of the four countries, the study has collected a wide variety of relevant archival material on both NORAD's and the NGOs' efforts there, and interviews have been made with both Norwegian and local NGOs working in the different countries and with donor agencies and government departments. In addition, a questionnaire was sent to all the organizations receiving Norwegian public support.

What should be the level of analysis? Since one aim of the study was to carry out an empirical analysis of one donor government's NGO policy, one level chosen was the Norwegian Government, Parliament and the state institutions handling official Norwegian policy on NGOs (including the Ministry of Foreign Affairs, the Ministry of Development Co-operation and NORAD). The study covers both development aid – meaning long-term assistance – and refugee as well as humanitarian aid.

A close reading of all reports to the Storting and parliamentary debates in the field has formed the basis for a reconstruction of political developments and how policy changes have been justified. These have then been compared with the way institutions have carried out state policy. The policy and administrative guidelines for the various state units, the public co-ordination of policy and relation with the various organizations have been studied (especially by reconstructing the history of NORAD's guidelines and discussions in NORAD Board meetings).

On the one hand, the objective was to present a broad description of the field and its history in one donor country – Norway. One method might be called an extensive, quantitative analysis. One area of study reconstructed in detail the government budgets and their distribution of funds to the different NGOs over time: the number and types of projects supported by the state, the geographical location of the projects supported, their profile, etc. In particular for the years 1981, 1987, 1991 and 1993 a considerable amount of data was collected and analysed.

In addition, the study set out to collect central documentation for the years 1988–91 from all the 99 organizations registered at the NGO Division of NORAD. Information was received from 83 of them; 12 replied that they had undertaken no aid activity in this period, and 4 did not respond. Their objectives, their total budgets for developing countries, government support as compared with own financing, project portfolios and the number of employees working with developing countries were registered and analysed. In Tvedt 1992 and 1993a a more or less complete picture of this Norwegian scene is presented.

Data about the organizations were collected at three levels. Nine organizations were selected on the basis of different criteria; Norwegian Church Aid, Norwegian People's Aid, Save the Children, the Norwegian Federation of Trade Unions, the Norwegian Missionary Society, the Strømme Memorial Foundation, the Latin American Solidarity Groups of Norway, the Norwegian Council for Southern Africa, the Norwegian Association for the Blind and Partially Sighted and the Norwegian Association for the Disabled. These organizations were chosen because they belonged to different categories of Norwegian organizations (see Chapter 5), and represented different working styles within these categories. Their annual reports, strategy documents and evaluation reports for every year in the period 1981–91 were collected and analysed. In addition, a questionnaire was distributed to these ten organizations asking for data on their working and learning methods and the administrative set-up and financial arrangements of different types of organizations (for this questionnaire, see Tvedt, 1993a).

Furthermore, four organizations were selected in order to carry out more in-depth organizational comparative studies (the Norwegian Association for the Blind and Partially Sighted, the Norwegian Missionary Society, the Latin American Solidarity Groups of Norway and Save the Children). Finally, in order to establish empirical data about the NGO channel in the four study countries a questionnaire was distributed to about 150 Norwegian and national organizations working there with Norwegian financial support (see Tvedt, 1995c). Almost all relevant organizations replied.

The main approach has been archival studies and close readings of different kinds of written material: Parliamentary documents as well as documents from NORAD and the organizations carry more weight as historical sources than statements in individual interviews This method was also chosen in order to achieve the greatest possible distance and independence in relation to the different actors and special interests within the field. A frequently used and less demanding method in evaluation studies – interviews – involves problems relating to memory and recollection, and the desire to gloss over the past, or to blacken it. Nevertheless, hundreds of interviews have been carried out in order to control and improve the interpretation of the written material and to fill in the gaps in our analysis.

Notes

1. Clark states that US$3 billion are disbursed every year (Clark, 1991 :47), while Smillie and Helmich suggest US$9–10 billion annually (Smillie and Helmich,1993: 14). The number of Southern NGOs estimated to be receiving support from Northern NGOs also varies between 10,000 and 20,000, a gap that illustrates the lack of knowledge and reliable data. Salamon gives the figure of 20,000 (Salamon, 1994: 111). It is unclear what sources these figures are based on and to which year(s) they refer. No reliable figures are available.
2. The figures vary enormously; 100 million is taken from Clark (Clark, 1991:51), while the figure of 250 million is according to UNDP's *Human Development Report 1993*. The figure of 100 million is obviously too low, and probably reflects an *a priori* and implicit definition of NGOs which focuses on only one type of NGO and excludes, for example, the Orthodox Church in Ethiopia (according to the Church itself it has close to 40 million followers), Muslim organizations and Catholic or Protestant church societies.
3. For a study of Norwegian images of 'the other' in the era of development aid, see Tvedt, 1990. Tvedt 1995a and b specifically deal with NGOs' role in this image-making process.

1 In Search of the Development NGOs

All around the world there is an upsurge in the establishment of private, non-profit or non-governmental organizations. We are, it is said, 'in the midst of a global associational revolution that may prove to be as significant to the late twentieth century as the rise of the nation state was to the late nineteenth' (Salamon, 1994: 109). From this point of view, the NGO aid channel can be described as a revolutionary factor in contemporary history. The causal role of development aid in this global surge in organizations has been far-reaching, because, with its financial resources and conceptual power, it has been instrumental in exporting NGO growth from Western welfare states to the world at large. But attempts at describing and analysing this 'global associational revolution' are hampered by the fact that there is no generally accepted transnational or transhistorical definition of what is an 'NGO', 'non-profit' or 'private voluntary organization'. This is a problem when the background and role of such organizations are being analysed at the national level,[1] but even more so when the aim is to assess the character and importance of this 'associational revolution' internationally. What are we really talking about and how should this phenomenon be analysed?

The need for a meaningful definition is urgent. Differences in national legal traditions concerning what constitutes an NGO, and different practices in providing for such organizations in legal structures, make official lists of such organizations notoriously incomplete on a national scale; they are also based on such very different variables as often to be incapable of comparison between countries. The definitional problems are compounded by a wide range of shifting relationships between organizations, the state and the market, and the sudden worldwide proliferation of development NGOs.[2] Some organizations are, or have become, state-directed, while others have been directly established by governments to serve state interests. In some countries there is growing competition not only among the NGOs themselves but also between 'for-profit' firms and traditional 'non-profit' NGOs for development or emergency contracts with governments. NGOs develop into for-profit firms, and for-profit firms establish a 'voluntary' arm in order to acquire profitable contracts. In a growing number of emergency and aid situations, military emergency units established by governments work in close contact with NGOs or in some of the same areas as NGOs used to work, and new types of NGOs are being established that are very similar to military units, although formally they are distinct from official military institutions.

Unclear ideas as to what NGOs stand for and what the term 'NGO' ought to include lead, of course, to unclear donor policies and inappropriate or relatively useless comparisons between countries. The ambiguity of the present term might politically be optimal, because one can put whatever one wants under this umbrella (the Grameen Bank in Bangladesh has been marketed as an NGO success, and governments may support business firms – dressed up as NGOs – as well as traditional humanitarian NGOs). To talk about the 'impact of NGOs' as if it were an easily distinguishable phenomenon, or of 'NGOs as representing civil society', or to propose that a certain share of official development assistance (ODA) should be channelled through NGOs because of their comparative advantage is rather meaningless and vague without a prior discussion and definition of what NGOs actually are. This is demonstrated, for example, in an influential OECD study of NGOs (Smillie and Helmich, 1993). That report is not as useful as it might have been because it lacks conceptual precision and consistency in the use of fundamental terms such as 'NGO', 'sector', etc. It therefore presents an erratic picture of the situation in different donor countries, and it is difficult to know to what extent the phenomena compared are actually comparable.

This book argues in favour of using the term 'NGO' – non-governmental organization – as a common denominator for all organizations within the aid channel that are institutionally separated from the state apparatus and are non–profit-distributing. At first glance it may look conventional and traditional, but if used in a stringent way it can be fruitful, with broad analytical consequences. It is a definition which can be employed internationally and which does not reflect specific political or ideological viewpoints as to what is a 'good' organization. At the same time it allows for organizational heterogeneity and historical changes in the ideology and character of different organizations.

Conceptual confusion

A great number of terms are in current use: non–profit voluntary organization (VO), charitable organization (CO), grassroots organization (GO), civil society organization (CSO), independent organization (IO), associational organization (AO), private organization (PO), private voluntary organization (PVO), community-based organization (CBO), quasi-non-governmental organization (QUANGO), and many more. The problem with all these terms is that they are culturally and politically loaded, and emphasize one aspect while downplaying others, and none of them captures the diversity and allows for the dynamics of the organizational scene. Nevertheless, despite all definitional problems, it is essential to employ a precise language with definitional categories because without such precision, knowledge cannot be improved and the channel cannot be analysed productively.[3]

A much-used characterization of these organizations in Western welfare states is that they are constitutionally separate from governments, are not primarily commercial or profit-seeking in purpose, have their own procedures for self-government and serve some public purpose (Gidron, Kramer and Salamon, 1992).[4] This definition includes 'universities, symphony orchestras, adoption agencies, day-care centres, and hospitals, but also trade associations, labour unions, political parties, neighbourhood organizations, self-help groups, and groups advocating for a wide variety of causes, from environmental protection to the preservation of civil rights' (ibid: 4).[4] It reflects a broad sectoral approach and can thus highlight differences between research on welfare states and discourses on NGOs in development aid. Political parties, universities and orchestras are not usually included when NGOs in development are being discussed.

The Central Evaluation Unit of the United Nations has presented an essentialistic definition which includes 'professional associations, foundations, trade unions and business associations', as well as 'research institutes dealing with international affairs and associations of parliamentarians'. The problem with this definition is that it will downplay national differences and make comparison difficult: in some countries trade unions are not allowed to register as NGOs, while in many countries business associations are excluded, as are research institutions. It also downplays the question of public registration (United Nations, Central Evaluation Unit, 1993). Others define NGOs as 'private non-profit organizations that are publicly registered (i.e. have legal status) whose principal function is to implement development projects favouring the popular sectors'. The source of their support is 'almost always non-government organizations themselves based in industrialized countries' (Pardon, 1987:69-77). This definition restricts the NGO term to 'correct' NGOs (favouring the popular sectors). Wellard and Copestake proposed that NGOs should be 'taken to refer to registered, private, independent, non-profit organizations', explicitly excluding grassroots organizations and commercial bodies (Wellard and Copestake, 1993:5). Bebbington *et al.*, in a book in the same ODI series, include grassroots organizations, called membership support organizations, and propose that the term might include the 'commercial private sector, although the label 'NGO' is rarely applied to businesses'. Since this sector does not deal with 'poverty alleviation', it was not considered in the study (Bebbington *et al.*, 1993:7). To choose one or other of these alternatives will have obvious and direct political implications, which is a problem when analysing the field as a whole. None of them creates sufficient clarity and stringency.

Instead of choosing haphazardly from among existing definitions, the criteria of definition should first be discussed. Salamon and Anheier (1992:134) have identified four types of definition of the non-profit sector. Although, as shown below, the sectoral notion is not very fruitful in our context, these typologies are helpful.

Typologies of definitions

a) The *legal definition*. Most countries have legal provisions for the establishment of organizations, and some also have provisions for classifying them. The legal approach defines and classifies a non-profit organization or an NGO according to what the law of a country prescribes it to be. From one perspective this is very handy and gives a legal framework for support to NGOs. From a comparative perspective it is less useful since the entities and the organizational landscapes are not comparable. In the United States such organizations are legally defined as 'incorporated entities that qualify for exemption from the federal income tax under any of the 26 specific subsections of the Internal Revenue Code' (Hopkins, 1987, quoted in Salamon and Anheier, 1992:133). Compilations of official documents in Bangladesh, Eritrea, Ethiopia, Nicaragua, Tanzania and Zimbabwe provided clear evidence of variations in legal procedures and requirements (some countries had not established legal definitions). In Bangladesh, an 'Organization/Person interested in carrying on with voluntary activities through receiving and utilizing foreign assistance shall have to apply for registration under Rule 3 (1) of the Foreign Donation (Voluntary Activities) Regulation Rules 1978 to the Director General NGO Affairs Bureau' (NGO Affairs Bureau, 1990). In Ethiopia NGOs are defined as 'humanitarian organizations which, using their own resources, participate in the country's effort to eliminate poverty and deprivation' (para 13 of the Directives, Transitional Government of Ethiopia 1993:31, quoted in Karadawi, 1994). The general policy regarding NGO operations is to specify 'the conditions relating to management, financial arrangements and operational parameters for the NGO. operations in the country'. Thus, 'every NGO desiring to render assistance must act in conformity with the general policy. Specific approval from the RRC should be secured if an NGO seeks to deviate from general policy on account of donor conditions' (ibid. para. 13.1). In Eritrea the 'indigenous NGOs' wishing to 'participate in rehabilitation and development activities are free to do so, but are requested to register and negotiate agreements with ERRA [Eritrean Relief and Rehabilitation Agency] so as to obtain the necessary permission, and to establish their contacts with relevant departments of the Provisional Government of Eritrea (PGE) through ERRA'. And such NGOs may only undertake projects 'falling within the parameters of the general national development plan' (ERRA, 1992). In Bangladesh persons and organizations interested in voluntary activities financed by foreign money are focused on, in Ethiopia 'humanitarian' organizations 'using their own resources', and in Eritrea the organizations' role in the government's plans.

b) The *economic/financial definition*. This emphasises the source of income, and is the approach taken by the UN System of National Accounts (SNA) (see Salamon and Anheier, 1992:133). The relevant organizations receive the bulk of their income not from the sale of goods and services in the market, but from the dues and contributions of their members and supporters. SNA regards an organization that receives more than 50 per cent of its income from government as part of the government. According to UN (SNA) definitions, the majority of Norwegian and Italian NGOs, for example,[5] and most development NGOs in developing countries, because they receive funds from bilateral donors even though channelled through Northern NGOs, will not be recognized as NGOs at all, but rather as government institutions. This definition would tend to keep the channel's most dramatic transformation outside the scope of interest. In Norway, for example, the large, traditionally independent NGOs are now engaged in contract work for the government on a project basis where the government may finance 110 per cent of their outlay. Nor is such a definition particularly relevant in developing countries, since many of the organizations that have mushroomed lately will not meet the criteria. This definition would be no more relevant if the percentage was allowed to rise to, say, 75 or 90 per cent, because political-ideological relations between organizations and states are often more important than what may be only temporary economic dependence.

c) The *functional definition*. This emphasizes functions, purposes and working methods, and is a common approach in the development aid field. UNDP refers to two broad types of organization: 'peoples' organizations and non-governmental organizations (NGOs)' (see UNDP, 1993:84). NGOs are 'voluntary organizations that work with and very often on behalf of others. Their work and their activities are focused on issues and peoples beyond their own staff and membership'. 'People's organizations', on the other hand, are 'democratic organizations that represent the interests of their members and are accountable to them'. They might be small, locally based and loosely established, but they need not be confined to the 'grass-roots'. A UNDP report states that NGOs can be 'quite different from people's organizations, often having bureaucratic hierarchies without the democratic charac-teristics or accountability of most people's groups' (UNDP, 1993a:84). Others focus on the positive functions, values and working methods of all NGOs: 'All NGOs – whether community-based, national or international – also share to some degree the organizational principle of voluntarism' (Bratton 1989, 574). Consequently, 'voluntarism sets NGOs apart'. This definition focuses on highly normative criteria that are difficult to apply vigorously in different countries and at different times. It is also an artificial distinction, which implicitly reduces the impact of donor funds on organizational profiles and set-ups.

d) The *structural-operational* definition. This is preferred by Salamon and Anheier. It emphasises not the purposes of the organizations or their sources of income but their basic structure and operation. A number of key features are identified:

- formally constituted, i.e. institutionalized to some extent. This means that *ad hoc* organizations, although important in the life of people, are not considered to be part of the non-profit sector.
- non-governmental in basic structure, i.e. private, institutionally separated from the government. They may receive funds from the government, but are not controlled by the government
- self-governing, i.e. equipped to control their own activities.
- non-profit-distributing. Profits in any one year are not distributed to owners or directors but recycled within the organization to further its aims.
- voluntary to some meaningful extent. This does not require that most of the staff must be volunteers. It might suffice that there is a voluntary board of directors (Salamon and Anheier, 1992:135–6). To qualify within the non-profit sector an organization must make a reasonable showing on all five components of these criteria (ibid).

This *structural-operational* approach is most helpful in our context, although it is employed here not to sectoral analyses but in order to understand the development aid organizations within the NGO channel. It does 'de-emphasise distinctions and similarities that reflect particular national, legal and political circumstances, while highlighting crucial common features' (Salamon and Anheier, 1992:148). What legally constitutes an NGO differs greatly among countries and states, and what legally constitutes development NGOs as compared with other organizations also varies from country to country. The economic and financial links to governments are not given more weight than they deserve in this definition, links which vary according to the traditions in different societies and according to the types of development activities, and because experience has shown that there is no direct causal link between the level of public sector financial support and actual organizational independence. It also plays down organizational functions and intentions, which always reflect changing political situations, the resource situation, etc. Since the channel is international it is important to employ a concept that has near-universal coverage. To the above will be added here two important criteria: a) that the organization *receives donor funds* through the aid channel; and b) the *time factor*, missing from all the above typologies.

Employing these criteria means that a) organizations not formally constituted are included. Although they may not be institutionally formalized organizations, they are included analytically as part of the wider NGO channel. To disregard them because they do not fit formal criteria is not advisable, especially in a situation in which Northern NGOs are often looking for such partners. b) Organizations involved in aid are strongly influenced by rapidly changing political trends and funding patterns. How organizations approach the problem of formality in constitutional affairs, institutional separation, their ability to control their own activities, the non-distribution of profits and voluntarism, is an important subject for study. It might be of more importance for the analysis of an organization or a whole national NGO community to be aware of these *changes* in financial dependence rather than the funding rate at one particular point in time. c) It is also necessary when applying the 'structural-operational' approach to consider the connection between how organizations score on different variables and the way they are linked with the aid channel and political, economic and social conditions in any particular country.

A new definition

The term 'NGO' should be used as a common denominator, a collective term, for all organizations within the aid channel that are institutionally separated from the state apparatus and are non-profit-distributing. It is an advantage that the term already has a strong position in aid circles and in the literature. At the same time it is important to avoid the 'catch-all' quality and the political flavour which past usage of the term has implied. It cannot be reserved for a certain group of organizations in the channel, whether on political, institutional or value-based grounds.

This definition of NGOs can be employed in different countries and in different development aid contexts. In Bangladesh, for example, the preferred term is Private Voluntary Development Organization (PVDO), since the most important organizations are run by charismatic leaders and usually have no members. There were many kinds of organizations – ranging from clubs to commercial businesses. PVDOs are non-profit organizations committed to the development of the poor. PVDOs were considered as part of the private sector, but of the non-profit part. No shareholders receive profits, but the organizations were set up privately, on the initiative of individuals (ADAB: no date).[6] This can demonstrate the analytical importance of employing a non-ideological NGO term as well as a term which makes it possible to distinguish analytically between NGOs involved in the aid channel and other national or third-sector organizations.

The structural-operational definition of the term NGO captures one overriding concern, namely, the relationship between these organizations and the state and governments; non-governmental organizations are not necessarily anti-governmental organizations (AGO), although some NGOs are. It helps to raise the problem of the NGOs' inherent particularism in development thinking and practice as opposed to the 'universalism' of governments. It also highlights the question of independence *vis-à-vis* contract relations with both donor and national states, as in structural adjustment programmes and as foreign policy instruments for states. It also focuses on the particular problem of accountability for organizations of this type. NGOs are also differentiated from for-profit firms or organizations. The OECD has a definition of NGOs which includes business ventures. This is too open-ended and will undermine a clear focus on this special type of organization and on the way the channel functions.

This definition also excludes some organizations that are, or have been described as NGOs in both research and policy documents, but which are not NGOs. Some organizations supported as NGOs by Northern NGOs and donor governments under the Sandinistas in Nicaragua were not NGOs, because they were mobilizing instruments set up by the state without even formal autonomy. The Eritrean Relief Association (ERA) in Eritrea is another example. It was an NGO until the independence of Eritrea, although in reality it had been led by the Eritrean People's Liberation Front and was its humanitarian arm, with the objective of securing foreign funds. But ERA was independent of the Ethiopian state and was therefore an NGO according to our definition. When Eritrea became a state, ERA became the Eritrean Relief and Rehabilitation Agency (ERRA), a public office for NGOs in the Eritrean state administration in charge of registering NGO activities on behalf of the Provisional Government. Some international NGOs were for years reluctant to accept this change in the agency's character, and reported on ERRA as an NGO partner, thus underplaying the shift of strategy this partnership implied, perhaps as a means of postponing a strategic reorientation of their work. The Grameen Bank, often hailed as an NGO in NGO and donor circles, is not an NGO but a bank, although a different type of bank. It receives money from the Bangladeshi Government and foreign governments (including Norway) as a bank, and not as an NGO.

The NGO concept as defined here is useful in analysing organizational hybrids which are a typical feature of the whole channel. Many NGOs are hybrids, combining many characteristics. The same organization may combine a strong market orientation with a strong social commitment, and part of its activities may be contract work for a Foreign Ministry while other parts may be entirely voluntary and independent. This diversity is not handled productively by introducing a number of new concepts which divide up into different parts what most productively should be seen as one system, as a single channel. To introduce DONGOS, QUANGOS or GONGOS (governmental NGOs) as distinctive categories of similar order to NGOs, is not useful. They should all be regarded as NGOs, but as sub-classes of NGOs. To the extent that they are non-governmental in basic structure and equipped to control their own activities, they should be regarded as NGOs. In some countries governments have created QUANGOs and GONGOs, with, for example, wives or close relatives of central politicians on the Boards, etc. Much NGO literature focuses on this aspect. Less widely discussed, but just as important in this respect is the fact that many Western NGOs also have leaders very close to the political elite on their Boards.[7] Closeness to government does not always imply loss of autonomy. The NGO sign has been used to obtain funds, not only in developing countries, as has often been highlighted, but also in donor countries. Actors outside the NGO community hope to retain the economic advantages which NGOs offer, whilst countering the political disadvantages which they represent by establishing their own organizations.

The contradiction between formal constitutions and regulations claiming independence and self-rule, on the one hand, and the growing dependence on state money, on the other, is apparent across the board, as is the growing tendency for organizations to become either service providers within government programmes or emergency operators in donor projects. But the organizations are still NGOs if they make a reasonable showing on the above criteria. The NGO concept as used here embraces these developments and dilemmas, and makes analyses of change over time possible. The term also makes it possible to analyse the development NGOs as a group and as part of a new type of international social system (see below), and also to examine how they articulate with donor communities, state administrations and different types of non-profit organization. It allows for fruitful analyses of how other NGOs and NGOs in the aid system interact and influence each other, since the distinction between them is systemic rather than definitional.

Of course, it might be possible to view the whole upsurge of non-profit organizations as a *global* third sector and 'drown' the aid channel in this broader context. Because of its great importance for the development of this global third sector, however, it is crucial to understand how a particular aid channel or system interacts with its organizational environment and with the rest of the organizations in the country in question. The NGO channel's strength and policies are influenced from 'above' by parliaments, governments and state funds, and the channel also influences public opinion, parliamentarians, state policies and funds. It influences the entire organizational landscape (to be or not to be a member of the donor-led NGO system makes important differences in terms of funds, accountability and policy directions) and the target groups in countries where it operates. The channel itself, on the other hand, is influenced by what national organizations are 'allowed' into it and with which target groups it is interacting. This system is not stable. It may be enlarged with new organizations, donors and geographical areas and it may contract and diminish, but it is a system knit together by a mutual language or rhetoric, resource transfers of a special kind (the gift economy) and a feeling of belonging to a thing apart: the 'NGO thing'. The system is, of course, full of contradictions and open and potential conflicts, but these contradictions are part of what forms its enabling and constraining structures. Such a perspective makes it possible to approach it as an international system within which donors, international, national and local NGOs interact among themselves and with their environment in complex ways.

A separate sector?

To get a clearer picture of the relevance and implications of this definition, a number of alternative approaches will be discussed. This also helps to demonstrate that choice of definition has political implications and that lack of clarity on this issue has created unclear research and policies bereft of direction. The above definition implies the rejection of the utility of a third-sector distinction in this particular aid field. The distinction between the state (the public or first sector) and the market (the private or second sector) has become accepted as a useful analytical concept (in spite of all the internal sectoral differences). It has also become increasingly usual to use the term 'third sector', especially in the US and parts of Europe.[8] In the literature it is agreed that this sector is a kind of residual category embracing the diverse sets of organizations that lie somewhere between the state and the market; neither government agencies nor primarily profit-seeking organizations,[9] and that it was discovered at a time when politicians were looking for ways of reducing state responsibilities. The sector term describes, however, an organizational development that goes beyond current political trends, and it has proved fruitful in analyses of Western welfare states.

The 'sector' definition has also been applied to NGOs in development aid. But do such organizations form or occupy a distinctive and identifiable social space outside both the market and the state – a space sufficiently important and consistent to be called a sector of its own? In other words, is such a term also useful in this context? That the issue is unresolved is reflected in aid documents: NGOs are simultaneously described as part of the private sector, as part of the public sector, or as synonymous with a third sector. The final choice has important strategic implications for the activities of NGOs, and for how their growth is to be understood, also because the third sector and its organizations have usually been described in terms that have clear ideological connotations in relation to aid. The notion of separate sectors has often implied a sharp distinction and implicit conflict between sectors which downplays the processes of integration and their interdependence (see, for example, Kramer 1992).

An influential World Bank study referred to three distinct organizational sectors, termed 'government, commercial and voluntary', each having 'distinctive and conceptually meaningful characteristics' (Brown and Korten, 1991:49). This definition emphasises ideological and motivational issues rather than economic strategies or material, structural features: the voluntary organizations (VOs) make up this sector, *because* they depend on energy and resources given freely by their members and supporters. The VOs believe in organizational missions, and do not act primarily on the basis of political imperatives or economic incentives.[10] The term that best characterizes the sector is therefore 'voluntary', and refers to 'actions taken by the free will of the actor' (ibid.).[11] The sectoral differences and characteristics are further explained by the primary options that are regarded as being available to organizations in mobilizing the resources on which their function depends; 'coercion and legitimacy in hierarchical systems, negotiated exchange in market systems, and shared values in consensus-based systems' (ibid.:49). A fundamental difference is said to lie in the fact that the voluntary sector organizations mobilize social energy and resources through the 'mechanisms of shared values and expectations' (ibid.:50).

This definition is also said to be important in understanding the special development potentials of those 'NGOs that are truly VOs' (ibid.). NGOs that are legally non-profit but are primarily concerned with market and financial incentives are classified as commercial agencies and thus defined as being outside the voluntary sector. Public service contractors (see Korten, 1990) are NGOs whose avowed purpose is to provide services to third parties, but which are driven more by market considerations than social values. These are market-oriented non-profit businesses, serving public purposes, and form part of the government structure. Such organizations, which are largely dependent on and subordinate to government authorities, are 'better understood as part of the government sector despite their non-governmental status' (Brown and Korten, 1991:50).

The term 'voluntary sector' is, however, not particularly applicable if the aim is to study the NGO channel in aid, because the degree of voluntarism is declining in the North and is modest in the South, with the exception of some religious organizations, while at the same time it is possible to talk about a worldwide proliferation of a diverse set of organizations lying between the state and the market. In Norway, as in most other donor countries, the extent of voluntarism and the political standing of the organizations concerned have been comparatively strong. A survey of 66 Norwegian NGOs working in developing countries showed, however, that they employed a total of 987 Norwegian and other expatriates and 4,381 local employees in 1992, while they had only 63 volunteers enlisted.[12] In a survey in 1992 of all local organizations receiving Norwegian Government grants in four selected countries, 87 organizations replied (see Tvedt, 1995c). Of these, 17 reported that they had no volunteers at all, 15 had 10 or fewer and 8 had 20 or fewer. The majority of those reporting that they had a large number of volunteers were Christian organizations (Ethiopian Evangelical Church Mekane Yesus, 50,000; Consejo de Iglesias Evangelicas Pro-Aliaza Denominacional, 120,000; but also the Zimbabwe Red Cross, 58,000).[13] Since these data are thought to be fairly representative although the actual figures may be inflated, the term voluntary sector would still in many countries be nothing more than another label for religiously motivated organizations, be they Christian or Islamic. This would drastically reduce the actual scope and role of the NGO channel in aid.

It is possible, of course, to restrict the discussion and analyses of the NGOs to charities (see Burnell, 1991). The problem also with this term is that a great number of development NGOs will be definitionally excluded from the NGO channel, and especially many organizations in Third World countries, since only very few of them are charities as the term is usually understood. In the perspective of this book it is thought to be more fruitful to regard charities as one group of NGOs. Other NGOs may strive to become charities and some charities have developed into state-funded organizations with few voluntary contributions.

NGOs have been considered a sub-sector of the private sector (Uphoff 1994:2). As a corollary NGOs become synonymous with 'private organizations'. Most organizations commonly referred to as NGOs thus belong to the private sector, 'albeit to the service (i.e. not-for-profit) sub-sector thereof' (ibid.:3). The result is a 'genuine', but narrower, third (voluntary) sector, which comprises what are called people's associations or membership organizations, and a second private sector which includes development NGOs as a sub-class. In this way a great many organizations involved in aid are 'lifted out' of what is considered the real NGO field and put into the private sector, because the great majority of organizations in the developing countries that receive funds from donor states and many in the donor countries depend on public financial support, and the degree of voluntarism is marginal.

To draw distinctions in this way implies that a major shift in the history of the channel is de-emphasized and that the size of the channel and its importance are accordingly reduced. A definition that fails to catch the ongoing transformation not only of the organizations individually but also of entire organizational landscapes in 'privateness' and 'voluntarism', both of which are better viewed as continuous variables than as firm categories, is not particularly useful. The above perspective has a further consequence; it implies a sharp analytical distinction between membership and non-membership organizations. But this is of marginal importance in explaining their role and impact.[14] To use the term 'people's associations' as a criterion for deciding which organization belongs to which societal sector is not advisable. How are we to decide who are the 'people' and how can we assess whether the 'people' own an organization? Are the 'people' the farmers or only the poor farmers, women's lib groups or groups fighting for the maintenance of the *status quo*, members of business organizations only or of trade unions as well, or vice versa? If the 'people' is broadly defined, it will include all organizations, and will therefore not be very useful as a definitional criterion. If the term is more politically and ideologically defined, i.e. that the people are the poor, the 'progressives' or those groups sharing the same 'correct' values (as the observer), one is truly left with a residual third sector. The concept of NGOs in development as an ideologically motivated and voluntary third sector implies that important parts of the existing NGO channel are left out and that the system's external impact and internal mechanisms cannot easily be analysed. To be or become value-oriented organizations is an available option, but an option that not all NGOs have chosen in the past or will most likely opt for in the future, and it should therefore not define the analytical category.

To group the NGOs as a separate private sector is not appropriate, since more and more money is coming from public-sector budgets, although channelled by private intermediaries. It has been estimated that total ODA funds transferred by and through Northern NGOs rose from US\$ 1 billion in 1970 to US\$ 7.2 billion – twice the rate of increase for international aid as a whole (UNDP 1993: 88). They also handle emergency funds and funds that have been channelled via the multilateral system. In Norway 22 out of 70 organizations obtained more than 80 per cent of their budgets from the state, a further 39 more than 60 per cent, while 23 received less than 40 per cent from the state (Tvedt, 1992:87), in spite of the fact that they collected a total of about NOK 800m in 1992, compared with an allocation of about NOK 1.3 billion from the state. A survey of all local organizations that received support from the Norwegian Government and from all Norwegian NGOs in four selected countries – Bangladesh, Ethiopia, Nicaragua and Zimbabwe – shows that out of the 87 organizations that responded to the inquiry, only 4 obtained more than 50 per cent of their funds from their own organization, and the great majority were totally dependent on donor funds (Tvedt, 1995c). There are also some large semi-official organizations that have a long and complex historical role, and which do not aptly fit into the 'private sector' definition. The Orthodox Church in Ethiopia (a central institution in the country's history for the past sixteen hundred years, most of the time in close alliance with the reigning emperor), the Catholic Church in Nicaragua or the humanitarian arm of such political movements as the Eritrean Relief Association (ERA), the Sudan Relief and Rehabilitation Association (SRRA) or the trade union movement and the missionary societies in Norway, have all been important actors in the recently established NGO system, but to call them 'private organizations' or to put them in a 'private sector' is not very appropriate.

The NGO scene presents a chaotic picture of a multitude of organizations. This heterogeneity should not be evaded by placing some NGOs in the private sector and other organizations in the public sector (without clear or easily applicable criteria), or by conceptually constructing a clear–cut voluntary sector between them (without solving the insoluble problem of deciding what actions are taken by the 'free will of the actor'). To group NGOs as part of government structures because of their financial dependence neglects, on the other hand, the important question of legal and formal independence. A useful analytical perspective has to include both charities and non–charities, state-friendly organizations and organizations determined to fight the state, voluntary organizations and organizations without voluntary labour, 'progressive' organizations and 'reactionary' organizations. To split them according to which are 'good' (those with a voluntary spirit) or 'bad', creates a societal sector on the basis of the motives and intentions of the actors. By drawing a dividing line that puts development NGOs into different sectors, the importance of analysing and understanding the particular impact of the aid relationship on organizations and on the relationship between those organizations receiving external funds and the great majority of formal and informal groups that are not supported by foreign donors will be underestimated.

The notion of a non–profit third sector has proved to be useful in research on welfare societies. But how relevant is it when analysing development aid? Has a global third sector emerged? There is a proliferation of organizations that provide a wide variety of service-delivery, advocacy, and information activities both in donor and developing countries. But while it is safe to operate with hundreds of thousands of organizations worldwide, only a small fraction of these are linked to the development aid system. In Bangladesh there are figures of about 16,000 registered nongovernmental organizations, but only a few hundred of these are registered as authorized to receive foreign funds (Amminuzzaman, 1993). In the Philippines there are said to be some 21,000 non-profit organizations and in Brazil nearly 100,000 Christian Base Communities based on local action groups, while 27,000 non-profit groups are reported in Chile (Salamon, 1994). Only a fraction of these are linked to the aid channel and the NGO aid system.[15]

In order to grasp the particular role and importance of the NGO channel in development aid (due to financial weight, external linkages, the hegemony of the development aid language in many countries), it is important not to neglect the boundaries and linkages it will always have with societies in general. Communities organize themselves for the utilization of resources and for protection against threats posed by man or nature, independent of the aid system.[16] What must be analytically interesting is to understand how the aid channel interacts with society at large, how it impacts on the organizational landscape in a particular country and how it is influenced by particular national traditions.[17]

If the third-sector concept is intended to refer only to a national context, the problems are not diminished. One method would be to formally restrict the sector concept to entities that are legally registered (see Salamon and Anheier, 1992).[18] This would limit the social importance and scale of the channel since it would be defined by different governments' political attitudes at any one point in time. Registration procedures have been, and still are, of such widely varying efficiency and coverage within the same developing country over time that it is difficult to use such formal criteria.[19] At present a number of countries are working on registration procedures and criteria for NGO establishments. In other cases organizations do not bother or do not want to register, but still receive support from donors. They are a part of the NGO channel, but not a part of this sector, if it is formally defined.[20] Analytically, it is also very important to grasp the point that, in many countries, the development NGOs differ from other organizations, especially in terms of size of budget, type of professionalism, international orientation or dependence, ideology and rhetoric, legal standing, etc. Furthermore, while it may be useful to talk about these NGOs being part of the NGO channel as part of a national third sector, for example in Norway (or in the UK or the US, for that matter), it would be less fruitful to talk about them as part of the third sector in different developing countries when they are working there. Northern NGOs implement many big projects in a number of African, Asian and Latin American countries, but their legal standing and *modus operandi* do not make them into a part of the particular country's third sector, although they are part of that country's organizational landscape. Nor is it appropriate to describe Southern NGOs, 100 per cent supported by, and established in response to, Northern donor money, as part of a national third sector, although they may be parts of an 'associational revolution'. They may develop into national third-sector organizations, but that will depend on their ability to put down roots in the society concerned, and in societies where there is a limited degree of social differentiation and economic development, organizations that seek to create a separate sphere of associational life may become integral parts of what might develop into a national non-profit or third sector.

While it is reasonable to talk about a third sector in some countries, in others it implies the imposition of a very new notion in Western social science on traditional agricultural societies, thus emptying the notion of any concrete meaning. It is not fruitful to use prematurely a concept which will tend to minimize differences in fundamental historical developments between states and regions. Moreover, since the concept of a single international sector implies that the organizations are more similar in aim, voluntarism, 'privateness', etc. than they actually are, and also downplays varying relations between various types of NGOs in different countries, the term should, at least for the time being, be avoided. Development NGOs do not usually make up a third sector in a meaningful sense of the term. NGOs that are foreign-sponsored institutions dependent on external injections of money and advice do not form a national third sector, although they might be very important for the development of society and of such a sector. This contrast – foreign-sponsored NGOs or non-profit/voluntary organizations, often with a 'third sector' background in the donor country, working in an environment without such an organizational sector – makes it urgent to search for approaches that do not miss the distinction between NGOs as part of the aid channel and other organizations in society.

Classification of Development NGOs

Classification systems always imply simplification, and to some extent give a distorted picture of what are complex realities and relations. Since classifications can be described as the system of languages used in communication about phenomena and are used all the time, consciously or conventionally, unclear thoughts on this issue will lead to unclear research and unclear policies. Neither the UN system nor the different donors have a clear, conscious language of classification, in spite of the efforts, money and political prestige put into the NGO channel, and the research on NGOs in aid has not given the question the theoretical and methodological attention it deserves.

The fruitfulness of employing some classification systems based on national traditions will be demonstrated. But in order to understand what is happening on an international basis a more general system is thought to be necessary. A discussion of existing classification systems shows that they are too Western-welfare-state-biased, too broad (like the OECD's DAC sector system) or too normative to enable a fruitful apprehension of the working areas and importance of different types of NGO. A proposal is put forward to advance more rational discussions of a 'global' NGO strategy and meaningful comparative studies. An attempt at developing new analytical tools must be important, and some of the dimensions focused on should be important in future, more developed attempts at classification. The suggested system is based on dimensions that form categories, and not on established categories, and these are seen not as normative ideal-types, but as empirically oriented classifications in a development perspective. Generally the extreme variations in the aims, scope, character and role of the organizations are neglected in such classification systems, and this becomes an even greater obstacle within the context of this study, which is not only the voluntary sector within a certain society but which should also be useful for a global NGO channel.

National classification systems

First a presentation of NGO landscapes and classification systems in different countries is given. These different systems show the massive array of NGOs, and indicate the problems of employing a more universal system, since such a system will de-emphasize the particular national political and ideological contexts. Although the NGO channel is analysed here as a new type of international social system, it entails sub-systems with national variations, which should not be neglected. National classification systems are useful when the aim is to cater for national histories and contexts. In the four countries discussed one can broadly say that four different dimensions have formed the fundamental basis for classification: a) 'community of interests' or 'shared values' (Norway), b) 'foreign' versus 'national' (Bangladesh), c) ethnic and religious cleavages and interests (Ethiopia), and in the Zimbabwean case a mixture of the first and second. It is important to continue to develop classification systems which capture the development and dynamics between NGOs and the state, NGOs and society at large and NGOs and the donor community; it will advance much-needed research on important aspects of countries' development potentials and constraints.

Donor countries

In donor countries, third-sector organizations operating nationally and within the aid channel have often been classified in different ways. For example, in Norway a government-appointed committee in 1988 categorized the organizations working on the Norwegian scene into ten sub-groups according to activities (NOU, 1988):

1 humanitarian and social welfare organizations

2 women's organizations, especially those promoting women's interests

3 sports organizations

4 cultural heritage organizations, environmental organizations, nature conservation societies

5 hobby organizations

6 religious organizations and convictional organizations

7 internationally oriented organizations, human rights organizations and solidarity organizations

8 local committees, local associations, housing co-operatives

9 *ad hoc* action groups, new social movements

10 other organizations and membership associations

This is a commonly used classification of the Norwegian organizational landscape. It is, however, not very useful in our context. Some of the categories reflect important aspects of Norwegian ideological and institutional history and are also adapted to challenges the organizations face in Norway. But like hobby organizations, for example, they may be somewhat irrelevant in relation to foreign aid. Category 7 implies that some organizations which are internationally oriented form a separate and exclusive category. In Norway there are organizations that only work internationally and others that only work nationally, but a striking feature of the Norwegian organizational scene is that quite a few of the biggest organizations with a predominantly national profile also work in development aid (e.g. the two biggest membership organizations – the Norwegian Confederation of Sports and the Norwegian Federation of Trade Unions – were both established for work in Norway, but are now involved in work in many developing countries).

The most frequently used classification of Norwegian organizations involved in aid is based on ideological criteria. They are grouped according to types of perceived 'shared values':

1 humanitarian

2 political–idealistic, often connected to political parties and solidarity movements

3 mission organizations

4 special interests groups and organizations that promotes social welfare

5 occupational associations and trade unions

This categorization has proved useful for many purposes; among them, they have served a government goal, to ensure that state grants have been disbursed to different types of Norwegian NGOs with different constituencies. It can illustrate how official classification in donor countries will often have to cater for national political considerations, which may have little to do with NGO-state relations or NGO efficiency or NGOs' sector priorities.

Norwegian NGOs may, of course, also be grouped according to diverse criteria such as 'organizational capacity', 'size', 'experience', the role of aid (in financial terms and of personnel, etc.) as compared with the total activity of the organization, 'information activities', 'policy aims', whether they are implementing or non-implementing organizations, nearness to the government, 'activity profile', etc. These classifications have been helpful when used to highlight different aspects of the Norwegian NGO landscape. They also make it possible to analyse the field from many angles (see Tvedt, 1993a). The 'shared values' dimension is important, however, both as an empirical classification in a development perspective and in the context of Norwegian aid policy, and it also constantly produces and reproduces categories and relationships in the Norwegian NGO community.[21] In spite of the 'Noradification' of the organizations – in important areas they have become more and more similar as a result of integration processes – they should primarily be seen as value-sharing organizations, representing a community of interests or a particular social group.

Developing countries

Some classifications will be given below that have been used in different developing countries. Here we are focusing not so much on what have been called national organizational styles as on striking features of the organizational landscape, encompassing relationships both among organizations and between them and the state and the donors. To limit the focus to internal inter-sectoral relations is not fruitful, partly because it will downplay the importance of the donor relationship and also because it presuppposes that concepts such as third and first sector are appropriate also in underdeveloped agrarian areas and societies.

BANGLADESH
NGOs have been classified in many ways in Bangladesh. The Islamic movement

tends to distinguish between Western (or Westernized local organizations), Christian and secular organizations on the one hand and Islamic organizations on the other. Radical political movements have tended to focus on the organization's attitude to the state and to political questions of perceived importance in Bangladesh. The Asian Development Bank classified NGOs in Bangladesh according to three major criteria: country of origin, area of operation and source of funding (Asian Development Bank, 1989). Another very common, basic classification is that of NGOs without foreign support, local NGOs with foreign support and international NGOs. The dominant classification has not been inter-sectoral, but in relation to the degree of foreign influence and background.

Most Western donors have tended to classify organizations by activities rather than by ideological or geographical background. This has been the case for NORAD, for example; in its categorization of the organizational landscape there are no Islamic or Christian organizations, and it does not include international NGOs. This partly reflects past practices, because NORAD, Dhaka, has had very little contact over the years with Norwegian NGOs. But it cannot be the whole explanation, since NORAD, Dhaka, has supported CARE and some other international NGOs. It lists Bangladesh Northern Evangelical Lutheran Church (BNELC), an organization heavily supported by Norwegian initiatives and funds, but not the Norwegian Santal Mission, which works in close co-operation with BNELC. This classification system may thus reflect a manifest unwillingness among donors to address the power issues involved. The unit of analysis and the basis for classification are unclear, and it mixes sectors in which the organizations do work with targeted groups.

ETHIOPIA

A classification system that is to reflect the Ethiopian NGO scene cannot disregard the ethnic and religious dimension, which has given birth to different types of NGOs in the country. The majority of Ethiopian NGOs were established after the fall of the Mengistu regime. They therefore reflect the post-1991 political and ideological atmosphere, and available funding patterns and Northern partners. An obvious particular trait of the Ethiopian scene is the proliferation of ethnic-based welfare associations, encouraged by the ousting of the Mengistu Government and the political charter of the Meles Government.

The importance of the religious question in the country has also been important for the formation of NGOs. Ethiopia's self-image has been nurtured by mythical biblical stories about Solomon and the Queen of Sheba, and it claims to have one of the oldest churches in the world. The Emperors and the Orthodox Church (and Western Christians) have for centuries regarded Ethiopia as a bastion for Christ and a buffer against an expansive Islam heading towards Africa. From the centres of world Islam across the Red Sea, Ethiopia has been regarded as a gateway for the spread of Islamic civilization. Conflict and co-operation between these religious and political forces have fundamentally affected the country. NGOs have been formed to foster different religious interests and agendas at the same time as they involve themselves in diaconal work.

Central political-ideological issues in Ethiopian society are conceived in religious and ethnic terms. It is therefore natural to employ a national classification system which pays heed to this, since NGO-formation in Ethiopia partly reflects this situation. The NGOs can be categorized into the following groups (building on Karadawi, 1994):

(i) *Religious NGOs*. The most important Christian organizations are the Ethiopian Orthodox Church (EOC), which claims to have more than 30 million followers (EOC booklet, 1990), the Ethiopian Catholic Secretariat (ECS), and the Ethiopian Evangelical Church Mekane Yesus (EECMY), which claims to have about 1 million followers and established a development department in 1962. The Christian Relief and Development Association (CRDA) is an umbrella organization for more than 90 organizations (including secular members). Islamic agencies arrived officially in 1991 and include the Islamic Relief Agency (IARA), al-Dawa al-Islamiya, the International Islamic Relief Organization and the Muwafaq charitable agency. They have assisted the Muslims in Ethiopia with building mosques, schools and clinics and improving their religious knowledge. Islamic organizations are also organized locally. Examples are Islamic organizations such as al Manar welfare association, al-Omimam Relief and Development Association, and al-Barbara Relief and Rehabilitation organization. IARA and Muwafaq were both created in Sudan by the fundamentalist political organization of the Muslim Brothers.

(ii) *Relief and development NGOs*. These are divided into two sub-groups:
a) NGOs associated with liberation fronts or ethnical political organizations. The Relief Society of Tigray (REST), formerly the relief arm of the TPLF in the war against Mengistu and mainly operating in Tigray, the Ethiopian People's Relief, formerly the relief arm of the Democratic Movement, working in Gondar and Wollo or what is now Region 3 Amhara (registered with the Relief and Rehabilitation Committee (RRC) in September 1991), the Oromo Self-Help Organization (OSHO) associated with the Oromo People's Democratic Organization (OPDO), which dominates the administrative structures in Region 4, the Oromo Relief Association (ORA), formerly the relief arm of the Oromo Liberation Front, which was banned soon after the transitional government took power in 1991, while ORA is a legally registered NGO and works in Wollega, Borana, and Hararghe, and the Ogadeni Relief and Rehabilitation Society associated with the Ogadeni National Liberation Front.
    Another generation of organizations was born in 1991, inspired by the experience of the humanitarian-relief arms of the liberation fronts. Among these are the Afar Relief and Development Association, the Bani Shangoul Relief and Rehabilitation Association, the Eastern Hararghe Development Agency, the Gergaar Relief and Rehabilitation Association, the Gondar Relief and Rehabilitation Association, Guardian (Ogaden), the Harar Relief and Development Association, the Relief and Development Group for Oromiya and the Wollo Development and Rehabilitation Association.
    This class reflects and coincides with the new 'ethnic' administrative policy. The strength of this group of organizations lies in their close links with political struggle for transformation.
b) In addition, there are less important NGOs in the Ethiopian context, classified

into independent NGOs, functional organizations and advocacy organizations.

The above classification seems useful and pays heed to Ethiopian traditions and important aspects of the political and religious situation in the country. It underplays, however, the crucial role of the international NGOs, and shifts the interest from economic sectoral activities to political or ideological backgrounds and motivation. The emphasis on NGOs associated with liberation fronts or ethnic political organizations makes it also not very comparable to the NGO landscape in other countries. It can, therefore, show the strengths but also the limitations of this type of national classification system.

ZIMBABWE

NGOs in Zimbabwe have been categorized according to the geographical area in which they have been working (the following is based on Moyo 1994). They operate at three levels: a) across the country, such as the YMCA, Christian Care; b) at provincial level, such as the Manicaland Development Association and ORAP; and c) at local level, mainly community or grassroots organizations.[22]

They are also often put into five other categories: Community-based Organizations (CBOs), Intermediary NGOs, Service NGOs, Trusts and Unions, and International NGOs (INGOs).[23]

(i) *Community-based Organizations (CBOs).* It has been estimated that as many as 60 per cent of the organizations in Zimbabwe are CBOs (see Moyo, 1994). Only a few of these are part of the NGO channel. Many are promoted by various government ministries, as well as by church groups and national NGOs. Others have an unclear legal status, and may not be registered at the national level under the Welfare Act, nor as co-operative societies. CBOs may be grouped into larger NGO umbrella associations such as the Organization of Rural Associations for Progress (ORAP), the Organization of Collective Co-operatives in Zimbabwe (OCCZIM) and the Manicaland Development Association. CBOs are largely self-help groupings and associations that most often exist in a particular locality for a specific activity. Since independence, there has been a mushrooming of two particular kinds of CBO, farming groups and collective co-operatives, The latter were ideologically supported by the post-independence ZANU (PF) Government and they have also attracted considerable funding from international NGO donors.

(ii) *Intermediary NGOs.*Intermediary NGOs exist to facilitate the activities of smaller groups or to mediate between such groups and governments and funding agencies. The largest intermediary organizations are Christian Care and the Catholic Development Commission (CADEC), whose national and regional offices identify rural projects to be presented to foreign donors. Both are also implementing NGOs. The Self-Help Development Foundation, the Association of Women's Clubs, and the Zimbabwe Women's Bureau, which mainly target women's groups in their programmes, are also intermediaries that implement projects.

Others are ORAP, which works in the two Matabeleland provinces, Midlands and part of Masvingo, and OCCZIM, which operates at national level and aims to unite all registered co-operatives under its umbrella. Its target groups are in the fields of manufacturing, agriculture, fishing, transport, security and printing, as well as in the retail and consumer sectors (NANGO, 1992). The National Council of Disabled Persons of Zimbabwe (NCDPZ) campaigns to protect the rights of disabled people.

(iii) *Service NGOs*. These NGOs provide an expanding range of support services. They assist in project formulation and execution, or engage in consultancy and research activities on behalf of donor agencies, regional groupings, other NGOs, and government institutions. The Zimbabwe Project is such a service NGO, set up to assist ex-combatants from the liberation war.

(iv) *Trusts and Unions*. A fast-growing category of NGOs are the trust funds, modelled on the Manicaland Development Association, which has demonstrated remarkable success in fund-raising (De Graaf *et al.*, 1991). Some trust funds, such as the Zimbabwe Development Trust, have been established by influential politicians. Included in this category are the various interest-group organizations, notably farmers' groups such as the Zimbabwe Farmers Union, which represents small-scale farmers, and the various trades unions. A growing number of trusts have been formed among small enterprises to improve access to credit and investment funds for income-generating projects and disadvantaged business people.

(v) *International NGOs*. Around 30 international and regional NGOs are registered. These engage in collaboration or co-ordination with local NGOs, but rarely involve the latter in project activities (Chinemana, 1991). In 1991 15 Norwegian NGOs worked in Zimbabwe, Redd Barna being the biggest with a staff of 30 people and 17 projects.

This classification system also reflects national characteristics. To have a separate class for CBOs is important in Zimbabwe, since it is one of the characteristics of the national scene, created as a result of popular mobilization, state policy and donor support. It is also natural to include Unions and Trust Funds as a category since trade unions and farmer unions are a part of the NGO channel in this country, whereas they have not been eligible for NGO support in, for example, Nicaragua or Bangladesh.

How to classify

There is a need for classification systems that can accommodate the extreme heterogeneity of the field and the variations between countries and within the same country over time. In order to analyse the NGO channel's character and role, and to capture the importance of global trends and power relations, it is necessary to establish more general classification systems. Comparative studies or a global NGO strategy cannot be carried out without the development of appropriate and precise conceptual tools, among them a way of handling the heterogeneity of organizations and their relations to other actors in a systematic way. The NGOs are seen here as one class of organization based on the definition of NGOs given above. One needs to look for criteria that enable different people to put the same organizations and their activities in the same category irrespective of time and place. Attention must be given to interesting aspects, and it must be possible to classify empirical cases other than those from which the system was developed. The task is to group these differences in a way which acknowledges heterogeneity, and does so in a productive way for both understanding and action.

Some available classification systems

WESTERN WELFARE STATES
To get a clearer grasp of the particularities of our field a comparison with and discussion of some alternative systems may be useful. They can demonstrate the available options, and also the need for economy, stringency and adaptation to the development aid field. Most classification systems have been developed for Western welfare states. A number of systems have been developed: the UN's International Standard Industrial Classification (ISIC) (United Nations, 1990); the European Community's General Industrial Classification of Economic Activities (NACE) and the National Taxonomy of Exempt Entities (NTEE); and a recently proposed alternative, the International Classification of Non-profit Organizations (ICNPO). The existing classification systems have not, of course, been elaborated with an eye to the development aid field. They were to serve other purposes and had a different background and perspective. It is therefore inevitable that they do not easily accommodate the NGO channel in developing countries and the way it functions.

ISIC's definition excludes organizations that receive half of their funds from governments. Thus it excludes the great majority of NGOs involved in aid, especially in the developing countries where many of the most important organizations have been and are totally dependent on foreign aid (very often from governments, although channelled through international NGOs). The system is further based on a notion of uniformity which the NGO actors in the aid channel do not possess. Moreover, it has no place for the 'empowering' and advocacy NGOs which have recently grown in importance within the development aid field, or for the great and growing number of projects aiming at institution-building and organizational support. Naturally, it has no category for Northern and Southern NGOs, since the model presupposes what is normal in Western societies: that the NGOs operating in a country are also from that country. Not all the categories are split into meaningful sub-categories, and there are some catch-all categories which do not differentiate between what are crucial differences in the aid context. The system does not cater at all for the emergence of development NGOs working across sectors and in some cases running whole districts. Nor does it include emergency work, which is becoming increasingly important for many NGOs in the aid channel.

Another, also much used, classification system, NACE, excludes organizations that receive a significant amount of money from governments. Non-profit organizations are by definition restricted to certain categories of service. Tourist information and a number of other activities which are somewhat irrelevant in a development NGO context are included. This system also leaves out important types of development NGO, especially grassroot organizations, which are subsumed under 'other community services'.

None of these systems cater for the fact that many of the big international NGOs are often 'jacks of all trades'. They work in all sectors, and can be so strong as not only to supplement but even to replace government services and erode the authority of the government itself in certain (unusual) cases. There is, therefore, a need in this field for a multi-sector category, which is rare when describing NGOs in Western welfare societies.

NTEE is a very rich classification system, divided into 26 major groups, each of them sub-divided into 17 common activities and up to 80 additional activities specific to the groups. As Salamon and Anheier remark: 'combinatorial richness is purchased at a considerable price in terms of economy. The differentiation of organizational types is so fine that it becomes difficult to make the distinctions called for' (Salamon and Anheier, 1992b:278). Furthermore the organizations are categorized on two bases at once; the 'product or field in which the entity is engaged' and 'what they do in that field' (ibid.:279). There is not much space for special types of development NGO, such as the CBOs in Zimbabwe or the many emergency organizations operating in Ethiopia and Bangladesh after the war and famine in 1984 and the war and cyclone in 1971 and 1974 respectively.

The ICNPO system put forward by Salamon and Anheier proposes a compromise between the level of detail that might be ideal for national work and the level feasible for comparative work, and argues that it does so while 'achieving a significant degree of organizing power' (Salamon and Anheier, 1992b:278). It focuses on economic activities, and uses 'economic activity' as the key for selection. The unit of analysis is the 'establishment' rather than the enterprise or organization, the reason being that an organization might run a number of establishments each of which might have its own economic activity. There are 12 major activity groups, including a catch-all category: 'Not elsewhere classified'. There is no attempt at standardization at the level of activities, because of the great diversity of the non-profit sector in the different areas.

This system is useful, but it lacks some categories that are very important in NGO aid, it downplays the importance of emergency and refugee work (one of three categories within social services), it gives insufficient attention to the difference between mission and other religious organizations in aid and it includes political organizations that are generally excluded from the NGO channel in aid.

Development aid

Classification systems for development NGOs are generally less sophisticated. The field is newer, the knowledge is scantier and past efforts have often been based on highly normative or aid-political criteria. Classification efforts have often been a method of distinguishing the fundable 'good' NGOs from the 'bad' NGOs. It is important to formulate some more enduring classification systems where NGOs can be put into the same class irrespective of the observer's ideological or political attitude, attitudes that also tend to change rather fast in development aid.

Clark (1991:34–5) distinguishes six categories of NGO (relief and welfare agencies, technical innovation organizations, public service contractors, popular development organizations, grassroots development organizations and advocacy groups and networks). This system does not, of course, differentiate between the functions, ownership and scale of operations as part of a sub-categorization of these organizations (Farrington and Bebbington with Wellard and Lewis, 1993:3), but more importantly, it is normative and therefore unclear: how should one define, for example, what are 'popular development organizations' as compared with 'relief and welfare organizations', and how can one establish between different observers' agreement in space and time on what these terms imply?

Farrington *et al.* state that a 'first step' in classifying such groups is to distinguish them according to their origins. Northern NGOs with activities in the South, their Southern-based branches or affiliates operating with a 'high degree of autonomy' and 'indigenous South-based organizations' are listed as three different basic categories (ibid.). This classification will tend to overstate the importance of origin and understate historical changes. There are, for example, a number of Islamic donor NGOs, not originating from the North, but still operating in countries other than where they were originally established. The term 'indigenous South-based organizations' is also unclear, because many of these organizations have been established by foreign NGOs in search of partners. This holds for many church-affiliated organizations, women's groups, environmental lobbying organizations etc., some of which may be totally dependent upon a foreign funder. The cross-national character of the NGO channel is certainly important, but to tie the question of 'origin' to that of 'independence' is problematic, also, because such issues may not be important either for the question of efficiency or for accountability.

The problem with this classification becomes more evident when the two latter categories are distinguished into 'grassroots organizations (communities, co-operatives, neighbourhood committees, etc.), organizations that give support to grassroots, and those that engage in networking and lobbying activities' (ibid.). By defining the categories in this way, the term NGO itself is redefined so as only to fit those organizations that have the same idea of what constitutes the 'popular' and the 'grassroots' as the observers themselves. It will also have both conceptual and political implications: a national church (like the Orthodox Church or the EECMY in Ethiopia) or an organization of private entrepreneurs favouring the interests of capitalists would simply be defined away.

Furthermore, they argue that in the South it is important to distinguish between NGOs 'according to the nature of their relationship to the poor', i.e. membership organization, following Carroll (1992) and Fowler (1990), and non-membership organizations. They argue that the two types of organization have different relationships to the poor, who are members of the former and clients of the latter. It is questionable whether this criterion is important for the 'relationship' to the poor, unless it is a tautology; organizations with poor people as members have a different relation to the poor because of this very fact. Secondly, it introduces a formal attribute (membership) to assess relational issues. And thirdly and most important, it only accepts certain 'politically correct' NGOs as being a part of the NGO scene in a society, a criterion on which there can obviously be no agreement. Different people in different countries at different times will definitely not put the same groups into the same categories.

NGO-state relations

Inherent in what is often called the 'New Political Paradigm' or the 'New Development Paradigm', giving NGOs a crucial role to play in advancing democracy and pluralism, and which is based on a dichotomous relationship between state and civil society, is a focus on classifications systems at whose core is the perceived zero-sum game between NGOs and the state – a competitive relationship in which one actor's gain is the other's loss. Classifications based on distinctions between QUANGOs, GONGOs, DONGOs CSOs (Civil Society Organizations, a new term now used by USAID in Bangladesh), AGOs, PCOs, GANGOs (Gap-filling Non-government Organizations) are common and also in some cases useful. Such relational variables about political nearness to or distance from governments neglect historical and cultural differences in these relations from society to society and from time to time (what is regarded as anti-government in some countries may be seen as pro-establishment in other countries and vice versa), and it also downplays the different role and importance of physical distance between the NGO and the 'centre' in different countries. The enormous differences in character of state formations and the size and character of the 'third sector' and the role of 'voluntary organizations' – if it is at all possible to talk about the third sector and voluntary organizations in many countries – make any classification of NGOs in regard to relations with government or state very difficult, if not impossible.

Strategic orientations

A highly influential proposal developed by Korten (Korten, 1987), classifies NGOs according to aid-strategical generations. The basis for classification is how the organizations think about development and development strategies. The generational pattern reflects the learning process over time. The system contains what was first described as three, now four, stages or generations of strategic orientation (Korten, 1990). According to the conception of historical evolution that forms the basis for this classification system, each generation of strategic theories was moving further away from alleviating symptoms towards attacking more fundamental causes. NGOs are classified according to a unilinear, evolutionary scale, in which the later ones are more mature than the earlier. Implicitly, they operate and change in a vacuum, unaffected by national political and cultural traditions, donor priorities, the impact of the structures of the NGO channel, individual actors, etc. This theory conceals important developments. More and more NGOs are becoming involved in emergency aid, i.e. development NGOs are 'reverting' to becoming 'first' generation NGOs because there are official funds easily available in this area (see, for example, data on Norwegian NGOs or think of perhaps the best-known NGO – Medicins Sans Frontières). Moreover, how can one classify an organization like the Orthodox Church (founded c.300 A.D) in Ethiopia or the Norwegian Santal Mission in Bangladesh (began development work among the Santals in 1867) in this scheme of things? The primary problem is not its implicit evolutionary developmentalism, but the fact that it creates a mythical historical development from good to better, while neglecting much more important and real divisions and reducing the complexity of the NGO scene. It also ascribes to the channel as a whole an agreement on normative thinking about the primary role of NGOs that is untenable.

Table 1.1
The International Classification of Development NGOs (IDENGO): summary table

Group 1: Culture and Recreation 1 100 Culture and arts 1 200 Sports 1 300 Libraries and Archives 1 400 Museums & Zoos	**Group 8: Philanthropic Intermediaries** **and Voluntarism Promotion** 8 100 Philanthropic intermediaries, umbrella organizations, etc. 8 200 Information organizations 8 300 Institution/organization building
Group 2: Education and research 2 100 Primary and secondary education 2 200 Higher education 2 300 Adult education 2 400 Vocational training 2 500 Research	**Group 9: International Activities** 9 100 International networking 9 200 International advocacy
Group 3: Health 3 100 Hospitals and rehabilitation 3 200 Primary health care 3 300 Veterinary activities 3 400 Other health services 3 500 Vaccination campaigns	**Group 10: Religion** 10 100 Mission organizations 10 200 Other religious congregations and associations
Group 4: Social Services 4 100 Social services 4 200 Income support and maintenance	**11: Interest organizations** 11 100 Business and professional associations 11 200 Trade unions, etc. 11 300 Peasant associations 11 400 Women groups 11 500 Others
Group 5: Environment 5 100 Environment 5 200 Animals	**Group 12: Emergency and refugees** 12 100 Emergency 12 200 Refugees
Group 6: Development and Housing 6 100 Economic, social and community development 6 200 Housing 6 300 Employment and training 6 400 Income-generating projects 6 500 Water development	**Group 13: Others**
Group 7: Law, Advocacy and Politics 7 100 Civic and advocacy organizations 7 200 Law and legal services	

Recently Brown and Korten have suggested another system. The unit of analysis is the organizational level, while the basis for classification seems to be differing types of welfare and development intervention. One class is termed 'voluntary service-delivery organizations' (Brown and Korten, 1991:58), as opposed to 'development-catalyst organizations'. This distinction is highly normative and unclear. Most big organizations are both; in some cases they are 'delivery organizations', in other situations they must be described as 'development-catalyst organizations'. There are no NGOs, at least no big ones, that can be fitted into only one of these categories. The term catalyst is used in an absolute, normative way. There are, however, NGOs and VOs that do not aim to become catalysts for overall development, but are concerned with fighting for particular interests *vis-à-vis* the rest of the society. They can be, and often are, more 'voluntary' than some of the more professional 'development-catalyst organizations', but at the same time they are interest organizations, and as such they cannot be fitted into this scheme because it does not contain this important category. Another distinction is drawn between what are called 'sector-support organizations' and 'networks' (the latter being 'self-help support systems, often with secretaries that provide services for their members similar to those provided by the sector-support organizations' (ibid.:61).

Yet another category called 'other types of social action NGOs' is introduced with two sub-categories: a) 'public service contractors' (PSC) namely, highly market-oriented organizations which evaluate their overall performance 'on such criteria as total funding level and market shares of particular types of funding' (ibid.:62). The difference between a value-driven NGO and a market-driven PSC is that the former defines its programme on the basis of its social mission and seeks the funds required to implement it, while the latter starts with an assessment of prospective funding sources and defines its programmes on that basis. Again, the problem with this classification is that it is not useful in categorizing the organizations, since most organizations act in both ways. It is not fruitful to use this as a borderline between different types of organization, and it will be less likely that different people will put the same organizations into the same categories. b) On the opposite side are the 'people's organizations'. They must meet three criteria: being *self-reliant* in that the organization's continued existence must not depend on outside initiative; being a *mutual benefit association* in that it exists to serve its members; and being a *democratic structure* that gives its members ultimate authority over its leaders.' (ibid.:63). A people's organization seems to be a kind of interest organization, but by prefixing the category with 'people's' not only does it distance itself from PSCs, but its opposite is 'non-people's' organizations, thus drawing a border line which is at best unclear.

One basic problem with these classification criteria is that they are all based on normative judgements, which means that different people in different countries will not put the same organizations into the same category. To measure 'self-reliance', 'democratic structure', 'voluntarism' is very difficult within a country framework (people will tend to disagree on what is what) and is well-nigh impossible at a global level.

The above has demonstrated that rigorous and clear classification systems proposed within a Western welfare state context or derived from research on Western welfare states have important limitations in relation to the NGO scene in developing countries and NGOs that are part of the aid channel. Classification systems put forward for NGOs in development aid have usually been less rigorous and more ideological, and therefore less useful in a comparative context. A suggestion is put forward below, building on Salamon and Anheier, which tries to take account of the particularities of NGOs in aid without making it so 'particular' that it has no relevance to other organizational fields. It is also more specific than the much-used DAC sectors, which are not very useful for analysing NGO activities, since most of them will fall into a couple of very broad main classes.

Salamon and Anheier propose that the appropriate unit of analysis should be the individual establishment and that the appropriate basis for classification should be the product or service it generates. The most homogeneous unit, and the most important classification factor, is taken here to be the organization. There is, moreover, plenty of data available at the organizational level. An alternative unit of analysis could be the activities of the organization or types of government-NGO relations. Bases for classification could be size, legal status, recipients, type of activity, ideology and aims, degree of professionalism, degree of grassroots orientation, etc. If the channel's varying roles internationally are to be understood, it might be fruitful to analyse NGOs according to all these roles. Here type of activity is chosen as the basis for the classification, but this is not sufficient in our context, because of the channel's international character. It is therefore important to have a system which also registers level of implementation and the national or foreign background of the organization. Basically, however, it tries to sort NGOs according to their area of primary activity.

The following comments can be made.

a) This classification does not classify NGOs according to value-orientation, 'correctness' in attitudes to participation, gender, the poor, etc. In different countries and for specific purposes such criteria may be very useful, and for organizations classifications of this type may encourage more reflection on where they belong or their 'community of shared values'. In a discursive and planning context it may be less fruitful, because observers will tend to put the same NGOs in different categories, reflecting the observer's subjective perspective or viewpoint.

b) It does not exclude any NGO on the basis of degree of independence of economic self-sufficiency. In a development aid context such a basis is not advisable, because so many would have to be kept outside the classification exercise. Many NGOs in developing countries are totally dependent on foreign funds, but they are still a part of, and often an important part of, the NGO scene. It does not distinguish between international and national NGOs, partly because many organizations are both national and international, and because many national organizations in this channel are totally dependent on foreign funding. When analysing the NGO landscape in a particular country it is, however, important to bring in this distinction.

c) It pays sufficient attention to the particularities of the development aid field as compared with the NGO scene in Western industrialized countries, and it avoids the broader categories which in general are used in development aid (for example, the OECD DAC system of classifying types of development assistance).

Notes

1   The difficulties involved in characterizing what is an NGO in the comparatively homogeneous context of Norwegian aid was discussed in Tvedt (1992:8).

2   Salamon and Anheier argue that the lack of 'attention to the third sector is a function less of the weakness of the sector than of weakness and limitations of the *concepts* that have so far been used to comprehend and define it' (Salamon and Anheier, 1992: 127). This does not apply to development NGOs; either in Norway or in many other countries. For example: Médicins Sans Frontières in France, OXFAM and Save the Children in the UK, the Red Cross, Redd Barna, Norway, Norwegian Church Aid and the other major Norwegian NGOs have a very strong position in public opinion and in the media. Analytically there is a deep lack of conceptual clarity as to what they are, but in the media there is not. But perhaps the problem of 'concepts' is still valid, since these organizations do not receive attention as third-sector organizations, but as societal organizers of altruism.

3   NGO directories suffer from this drawback. The *Directory of NGOs in Bangladesh 1993* makes no effort to define what it is a directory of. In consequence, this NGO directory also includes 'diplomatic missions, professional associations, cooperative sectors, corporations and various ministries and departments of the Government' (ADAB 1993). The Christian Relief and Development Association in Ethiopia published a directory of its members stating that it is a 'non-profit organization open to all churches and agencies (with agreement with the government of Ethiopia) working for the welfare of the people of Ethiopia' (Christian Relief and Development Association, 1993). The Zimbabwean National Association of Non-governmental Organizations (NANGO), 1992, *Directory of NGOs in Zimbabwe 1992*, makes no attempt to clarify the criteria required to deserve the NGO label. TANGO's Directory in Tanzania defines NGOs as 'private, developmental, non-profit and apolitical organizations and are accountable to their respective Boards/Executive Committees and beneficiaries' (TANGO, 1994: xxii).

4   No distinction is made here between organizations and institutions. It is however, an important division, although the two terms may overlap. In the Norwegian context, the development NGOs are only organizations and not institutions (universities, orchestras, etc. that are involved in aid are not funded via the NGO chapter).

5   According to data on 67 out of 98 registered development NGOs, 46 out of 67 Norwegian NGOs recovered more than 50% of their expenditure on development projects from government grants (Tvedt *et al.*, 1993a: 38). On average, the Italian Government covers 52.34% of the contributions to Italian NGOs, excluding grants from the EU and other international institutions (Smillie and Helmich, 1993).

6   Lack of definitional clarity also makes the number of NGOs uncertain. According to official figures given to the Bangladeshi Parliament in January 1990, 11,701 organizations were registered with the Department of Social Services in Bangladesh. Some NGO observers have operated with figures of 16,000 or more NGOs in Bangladesh, but sources and definitions are not explicit. UNDP writes that 'at the start of the 1990s at least 12,000 local groups were receiving financial and technical support' (UNDP, 1993: 92). Whatever the total number of what might be termed 'third-sector' organizations, only a small fraction of them are registered with the NGO Bureau and are thus permitted to take in foreign currency.

7   *The Economist*; 6 August 1994 (pp. 31–3) had an article on 'How to control the quangos', focusing on the emergence of a new class of 'quangocrats' in many parts of Britain. 42,600 quangocrats were appointed by the government to run what were called 'quasi-autonomous non-governmental organisations'. (31–33). Many of the unelected leaders of these organizations owed their jobs to 'government favour'. In Norway development NGOs appoint their own leaders and their own boards of directors, but those appointed are often former members of the government, members of the Storting and so on.

8   In Norway it was first introduced as a concept in 1989 by the Labour government in its Long-Term Programme (see, Kuhnle and Selle, 1992). It has not yet been used in White Papers on development aid. The term was first used by US scholars in the early 1970s and was made

influential by the Filer Commission, initiated by John D. Rockefeller.

9 Initially, the term was intended to express an alternative to the disadvantages associated with both profit maximization and bureaucracy, by combining the flexibility and efficiency of markets with the equity and predictability of the public sector (Anheier and Seibel, 1990:7).

10 Bratton describes the voluntary sector in the same vein: 'The voluntary sector thus provides a home for new ideas and helps to legitimize them so that they are not immediately branded as subversive. As institutions emerge that offer work for social transformation as a professional option, adherents to unofficial viewpoints can find opportunities for employment and expression that would otherwise be closed to them by the state' (Bratton, 1989:575).

11 To focus on the actors' 'free will' is an unusual way of defining an organizational sector in society (the implicit causal link between individual actors and collective institutions, or between ideas or intentions and material structures, or what is meant by 'the free will of the actor' or how this relation between intention and action can be observed is not discussed), and no advice is given as to how this criterion could be employed in deciding what belongs to the third sector.

12 Staff working in Norway are not included here. The information is based on a questionnaire sent to all Norwegian organizations in 1992.

13 Such figures usually turn out to be inflated because voluntarism is regarded as a 'market asset', and also because it is difficult to define voluntarism. A study of rural NGOs in Zimbabwe shows that 69% had either no volunteers, or only one or two. Of those that reported one or two volunteers, almost half were foreign and were recruited and supported by an international agency (which means that they were not volunteers in the original sense of the term). Some of the few organizations which reported large numbers of volunteers counted all former beneficiaries as volunteers, giving them the role of 'spreading the word'. According to this survey, a few relied on volunteers for a substantial proportion of their activities (Vivian and Maseko, 1994: 11–12).

14 To draw a sector line between member organizations and others is not advisable, because the criteria have marginal influence on aid conduct and aid profile. Take two of the most important Norwegian NGOs; Redd Barna (Save the Children, Norway), a powerful membership organization, and Norwegian Church Aid. Redd Barna is a firmly and formally constituted organization with a Board led by volunteers and a number of local cells around the country which mobilize children and others to arrange bazaars, parties, etc. to collect money for aid. It has worked in most sectors (health, health-related research, primary and secondary education, social services, culture and arts, emergencies, income generation, etc.). Redd Barna started working in development in 1961, and in the early 1990s it ran development projects and relief operations in more than 30 countries. Its total expenditure on development activities abroad (including emergency aid excluding administration at home) in 1981, 1986 and 1991 came to NOK 38m, 101m and 209m, respectively (budget). Norwegian Church Aid (NCA) was established in 1947. It is not a membership organization, but is governed by a Board appointed by a Council that in its turn is established by various institutions, including one from each diocese in Norway, and one from Norway's annual Church Meeting, plus other institutions, clerical as well as secular. It started operations in developing countries in 1962. In 1991 it worked in 61 countries. Total expenditure (excluding costs in connection with the running of the international network: Emergency Relief Desk) in 1981, 1986 and 1991 were NOK 82m, 298m and 369m, respectively. NCA works primarily with local churches, while Redd Barna primarily implements its own projects.

   In Ethiopia Redd Barna's revised budget for 1993 showed total cash requirement of NOK 23,295,000, comprising funds for 17 projects in a number of warradas (i.e. districts), with a staff of more than 300 people. NCA co-operates mainly with the Ethiopian Evangelical Church Mekane Yesus (EECMY). Since 1986–91 NCA has supported EECMY with NOK 43.959m in nominal terms. In Eritrea Redd Barna and NCA are both working very closely with the government. In Zimbabwe, Redd Barna has good relations with the government, and tries to work through community-based organizations. From one perspective these organizations are 'many' types of organization, and fit many of the most commonly used terms.

15 The total number of Northern NGOs involved in aid in 1987 worldwide has been estimated at 2,450 (OECD, 1988). Presumably this was a gross underestimate, for it is now said to be about twice as many. Even so, the organizations in aid constitute only a fragment of the entire organizational landscape in the donor countries. Even in Norway, where organizations have

been mobilized to take part in aid to a greater extent than in other donor countries, it has been estimated that there are 1,685 voluntary organizations (Raaum 1988:303). About 140 of these are involved in development aid or in development information.

16 One of the best-known community-based institutions in Ethiopia, for example, is the Iddir, to which the bulk of the population subscribes, particularly in towns. As defined by one observer it is an association of persons united by ties of family and friendship, by living in the same district, by jobs, or by belonging to the same ethnic group. The Iddir is a sort of 'insurance programme run by a community or a group to meet emergency situations' (Karadawi,1994). In Addis Ababa the number of Iddirs grew from 600 in 1969 to 1213 in 1983 (ibid.). Other such grass-roots organizations include the Equb (credit association), the Debo, (rural mutual support organization), organizational types which could be defined as part of the 'informal' sector, or if preferred, as a 'third sector', but are not part of the NGO channel.

17 In Zimbabwe, registration has been compulsory for NGOs, but not for the hundreds of community associations and co-operatives. It has been said that there are 'certainly thousands of either governmental or private "organizations" involved in some way in promoting or initiating development projects or programmes in Zimbabwe' (Muir, 1992: 12). This figure might be exaggerated, but only a minority of these organizations are linked up to the NGOs working in aid. Some of the NGOs have been registered with the Ministry of Health, some with the Ministry of Labour, Manpower and Social Welfare and some again with the Ministry of Finance, Economic Planning and Development.

18 The same proposal has been put forward with regard to a definition of NGOs (see Wellard and Copestake, 1993:5). This formal solution to the problems of definition neglects state weaknesses in many Third World countries, and the lack of stability in their political systems.

19 Ethiopia can serve as an example. During the Derg regime local NGOs were not allowed to register to receive foreign funds, although peasant associations mobilized around government policies were encouraged. In 1994 more than 150 NGOs were registered, while hundreds were said to be awaiting registration. Officially it has been argued, however, that 'the concept of NGO, as a distinct entity, is not known to the Ethiopian legal system' (Ato Shiferew, former Minister of Justice, to Brother Augustine O'Keefe, CRDA, 6 September 1993, in *Redd Barna, Ethiopia, Bi-Annual Report* No. 2/93, Appendix 1.12. 'The formation and operation of NGOs in Ethiopia', Addis Ababa: 1993).

20 REST in Tigray and ERA in Eritrea are, of course, prominent examples. They were illegal organizations and for that precise reason they therefore became important as partners of Northern NGOs in the particular context of war and famine in the Horn of Africa. In the Southern Sudan in the 1980s many organizations did not register, although they were formally obliged to do so. UNHCR co-operated with organizations as implementing agencies, although they were not officially registered. To use registration as a criterion presupposes a conflict-free, stable situation that is not always present.

21 The mission organizations have come together in one umbrella organization: the Bistands-nemda. The big humanitarian organizations have frequent top-level meetings and also meet regularly with the Foreign Ministry in the Katastrofeutvalget (Catastrophe Committee). Some of the political-idealistic organizations have joined forces in publishing a magazine (called X) on North-South issues.

22 Organizations vary greatly in size, from the large membership NGOs like ORAP with over 100,000 members, to small community-based organizations (CBOs) with 10-100 individual members or households (De Graaf et al., 1991).

23 Moyo 1994 also discusses other ways of classifying NGOs: by size, budget, geographical location, sector of operation, particular activities undertaken, etc. Here the focus is on organizational types, for comparative purposes.

2

Why do Development NGOs Exist?

Why do development NGOs exist and what decides the distribution of functions between the state and the NGOs or between different sectors in society? A dominant explanation has been that NGOs (here we are talking about NGOs in general, and not only NGOs in aid) emerge as an institutional response to market or state failures. They occupy a niche not served or already filled by the for-profit sector or the state. This chapter will discuss the extent to which such functionalist theories about the role of non-profit organizations in society are useful when trying to understand the NGOs in development aid in a donor country and the NGO channel's role and position in different aid-receiving countries. To explain the existence and growth of third-sector organizations by means of functional theories, means that they are regarded collectively as a natural phenomenon, being a functional response to the shortcomings of other sectors. As long as organizations in donor and developing countries are perceived in this way, the particular role and impact of the NGO channel in aid will be missed, and there will be no need for donors, governments or the big international NGOs to formulate country-specific strategies on how to stimulate the growth of national third sectors or how to influence state-society relations: *Ad hoc* support for 'naturally' emerging groups becomes sufficient. This functional perspective also tends to assume that there is a permanent and basic conflict between the public and the voluntary sector, and the theory therefore plays a clear political role in the international debate on the role of the state in society.

Influential theories

The most influential theories about the voluntary sector have been developed within an economic theoretical perspective.[1]

The *public goods theory* or the 'performance failure theory' states that NGOs exist to satisfy the residual unsatisfied demand for public goods in society (for an overview of this school (see Weisbrod, 1988). It argues that the state tends to provide public goods only at the level that satisfies the median voter. Where a significant minority wants a kind or a level of public goods for which majority support is lacking, the government cannot help, and NGOs step in to fill the gap. Some parts of the population may want more public goods than the government is willing to provide. They can obtain them by organizing themselves, demanding more social services for their particular group, organizing their own community schools, or mobilizing local people for a collective campaign of some sort. From this logically follows a theory arguing that the more heterogeneous a society is, the larger this other organizational arena is likely to be (James 1990, 23).

Another influential and related theory is the *contract failure theory*.[2] This suggests that NGOs arise where ordinary contractual mechanisms fail to provide the public with adequate means to assess the services firms produce. This lack of adequate information to control producers in this way is called 'contract failure'. When contracts are difficult to define, people will trust non-profit organizations or NGOs more than commercial firms, because the former are seen as having fewer incentives to take advantage of the consumer's ignorance. The 'transaction cost approach', being based on the contract failure theory, explains institutional choice by the cost of alternative contractual arrangements. The 'new institutional economics' (see, for example, Williamson, 1985) aims at understanding, within a functionalist perspective and on a general level, why some transactions are handled by organizations and others by the market.

The above theories explain the existence and the role of NGOs as resulting from various forms of failure by the market or state. They have been developed in research on the welfare and social fields in Western welfare states.

An influential World Bank book on NGOs (Paul and Israel, 1991) describes such functional perspectives as being useful also in explaining NGOs in development aid and in Third World development in general. In their contribution to the book Brown and Korton argue that since markets tend to be 'especially vulnerable to failure in developing countries', organizations might, as 'remedies for market failures be particularly relevant there' (Brown and Korton 1991:47). They also bring in a different perspective, what is called the 'lens of political analysis'. This tends to focus on the role of NGOs in filling niches created by government failure, particularly in the production of public goods. NGOs exist primarily because of the 'reality of social diversity and otherwise unmet needs for experimentation and flexibility' (ibid.). It is problematic for governments to respond effectively to social diversity, since this will create different constituencies making different or contradictory demands for services. NGOs therefore arise as a response to a situation where people are sovereign but diverse – with competing and sometimes contradictory wishes. This theory stipulates that where there are many competing and contradictory wills, a great number of NGOs will eventually grow up to meet and institutionalize this social diversity (Douglas, 1987). Brown and Korten also point out that 'a widely recognised failure of large-scale government bureaucracies is their inflexibility and conservatism'. This political form of state failure creates a situation in which NGOs emerge as innovative responses to novel problems, because of their abilities for experimentation and flexibility (Brown and Korten 1991:48). In other words, NGOs emerge because of their ability to respond to problems the state itself is unable to solve in a satisfactory manner.

The introduction to the World Bank book, quoting Douglas, 1987, states that 'studies of the politics of the nonprofit sector have focused on the reason that NGOs perform public functions that normally fall within the purview of the government'.[7]

In line with the dominant perspective, and written in typically functionalist language, the implications are summarized as follows: voluntary action of this kind is seen as an 'adaptive response to the constraints of the majority rule and equitable distribution criteria of the state' (Paul and Israel, 1991:4).

The theories and the NGO channel

There are theories about what 'environmental niches' the non-profit organizations thrive in, and why they move in to occupy them. They may be useful in industrialized, capitalist countries, and in certain micro-contexts. They have not, however, been tested empirically in the development field or with respect to the emergence and existence of the third sector in different non-industrialized countries. This chapter will argue that these theories are not particularly useful in explaining the variations in NGO roles in either donor or developing countries.

Studies of NGOs in development should not neglect the fact that the type and form of these organizations vary between different organizational fields within the same society. The development aid field has important particular characteristics and dynamics that differ from other segments in society. This study emphasizes organizational fields rather than sectors of society, regarding the sector-term as too broad and vague in this connection.[3]

The discussion is in two parts: one focuses on donor countries, the other on aid-receiving countries. This structure does not reflect the conventional conceptual dichotomization of the world, with developing countries on one side and developed countries on the other, as if they were clear-cut, empirical and analytical entities. Neither states nor organizational structures differ fundamentally according to the distinguishing line introduced by this dichotomy. The purpose of the present distinction is to highlight what is a real and crucial difference: the relationship between donor states and their NGOs in Western countries on the one hand, and that between NGOs and sectors in developing countries, on the other.

The donor country which will be focused on is Norway.[4] The Norwegian case is seen as unique, but at the same time it is contended that some of the same processes have been of great importance in other donor countries as well. Secondly, these theories will be shown to be not very helpful in explaining the great variations in size, role, extent and type of link between NGOs and other sectors in developing countries. In other chapters the Norwegian NGO channel will be analysed to show how integration processes between the state and NGOs may develop and how a donor state's NGO policy has been formulated. The Norwegian scene will also serve as an example of how these questions can be studied.

The NGO sector in Norway[5]

Although the government has played a central role in the history of the modern Norwegian welfare state (the concept of 'the Scandinavian model' captures these characteristics),[6] the voluntary sector has been rather strong (see, for instance, Kuhnle and Seller, 1992). It has been said that, 'especially the Scandinavian social democratic model provided social welfare with no ideological space for voluntary organization' (Lorentzen, 1989:11). In the case of development aid, the growth in official aid has definitely not rendered the voluntary organizations redundant (see Tvedt, 1992).[7] On the contrary, the substantial growth in ODA has led to an even stronger growth in government support to NGOs, and their ideological space has been enlarged.

What needs explanation is the emergence of this rather large sector within the field and the significant growth in NGO activities from 1963 to 1993. For the present purpose, the development of Norwegian aid NGOs can be divided into four phases (for a more detailed, empirical description of the sector's history, see Tvedt 1992): a missionary phase (1860 to the 1960s) where the focus was on diaconal matters and the work had little or no financial public support, and three later phases all related to NGO-government relations – an establishment phase (1963–78), an expansion phase (1978–92) and a consolidation phase (from 1992). Since 1992 the number of organizations has slightly decreased, and during the last few years very few new organizations have entered the field.

NGO growth

Norwegian missions had been working since the middle of the last century in countries like Madagascar, South Africa and China. Their aim was, of course, to spread the Gospel, and as part of their strategy they established hospitals, schools, etc., supported financially by their congregations at home. Before 1963, 20 organizations worked in developing countries. In 1963 the state for the first time channelled money through what the Storting called 'private organizations'; seven Norwegian organizations obtained a total support of NOK 3 million for their seven projects. Reports to the Storting in the 1960s and 1970s argued that NGOs should be mobilized to take part in development aid and especially in informing the public about its importance. The state therefore mobilized the organizations to become some kind of propagandists for the state-directed aid project, in accordance with US and UN initiatives in 1962 (see below). Both the state and the organizations stressed the importance of the organizations maintaining their special character and identity; both were aware of the problem which later in the social sciences has come to be called 'institutional isomorphism' (DiMaggio and Powell, 1993:147).[8] It was there-fore not a question of filling niches; rather it was planned complementarity, financed by the state. The establishment of the NGO Division (a direct English translation would be the 'Office for Private Organizations') in 1978 made it clear that the state aimed to institutionalize the support of Norwegian NGOs. In that year NORAD supported 34 Norwegian organizations, and the total budget for NGOs was almost NOK 50m – four per cent of Norwegian bilateral aid. At the same time policy and guidelines for the NGO field were fundamentally revised (in 1977 and 1979). The first experimental phase was over.

During the next decade the support 'exploded'. In 1981, NORAD supported 70 organizations with NOK 80m. In 1982 it allocated an extra NOK 64m. New guide-lines were put forward under which NORAD could directly support local NGOs in Norway's main co-operating countries and international organizations. 'Framework agreements' with the largest Norwegian NGOs, (rotating over three years) were also initiated at this time. By 1991, 134 Norwegian organizations, many hundreds of local organizations and between 20 and 30 international NGOs working in about 100 countries were supported by the Norwegian Government to the tune of about NOK 1.2 billion. While the NGOs in 1963 received NOK 3m and their share of the total aid budget averaged 7.2 per cent for the whole period 1963–81, it was increased during the 1980s to 25 per cent of the total bilateral aid in the early 1990s. In 1981, 98 projects were supported, while in 1991 the figure was 1,058. About 43 organizations started work in developing countries in this decade. The target-oriented basic needs strategy which the Storting put forward in 1984–5 gave them increased space and importance. In many cases they were given support to operate more or less on their own, with no interference from the government or from NORAD offices in the countries where they worked. In the same period the state–NGO relationship was not only broadened in scope but also became more routinized and bureaucratized. At the end of the 1980s the state aimed at improved co-ordination, efficiency and control, and NGOs were subsequently defined as both operators for and partners with the state. Gradually it became more and more common for them to take on contract work for both the Foreign Ministry and NORAD, especially in relief and emergency and in specific programmes such as AIDS, the Sahel programme, etc. Not only had the size of the NGO channel increased dramatically since 1963, but some organizations were now carrying out projects that were 100 per cent financed by the state. A logical outcome was that the organizations, or at least some of them, by the end of this period had become close to what can be called non-profit organizations up for hire.

In 1992 a consolidation phase was initiated. The Foreign Ministry launched a major review and NORAD broadened its reappraisal of past NGO policies. Many of the organizations also felt the time had come to reassess their profile and working methods. Although support to the NGO sector was still on the increase, the growth in budgets and official transfers was flattening out. The number of organizations involved was decreasing, while support to NGOs in developing countries continued to be a growth area. Few new Norwegian organizations were entering the field. The state was aiming to professionalize the organizations, partly by streamlining their administration and partly by stressing the need for them to maintain and strengthen their autonomy and identity. At the same time, the overall policy aimed at stronger co-ordination between NORAD and the Norwegian NGOs, and an alignment in policies and geographical areas. On their side, the NGOs discussed plans to organize a lobbying body for voluntary activities within the aid sector.[9]

STATE FAILURE OR STATE INITIATIVES?

This history of NGOs in Norwegian aid policy cannot meaningfully be explained as the result of an adaptive response from society or groups in society to market or state failures, or as a functional response to social diversity, or as innovative responses on the part of the society to novel problems. The introduction of NGOs into the field and the growth of the NGO sector were brought about by conscious government decisions. In the early 1960s – when government-to-government aid was undisputed as the main and best form of aid – they were invited into the arena by the state and did not occupy a niche in competition with other sectors. The initial government decision gave the voluntary organizations a well-defined role: they were to co-operate in government programmes and preferably to carry out their own projects, but more importantly their main task was to help broaden the support among the Norwegian public for development aid in Norway in general.[10] The state deliberately involved them in order to achieve a broader aim: the internationalization of Norwegian society.

The organizations did not therefore occupy a niche created by government or market failure; instead they were invited in as a channel for government money and as a junior partner with special responsibility for information in Norway – a role they were generally happy to take on.[11] At the same time the government tried to involve the for-profit sector, but with little success – not because of questions of trust or market failures, but because the business organizations were hesitant to involve themselves with NORAD in overseas activities. During the late 1970s and early 1980s the state and NORAD deliberately issued a number of offers which the organizations supposedly could not refuse, by reducing the demands for own contribution and by increasing the financial support for administration and management. The initiative was generally in the hands of the government, but the NGOs soon acquired enough political leverage to exert considerable influence on parliamentarians and the aid administration on policy issues and in defining their space within overall ODA. In some cases the original junior partner called the tune, invading niches which NORAD had not planned, but this development had less to do with economics and failures than with political and ideological alliances between organizations and politicians.

The organizations were gradually given an ever-expanding arena by the government, and not because of under-supply as the above theories tend to argue, namely, that the increasing importance and enhanced role of the NGOs can be seen as the result of their occupying a niche created by under-supply on the part of government services. Rather, it was stimulated by over-supply. Pipeline problems in government-to-government aid (the spending imperative), coupled with rapid growth in emergency budgets, the need for legitimation of, and information about, aid in Norway, the demand for alternative channels to politically sensitive areas and groups (Frelimo, ANC, Palestine, etc.) and the government decision to launch aid programmes to countries affected by the Sahel drought outside the traditional areas of Norwegian bilateral aid all required alternative channels. The use of the NGO channel was a convenient administrative and political solution for the state – and a solution that would be welcomed by influential NGOs.

THE STATE AS NGO-SUPPORTER

Growth in the NGO sector cannot, in this case, be seen as a response from the society itself or from 'civil society' to the problems of majority rule or as an institutional reflection of social diversity. On the contrary, the NGOs were invited into the field and encouraged to become central actors by the ruling majority government. They responded positively to the state's relatively unified demands. To explain their growing importance by referring to them as being regarded by consumers or tax payers as a more trustworthy alternative, as the theory would suggest, is not particularly relevant. In 1984–5 the Conservative-Christian Democrat government formulated a basic needs strategy which made NGOs central actors in policy implementation (Report to the Storting No. 36 (1984–5). The government argued that it was important to reach the poorest among the poor and the most vulnerable groups, if necessary by bypassing state structures in the recipient country. The NGOs were put forward as an alternative by the state itself, especially in view of their flexibility and their ability to pursue a grassroot-oriented policy. This reflects a general development in most donor countries and is very similar to what took place in other Scandinavian countries. But the rapid growth and the form it took were influenced by special factors. For example, the Minister in charge of development aid, Reidun Brusletten (from June 1983 to May 1986) with a background in voluntary missionary organizations, was instrumental in bringing NGOs to the centre stage in NORAD's development policy. Jan Egeland, Personal Secretary to the Foreign Minister and later State Secretary in the Foreign Ministry (from 1991) with a background as International Secretary in the Norwegian Red Cross, also played an important role in enlarging the space of NGOs in Norwegian foreign policy.

The functionalist theory about why organizations manage to occupy such niches, implies an assessment of their comparative advantages *vis-à-vis* the public sector: the state is regarded as bureaucratic and hierarchical in structure and monolithic in form. While this is a generally valid viewpoint, it is not very appropriate in this organizational field. Seen as a whole, the Norwegian state, of course, represents a formidable structure and power as compared with development NGOs. But development aid in Norway has, to a large extent, been an organizational field detached from other state interests and functions, because the Norwegian state has had few and not very important political and strategic interests in the developing world and the Norwegian business community has had relatively few economic interests in these same countries. Since its start in the 1950s, development aid has been a field reserved for 'good-hearted', altruistic and mission-oriented Norway. Historically speaking and on a general level, there has been a close relationship between the state administration and the organizations within this sub-sector, as is reflected in many ways, not least the fact that senior personnel have alternated between working in NGOs and working for the state.[12] People working in these state offices, and especially in NORAD, have often regarded themselves as spokesmen for the NGOs *vis-à-vis* the state machinery. Secondly, those state institutions working with the NGOs – the NGO Division, the Emergency Division, the First and Second Political Divisions in the Foreign Ministry – have been small, anti-bureaucratic, less hierarchical and less monolithic than some of the bigger organizations in Norway. Compared with many international NGOs like CARE, the Ford Foundation, etc. this goes without saying. The point is that some of the bigger NGOs have more organizational stability, a bigger and more professional administration, more money and are more conservative in many respects than some of these state offices. In many cases the state has been more interested in experimentation and more flexible than many of the NGOs, both because of the latter's financial vulnerability and because some of them have had a very firm ideological agenda.

The growth of this sector in Norway cannot therefore be explained by the failure of the state because of its ascribed characteristics such as hierarchical structure, bureaucracy, etc. Rather, it is the outcome of the combined effects of state achievements in inviting and mobilizing Norwegian voluntary organizations to broaden their work to include development aid. The state has been especially successful in getting national welfare and interest organizations to take on international development aid work (for example, the Norwegian Confederation of Sports, the Norwegian Housewives Association, the Norwegian Union of Teachers), and in opening the channel to what were originally solidarity organizations, which developed into service providers for official Norwegian aid. Many of the NGOs do not represent social strata in an economic sense or consumer interests, but are groups with different and competing political and ideological values; in other words, they are linked more to ideological agendas than to social diversity and consumer positions in Norway.

According to Weisbrod (1977, 1988), the non-profit sector is only a substitute for government, providing goods and services that the fully political community has not endorsed (government failure). In this case, the non-profit organizations have not taken upon themselves tasks that the government did not support. On the contrary, all Norwegian governments have emphatically supported the NGOs' role in aid. Within the above perspective government support for non-profit organizations cannot be explained either theoretically or empirically. What is of great importance, and a factor which has influenced the particular role of the state in supporting the NGO channel in development aid in most donor countries, is that at about the same time as aid was institutionalized, the state in most Western welfare state countries started to delegate functions via grants or contracts to NGOs.[13] Theories based on dichotomizing relations between states and 'civil society' can explain neither actual developments within the field nor national and regional variations in the NGO sector. The role and place of the organizations cannot be understood as one organized response to unsolved social problems because there is no simple one-to-one relationship between state and market failures and the number, character and types of NGOs in development aid.

NGOs in other donor countries

The initiative behind aid as a project, and also the plan to involve voluntary organizations with government support came from the US governments in the post-World War II period. Truman proposed the 'Point Four' programme, but already in 1946 his administration wanted 'to tie together the government and private programs in the field of foreign aid'. In the same year he appointed an Advisory Committee on Voluntary Foreign Aid attached to the Department of State and composed of representatives from the voluntary organizations and the government (Smith, 1990:45–6). This started a period of co-operation between US NGOs and the State Department which has continued up to the present day. The general argument from the government and Congress has been that support for private organizations would heighten their visibility and thereby, it was hoped, increase the support for all foreign assistance programmes, governmental and private (ibid.). In addition, the help would more efficiently reach the most needy (bypassing corrupt governments, and UN organizations, where the Soviets had a hand in the administration of resources, which could mean setbacks during the Cold War), and would also act as a useful channel for getting rid of surplus agricultural produce as food aid. The majority of American NGOs accepted their role, and were important supporters of American policy during the Korean and Vietnam wars.[14] Since the US Government asked its allies in 1962 to start giving support to voluntary or private organizations in order to widen and deepen the support for official development aid in the donor countries, all Western governments have adopted a policy of public support for development NGOs. The size of the support varies, as does the year when the different governments began to pursue this policy, but during the 1980s most states had established their own national NGO channels.[15] Apart from Smith 1990, however, there are very few historical-empirical studies about how the channel developed in the donor countries, the types of organization involved and their degree of financial dependence on the governments.

There is a clear tendency for states to have been instrumental in mobilizing the organizations to take part in aid, and government support has risen as a proportion of total NGO expenditure, although strict comparisons are difficult to make because of different national traditions and legal provisions regarding what are considered to be NGOs and in government funding. There are figures on income, but not expenditure, that can indicate the role of states in building up the international NGO system, as shown in Table 2.1.

Table 2.1
Some estimates of the percentage of NGO funds derived from official sources

Sweden	85%	(1994)
Belgium	80%	(1993
Italy	77%	(1991)
Canada	70%	(1993)
United States	66%	(1993)
Australia	34%	(1993–4)
France	15-22%	(1993)
Austria	10%	(1993)
UK	10%	(1993)

Sources: Smillie and Helmich 1993; Riddell *et al.*, 1995.[16]

NGOs in some developing countries

Salamon has described the growth in NGOs worldwide by the phrase 'everyone's doing it' (Salamon, 1994:111). In developing countries there has been a very significant growth, but the formative role of the NGO aid channel should not be underestimated. It seems it is, in particular, members of the educated middle-class, who come into contact with the aid channel, who are 'doing it'.

The present short analysis bases itself on empirical studies of NGO-government relations in Bangladesh, Ethiopia, Nicaragua and Zimbabwe, by a research team, plus a compilation of central legal documents and directories and official guidelines for the NGO sector in these and other developing countries by the author, and personal interviews with leading officials both in government and in the NGO community during five field visits to three of the study countries. It also draws on data collected by an extensive questionnaire survey to 119 organizations receiving support from the Norwegian Government and Norwegian NGOs in Bangladesh, Ethiopia, Nicaragua and Zimbabwe. In addition, information from secondary sources will be discussed. Empirical knowledge of the development of state-NGO relations in these countries is still very scanty, however. The following aims to show that the functional theories described above are not very useful when these NGO and organizational fields are to be explained or analysed.

Bangladesh

Bangladesh has a large number of different types of NGO. In 1993 at least 12,000 groups were registered. The NGO movement began after the war of independence in 1971 and the famine of 1974. Some NGOs with clear international connections started before then, for example, CARE International (1955) and East Bengal Evangelical Lutheran Church (1959). According to government sources there were only 122 international and 650 national NGOs registered in the country, under the Societies Act of 1860 and the Voluntary Societies (Registration and Control) Ordinance of 1961. In the early 1990s around US$100m was channelled to NGOs from external sources (about five per cent of total aid flows, UNDP, 1993:92). Others have argued convincingly that the percentage was around 15 per cent of the total aid flow. Whatever the exact distribution of support between the two sectors, the support for NGOs has been conducive to building up a strong and vocal NGO community. The most influential organizations in the country are part of the NGO-donor channel and are supported by foreign funds (our knowledge of Muslim NGOs and their link to Islamic funding sources in the Middle East is scanty).

The proliferation of small rural organizations in Bangladesh is, of course, partly a result of market or state failures. In a country like Bangladesh there are a lot of niches that need to be, and can be filled. But who has occupied them at a certain point in time is not decided by the market or the sectors' comparative advantages, but is primarily affected by decisions taken by donor governments and the Government of Bangladesh, and the ability of NGO leaders and potential NGO founders to communicate with the donors. Pervasive corruption during the Ershad regime was one reason why international donors swarmed around local NGOs, seeking alternative avenues for funds. This has led to a situation where most NGOs depend almost completely on external funding. At the end of the 1980s and the beginning of the 1990s the government sought to control what its predecessor had unleashed, which led to serious strife between the government's NGO Affairs Bureau and the NGO community.

The state and the NGOs are competing (and also collaborating), but the price is not so much market niches or political gains as foreign funds. The state is the winner and at the beginning of the 1990s was still receiving between 80 and 90 per cent of the foreign aid funds, but a gradual shift has taken place in the last few years. What counts in defining this division of functions is the institutional choices of the donors – and not of the consumers – as the theory would have us focus. Nor is it a zero-sum game, since aid for the government is partly made dependent upon its allowing foreign grants to Bangladeshi NGOs or 'Civil Society Organizations', as the Americans now call them. The point here is that in order to understand the NGOs' growth, it is insufficient and not particularly useful to focus on the market's or the government's failure in providing services, since that failure has existed for decades. To regard them simply as a functional necessity, as society's response, is no help in understanding the profile of the NGO community, or in analysing why these same organizations are issues of political strife. By some they are regarded as weapons of imperialism, of Christianity, of anti-government policies, or of pro-Indian policies, etc.[17] Others see them as expressions of pluralism, rationalism, and people-centred development.

Zimbabwe

NGOs in Zimbabwe mushroomed in the late 1980s and the early 1990s, but not as a result of government or market failures as such. In the 1980s it was the policy of Mugabe's party to mobilize the people by encouraging farmers' unions, trade unions, women's groups, etc. By the end of the 1980s external pressure was put on the Zimbabwe Government to restructure its policy, reduce state involvement, reduce social benefits, etc. By encouraging NGOs in this new context it became, and becomes, possible to achieve an important policy goal: to reduce the number of state employees and cut public budgets. There is no evidence to suggest that Zimbabwean consumers (at least not the poor rural households to which the NGOs direct their attention) have been against what the state has provided or that they have preferred relations with NGOs. It is primarily the World Bank and other donors that have been dissatisfied, and their leverage has changed the environment and space for both indigenous and international NGOs. The gap they have to fill has gradually been widening, not so much because of the laws of the economy, but because of external funding opportunities. Similarly, the NGOs that existed prior to independence were also the outcome of policies, at that time by the racist government, which banned black organizations, apart from 'apolitical' burial societies, etc.

Ethiopia

The growth of NGOs in Ethiopia has also been influenced by internal politics. First, the years 1973–91, marked by the authoritarian one-party regime which carried out systematic suppression of opposition of any kind, made it impossible for NGOs to emerge, unless illegally, like REST, ERA and ORA. Since the EPRDF takeover in 1991, there has been an environment conducive to increased national NGO activities. NGOs are expected to play an important role in rebuilding society and helping to create conditions for sustainable growth and democracy (the Ethiopian Government's Plan of Action towards implementing the national policy on disaster prevention and management, in *Redd Barna, Ethiopia,* 1993). The World Bank regards assisting private sector initiatives at all levels and the channelling of ODA for grassroots development as being among its main priorities.

In the period 1973–91 there was a growth of NGOs associated with liberation movements and NGOs wanting to assist refugees who had fled from Ethiopia. The combination of war and drought in 1984–5 caused both national and international NGOs to move in where the government was absent (for example, during the war and drought situation in 1984–5 they actually sought to support the 'closed', i.e. rebel-held, areas). Since 1991, the growth has entered a new phase. Now the government wants the NGOs to act as contracting partners and it also wants to monitor and control their activities more than before. The government and the NGOs are competing for funds, on the one hand, and on the other hand the government wants the NGOs to undertake operations. The donors, with the World Bank as the leading agency, have demanded a reduction in the role of the state. NGOs are encouraged, and since 1991 they have been officially encouraged, to form on the basis of ethnic allegiances.

It is therefore more useful in general to focus on market-external factors. The amount, and earmarking, of foreign funds is important. This partly reflects the number of catastrophes and their aid-mobilization character; if the BBC had not discovered the Koren camp in 1984, the Ethiopian NGO landscape would have looked very different. At a time when television seems to be a driving force behind international humanitarianism, the interest orientations of the media and individual journalists may have a more profound effect on countries' organizational landscape than theories about adaptive responses and niches will ever discover. Also important is the size and strength of the middle classes and the intelligentsia in the country, in other words, whether there are social groups capable of, and interested in, the formation of NGOs which satisfy donor notions and expectations, government policies and the recurrent trends followed by the international aid communities.

Nicaragua

In Nicaragua NGO activity developed more slowly than in other Latin American countries. At the end of the Somoza period there were only seven or so indigenous NGOs. The revolution changed the context radically. The existing NGOs received legal status, and new ones emerged. In this new climate the NGOs worked closely with the Sandinista Government in designing and implementing projects, and some of them were government instruments in disguise. Since the elections and the change of government in 1990, there has been an explosive growth in the number of indigenous NGOs. At the same time, their relationship with the state has changed to one of competition and confrontation. The conflict stems from, among other things, disagreements between the state and the NGOs on development objectives, the state's loss of social legitimacy, the emergence of stronger and more autonomous social movements and the withdrawal of the state from the social sector. Assessing the growth of NGOs, one finds a clear lack of complementarity. The failure of the market and the state has, on the one hand, created too broad a gap to fill, at the same time as there is a dissonance between NGOs and the state on which problems to solve, and by whom (Bebbington and Rivera, 1994:5–7). The amount channelled through NGOs increased from US$ 35–40m during the 1980s to US$ 100m in 1992 alone (estimates referred to in ibid.:7).

Functional theories – a 'mental blinder'

The theories of market niches, lack of government flexibility and other state failures confuse our understanding of the concrete historical development of the politico-economic context in which these organizations have mushroomed. To explain the growth of NGOs in these four countries by regarding them as a societal response to internal market or state failures is not very helpful. Rather, the majority of local NGOs have emerged as a response, not to internal conditions, but to growth in political and financial initiatives on the part of the donor community and the ongoing competition among donors for suitable and good local partners.

Care must be taken in transferring theoretical generalizations from one level or field to another or from one country to another. The functionalist theories might be fruitful in some countries and for some fields, but they provide little rationale for the character and growth of the NGO channel in aid. When the World Bank discusses growth in NGOs independent of conscious changes in its own policies, and explains its increasing support for NGOs in developing countries more or less as an organic outcome of its interest in poverty eradication (Paul and Israel, 1991:5), it is mystifying. The Bank's policy of reducing expenditure and state responsibility for social services in developing countries as pursued in the structural adjustment programmes, might be good or bad for a country's development (it is not an issue for this study), but without doubt it has fitted very well with giving NGOs an increased role. By employing the theories outlined above, the NGO scene is viewed through conceptual lenses that miss important aspects of both their role and their *raison d'être*. Their importance has mostly been evaluated in theoretical frameworks designed to review organizations in the commercial and government sectors (see Brown and Korten, 1991). But more importantly here, their origin and position – as a social phenomenon – cannot be explained and understood in this perspective.

Since NGOs are regarded as a functional response to failure, inherent weaknesses in the NGO channel itself have been underestimated or neglected, because the NGOs are seen as being functionally necessary. The theories support a dominant paradigm which portrays the relationship between government and the third sector in terms that are close to what economists would call a zero-sum game. Implicitly it tends to see a fundamental conflict between the NGOs – representing the voluntary sector or a 'civil society'– and the state. Some have argued that this conflict is 'the real conflict in modern political history' (Nisbet, 1962:109), but this is definitely not so within the aid organizational field. Rather, one might argue that most governments have discovered that NGOs can offer a relatively efficient means of furthering government interests and policies, interpreted broadly. On their side, the organizations, in order to become stronger, need institutional and financial support from the very government or firm to whose failure they are said to be a response. Governments in developing countries regard many NGOs as a convenient gap-filler, as a way of carrying out some services in areas from which they have withdrawn. The organizations generate a number of economic, political and social activities, but often closely integrated with the states. In many cases the governments can be regarded as purchasers of services, and in the structural adjustment programmes, the donors are the purchasers while the host governments comply with their conditions. The development arena is an arena for both private and public intrusion, and a meeting place which again influences both the private and public arena. The zero-sum model has had a strong influence and has prevailed, in spite of empirical data confirming beyond doubt that the situation is often one not of confrontation or competition for niches, but of overlapping functions. It is therefore not sufficient to focus on utility functions or incentive structures, but state policies must also be taken into consideration.

What has taken place cannot be ascribed to market failures, because there are no market conditions for the field as a whole. The competitive paradigm, enshrined as it is in political rhetoric, is not able to cope with the realities described above. It is not necessarily the case that the organizations are subject to 'competition with the state' (Douglas 1987:43). The relationship between the two sectors in most donor countries can rather be described as one of partnership and complementarity, although there also is competition. Growing donor government reliance on non-profit organizations is the rule rather than the exception. In many developing countries they are, however, competing, but that competition is related not to free market conditions but rather to the funds given by the international donor community. And the competition is as much among the NGOs, as between the NGOs and the state.

What has been called the 'administrative dilemmas approach', assumes that contradictory organizational principles are at the root of the processes of institutional choice. It has been argued that the performance failure and the transaction costs approaches both assume that institutions emerge as a result of choice processes. But since all governments involved in development aid and all governments in developing countries continually face situations where not all the services needed by the people are provided, they all – according to the theory – should want to ease their burden by handing over responsibility and power to NGOs. This theory cannot explain the important differences between countries or the way the variations actually take place. Moreover, although the governments of most developing (and some developed) countries face situations where a number of needed services are not provided, they refuse to give more power to NGOs, for political reasons. To ease the burden in the short run may make the burden of governing heavier in the long run.

These theories tend to leave unanswered a fundamental question: who makes the choices about what sector should be involved in aid? In the world of development aid it is irrelevant to build a theory on the assumption that individuals decide on their contractual arrangements. The different actors do not negotiate about the best institutional form as if it were a question of the provision and transferral of commodities between economic agents. While the dominant theory assumes free market conditions, these do not exist within the sector focused on here. The taxpayers in donor countries or the beneficiaries in the recipient countries do not have the power to determine what kind of institution is to be the provider of goods and services. The NGOs in donor countries which are involved in development aid have to a large extent become actors on the scene because the donor states have wanted them to do so. The manner in which they have been involved reflects different combinations of broader political aims, ideological trends and national traditions. What is needed, therefore, is a close investigation of the particular 'demand and supply aspects', to borrow concepts from these theories, of different settings for institutional choices, within a particular historical context. While it might be possible to understand the third sector in other fields as partly an organized response to unsolved social problems, this is not fruitful in this case. Here it is less a question of organized response, than of deliberate government policies, creating the arena for organizational establishments.

The theories outlined above take the form of a global model of hierarchical or sequential institutional choices, disregarding both national histories and particular political and economic contexts. This chapter has shown the importance of moving the analytical focus to particular historical contexts, the role of different governments and individual actors in these governments, the traditions and willingness of people to organize themselves to improve their livelihood, the importance of pressure from Northern NGOs and from national NGOs, as religious bodies, political parties, ethnic groups, etc. Since the aid sector is 'decommodified' and the whole project is a non-market system, theories which ultimately rest on the assumption of a free-market situation are not particularly relevant. The above theories disguise the question of power relations and diminish the role of the individual actor and the importance of the particular context in which NGOs develop.

Notes

1 There is a poverty in social science analyses of this field. Political science has specialized in the study of government. Economics has concentrated on the study of market-oriented institutions. Both of them have recently 'occupied' part of this field. Historical perspectives and historical research have been almost non-existent, as have anthropological approaches, in spite of the channel's role as a meeting-place between cultures both within and between societies.

2 This theory was first presented in an essay on day-care in the United States by Nelson and Krashinsky (1973). It was later generalized by Hansmann in 1980. He argued that NGOs 'of all types' typically arise in situations where consumers feel unable to evaluate accurately the quantity and quality of services a firm produces.

3 For a broader theory of the segmented state, see Powell and DiMaggio, 1991.

4 Norway is a country where the quality, quantity and availability of data and historical sources are sufficient to undertake such analyses. Tvedt 1992 and 1995 present large amounts of empirical data. The research team had open access to the archives of NORAD, permission to study very recent material in the Foreign Ministry and was met by the relevant NGOs with general openness regarding archival research.

5 The empirical data are taken partly from Tvedt, 1992 and partly from Tvedt et al., 1993.

6 The concept of a Scandinavian model has been elaborated by many when it comes to analyses of the welfare state, see for example Kuhnle, 1989 and 1992 and Kramer, 1992.

7 This section is based on detailed reconstruction of all government disbursements to NGOs in 1981, 1986, 1991 and 1993, collection of central policy documents, annual budgets and reports for 80 organisations for the years 1989,1990 and 1991, compilation of central policy documents, annual budgets and reports for ten selected organisations for the ten-year period 1981–91, and three questionnaire-surveys. In addition, extensive archival studies in NORAD and interviews with almost all leading actors of the Norwegian NGO scene.

8 NORAD's General-Secretary, Andresen, wrote in a memorandum on 17 August 1962 that the state should have only a supportive role and that the organization should provide at least half of the project funds itself. If not 'the natural distinguishing line between private and official projects will be rubbed out, and that might also create problems about who has the responsibility' (quoted in Tvedt, 1993a: 40. Translated by author).

9 This development is similar to what has taken place in other donor countries. The DANIDA/CASA report notes that 'SIDA is emphasizing the importance of the NGOs maintaining and developing their own identities and ideologies and wants the NGOs to consider their individual ideology and approach as an advantage...', DANIDA/CASA, 989: 154.

10 Allocations from NORAD to Norwegian voluntary organizations, information on developing countries and Norwegian aid in general have been generous since the start in 1966. In 1980, NOK 7.2m was allocated to 12 organizations under framework agreements (six of them were political parties) and to 41 other smaller campaigns. This amounted to 66% of the NORAD budget for information. In addition, 17 journalists received travel grants to developing countries that year from NORAD. In 1990, 22 organizations had framework agreements and 44 ad hoc

campaigns were also given money. The support to NGOs amounted to NOK 24m or 71% of the total NORAD information budget.

11 There were, of course, some disagreements between the state and the organizations even in the formative years. These disagreements were, however, mostly connected to debates between one type of organization and the state. The mission organizations wanted freedom to evangelize while NORAD introduced guidelines which made this illegal. NORAD's arguments were twofold: Norway should not interfere in other countries' internal and religious affairs, and NORAD wanted to establish development aid in Norway as a project which could be supported by the whole population. The image of aid as a continuation of missionary activities was not conducive to a policy of rooting aid as a national project.

12 There are many instances of personal unions between the political milieu, the state bureaucracy and the NGOs. In Norway this is more evident than in many other countries. Vesla Vetlesen, Norwegian Minister of Development Cooperation 1986–89, Hans Christian Bugge in the same ministry and Jan Egeland, State Secretary in the Ministry of Foreign Affairs, all had an NGO background. It is also quite common for MPs to be members of the boards of NGOs. Leaders of NGOs might often become employees of the NGO Division in NORAD or work for NORAD abroad, at least for short periods.

13 Even in the US, by 1975, the government had replaced private donors as the largest source of non-profits' revenues (DiMaggio and Anheier, 1990:143).

14 CARE, the Catholic Relief Service, World Vision, the American Red Cross, Lutheran World Relief among others were all active in Vietnam, with considerable support from the US Government. A delegation of representatives from different organizations visited Saigon in 1965, when President Johnson was about to step up the war effort. They declared that the role of the voluntary agencies, 'whose programs vary considerably from one to another, is supplemental to that of the government.... There should be no slackening of support for both types of activity, governmental and private, especially since they are working in increasingly close and effective collaboration' (D. Marr, 'The politics of charity, *Indochinese Chronicle* (October–November, 1974, cited in Smith, 1990:65).

15 New Zealand can serve as a typical example. The Voluntary Agency Support Scheme fund was established in 1974, administered by the Ministry of Foreign Affairs. The Foreign Affairs document that initiated the programme stated: 'A sustained national effort by the whole of New Zealand is required if New Zealand is to approach attainment of the international aid target of 1% of gross national product for total aid (official and unofficial) to developing countries. In addition to doing its best to ensure early achievement of the 0.7% target for official development assistance, Government has instituted a programme designed to promote private aid flows to developing countries. Under the scheme Government provides up to one third (as compared with one-half in Norway when the Norwegian system was established in 1963, author's comment) of the cost of approved projects undertaken in developing countries by non-governmental agencies' (quoted in 'New Zealand Coalition for Trade and Development' under the auspices of New Zealand's Official Development Assistance Programme, 1987:5). The same report quotes another document produced by the Ministry ten years later: 'The Voluntary Agency Support Scheme (VASS) was established in 1974 with a view to encouraging voluntary agencies to undertake approved aid projects which they otherwise may not have considered to attract financial support.' The Project Selection Committee comprised four NGO representatives selected by the organizations. A member of the staff of the External Aid Division of the Foreign Ministry acted as secretary to the committee and the Chair of the Foreign Affairs and Defence Committee was an ex-officio member (in 1987). At that time the state also introduced a subsidy of up to 75% for approved projects.

16 A study of Australian NGOs show that these figures for Australian NGOs as a whole are somewhat skewed by the large proportion of the totals which are accounted for by the two largest agencies: World Vision Australia and CARE Australia (both international NGOs). For the rest of the NGOs government support rose from 28% of their income in 1988 to almost 40% in 1992.

17 During the tug of war with the NGO community in July 1992 the Bangladesh Government made a list of 52 NGOs which were described as being engaged in missionary work, especially in proselytization.

3 How to Analyse an NGO Scene-I: Some Alternative Perspectives

How can one most fruitfully analyse the character and role of voluntary or private organizations in a particular country, and the manner in which this organizational scene affects and is affected by the NGO channel in aid? Why does the importance of NGOs, and their character, vary from one society to another, and how can the division of labour betwen NGOs and the state be explained? These questions have rarely been asked in studies of development NGOs. There have been few efforts at discussing theories and methodologies which could support such an analysis. On the political level this faint-heartedness is reflected in the fact that governments and donors have rarely attempted to formulate analytically comprehensive country-specific strategies for support to local organizations, giving sufficient thought to both state-society and donor-NGO relations. Reliable empirical data about the number and size of organizations, the scope of their activities, the degree of voluntarism, their ideology and their working methods are also rare.

The dominant interest has been in NGOs in micro-level development, in studying project effects and cycles rather than their role and impact at the regional level or in state arenas. For example, all 105 registered evaluation reports assessing the work of Norwegian NGOs up to 1991 dealt with project effects at the micro level (Tvedt, 1993a). This confirms the findings of Tendler concerning USAID-supported NGOs ten years before (Tendler, 1982), and according to other studies and a number of interviews in seven countries this was the general situation at the beginning of the 1990s. This finding underlines the prevalence and strength of the project perspective. Nevertheless, NGOs and other organizations are increasingly regarded as crucial actors in advancing democratization, advocacy and development, not only in the local setting but even nationally and globally. This gap between ascribed attributes and actual knowledge – against a background of a weak analytical tradition – makes it urgent to debate analytical and empirical approaches to understanding this field in development aid.

Functionalist approaches

The functionalism of the influential micro-economic school is not very useful in this context. It argues that the emergence of third-sector organizations is a functional necessity, or a natural societal response to state or market failures. Since niches created by such failures will be a universal phenomenon, it has also been regarded as normal that such organizations should emerge in all countries by conquering these niches. The focus of interest has therefore been their general comparative advantages, based on criteria of economic efficiency and assumptions of organizational flexibility and innovativeness. But the social choice processes and utility functions emphasized by economists are not particularly relevant, since they cannot account for the difference in size and character of the organizational landscape in both donor and developing countries. For example, there are many more voluntary organizations in the US, Britain and Norway than in countries like the Sudan, Pakistan and China, but this cannot be interpreted as the result of more state and market failures in the former group of countries. State and market failures are fewer in many Latin American and Asian countries in the 1990s than in the 1960s, yet the number of associations is still growing rapidly.

The literature also refers to 'service imperatives', i.e. that there are general service imperatives associated with particular tasks in society which create common organizational forms in various countries. The argument is that there are strong similarities between the nature and dynamics of each such programme area in each country (Hood and Schuppert, 1990:99). What is called the 'transactional approach to institutional analysis' (see Hood, 1986) is expected to 'predict under what circumstances one rather than another type of enterprise will tend to be appropriate, and it will also explain why forms of organizations other than core public bureaucracies have expanded in an apparently one-way manner' (Hood and Schuppert, 1990:104). The focus of this theory is Western Europe, but the way in which it is formulated makes it reasonable to test its explanatory power also in the development aid field. This theory of common organizational forms as a result of general service imperatives, may highlight some of the particularities of this field. The differences in ecology and social organizations are so great that the theory implicitly has to overlook fundamental differences in environment and societal structures between, for example, nomadic people on the fringe of the Sahara and dwellers in modern megacities. The transactions involved are too different to of themselves demand similarities in institutional choices. The theory has, however, influenced donors' NGO policies: the similarities in strategies in all countries and in all areas of countries determine common organizational forms. Institutional isomorphism is created, but – in this case – it should not be interpreted as a functional response to social service imperatives.

A more politically functionalist theory (Seibel, 1990) argues that NGOs and other non-profit organizations provide the state with unique opportunities to discharge insoluble social problems which may prove politically risky. Seibel mentions poverty alleviation and help to the handicapped, problems explained by inefficiency and lack of responsiveness on the part of the state. Again, there are examples of governments employing NGOs to undertake both insoluble and politically risky tasks, but this theory cannot explain intra-state variations or variations over time in the NGO sector in the same country.

Functional explanations should not be abandoned altogether in this field. But historically and empirically there are no clear or necessary causal links between, for example, a state's policy of minimum public power and a proliferation of NGOs in development. For example, the state's policy of 'minimum public power' in Norway in the middle of the last century, was one among many reasons why organizations developed relatively fast and gained influence (see Steen, 1948, Seip, 1984). The decay and demolition of state power in the rural areas in many African countries has not led to the same social response. On the other hand, it was a state, seeking maximum power through its aid policy – the US government under Truman, Eisenhower and Kennedy – that initiated a process that later led to the proliferation of development NGOs in donor countries. Functional theories cannot explain why in some countries the role of NGOs should be seen as the outcome of a conscious move to strengthen state and government control by proxy. NGO proliferation may in other cases be seen as an effort to maintain government influence by adapting public policy to changing financial and political environments, or as the outcome of private societal responses to World Bank structural adjustment policies, but responses made possible and financed by donor governments.

Implicitly these theories have held that organizations adapt easily and quickly to changing environments. The organizational landscape which exists in a particular country at a particular point in time will therefore be regarded as a mirror or reflection of existing failures or niches in the society. The institutions involved are simply regarded as institutions executing necessary social functions, and not as organizations of human agents with identities, objectives and histories. So long as this perspective has prevailed, a historical or cultural perspective has been regarded as irrelevant. A useful approach should facilitate explanation of both the growth of the field and variations in the development aid sector in donor as well as developing countries, and how they interact with and influence each other and the society at large.

The national-style approach

Within this analytical perspective the organizational structure and landscape in a particular country are seen as a reflection of its cultural and historical characteristics, rather than as functional products of market and state failures. This perspective has been called 'the national-style approach' (see, for example, Hood and Schuppert, 1990). National organizational culture is regarded as a crucial explanatory variable, since historical contingencies have a fundamental impact on institutional choice. The size, role and character of the organizational field are analysed and explained by referring to the unique historical circumstances of societies and cultures. DiMaggio and Anheier write: '... nonprofit-sector functions, origins and behaviour reflect specific legal definitions, cultural inheritances, and state policies in different national societies' (ibid.:137). They continue: 'One can predict the legal form of most organizations if one knows the industry and nation-state in which they operate' (DiMaggio and Anheier 1990:139). Since institutional design is regarded as something deeply rooted in tradition, it will be explained by factors which change only slowly in the society. What is required is a 'deep and holistic understanding of the individual political system within which these political decisions are made' (Hood and Schuppert, 1990: 95). Analysis of the relationship between such organizations and the state or the position of the 'third sector' tells the way 'in which societies "choose" to govern themselves' (Anheier and Seibel, 1990:2). Most work on the third sector and NGOs in Western welfare states has been in a 'national style vein' (Hood and Schuppert, 1990: 95), and the explanation of institutional patterns has been done on a country-by-country basis (see, for example, Anheier and Seibel, 1990). For the third sector in developed countries, which are characterized by a certain stability in constitutional rules and state/society relations, this has proved to be a useful perspective.[1]

The questions are: how useful is this approach in explaining the organizational landscape in developing countries and how does it cope with the megatrends in the development aid sector in donor states? And to what extent will it disregard the crucial importance of international factors in shaping the NGO landscape and the third sector in developing countries? And how useful is this theory in explaining the development and functioning of the NGO aid system in donor countries?

The national-style approach in donor countries

There has recently been a growing interest in the national-cultural background to the NGO field in development. A rather recent OECD study (Smillie and Helmich, 1993), suggests that different institutional patterns in different donor countries should be explained by distinctive national cultures. It focuses on 'the organizational culture in which voluntary action develops, or does not' (ibid.:16). As the study demonstrates, an advantage of such an approach is that it draws attention to the varied history of relations between NGOs and governments and also between organizations at large and the state. It also implicitly questions what has become a mania in development research; the tendency to produce generalizations of 'African NGOs', the 'Asian NGO scene', etc., abound in the literature.

Three arguments are of importance. First, by focusing on culture, which is difficult to define (the OECD study evades this problem by not defining it), and even worse to identify empirically in a national context, the approach will tend, within the politicized setting of organization-state relations, to encourage superficial descriptions of countries' past and create stereotypes.[2] The OECD study argues, for example, that Norwegian culture can explain NGO-state relations in aid; 'Norwegian corporatism' is contrasted with 'pluralism or democratic pluralism' in the US and Canada, where voluntary associations help to ensure that no single interest or interest group will prevail over others on a given issue (Smillie and Helmich, 1993: 16-17). The pluralist approach is 'rooted in a clear separation of powers between government, political parties and interest groups' (ibid.:217) whereas in Norway and other Scandinavian countries the organizations work together with the government 'to develop a consensual approach to policy and governance'). The problem with this analysis is that it downplays a similar development in most donor countries regarding the NGO channel in aid – a closer integration between the state and the organizations and the prevalence of a predominantly collaborative relationship between governments and development NGOs.

In descriptions of political cultures and national traditions, fundamental notions like 'state', 'civil society', 'NGOs', 'democratic pluralism' and 'corporatism' are metaphors. Moreover, the dynamics of their interrelations do not constitute suprahistorical phenomena, but must be given a concrete meaning in a specific historical and geographical context. Since the notions and concepts against which this history is assessed are often injected with highly ideological values, the national-style approach may encourage politically or ideologically convenient inventions of a country's cultural past, and also a tendency to explain the past by the present, or present NGO roles simply by past national cultures and traditions.

Secondly, the development of the aid sector in Norway reflected general ideological trends internationally as well as in Norway. Support for NGOs started in the 1960s in all OECD countries as a result of US and UN initiatives. NGO divisions were established in most donor countries. The 1980s was the NGO decade both internationally and in Norway. In all countries a growing proportion of NGO funds came from the state. The main lines in the Norwegian development were thus very similar to those in other donor countries. Research has shown that, since the end of the last century, many of the most influential NGOs in the US have been dependent on public support.

Moreover, the NGOs in aid were recognized as important actors earlier than were voluntary organizations in many other organizational fields in Norway. Their ideological breakthrough came with the Report to the Storting, No. 36 (1984–5).[3] Already in 1977 the Norwegian state had decided to give direct support to organizations in the main co-operating countries,[4] even organizations representing a clear opposition to their own governments and with minimum NORAD control of what they were doing.

The history of voluntary associations in Norway dates back to the the middle of the nineteenth century (see Steen, 1948; Seip, 1984). When the NGO decade started there were many strong organizations working in close co-operation with the government. National traditions can account for the breadth and hetereogeneity of the organizational field. But the rapid increase from seven aid NGOs in 1963 to more than 140 working in developing countries in 1991, and the growth in relative importance from about seven per cent of total bilateral aid in the 1970s to more than 25 per cent in the early 1990s cannot be explained simply within a national style approach, but must be seen as the result of truly international mega-trends in the donor community. The political and ideological environment was increasingly favourable to voluntary associations generally, and to NGOs in aid in particular. The ideological climate in the late 1980s and early 1990s idealized the voluntary sector in general. It is problematic to describe this as an organic outcome of a national tradition, since it represented, as shown, a break with this tradition.

Thirdly, national traditions are not simply reflected in the aid sector, because of the sector's particular nature and mechanisms as compared with other areas in society. Let us assume that the dichotomized description in the OECD study – of corporatism as the organizational culture in Norway and pluralism in the US – is apt. The problem is that this information is not very helpful in analysing Norwegian or US NGOs in development aid. The US Government has used and contracted NGOs for policy purposes since World War II (see Smith, 1990). The role of CARE as a weapon in US policy against President Nasser in connection with the Suez crisis in 1956 is well documented, as is the pro-government role of US NGOs in Vietnam and Korea during the wars there. It is not difficult to show that US organizations have not only co-operated with the government, but have willingly functioned as a cover-up for espionage and clandestine policies. This is natural, because the US is a superpower with global economic, political and military interests. Similarly it is easy to list many US NGOs which have followed a strongly independent line *vis-à-vis* their own government's foreign policy initiatives. Norwegian NGOs have in general been more sheltered from interference or demands from the Foreign Ministry. The NORAD representatives in most countries where Norwegian NGOs have been working, have had very superficial knowledge about what they were doing. Until the late 1980s NORAD was not particularly interested in co-operation or co-ordination with Norwegian NGOs in developing countries, partly because of capacity problems. Moreover, the Storting has clearly stated that Norwegian NGOs are to work independently of interference from the Norwegian state.

There are therefore no one-to-one relationships between 'pluralism' and 'corporatism' in the donor country and the extent to which development NGOs are instruments of state power or 'corporate will'. The organizational and political distance between the US embassy and the US NGO is generally much shorter than that between the Norwegian NGOs and their embassy or NORAD office, and the need for policy co-ordination arises more often in a US than in a Norwegian context. It is therefore not a paradox that a donor country with a corporatist culture can, because of a host of factors unrelated to national cultural traditions, support Northern NGOs that act more independently than NGOs from pluralist countries may do. In order to analyse the relationship between NGOs and the state in donor countries and how these actors interact with organizations in developing countries, it is therefore necessary also to include such factors as state power, economic interests, strategic interests, distance, the donor state's capacity and competence.

The national-style approach de-emphasizes the particular context and political history of the development aid field. The role of NGOs in this arena can be, and often is, very different from that of voluntary associations in other organizational fields in the same country. In many countries the aid system is a relatively autonomous system, with its own developments, norm systems and value orientations. There have been different conditions for the construction of the NGO aid system than for other systems within the third sector. (This relates to the system as a whole; it emerged as a foreign policy issue. It also relates to the individual organization; there are important differences between the growth, ways of functioning, etc. of local sports associations while working in the donor country, and the background to how they became involved in aid and how they operate in this arena.) The focus on deep-seated cultural traditions will tend to miss these differences between sub-systems within the same countries and between countries.

The OECD report argues that by contrasting the cultural traditions of 'corporatism' with 'pluralism' or 'democratic pluralism', one can find the most important variable and focus point in future NGO policies. If this materializes, the question of defining and assessing national culture or national style becomes a question of immediate political importance. A contrastive discussion between corporatism and pluralism is identified as the most useful way of 'approaching the question of where NGOs fit in society, and why they differ from one country to another' (Smillie and Helmich, 1993:217).[5] This dichotomy therefore assumes that corporatism and pluralism are cultural properties and mutually exclusive categories in any one given society, that it is a fundamental issue in all countries, and that cultural traditions decide the role of NGOs in a society.

The national-style approach in developing countries

An analysis of the role of NGOs and the third sector in developing countries must, of course, take account of national traditions. Different historical patterns in religion-state relations, the degree to which the state is subordinated to interests originally rooted in religious traditions or differences, the strength of state structures, the level of communication and contact between state and society and the type of legal system, significantly shape the role that NGOs have played. A focus on such traditions will also enable questions about NGO potentials in different countries. For instance, it is obvious that the potentials for NGO growth and influence have been much stronger in India than in the Southern Sudan, due to differences in level of education, experiences in organization, etc. Political cultures may also influence the extent to which NGOs may be able to implement 'bottom-up strategies', because the task will be different in very hierarchical societies from that in societies with more equality. National cultural traditions, for example, also form an environment for what Northern NGOs might achieve: the constraints and potentials of the Lutheran Mission as a development NGO may be affected by working in a Muslim, Orthodox or Catholic country. The problem of differences in culture and traditions and how these create unique structures for NGO activities in different countries and regions has not been discussed very much in NGO literature.

The methodology and approach of the national-style approach in analysing development NGOs are inappropriate. Firstly, to talk about deep-seated cultural traditions as decisive while paying no atttention to the implications of abrupt political and economic changes and instability for NGO work, neglects an important aspect of many (but by no means all) developing countries. Recurring revolutions in the state apparatus and state policies will have important consequences for relations between the state and society and for the space available for NGO formation. Ethiopia under Mengistu and Meles and Nicaragua under the Sandinistas and Chamorro, for example, fundamentally changed relations between the state and the NGOs in both countries. Traditions in such contexts should not be defined only as 'deep-seated cultural notions', and the historical perspective should embrace analysis of political actors and events.

Secondly and more important in the context of this study, a purely national focus will downplay the impact of external influence on the organizational landscape through the aid channel, and thus divert attention from a crucial question of long-term development: the relationship between the entire organizational landscape in the country and the NGO channel's role and potential within it. From 1970 to 1990 the total funds transferred by and through Northern NGOs rose by twice the rate of increase for international aid as a whole (UNDP, 1993:88). Between these dates official aid via NGOs (excluding emergency and relief budgets, which in Norway and many other countries have been higher than those for long-term development aid) rose tenfold in real terms. The number of Southern NGOs receiving funds also increased dramatically. In recent years Southern NGOs have become the new darlings of development aid, not least as central agents in realizing what is called the 'New Development Paradigm'. NGOs are mushrooming at what is – when compared with the past or national traditions and organizational culture – a very high speed. This holds for both national and international NGOs. These dramatic and global changes cannot therefore be explained by national traditions, alone.[6]

The present organizational landscapes are not organic outcomes of long-term, deep-seated traditions. Compared with the time and processes of *la longue durée*, they are in many cases superficial present-day products, characterized by weak roots in the society in which they operate. It is crucial therefore to develop an approach which takes into account the fact that the institutional choices in a recipient country are often donor-led and that the position of the NGO community, and therefore the whole third sector, not only reveals the way in which a society chooses to govern itself; it is also fundamentally influenced by political decisions by foreign governments, and that it is therefore necessary but insufficient to acquire a 'deep and holistic understanding of the individual political system within which these decisions are made' (Hood and Schuppert, 1990:95). For more than a decade there has been a rush among donors to find fundable national NGOs in the developing countries. To a large extent they have mushroomed in response to external funds and rapid political changes, both concerning types of organization, value orientations, development rhetoric and in which sectors they work. (A simplified chronology would be: co-operatives in the 1970s, women's groups in the 1980s, environmental groups in the late 1980s, AIDS-groups at the turn of the decade, civil society organizations in the early 1990s.) At the same time their working style, their nearness to the state, and their degree of integration with society and the public sector may express cultural traditions and national institutional environments.[7] To capture the dynamics between the overall organizational landscape and the role of NGOs in aid, we shall argue that it is fruitful to approach the NGO channel analytically as a new type of international social system. This approach rejects analyses which argue superficially that the 'existence of NGOs, their types, interests, activities, etc., is an indication of the situation of civic society *vis-à-vis* the nation state' (Fowler, 1988:2).

To analyse particular national traditions and organizational cultures might help in understanding the particular character and size of an NGO landscape. But an underlying assumption – that the historical-political context is the same as the *national* political-cultural system, or that this history will have the same effect on the development aid arena as it has had on other areas of third-sector activity – is not a necessary implication. The national-style approach, if it allows for more attention to individual actors and particular historic events (and not only structures), may be helpful in explaining cross-national differences, but it is less useful in explaining obvious similarities in developments within this field.

An international social system approach

What are often described as unique and distinctive national 'styles' are often reflections of general international trends – mega-trends. In aid, formal organizational types and policy directions are influenced by 'universal' trends. In general the emergence and formation of NGOs in developing countries have been described, based on implicit theories which regards organizations as an expression of the particular interests or objectives of groups within the body politic. The existence of NGOs, their types, interests, activities, etc. have also been analysed within a state/ civil society dichotomy, where the organizational space is seen as an indicator of the relation between state and society in the country. Functionalist perspectives have not paid much attention to the background of the NGO aid sector.

Many NGOs have also, of course, experienced a relatively benign but pervasive dependency relationship with most donors. It has generally been said that institutional designs tend to be deeply rooted in tradition, linked to 'fundamental constitutional rules and legal assumptions, which themselves change only very slowly' (Hood and Schuppert, 1990:94). This universal description presupposes the existence of a strong state authority, able not only to formulate such rules, but more important and more difficult, to enforce them in relation to international and national NGOs. Moreover, these rules are not only a national product in today's NGO world: they are the outcome of negotiated values and compromises among NGOs, governments and donor communities and institutions. Since many developing countries have weak states with often feeble authority for efficient rule making and enforcement, the space for NGOs may be larger than fundamental legal assumptions and traditions should assume.

An unmixed national-style approach might therefore legitimize the current rhetoric; if the NGO scene we see is the implicit outcome of national traditions, an equal partnership between donors and local NGOs or between foreign forces and national groups has already been established. This approach may also downplay the importance of a globalizing ideology, with consequences for institutional choices and institutional isomorphism: the NGOs mushrooming in the developing countries do not necessarily express societal needs and values in a particular country, but mirror needs and values expressed at UN conferences, donor conferences, etc. The approach does not explain or take sufficient account of the impact of the NGO decade worldwide. Despite different traditions and cultures, during the 1980s there was a very significant growth in NGO activities across most countries. To account for this global trend one cannot limit the focus to national arenas. This perspective will also tend to neglect the important role of international NGOs, supported by a number of different donors, the 'home-government', the UN-system, other governments and other NGO networks. Their great number, the high level of activity, their size of funds and the fact that they are the managers of the international NGO language, influence in fundamental ways the institutional design and organizational map in developing countries. A national-style approach cannot account for the processes of homogenization or isomorphism across national boundaries.

What is crucial is the need for combining domestic and international structures in the analysis. The domestic or national context affects the nature of the NGOs and of the NGO-government relationship and the institutions with which the NGOs interact. It is not a good guide to rely only on the national past in seeking to understand this particular area of third sector–government relations. Nor is it fruitful to introduce static, ahistorical terms such as 'indigenous NGOs' as opposed to 'not-indigenous NGOs' (see Fowler, 1988:2), since most organizations are the outcome of internal traditions and external influences. This applies to donor countries; some of the most influential organizations in Norway – the Norwegian Trade Unions and the National Sports Association, were founded in the last century, under strong influence from the rest of Europe. And it applies also to developing countries: some of the strongest NGOs in Africa, Asia and Latin America, both financially and as regards popular backing and the degree of voluntarism, are religious organizations, often imported from Europe or the Arabian peninsula. By combining a national-style approach and the international social system approach the complex development processes shaping the NGO scene in the aid area can be taken properly into account. Development aid is different from social service provision in welfare states. It is less embedded in national traditions and the subsequent type of institutional inertia. The international context and the donor structure have influenced the organizational landscape. Structural, institutional history has to be combined with an analysis of the concrete, historical process of how the system produces and reproduces particular relations and practices in interaction settings. By employing this perspective, the object of analysis can be constructed in a new, and it is to be hoped, more fruitful way.

Analysis of the NGO sector should therefore rather be looked upon as one social system, and a social system of a particular kind. It is a global system, donor-led but with a great number of supporters in the developing countries, which helps to transform the conceptual horizons of millions of poor farmers. This happens in parallel with a general increase in the influence of donors in overall economic policy discussions, implicit in the liberalization programmes announced by the World Bank and the major donors in the mid-1990s. To limit the focus to functional theories or to national-style approaches is to disregard the fundamental way in which the system operates and develops, and how the channel interacts with and transforms societies. Analytically the function of the theories may be to conceal fundamental power conditions influencing the relation between state and society in different societies.[8]

Some examples of how the NGO scene in such a perspective and related to the four study countries, Bangladesh, Ethiopia, Nicaragua and Zimbabwe, can be approached, will be discussed below.

The development of the NGO landscapes cannot be explained by the particular country's national or political culture alone, but the connection between dramatic political changes, often caused by individual politicians and political forces, and the intervening role of foreign NGOs and funds must also be analysed.

The modern NGO story in *Nicaragua* starts with the establishment of Caritas-Nicaragua, a Nicaraguan Catholic Episcopal Conference which began to operate in the mid-1950s (this section is based on Skar et al., 1994 and Bebbington and Rivera, 1994). The earthquake of 1972 gave birth to the largest NGO in Nicaragua today, CEPAD – the Consejo de Iglesias Evangelicas Pro-Alianza Denominacional. During the Somoza dictatorship organizations like INPHRU (Instituto Nicaraguense de Promoción Human),1966, CEPA (Centro de Educación y Promoción Agraria), 1974 and the ERN (Escuelas Radiofonicas de Nicaragua), 1966, began literacy work and organizational activities. The Bishops' Conference at Madeleine in 1968 declared its 'option for the poor', and gave support to such activities. This development was influenced both by national traditions, natural catastrophes and political and ideological trends in the Catholic Church internationally, plus the popularity of Paulo Freire. At the end of the 1970s, another group of NGOs began to appear, such as ADP (Associación para el Desarrollo de los Pueblos) and CRISOL, the Christian

Committee in Solidarity with the People of Nicaragua, together with CEPAD, FUNDE and the Red Cross.

Thus during the years of insurrection against the Somoza dictatorship (in the 1970s), many of the present NGOs emerged and were consolidated. Examples are the Sandinista Defece Committees, the beginnings of the women's organization AMPRONAC (Associación de Mujeres Frente à la Problematica Nacional), the Association of Farm Workers (ATC), which later continued as a farm workers' organization with a spin-off, UNAG – the Nicaraguan Union of Small Farmers and Ranchers – and the urban union movements, especially industrial, teachers, health and other public sector workers. At the end of the Somoza period, in 1978, there were six or seven national NGOs supported by the international community and international NGOs.

During the Sandinista period the context of NGO work changed fundamentally, partly because of the change in government policy. Important NGOs that had been established in the 1960s and 1970s were further consolidated. Officials from some of the major NGOs accepted important positions in the Sandinista Government.[9] Several major new NGOs were created. The Augusto C. Sandino Foundatio (FACS) was established in 1980; it aimed at channelling support to Sandinista-affiliated mass organizations.

The Manolo Morales Foundation, affiliated to the Christian Democratic Party, was founded in 1982, and began working in development projects with trade unions and peasants. A few NGOs, such as the Centro Antonio Valdievieso (CAV) and the Eje Ecumentico, were created and began to specialize in development projects with Christian-based communities. In general, the NGOs were very pro-government, as was the international NGO community.

Foreign NGOs were attracted to Nicaragua by the Sandinista revolution. No less than 120 offices of international NGOs were opened in Nicaragua during the 1980s, and many of them established direct relationships with popular organizations or with the government. Coupled with the enormous growth in donor funds for NGOs and the government's policy of mobilizing the masses, this shaped the NGO scene during this period. Significantly, many Nicaraguan NGOs opened offices for international relations and began to negotiate projects directly with international NGOs. Relations with the government were very good throughout the 1980s for the majority of NGOs. NGO co-operation represented one of the major sources of dollar liquidity, as Nicaragua was starting to feel the consequences of the economic and financial boycott by the US and most of the multilateral financial institutions. It was rare to see an NGO development project which did not have a strong component of local support from the government. In some cases, NGOs channelled funds from international NGOs to government projects. As a rule, the major national NGOs received the majority of their financing via international NGOs.

When Dona Violeta took power after the victory of UNO in 1990, as many as 350 new NGOs were registered (Skar et al., 1994:15). The deep-seated cultural traditions did not, of course, change overnight, but in the early months of 1990 outgoing members of the Sandinista-dominated National Assembly, hastened to register civil legalities which could provide both alternative employment for those out of power and para-political platforms. Only about 150 of these NGOs have survived.[10] New NGOs were established by those with connections to the Violeta government, often led by people returning from exile in the US. The government also established some NGOs of its own to channel services out of the state arena.

The shifts in orientation and the rapid growth in numbers indicate the importance of external funds. When first published in 1991, the Directory of NGOs in Nicaragua reported a total of 174 local NGOs (based on the available lists of existing NGOs and the lists of the newly approved NGOs from the National Assembly). Two years later, the Directory was re-edited. Approximately 100 of those previously identified had disappeared and 53 new ones had been established, the majority of which had begun work in 1991.[11] The 39 organizations receiving support from Norway had more than 1,600 employees in 1992.

The external linkages developed in new policy contexts. The government was trying to roll back the state to a minimum. It reversed the past policy by pursuing a neo-liberal policy. From a decade of state-led development in a war economy, Nicaragua has been developing according to a policy of rapid state retrenchement. Within a couple of years NGO-state relations have changed from a situation of collaboration to one of confrontation and competition. The government has been ideologically in favour of private organizations. The problem is that some of these NGOs have also been platforms for the political opposition. A fact which illustrates this situation well is that in 1993 the most important government administrator in NGO affairs used to be a spokesman for the Southern Contras in Washington during the war.

In *Zimbabwe* an analysis of the NGO landscape or of the NGO–state relations has to take account of the impact of the racial policies of the settler state. (This analysis is mostly based on Moyo 1994.) The UDI government restricted most forms of non-governmental organizational work by law. Only social clubs were allowed among blacks. The white-run NGOs that existed maintained the missionary 'civilizing' tradition. Christian Care and the Catholic Development Commission (CADEC) were the main channels for NGO assistance. When Ian Smith's rule ended, there were hardly any NGOs concerned with the problems of the black majority.

After independence the environment for NGO establishment changed fundamentally. A growing number of black NGOs emerged, with the declared aim of contributing to the country's rehabilitation and reconstruction. They developed close links with government agencies, particularly departments concerned with improving the welfare of the citizens. From the outset these NGOs were supported from abroad, and these external linkages were one reason why the government's attitude in the first years was one of distrust.

The volume of funding to NGOs in Zimbabwe has grown rapidly since 1980. The foreign support for NGOs has been estimated at US$ 40m a year, representing one-tenth of all foreign assistance to Zimbabwe. It was estimated to be equivalent to between 15 and 25 per cent of total ODA in 1990, and probably represented 20 per cent of the official foreign currency aid inflows at that time (Moyo and Katoure, 1991:58).[12] There has been a wide range of sources of funds available to the NGOs. NOVIB, Netherlands, was found to have contributed 27 per cent of the NGO assistance recorded. OXFAM, Save the Children, (UK and Norway), and Norwegian People's Aid have all established country branches operating in Zimbabwe. Church-based NGOs, such as the World Council of Churches, continue to raise significant levels of funds. Secondly, there are foreign government agencies such as NORAD, SIDA, ODA, CIDA, USAID. Since 1986 NORAD for example, has channelled about US$3m annually to a total number of 45 local NGOs. A third source of funding is the multilateral agencies, although in Zimbabwe they play a rather marginal role. The European Union is the biggest multilateral funder; its annual allocation has risen from about ECU 1.5m in 1989 to over ECU 2m in 1994.

The importance of foreign funds can be seen in the number and types of NGOs that exist. As some donors have reduced their contributions (Sweden cut back its foreign aid by ten per cent in 1992, while the UK froze its ODA), some NGOs have been obliged to change both their aims and their profiles; some transformed themselves into a sort of consultancy firm or started income-generating businesses. Many also shifted their focus from a local level to national and regional levels. The structural adjustment programme (ESAP), introduced in 1991, affected the NGO community. NGOs faced increased competition with the deregulation of agricultural markets and the liberalization of imports, but, on the other hand, their prospects as 'gap-fillers' increased.

The relative importance of external linkages is, of course, affected by the alternative funding sources nationally. In Zimbabwe private sector funding amounts to less than ten per cent of the overall NGO funding (Moyo, 1994). The government's development policy and strategy are not designed to target NGOs as a channel for financing development. Government financial support is mainly available through the payment of salaries in private mission hospitals and schools. Otherwise, NGOs gain access on an *ad hoc* basis to the use of government expertise in the design and management of their projects, and to the use of government offices, schools and facilities. The government has also entered into direct joint ventures with a handful of NGOs (ibid.:67) The most obvious way in which the government indirectly supports the NGOs is through the legal provision for their exemption from overall income taxes and some import duties. Taking all these sources together, they are insignificant, and will be so for a long time to come in comparison with the funds from foreign donors. This external dependency has produced an identity crisis for many Southern NGOs. More often than not their creation was directly linked to Northern NGOs, 'SADEC NGOs have tried to assume the characteristics of their Northern counterparts in an attempt to create a look like [*sic*] NGO' (Moyo and Katerere, 1991:1). Since donors have consciously prioritized what are called development NGOs, and not traditional, more welfare-oriented NGOs, they have not only had a substantial impact on the whole fabric of Zimbabwean society, but they have helped to reshape power relations between different organizational types in that society.

In *Ethiopia* there have been, historically speaking, weak traditions for organizations or voluntary organizations, outside government or church control. After World War II Haile Selassie gradually allowed the formation of associations, provided they were in accordance with the constitution of the Empire and the relevant specific legislation. He also opened the door to Western missions. Welfare associations emerged in the 1950s to serve their home areas, and through such home-area organizations several schools, clinics and roads were built. Basically these organizations were ethnically-based welfare associations. From one point of view, these may be seen as the forerunners of the present proliferation of ethnically based NGOs.

The history of the Ethiopian NGO field can be divided into three periods: a) the Haile Selassie period, b) the Mengistu period and c) the period after the EPRDF took over in 1991. Two events are especially important, the drought of 1984 and the Charter of the Meles Government. Even before 1984 NGOs were active in the country. Redd Barna, Norway, started in 1969, the Norwegian Lutheran Mission has had support from NORAD since 1963, Norwegian Church Aid arrived during the mid-1970s. A number of mainly Christian-based NGOs were working in this period. The Relief and Rehabilitation Commission (RCC) was established in 1974 in response to the need for relief in Wollo; it was charged with the responsibility of co-ordinating relief efforts. In spite of clear guidelines from the government, this body was unable to control or evaluate the NGOs, because of lack of capacity.

The drought of 1984/5 created a humanitarian outcry in Britain and the US Band Aid was started. Michael Jackson, Bob Dylan and others sang charity songs for Africa and a great number of new NGOs went to the Horn to help. The BBC's discovery of the Koren camp thus had a significant impact on the Ethiopian organizational landscape. The pattern of NGO development was directly influenced by the government's refusal to grant international agencies safe passage to areas under the control of guerrilla movements in the north. The Ethiopian Government wanted to command the distribution of relief, as a political and military weapon, officially an estimated 40 international NGOs took part in this relief operation. Presumably the true figure was nearer to 100. Although unclear criteria make it difficult to obtain exact figures, more than ten Norwegian NGOs worked in the area and many more collected money to alleviate the crisis.

Some local NGOs also emerged, but apart from those attached to guerrilla movements, these were very weak (also because at that time it was not usual for donors to channel money to local NGOs). The total number of NGOs in Ethiopia is unclear. The FINNIDA report says 'more than a hundred', 'most of them international or foreign' (Satokoski et al., 1994: 3). In March 1993 there were more than 90 Ethiopian organizations (92 registered by the RRC in 1994, six awaiting registration).[13] According to figures from the Relief and Rehabilitation Commission, there are currently (August 1994) 229 NGOs, 134 of them indigenous and 95 international. Until 1990 only seven Ethiopian NGOs were registered by the RRC, while in 1992 alone 21 were registered. In 1994 the government estimated that about US$200m were transmitted through NGOs (Karadawi, 1994). Currently 97 international NGOs are registered with RRC and with the Ministry of the Economy and External Cooperation (MEEC).

The emergence of strong liberation movements in Ethiopia and Eritrea created NGOs of a special type. They not only distanced themselves from the state and the government, they also fought to bring down both. Most opposition groups, often organized along ethnic lines, now have an NGO, because everyone knows that – at least in the past – this was the most efficient way to mobilize funds. One example, the Tigray People's Liberation Front (TPLF), operating in the western part of Tigray, drove the Ethiopian Democratic Union out of Tigray in 1977. Its political and military line was to mobilize the rural people around its programme for rural transformation and national liberation. In this policy the role of its NGO, REST, in providing material benefits for the population cannot be overemphasized. REST was established in 1978, initially to start health and education projects. Due to the escalation of the war after 1978 and the onset of droughts and famines, REST became responsible for co-ordinating the largest relief programmes in the area. By the early 1980s, it had gained the confidence of European and US aid agencies. By 1982 it was officially registered with the Sudanese Government as a humanitarian NGO. This was a crucial event, which gave it access to the international donor market. The Emergency Relief Desk (ERD), led by Norwegian Church Aid from Khartoum, transported enormous amounts of food across the border. REST's standing and role overshadowed those of other NGOs in the area. Its success was one reason behind the power shift in Addis Ababa after the war.[14]

The Christian Relief and Development Association (CRDA) illustrates this internal-external relationship. It was formed in 1973 in response to the Wollo famine and was originally an *ad hoc* co-ordinating body for foreign Christian NGOs (called the Christian Relief Association). As the need for continued assistance failed to abate, the CRA evolved into the CRDA in 1984, since when it has acted as an umbrella agency (with a membership of about 90 NGOs in 1993). The CRDA is not operational in the field, but functions as a transmission belt for money through its member NGOs. Its strength has derived from it being a broad forum for church NGOs as well as international secular and indigenous independent NGOs, and now also the relief arms of political movements such as REST, ORA, and ERO. The CRDA embodies in one organization national style and international social system, at the same time as it excludes other types of influence (Islamic groups cannot become members).

A brief case history may illustrate the mechanisms from another angle. The history of the Ethiopian Evangelical Church Mekane Yesus (EECMY) dates back to the second half of the nineteenth century when the Swedish Evangelical Mission in co-operation with the Evangelical Church of Eritrea (also established by Swedish missionaries) sent the first missionaries to work among the Oromos in south western Ethiopia. Since 1868 when the first missionaries were established in Boji, and especially in the last few decades, Protestant Christianity has witnessed constant growth in south and south-west Ethiopia. The EECMY was established as an Ethiopian church in 1969, and its different Synods were marked by the different mission organizations working there.[15] For more than a decade it has also been a local NGO, registered with the RRC (the Orthodox Church has more recently done the same; it established a development department, and became an NGO as well), and is regarded as a suitable local partner for Western missions and church groups. The EECMY is also a member of the CRDA and the Joint Relief Partnership; thus it is involved in both relief and development programmes. It receives finance as well as personnel from missions in Germany, Denmark, Norway, Sweden and the US. The church was established before the development aid era, but it has increased its strength and its development orientation, strongly helped by donor funds. The Norwegian Government is still the main funder in two of the most important Synods, through Norwegian NGOs. By breaking out of a narrow national perspective the relationship between national traditions and foreign funds in creating a Lutheran minority church in Ethiopia can be studied and analysed.

While a few NGOs existed before 1971 in *Bangladesh*, the growth of the NGO scene came in the wake of the War of Liberation, when a great number of international NGOs established themselves in the country. Two national organizations founded at that time have come to dominate the Bangladeshi NGO scene. The leaders of both of them were living in Britain, but returned to fight for development and improvements for the poor, and BRAC and Gono Shasthyo Kendro were established, both receiving support from OXFAM from the beginning.

New organizations were formed, supported by Northern NGOs. Gono Unnayan Prochesta (GUP) got support from Quaker Peace and Service and Friends in Village Development (White, 1991:12). In 1974 the Canadian NGO, Canadian Universities Service Overseas, set up a project to launch the concept of a service NGO. This was called 'Proshika', and was supposed to support small organizations, but it became a programme, and an organization itself, which split into two separate and very influential organizations.

It was in 1978 that foreign funding first became an issue, when the Foreign Donations (Voluntary Agencies) Registration Ordinance was passed, followed in 1982 by the Foreign Contribution (Regulation) Ordinance. This required for the first time registration of all organizations receiving foreign funds, and also annual approval of foreign-aided projects. These legal instruments did not change the direction, however. In 1981 there were 68 foreign NGOs working in Bangladesh, and by 1993 there were 109. In 1981 there were 45 foreign-aided national NGOs, while in 1993 the number had risen to 513 (Aminuzzaman, 1993:6). The NGOs in Bangladesh in the mid 1990s received about 15 per cent of foreign funds as compared with one per cent in 1972–3.

Notes

1 The following distinctions have been proposed by Anheier and Salamon, 1990: a) between liberal and conservative regimes (dating back to the nineteenth century) and the social democratic regimes (of the twentieth century); b) the importance of the degree of religious homogeneity/ heterogeneity, whether a Catholic or Protestant hegemony exists or whether the population is religiously heterogeneous; and c) the degree of centralization or decentralization of public welfare state activities. Obviously these distinctions are not very well suited to many developing countries, because they do not take account of other types of religious affinities, the importance of ethnic cleavages and contradictions, weak or non-existent states, etc. The typology therefore demonstrates the problem of employing universal concepts and approaches. To develop similar kinds of typologies for developing countries is futile because of internal variations.

2 The OECD study states, with regard to Italy and other Catholic countries, that 'voluntary action has grown almost entirely out of the church, and from an alternative, anti-statist mentality, to which leftist anti-government views were later added' (Smillie and Helmich, 1993:17). Other researchers underline exactly opposite cultural contradictions; 'traditional religious cleavages in the Netherlands, the Fascist-era experience in Italy, pragmatism in Scandinavia, the doctrine of an apolitical civil service in the UK', etc. (Hood and Schuppert, 1991 :96). While some contrast the Netherlands with Norway where the former has strong anti-state traditions (Kramer 1992:46), Smillie and Helmich describe both as being corporarist countries *per se*.

3 Studies of all Norwegian long-term government programmes since 1953 show the change in emphasis given to voluntary organizations (this description is based on Kuhnle and Selle, 1990). Until 1969 the organizations were almost invisible. The programme for 1982–5, presented by a Labour government, stated that for the first time the state should encourage voluntary organizations. Important tasks could be performed by them without the government escaping responsibility. Co-operation between organizations and government should be developed. The

Conservative government (1981–5), underlined more strongly the importance of voluntary organizations. For the first time a sub-section (in the revised long-term programme) dealt with voluntary organizations. The organizations were given many of the same positive attributes which were common in aid literature worldwide, but with an important difference: NGOs in aid were given a clearer political, mobilizing role, not least as the spokesmen of the people or the grassroots *vis-à-vis* governments. The long-term programme presented by the Labour Party minority government in the spring of 1989 for the first time introduced the concept of the third sector, redefining the role of the organizations as a group. The voluntary organizations were described as significant for society as they play a 'pioneering role, are schools in democracy, further participation and activity, maintain and transmit traditions, norms and values in our culture and keep up the fruitful interchange between public welfare authorities and voluntary and ideal organizations' (quoted in Kuhnle and Selle, 1990). This development in government attitudes is confirmed by other studies (see Lorentzen, 1993).

4 Direct support for local NGOs was initiated in 1977 by NORAD. This support system has gradually grown in importance. In the early 1990s NORAD channelled about NOK 100m. annually to more than 200 organizations.

5 Quoting de Toqueville from 1835, Smillie and Helmich illustrate the highly political-ideological nature of this exercise: 'A government by itself is equally incapable of refreshing the circulation of feelings and ideas among a great people, as it is of controlling every industrial undertaking. Once it leaves the sphere of politics to launch out on this new track, it will, even without intending this, exercise an intolerable tyranny' (quoted in Smillie and Helmich 1993: 18).

6 The Southern Sudan can be a case in point (see Tvedt, 1994a). The great number of international NGOs in the Southern Sudan in the early 1980s simply reflected the fact that the region had become an area where many foreign NGOs had decided to work. These actual institutional choices had, of course, very little indeed to do with internal or local traditions. The NGOs and their activities did not reflect historical contexts or social and ethnic criteria in any way.

7 This process has its forerunners. Christian organizations in the Middle Ages developed in different areas as a result of the work of the Catholic Church. Similarly, Islamic groups and welfare societies can also be seen as exported from a heartland and imported by Islamized peoples. The Communist International and the Socialist International are two more recent organizations working to expand worker organizations all over the world, with the help of funds, political advice, etc. The first recorded international relief action in north-east Africa was that of the Swedish Evangelical Mission and Catholic missions in Eritrea during the great famine of 1889-91. Voluntary fund-raising in Sweden raised 24.000 Swedish crowns which were used in their mission station in Monkullu for the upkeep of 800 destitute families (see Arén, 1978:319–23).

8 By regarding it as an international social system, it becomes clear that a small state like Norway and Norwegian NGOs play important, but neglected, roles in influencing the social fabric of other societies. The Norwegian state in in 1993 gave about NOK 200m to NGO work in the four study countries, and almost 50 Norwegian NGOs worked there. Since 1990 more than NOK 1 billion has been used to support indigenous and Norwegian NGOs.

9 For example, top-level people from INPHRU, many of them militants of the Popular Social Democratic Party, assumed positions as vice-ministers or ministers in such ministries as Labour, Social Welfare and the International Reconstruction Fund (FIR) which later became the Ministry of Foreign Co-operation (Skar, *et al.*, 1994). Leading members of CEPA went on to occupy important positions in the Ministry of Agriculture and Agrarian Reform.

10 This is according to a Directory of Nicaraguan NGOs, published by *CAPRI* in 1990.

11 12 of the NGOs supported by NORAD as part of the grant to local NGOs were established in 1990 (according to Questionnaire I, 39 organizations replied to the questionnaire. two did not give year of establishment). 29 were established after 1980. Only six of the 37 organizations were established before 1980. 12 organizations were established after 1990. The organizations supported by NORAD and the Norwegian NGOs were in general not the same. Altogether the organizations had 1,628 employees. (two organizations did not answer this question.) The organizations established in 1990 or later had 137 employees and those established after 1980, 1,000 employees.

12 These proportions changed because of the large inflow of official foreign assistance since

Zimbabwe adopted ESAP in 1990, so that the proportion of foreign aid accounted for by NGOs will have decreased considerably (but not the total amount received by the NGOs).

13 According to a written list given to the author in March 1994. The only list available giving the names of the registered organizations dates from March 1994, hence this is the basis for the categorization.

14 In 1994 some NGOs wanted to weaken REST's monopoly of work in Tigray. Some of the religious denominations wanted to work through their own structures (parishes) and not through the baitos, and to achieve this, they had to appeal to the donor community to redress the imbalance which they thought the donor community created inside Tigray.

15 The name EECMY was first used at that time, but it was not allowed, since there should be only one church in the country, the Orthodox Church. After the overthrow of Haile Selassie this church lost its position as the state church, and EECMY became the official name.

4 How to Analyse an NGO Scene-II: An International Social System

In this chapter the NGO channel will be analysed as a distinct international social system. This approach should not be seen as an alternative to the national-style approach or to empirical studies of individual NGOs' development projects, but as a complementary perspective which, it is hoped, will deepen understanding of the complex factors affecting all national organizational landscapes and every modest project in the remotest corner of the world. If the aim is to understand the development NGOs as an important aspect of what is called a global, associational revolution, such a perspective is thought to be indispensable.

But is not the NGO arena too chaotic to be analysed as a single entity or system? True, the NGO scene is extremely heterogeneous, not only within countries but even more so in an international, global perspective. The explosive growth in activities, roles and public attention makes it important, however, to try to identify some more general and institutionalized features and charactertistics shared by enough actors to be of universal relevance. While aware of the simplifications involved, it is possible to analyse NGOs in development fruitfully as part of a distinct social system. The conventional name 'channel' itself indicates structural characteristics, properties and 'systemness'. It has features and properties which create stability in relationships and functions across time and space within the NGO system, and seen in a historical and comparative perspective, it has encouraged important features of institutional isomorphism among a great many NGOs all over the world in an astonishingly short period of time. In a few years thousands of NGOs have been established in the urban centres and the remote rural areas in many European, American, Asian, African and Latin American countries, which share the same development language and which are attached to, and have, to a varying degree, become integrated with the same donors or more or less the same donor strategies for NGO support. A discussion of the NGO sector which omits this aspect will also underplay the channel's role as a transmission belt of a powerful language and of Western concepts of development, and at the same time as one arena for struggles between different development paradigms and ideologies. The discussion takes as a starting point that it is a donor-led system, because of the inequality in power and resources that historically gave birth to the aid relation as such and which still maintains it, and one which creates and reproduces some systemic relations and practices that cut across space and time.

In system theories there is, of course, a conflict between two different ideas about actions. Social actors are either viewed as the essential force which structures and restructures social systems and the conditions of human activity, or they are reduced to faceless automata following the iron rules of optimal choice theory in a world of constraints over which they have no control. What is focused on here, however, is how the system of properties has affected the working of NGOs internationally, and not these structures' constraining and enabling roles in varying circumstances. The order of this complex system may be discovered by identifying and explicating some of the systemic relations that cut across time and space. The study will discuss some of these central institutionalized practices of the channel, and their (often unintended) consequences which reproduce a system of a distinct character. The aim is also to focus on system structures that have an impact on how NGOs' project routines in general are carried out. This approach will be used to throw light on three crucial stages of what, for analytical purposes, may be called the NGO channel's ideal typical project cycle: a) assessment of needs, b) implementation and c) evaluation, and how shared discursive language, the role of power and other fundamental system characteristics affect these routinized practices. The project cycle may aim at (and succeed in) helping the poor or supporting the oppressed, but it is also part of the reproduction process of the NGO system itself. The project cycle may also be changed by the actors themselves, and is constantly affected by organizations, donor governments and recipients.

An advantage of the system perspective is that it allows a description of the channel not only as a channel of resources and authority from the core to the periphery in the system, but also as a 'transmission belt' or channel of information and legitimacy from the periphery to the core, or from the bottom up. Furthermore, it makes it possible to describe the NGO scene in the language of ordinary social science and thus liberate it from the normative jargon of the NGO community. It focuses on power, but not in a mechanical way, since power may be negotiated and there are cases where quite small Southern NGOs, because they are seen by the donors as valuable organizations from a political or image-producing point of view, have made big Western donor governments dance to their tune. It is certainly a channel, but the water may also run upstream.

The system and its borders

The system as it is defined here embraces not only the development NGOs, but also the donor offices that provide funds and assess their performance. The NGO channel and the government offices which deal with them are regarded here in the same way as a river and its feeders. A river system consists of both channels (rivers) and reservoirs, and this social system consists of both the NGOs as diversion channels and the donor offices and funding sources as reservoirs. The channel as a whole is regarded as a distinct organizational field. For example, the Norwegian sub-system includes the people working with NGOs in the ministries, in the Norwegian NGOs, and in the Southern and international NGOs receiving support from the Norwegian Government. This Norwegian (or Swedish, British, etc.) system, moulded by a particular national history, forms part of a bigger multinational NGO system, intermingling with the sub-systems of other donors at the core.

The actors in this system are structurally integrated primarily via resource transfers and communication exchange. Research has proved that donors and NGOs share more or less the same ideas about NGO roles and NGO activities.[1] Parts of the system are socially integrated via a continuous exchange of personnel between the NGO leadership and the government offices working with NGOs. Its 'systemness' is also produced and reproduced by means of a great number of conferences and gatherings at international or regional level: NGO leaders from a wide variety of countries, from both the North and the South, meet donors and consultants. These get-together meetings play a very important integrative role, and can explain why the channel's 'buzzwords' travel so fast to all corners of the world, transcending the borders of the national sub-systems. The actors basically learn and rhetorically internalize the same language and 'symbolic orders' as they are socialized in the channel's routinized practices.

The system is internally heterogeneous, while externally marked by quite clear boundaries. The crucial internal link which produces and reproduces it is the flow of funds, and the character of this resource transfer. The international system was established by official donor money in the early 1960s. It expanded dramatically in the 1980s and early 1990s because of the availability of more donor money earmarked for the channel. The money and resources are transferred as gifts, but this does not imply that they are not tied or that the donor does not, or cannot, expect reciprocity. The present description focuses, however, on one crucial factor: that immediate gain or monetary reciprocity has not in general been expected. This affects in a particular way how the boundaries of this system are drawn and accommodated. The boundaries of the money flow produce a closed system, in the sense that the actors have to apply formally to be included in it, or to cross the boundaries. It is also rare to be ejected from the system (unless one leaves voluntarily or reveals a praxis which the donor for one reason or another cannot tolerate). One is either inside or outside, perhaps looking in; at the beginning of the 1990s thousands of organizations worldwide were knocking on the door trying to join the system. Precisely how the borders are maintained and where they are drawn varies, however, partly reflecting individual donor policies and the national context. In Scandinavia, for example, the system has been based on a primarily altruistic legitimation, which means that for-profit firms have not been able to join the system, unlike the practice allowed in the World Bank and according to the OECD definition of an NGO. In some countries trade unions and interest organizations are eligible for support through the NGO channel, while this has not been so in Bangladesh and Nicaragua. It is therefore also generally the case that *ad hoc* or small grassroots organizations have to transform themselves into more formally established NGOs, and adopt the language of the relevant donor sub-system in order to be able to join the system on a permanent basis.

The environment of the system is also in a constant state of change, both the beneficiaries and those who provide the funds. The system depends, to an unusual extent, on how this environment perceives it, since what constitutes it – gift money – comes from outside the channel itself. The channel receives funds from the political environment (parliaments and the public) and returns legitimacy to the whole aid project as such. The original justification given by Western governments for support to NGOs in development aid was precisely this: that they ought to broaden the support for aid to the undeveloped countries. This argument is still much used in political and public debates about the advantages of NGOs. The NGO system interacts with other (aid) systems and vice versa. By entering at the lower end of a hierarchy of systems, by representing the grassroots, so to speak, in a state-led, elitist system (be it individual governments or the UN), this channel helps to bestow legitimacy on the system as a whole and thus creates opportunities for it.

A symbolic order – a shared language

One of the most important structural characteristics is the actors' discursive internalization of what are conceived of as the shared values of the channel. They have employed a common language as a means of communication, although they have not necessarily internalized its conflicting norms.[2] In NGO literature since the mid-1980s, the basic concepts have been shared.[3] This does not presuppose an untenable position – that, irrespective of time and place there has always been a value consensus among NGOs and between NGOs and official donors. On the contrary, there has been, and is something which can be called 'NGO-speak' (employed by NGOs, donors and NGO consultants alike), in other words, a language which has functioned as a symbolic order within the whole system, organized around a dichotomy, a rhetorical code with two values: good development and not good development.

This system has been recreated and reproduced via the means with which the system-members have expressed themselves as actors within it and in relation to the outside world. It has been knit together and held together by common rhetoric. This special type of value consensus can be understood as norms which also establish boundaries around the NGO channel, but a consensus to which a variety of different and in reality competing, value agendas and even manipulative attitudes have been attached (government organizations posing as NGOs to attract funds and legitimacy, for-profit firms dressed up as NGOs to earn money, mission organizations acting within the development aid channel while using it as a shield for achieving their main aims, political parties and movements establishing a neutral humanitarian arm to compete for funds, etc.). While the resource transfer has made it into a system, one might say that it is this rhetoric and the way it has been handled which has made it into, and reproduces it as, a social system. The rhetoric which has influenced the whole NGO scene can be analyzed as being functional for the maintenance of the system as it has functioned in the past. (This does not mean, however, that such language is necessary for its continued existence.) Because the system exists in an environment on whose perceptions and attitudes it is highly dependent, this rhetorical language may endanger the future of the channel, because it presupposes that conflictual aims and more realistic assessments of their diversity and achievements remain muted.

The relationship between this type of resource transfer and language makes it important to study how actors have related to this symbolic order, and how NGO actors in the donor states have exploited what can be described as an 'image-monopoly' in portraying the poorest among the poor and their development needs in Western donor countries.[4] They have never, of course, had an information monopoly, but the NGO channel has in recent decades been an important 'transmission-belt' of value-laden images,[5] partly because of its information support and activities, partly because of its ability to use journalists, newspapers and TV-stations in its fund-raising campaigns and partly because the image of the 'white good-hearted altruist' is an image that 'everybody' in the donor countries wants to embrace. Donor assessment of the efficient use of the funds transferred may therefore be linked less to the NGO's delivery and achievements in developing countries than to its management of language and information at home.[6] Few phenomena in society rely more on image production and handling than NGOs, since their activities take place so far away and are so difficult for the public to have an independent, empirically based opinion about. The question of image management will tend to increase in importance, as the organization grows and competition increases in the NGO market place.[7] The conflicts within the channel are therefore often a struggle not between openly conflicting ideas, but about who is best at expressing the shared NGO virtues. Internal conflicts will thus paradoxically tend to strengthen the systemness of the channel.

This social system has no fixed geographical boundaries (unlike a state, an urban community, etc.), although at any point in time it has relatively clear-cut physical boundaries. Growth in budgets and staff and improvements in communications have made it possible for the system to expand continuously.[8] Geographical expansion is most likely to continue rather than to contract. A marked feature of this system is precisely that it spans all continents and all countries. Although the system has been enlarged in physical space, there has at the same time been an important shrinkage in distance in terms of the time taken to move from one location to another, and to communicate from one area to another or from the field to headquarters.[9] This shrinkage is a major change which fundamentally affects the NGO channel, but is not so easily detected on a day-to-day basis. The shrinkage in distance is, however, not equally universal. It is more noticeable between the headquarters and the field than within the countries where development activities are carried out. Mission history is full of examples where missionaries could be left alone in the field, without contact with their headquarters, be it in London, Rome or Oslo, for long periods of time. When NGOs started their work overseas in the early 1960s, there was sporadic communication with the home country and the home office. Faxes, telephones and E-mail have changed the way the system is integrated, and continuously furnish more information and therefore language domination, power and sanctionary possibilities to the upper parts of the channel, but they also encourage the potential for more information from the bottom-up.

The system has been integrated through a common language, a reporting system, an evaluation system, and an information flow. A growing social integration, made possible by conferences and field visits, has also taken place. This integration is not without problems. There are differences and conflicts between expatriates and local partners,[10] as there are differences among local partners, but these are checked by organizational sanctions.[11] There are contradictions and conflicts between field personnel and the home administration. Often the field staff regard the home administration as unnecessarily formal and bureaucratic, while, in other cases, they feel overburdened when the home office asks them to take initiatives in emergency situations because their domestic members or supporters have wondered why their organization is not doing anything when 'everyone else' is. There are a number of examples showing that field offices have been forced to draw up emergency projects and applications, primarily because public opinion at home requires it. There are conflicts between official donors and NGOs, regarding policy, autonomy, the kind of control and dialogue, etc. There are, of course, important contradictions among different NGOs, because of both value orientations and market considerations, as there are conflicts among NGOs in the same country because of ethnic, religious and ideological differences. All the travel, seminars, field trips, faxes or internet messages in the world cannot undo contradictions inherent in the channel, but they make an impact on the balance between them and create means of handling these contradictions in a productive, systematic way.

Like other systems, the NGO channel as a system is pre-eminent over its individual parts. The system's origin is not focused on here. It should be stressed, however, that in describing these structures there is no explanation of how individual organizations or actors have acted or are likely to act, nor is the system's origin explained. The history of NGO work both in developing and in donor countries demonstrates the importance of the individual actor in shaping the profile and work of his organization and institution. Again, some of the same factors that create the constraining structures (value consensus, separation of policy-making from implementation, distance between assessors and implementation, knowledge gap between professionals and the rank and file) are the very factors that give ample room for entrepreneurial manoeuvring and action.

The NGO channel can be seen to be an international social system, consisting of a number of sub-systems (one of which is the national NGO channels, in other words the Norwegian channel is a sub-system with Oslo as its geographical core). This system has its own boundaries, defined by the character and profile of the resource transfers or allocations of money as gifts. It is structurally integrated through hierarchies of knowledge and sanctions and by a shared NGO language, and socially integrated through seminars and other forms of internal communication which spreads the 'social glue', i.e. the symbolic language. It is dependent on the environment's perception of it, and therefore also on images and image-management. It does not develop according to laws or rules in the market-place or in political life, but according to the management of conceived political and moral dilemmas and conflicts within the channel itself. In spite of contradictions between, for example, NGOs aiming at mobilizing the poor through project or advocacy work and public funding institutions, there are sufficient overlapping interests among the partners to provide a common ground for consensus.

System mechanisms and the ideal-type NGO project

The position and standing of the NGO channel within the aid context, and an important element in its self-understanding, rest on what can be described as the three 'articles of faith': 1) NGOs are able to respond to the needs of the poor and vulnerable groups, because they are closely in touch with the lives and the needs of ordinary poor people. These needs decide the project profile and the planned aid intervention. This NGO-driven process is flexible. It is responsive to the emerging needs of the poor, the disadvantaged, changing environments and lessons of the past. The NGOs are in this perspective a 'transmission belt' (Keen, 1994). Because of their grassroots orientation they can channel information on needs up the system, and because of their nearness to donor money they can channel resources downwards through the system. These given characteristics create an ideal-type project history. First the needs of vulnerable groups in recipient countries are assessed; this is the task if the NGO (be it a national or international organization). Plans are drawn up which are based on such assessments, echoing the needs of the poor and oppressed. Then, the goals and capacities of the NGOs, or the 'needs-expressing' organizations, are assessed; this is the task of the donors. 2) While the NGOs let the grassroots speak, the donor organizations assess and implicitly secure the capacities and capabilities of the NGO, measured according to a set of criteria on which the channel (both organizations and donors) tends to agree. During the *implementation stage* the NGO, due to what is regarded as its comparative advantage, demonstrates flexibility, efficiency and grassroots orientation. During the process the target population is involved in the execution of the project, enabling the NGO to realign its direction under way. 3) The final stage is *evaluation*, where the project results are assessed by donors, NGOs and independent evaluators. Lessons are summarized and become the basis for future decisions: needs assessments, funding policies and project implementation are improved and all the actors in the channel change their behaviour accordingly.

How do structural characteristics of the international social system affect this ideal-type project model?

Needs assessments

The needs assessment stage is affected by the way the environment (the beneficiaries) and the system meet. Ideally organizations meet the people face to face to detect their collective will, but it is always individuals the organizations meet, and not representatives of a collective will. The needs expressed may speak or not speak on behalf of one or another group of people. Depending on the socio-economic and socio-cultural context there might or might not be organizations already established in the area where the NGOs have decided to work. Frequently NGOs, and not least Scandinavian NGOs, are reaching out to areas where such organizational cultures and traditions do not exist. To the extent that they are targeting the poorest among the poor they are targeting groups, especially in the African rural areas, where socio-economic conditions have not been conducive to the development of formal organizations. In general there are no organizations established as economic or social actors to forward people's or groups of people's interests. There might, however, be institutions promoting religious interests (churches, etc.) and informal associations that might fight for ethnic, clan or other particularist interests.

The way people articulate their needs greatly depends on their perceptions of the person who asks the question and their potential offer. Those being assessed will be tempted to tell an NGO (whether international, national or local) what it wants to hear. Since the resources are gifts, this is the most efficient way to get access to the inputs an NGO might dispose of. A women's organization will generally receive requests concerning women's issues and an organization for the disabled will get requests for aid to the disabled. The donor agenda and the language in which needs are assessed exist prior to any actual assessment activity. The act of asking the people (which in reality will mean persuading the beneficiary to agree with the assessor, or to agree with him to the extent that a project can be implemented with this NGO's competence, capacity, time-plans, etc.) implies therefore institutionalizing a form of dependency, rather than expressing equity. It is a form of control rather than a real bottom-up-process. This is unavoidable because the one who asks, controls the accessible resources. The shared language and internal hierarchical system of the channel have put limits on the extent to which organizations can have an ear to the ground approach. On the other hand, since donors are in need of good projects and good partners, this relationship also offers opportunities for the assessed, or for the structurally subordinate partner in the system. By mastering the language, a form of equity may be established, not because the assessed express the people's needs, but because they know how to express their needs in the language of the NGO system. Just as local organizations may be more powerful than Northern NGOs or big bilateral donors, local people may make themselves indispensable to the donor in the long run. By embracing NGO-speak, opportunities are created that were not there before. By supporting the 'value consensus' or the 'norm', the inferior may manipulate it for his or her own betterment. There are examples of local people who have embraced the language of a neutral NGO in order to use the funds for political objectives, and of local people who have joined NGO projects aimed at 'conscientizing' and political reform, in order to change them afterwards into ordinary social service projects.

Bureaucratic routines, categories and system requirements in the NGO channel make a powerful impact on the actual assessment of needs, as well as on the political, religious and economic goals of the assessors. Needs assessment is not done according to fixed, neutral criteria. No such criteria are available. On the contrary, this is a field with fast-changing catchwords. One year it is 'women', another year 'ecology' and a third year 'civil society' and 'advocacy'. Most NGOs, also national NGOs, represent not the local people but sectarian or particularist interests or perspectives. The organization of the channel is diverse in value orientation, although it shares a more or less identical symbolic language. This means that NGOs (perhaps more than more rule-oriented, universally oriented institutions, like state bureaucracies and UN systems) will be less inclined to give unbiased reports on the needs of the people. An Islamic NGO will probably not report on the need for a project in response to the population's demand for more churches in south-east Ethiopia or Christian NGOs will not focus on the people's felt need for mosques, and an ethnically based organization will most probably not advocate the expressed demands of another ethnic group in the same area, or a secular-oriented women's organization in a Muslim country will not be a mouthpiece for women's expressed wish to veil themselves. An organization's own agenda enters into its assessment of what people lack or are seeking to do, and its role in assisting them in these endeavours. NGO staff may consequently, although unintentionally, be controlling beneficiaries in order to assist them in particular ways. In a situation where NGOs aim at scaling up their political importance and developing into advocacy organizations, this need for control of the assessment stage may paradoxically become stronger as their mobilization for a more just world is deepened. In order to access donor money, the NGO will tend to describe the local needs in the aid language prevailing at any one point in time, as a means of maintaining organizational activities as well as for the sake of the assessed.

The upward transmission of needs through advocacy and lobbying is gradually becoming a more important legitimation of NGOs.[12] The point is, however, that on the whole advocacy is, and must to a large extent be, advocacy of the ideas of the organization and, to a gradually larger extent, ideas that are acceptable to the donor state with which it is collaborating. The force of this endeavour has often been weakened by the need for legitimization by the will of the recipients. Organizations with no shared values to transmit may be opportunistic NGOs, in the sense that they may very easily adapt to changing fads and fashions. Many organizations that have their own agenda although they employ the common aid rhetoric, are not able, or willing, to transmit the expressed needs of the beneficiaries. From one point of view, international NGOs might be more able to transmit such needs than locally based NGOs, precisely because their value-sharing identity might be less enmeshed in local politics and contradictions. The need-assessment myth has therefore reduced the potential pluralism of the channel, but at the same time has served to legitimize the system as such.

This assessment distortion may be enlarged in the case of the big NGOs, but to argue that the crucial variable is organizational size in relation to organizational responsiveness to the needs of the local populations, is too simple and disregards system mechanisms.[13] There have been warnings about the scaling-up scenario, because it will distort the need-assessment stage. This argument overlooks a feature of the channel's structure, namely, that NGOs and NGO leaders will want to expand. This holds for Northern as well as for Southern NGOs. BRAC in Bangladesh wants to expand both in its country of origin and abroad. Again the main problem is the channel's rhetoric. Parts of it have identified with the slogan 'small is beautiful', and government is ugly because it is big. Development up to now shows that most NGOs want to become big – or to put it in another way, to ensure a continued role for their own organization in the aid process. NGOs behave, it seems, like most other organizations in this respect.[14] The issue therefore is checks and balances regarding the growth process, and not size itself, which is of less importance in this regard.

On the one hand most organizations are dependent on public donors and employ the official aid rhetoric of the system and copy what the NGO community considers political and organizational successes. On the other hand, due to physical distance and the knowledge gap between the funders and the actual work, they have often had considerable independence in the field. One of the attractions of working for an NGO is precisely the possibility of exerting considerable personal influence, of being little kings or local strong men, not only in taking decisions involving budgets of tens of millions of dollars outside ordinary bureaucratic checks and balances, but perhaps especially in being 'the entrepeneur in the bush'. This opportunity to exert personal influence is one factor which in some situations makes NGOs more flexible and responsive to changing circumstances than many larger organizations. To be a local strong man in an aid context (in the home country the same individual is often a marginalized lower-middle-class person) can, of course, also create the opposite relationship: the NGO entrepreneur knows best, although paying lip service to local needs or reporting home that what the organization is doing is expressing the people's needs, when in reality it is executing his own ideas. Because of the distance between the field and headquarters, the field and the funder and the field and the media, it is possible to implement the donor's agenda, the entrepreneur's agenda and the people's agenda, all within the same rhetorical language.

Organizations and their leaders face dilemmas between, on the one hand, the genuine wish to formulate projects in line with what the people suggest, and, on the other hand, the need for a strategy, also regarding needs assessment, that will help to maintain or perhaps strengthen and broaden the role of the organization. Changes of direction can therefore also be analysed as a kind of organizational coping strategy. Organizations vary in their flexibility and pragmatism in this regard. Organizations' principles may be pragmatically implemented. Many international NGOs adopt a flexible approach to this issue. The differences in fundamental approaches are not so much a reflection of the people's wishes, but of a pragmatic and concrete analysis of the space available to NGOs in different contexts.[15] Organizations' profiles (for example, the political profile in relation to the state) have often been more the result of the organization's history in the country than of a definite policy line.

NGOs acknowledge, of course, that external factors intervene in the project cycle and the assessment of needs. The effect of the media in influencing the project cycle and setting donors' priorities is often criticized. This emphasis neglects the fact that the NGOs themselves are major actors in influencing what the media are focusing on; in other words, NGOs are often instrumental in creating the image they criticize the media for producing. They are caught in a trap; on the one hand they live on tragedies, on the other hand they want the media to reform people's way of thinking. How long can they continue to play this double role? NGOs do not in general invite TV-cameras and journalists for events that are not directly related either to their projects or to issues that are connected with their interventions. NGO spokesmen are in fact 'shooting the pianist', while all the time maintaining the hero's role for themselves, thus underplaying the structure of the system itself.

The NGO channel is a social system in which each party (those who fund and those who are funded at all levels of the hierarchical set-up) pays homage to certain key concepts like 'the environment', 'sustainability', 'popular participation', 'empowerment', 'reaching the poorest among the poor'. By being so enmeshed in rhetoric (for example, the language of popular participation), actual interventions may be described with the right words, while unequal relations are maintained. The concepts mean very different things to different actors, but so long as more precise definitions are evaded, this is no problem and gives the channel space and freedom. In the absence of real 'participation', 'sustainability', 'equality', etc. it may give the impression that there is participation, sustainability, equality, where there is none.

To formulate projects based on the will of the local people is both theoretically and practically impossible. But few NGOs will accept a policy of implementing or proposing to fund projects decided at NGO headquarters or in government offices, irrespective of local feelings and wishes. Most NGOs strive to implement a bottom-up strategy. In these endeavours the system characteristics of the NGO channel, on the one hand, open up possibilities that most government or UN structures do not possess. On the other hand, the system itself has features which make the aim much more difficult to accomplish than the rhetoric would suggest, because of power relations and organizational survival or expansion strategies.

Donor assessment of the NGOs

Government donors have assessed NGO interventions using a set of pre-established but rapidly changing criteria. The systemness of the system is illustrated by the way the 'buzz words' change on a global level and in both the offices and the declarations of NGOs and official donors. The changing fashions in aid policy do bring home the fact that the process is often driven not by the demands of the most vulnerable but by the needs or ideas of the donor community. Popular slogans have tended to substitute for detailed knowledge: a donor often has few opportunities to assess the efficiency and fruitfulness of the countless projects properly,[16] and has relied, therefore, on the NGOs' ability to accommodate prevailing policy signals. As long as the donor or government can believe that the NGO is working according to declared policies and profiles, and the organization manages to communicate its ability to accommodate changing donor requirements both to the donor and the public at large, the donor-NGO relationship can be maintained.[17]

In this system the issue of how donor assessments have been functioning is fundamentally related to the particular conditions of time and space. The distance between the donor institution in the Western capital and the project site (conceptually, geographically, temporally) creates particular frameworks for donor assessments (information about the project can theoretically be transmitted daily, but it is transmitted by actors within the system itself – to quite another extent than is the case with policy development within the donor countries in other areas). As is the case not only with NORAD and the NGO Division, but is reported as a general problem in most donor countries (see Keen, 1994), staff in donor offices are overworked and have few opportunities to get to know the situation in the country, region or locality where one of the many projects is undertaken. Programmes and projects are usually assessed according to general policy guidelines – or, for example, the needs of women, preservation of the environment, poverty alleviation and more recently the extent to which they will contribute to human rights and democracy – and the organizations according to more administrative requirements. Since the people working in these offices are in general in no position to acquire sufficient knowledge about the individual project, the project area, the socio-economic conditions in the area and in the country, etc., they have to rely on how the project is described, i.e. on its relation to the 'symbolic order' of the system (the demand for more precise reporting on numbers of beneficiaries, etc., does not change the system as it is conceived here, only the manner in which it operates).

The need for spending allocated money also intervenes in this process. The gap between different kinds of demand requires mutual trust. Donors try to solve this problem in different ways (the problems are more or less of the same type in most donor countries, see Keen, 1994). They enter into different types of agreement with different types of NGO, according to the degree of nearness between the activities and policies of the NGO and the state, and they tend to allocate more money to big organizations. The tendency for a few organizations to get more and more is marked in most donor countries. With the need for mutual trust, and especially for donors to be able to trust the organizations, there is a common interest in keeping controversial issues, hidden agendas and project failures in the background. It is a general trait that there is little incentive for a bureaucratic organization to achieve an accurate picture of the world or of its impact on the world. Errors or failures do not have direct economic consequences for the guilty official, and generally not even for his position within the system. The activities and the resource flow of this system are primarily dependent on their media image (and not on efficiency, cost-efficiency, etc.), and mistakes have therefore been kept away from the public eye at home in the interests of maintaining the system.

Donors do have criteria for support, but experience shows that these can be used pragmatically. Donors (as well as NGOs) have proved capable of giving benevolent reasons for whatever course of action they choose. Mission NGOs may co-operate with churches aiming at evangelization, while describing their project activities as if they were ordinary secular development activities. Government donors involved in direct support for local organizations tend, if possible, to support those organizations that conform to the development jargon of the day. But equally importantly, a number of factors other than assessment of achievements enter into decisions about which project or which NGO is to get support. For example, NORAD's profile of direct support to Zimbabwe shows that what has actually happened is not in congruence with stated goals, because unclear criteria, undeveloped strategies and historical legacies have intervened and put constraints on free assessment. Nevertheless, the activities have generally been described as being in line with this same policy. Moreover, since the birth of the system, NORAD has had as a guideline that it should not support projects that favour particular religious or political groups; nevertheless it has supported both mission and solidarity organizations and organizations aiming precisely at promoting particular interests. In Zimbabwe NORAD has supported urban elite-based organizations rather than those people's organizations in rural areas which the basic assessment criteria would suggest had been supported. The power of NGO-speak and prevailing perspectives have partly made NORAD conceptualize these developments as being in line with declared policies and aims, and partly given it an instrument with which to legitimize whatever action has been taken, in a language that suppresses or ignores gaps betwen rhetoric and reality.

The above demonstrates that it is unlikely that the NGOs that get most money in the donor countries and in the co-operating countries are those with the best projects. What is considered best changes according to ideological trends. The donor does not have the capacity or competence to assess. A number of other considerations will always intervene in the assessment process. Historical legacies will tend to maintain the funding profile of the past, etc. On the other hand, this does not imply that the NGOs that get the most money are those with the worst projects. The point here is to underline one thing: systemic characteristics of the NGO channel do not give the present donor-NGO funding-assessment profile legitimacy based on evidence.

Implementation

A characteristic of the NGO channel is that it distinguishes between overall policy formulation and implementation. Parliaments and governments, being outside the system, draw up the main policy frameworks. Within the system the official donor offices develop the more detailed guidelines and strategies, and are formally accountable to Parliament. How will they tend to manage the real problems of establishing control over NGO activities, due to the different system levels and the complex upward and downward accountability mechanisms? In a situation where aid is under scrutiny, this separation of policy formulation and implementation might be an important aspect of the channel's attraction. In certain cases it has been obvious that NGOs have served as the fall guys of donors, especially in undertaking types of relief operation where governments do not wish to become involved. (The US Government's use of the ERD in Eritrea or of Norwegian Peoples' Aid (NPA) in the Southern Sudan can be a couple of many such examples, where efficient NGOs made efficient cross-border operations possible.) Donors may delegate politically sensitive tasks to NGOs, and if the need arises drop them later on.

Donors (governments, the UN system and international NGOs) exercise, on the one hand, power conferred by their financial wealth. On the other hand, they are in a weak position to check on what is happening on the ground. Efforts to design 'rules of the game', which partly keep them in control and partly exempt them from blame, affect the way the system in general operates. Bilateral and more recently also multilateral donors have defined themselves explicitly as non-implementing organizations. At the same time they have different control mechanisms, which in some cases are getting stronger. To maintain old policies by buying others to implement them has been one way the channel has functioned because of inherent power relations and resource transfers. The control mechanisms might also be more of a brushing up of the façade, where the donor (government or NGO), in order to please the external environment, puts emphasis on the formal correct handling of money, since that is controllable, while the idea behind, and the aim of, the intervention are de-emphasized. In emergency aid both official donors and Northern NGOs are still actively in operation. One reason is the claimed advantage compared with other actors within the channel, such as the local NGO or the national government. This activity is also more rewarding media-wise and entails less danger to the implementing agency since the work is short-term and less complicated.

Institutional interests will also intervene in relation to implementation and co-operation with local partners. It has been said that it is not in the nature of organizations to work for their own removal. This statement has to be modified in the context of this study. Organizations may easily withdraw from one country, area or target group, and have often done so, without jeopardizing their institutional survival. A particular withdrawal may be dictated by funding or capacity considerations rather than by an assessment that the local people are ready to manage a particular project themselves. The history of NGO aid is also a history of deserted projects, because of shortage of funds, changes in personnel, changes in fads and fashions, etc. and also the fact that other areas – for different reasons – become more important. As long as resources are limited, new disasters and emergency situations will tend to move organizations from one area to another. This right to end projects unilaterally is a characteristic of the voluntary sector in general.[18] In other cases NGOs will have a particular interest in staying on in order to secure the existence of the organization, job opportunities, etc. In a situation where other donors are invading the arena of the local NGOs, it might also affect the willingness to strengthen local NGOs. Strong local NGOs may represent a danger to operational Northern NGOs or to NGOs coming from a donor country where they compete with the state in funding the local NGOs.[19] This concern is real, also because many local NGOs prefer government agencies as funders (for example, some Zimbabwean NGOs prefer NORAD to Norwegian NGOs, because it is seen as more flexible, which in some cases means that it has less time for control and monitoring).

A structural factor which influences both assessment and who should implement is the spending imperative, or the way funds are transferred. The channel as a whole is expected to be an efficient transmission belt of money. Parliaments, official donors and the public share this attitude. After big emergency aid campaigns the press asks: 'Has the money been spent?' If not, the organization responsible is criticized. Few would criticize a state institution or a for-profit organization for postponing investments until conditions are optimal. NGOs, however, have to act very fast because they obtain money based on the grounds of urgency, effectiveness, flexibility, etc.[20] An NGO, or a group of NGOs, can thus be criticized and be less eligible for support as an implementing agency, because it uses money with care. An important argument in favour of local NGOs as a channel, has been their capacity to reduce pipeline problems in government-to-government aid. They have provided an outlet for excess money, since they were so many and the projects appeared so good or so small that to support them would not create some big media scandal. In this perspective the question of how much development they achieve becomes less important.

NGOs may implement good projects, and, not least, they are often better able to work among the poor than are governments. They may also in some cases be more cost-efficient, flexible, etc. There are, however, a number of factors within the channel itself that intervene in certain ways in which implementation is carried out. Organizational agendas, funding cycles and the handling of accountability within the system are some of these factors that intervene and make the implementation process different from the one originally proposed.

Evaluation

Evaluation can be described as the institutionalized reflexive monitoring of actions. Since the activities of the NGO channel are stretched over long periods of time, and take place in extremely different situations and fields, its continued existence as an international system depends on repeated rationalizations, for both external and internal use. Evaluations are not only an important way of learning from past experience, but also an activity which helps to give the system legitimacy *vis-à-vis* the environment, and which creates a sense of 'systemness'.[21] They help to bridge the time and distance gap between different actors in the system, between the policy makers and the implementors, and between NGOs through communication about an experience they have in common.

Monitoring action, no matter if it is by the donor government, the international NGO or the national NGO, is also a way of exercising control. When governments, the World Bank or big multilateral organizations are the actors, it can be seen as an effort at controlling a highly generalized scheme of system reproduction. Since the same actors, to an unusual degree, control both resources and normative sanctions, evaluation findings are instruments of power within this system of structural assymetries of domination. Good evaluations can also be regarded as a method of counteracting the selective information filtering that is endemic to this, as to other, systems. Strategically placed actors may use such evaluations to seek reflexively to regulate the overall conditions of system reproduction – either to keep things as they are or to change them.

The system function of evaluations does not, however, imply that all projects or all NGOs are involved in evaluations. Of close on 400 programmes in Bangladesh, Nicaragua and Zimbabwe, 56.6 per cent in Bangladesh, 35 per cent in Nicaragua and 60.7 per cent in Zimbabwe had been externally evaluated by 1992. In addition, two-thirds of the programmes had reportedly been self-evaluated (see Tvedt, 1995c: Table 3.30). Evaluations have certainly become an important activity within the NGO channel. Evaluations of NGO activities have in general been very limited in scope. The assessments have been assessments in which basic presuppositions or existing development strategies have been regarded as unproblematic. Thus the function has become to reproduce the basic assumptions, by showing the bad effects of praxis deviating from what is thought to be right. Evaluations have therefore often served to reproduce basic ideas and relations and the symbolic order.[22] They have been very project-oriented, and only in certain cases have they studied how particular organizations are working.[23] They have assessed whether objectives are achieved and usually discuss some aspects of obstacles to implementation, but these obstacles are not so much based on socio-economic and historical analysis as on a mirror list of the assessors' own convictions. Impact assessments have been carried out, but most of them disregard how system mechanisms and national and local contexts affect NGO activities and potentials. The evaluation procedures of international NGOs have been very weak, but this is perhaps an even bigger problem for local NGOs, which are even more dependent on donor assessments, since most of them are totally dependent on foreign aid. Moreover, the evaluation stage crystallizes power relations within the channel, and the way it is conducted and by whom and the interpretation of the results will reflect power relations.

In spite of their narrow perspective, evaluations have often dealt with the unsolvable question: to what extent has a particular intervention effected a change in people's well-being? This simple question is very difficult to answer. First, an assessment of the impact of aid requires what is often missing – a baseline study providing information on the position of people before the intervention. It also requires information on a control group or groups, of people who are in a comparable position to the designated beneficiaries, but who have not received aid (Keen, 1996).[24] This is not easily available. When some change is registered this is usually called a success, but what happened could be the result of very different factors from the project itself. When the situation of the target group has not improved, this is often blamed on the project. But other factors can have been more important, and the situation might have been much worse, had it not been for the NGO aid. In only the best evaluations is it likely that conclusions have been tested against alternative or opposing views (Riddell, 1990:20). Secondly, one of the characteristics of NGO interventions is that projects tend to be on a small scale. The 1986 CIDA report found that half of the NGO projects studied were serving less than 1,000 people (CIDA, 1986:23). Thirdly, what should be the time horizon and what is a good project? A company is successful if it makes enough money. An NGO can implement what is regarded by some as a bad project, but it may be assessed by others as a good project because of competing values among observers. Moreover, what is regarded as an unsuccessful project at one stage may turn out to be a very good project after five, ten, twenty or forty years. Since these issues are so seldom problematized in what is a growing NGO evaluation business, the evaluations should to a large extent be analysed as a system producing and system maintaining ritual.

Although altruistic motives will often play a considerable role in voluntary organizations, donors' self-interests should not be overlooked. This is important where donors or NGOs are competing for media attention. Since intermediate organizations (whether international or local NGOs) are likely to be held accountable to donors rather than to the would-be beneficiaries, they may also have an incentive to emphasize the appearance rather than the reality of assistance. Support for the Rwandan refugees in the Goma camp can be evaluated as good by the environment, because of the efficiency in delivery seen on the TV-screen, but what actually happens on the ground or the consequence of the assistance are not assessed or evaluated to the same extent. More broad-based and critical evaluations may, because of the market factor, be increasingly regarded as a threat (at least if the aim is to expand) to the individual NGO's future. But they may also endanger the status of the channel itself and the politicians supporting it. If NGOs (either local or international) or donors feel that their funding and policies are vulnerable to scrutiny and potential cut-backs, critical evaluations may be seen as particularly threatening.[25] Consequently, their activities are often described in a more positive manner than the data would allow. In some cases evaluations have been very critical, even evaluations undertaken by the organization itself. But this seems frequently to coincide with a situation where the NGO has already decided to change or modify its course, and the critical assessment therefore only adds to the legitimacy of the organization. An evaluation may function as a very important ritual by institutionalizing a routine reflexive monitoring of conduct, solidly anchored in NGO-speak.

Notes

1 NGO staff in Sweden, Denmark, the Netherlands and Canada stressed that there were few areas of sharp disagreement between themselves and official aid agencies (see Keen, 1994). A study of the relationship between Norwegian NGOs and the state offices dealing with NGOs showed that in many cases there were more important ideological differences among the organizations than between the organizations and the state institutions or officials (Tvedt, 1992). It is a system in which governments and NGOs tend to develop what has been called a cosy relationship (Keen 1994), in which everyone tends to praise – or at least apparently agree with – everyone else.

2 The like-minded group of donor countries (Scandinavia, the Netherlands and Canada) use more or less the same words, and change them more or less at the same time. One Canadian aid agency worker expressed considerable frustration at the rapid changes of priority within CIDA: 'At the moment it's gender, then it's the environment, then it's sustainable development and God knows what the year after that' (quoted in Keen, 1994). This could also have been said in Sweden, Denmark and Norway. This is not only a donors' phenomenon, because these fads and fashions are just as strong in the research milieu, the consultancy milieu and in the NGO community.

3 Tvedt et al. 1993 shows how Norwegian NGOs have employed the same language in describing their aid projects, their goals and achievements, etc., whether they were mission organizations,

formerly anti-imperialist solidarity organizations or mainstream humanitarian NGOs. As a leader of one of the Norwegian mission organizations said: 'each year has its own fashionable word. When we write applications, we have to be sure that we put the right words in the right place' (quoted by Morvik in Tvedt, l993a and Tvedt, 1 992:90).

4 There are many examples where NGOs or NORAD invite journalists to come to a particular country or area to cover a drought, a crisis situation or a project achievement. In Norway this plays a relatively important role. The point is not that the journalists necessarily write what the organizations tell them or wish them to do, but that by reporting on such issues they produce and reproduce an image of the world where NGO interventions will be seen as unproblematic and natural.

5 Such a monopoly has fostered different images at different times according to the image producers' relation to the object, and the image-monopoly of those returning from the field is, in a historical perspective, gradually weakened because of the revolution in communications. The images inherent in works by the priest Johannes Flood indicate the role such cross-cultural representation had for the mission idea and its support in the population at the turn of the century. He published in the last decades of the nineteenth century *Billeder fra Missionen blandt Hedningerne* and *Missionsbilder fra Afrika* and was the publisher of *Maanedsskrift for Missionsvenner.* The books are more or less a compilation of the worst horror-stories about cannibalism, human sacrifice, barbarism and the fear the heathen are living with. The front cover portrays a native on a beach, with begging hands crying out in the direction where the mission-boat is sailing in: 'Come and help us'.

6. The success of the Norwegian Red Cross in relation to Rwanda is a case in point. They won the struggle for media coverage and therefore also for the public's money. Due to different and happy circumstances and good personal networks, they were able to send planes chartered from the Army with a hospital, even before the advertisement campaign started. This was the important thing. Whether what they did was the most useful thing to do or more productive than what other NGOs did, nobody knew – and it did not matter. Some argue that they have been very efficient, while the BBC World Service reported that the main task of the hospitals was to keep the killer-soldiers alive. Owing to time–space relations, success within the system is primarily measured by popularity in the donor country.

7 Typical of this development is the fact that Norwegian NGOs now employ professional consultants to assess how they are conceived of in the market-place, i.e what the ordinary Norwegian has thought or seen about Redd Barna, the Norwegian Red Cross, etc. in the last couple of months. This partly reflects a general trend in society, of course, but this focus on and investment in image management would most probably have surprised the NGO pioneers.

8 Some examples: Norwegian Church Aid, which started its first project in Germany just after World War II, and in developing countries in 1962 (Nigeria), is now working in about 60 countries. Norwegian People's Aid continues to expand, and is now working in 30 countries. NORAD has given support to organizations working in 100 countries, and in the last couple of years there has been a tremendous increase in the number of NGOs working in Eastern Europe (see Tvedt, 1992, 1993a, 1994b).

9 Giddens' principal concept of time-space is too blunt an instrument to capture the temporal and spatial interdependences between these social entities, which possess great, and yet historically and spatially contingent, causal powers.

10 The Norwegian Santal Mission had still in December 1993 a sign on the wall in their guest house in Dhaka, declaring that nationals were not allowed to enter the house unless accompanied by Norwegians. The dining hall of Norwegian Church Aid at their headquarter at Hilieu, in the Southern Sudan, was only for expatriates until the mid-1980s.

11 In Pakistan, especially in organizations working in Afghanistan or with Afghani refugees, there are often conflicts between Pakistani and Afghan NGO employees. These contradictions are partly of historical origin, but they have also become relevant in a new way since the Pakistan Government asked NGOs to lay-off non-Pakistani nationals, because of their declared policy to fight what is called Afghan terrorism, etc. A number of NGOs working in areas with many ethnic groups have, of course, experienced contradictions among the target groups, and have consciously aimed at reducing these tensions by their employment policy and by trying to organize them around the NGO's language and values.

12 A spokesman for this trend, John Clark, has argued that any effect NGOs can have on the

broader political causes of suffering is more important than the impact of concrete, small-scale practical interventions (Clark, 1987).

13 Evidence indicates that all types of organization develop this attitude. Keen reports that NGO staff were increasingly asking CIA what kinds of project application had the best chance of success (Keen, 994). There is a growing awareness of the fact that NGOs tend to copy or follow donor agendas closely.

14 The 1993 *Human Development Report* of the UN Development Programme observed: 'The order of priority today is probably staff, trustees, donors and, finally, beneficiaries. Many organisations refer not to "beneficiaries" but to "partners", though the equality of this partnership is sometimes open to doubt' (UNDP, 1993:90). David Korten has also argued that NGOs in this position tend to focus on what is fundable (cited in Danida/CASA, 1989: 128).

15 To take an example: Redd Barna, Norway, employs the same language as other NGOs and the same language in the different country plans (in general), but in Ethiopia it implements projects itself, in Eritrea it works closely with the central government and the government implements some of its projects, while in Zimbabwe it has implemented its own projects with the build-up of a strong Zimbabwean staff in close understanding with local government structures in particular. In the 1980s it called its projects Integrated Rural Developmental Projects in line with dominating ideas; in the early 1990s the same projects were called Child-Centred Projects, because of renewed attention to their child-oriented profile. This is a general feature of NGOs. For example, Ibis, Denmark, has made a joint agreement on co-operation with the Mozambican Government, and it has worked with the provincial government in Zambia. In Namibia, Ibis is co-operating almost exclusively with government institutions, and has staffed part of the Ministry of Education with advisers since independence. In Nicaragua, Ibis has a mixed approach, working with national NGOs and some local authorities. In El Salvador and Guatemala, it has worked exclusively with NGOs (see Keen, 1994).

16 In 1991, a normal year in the Norwegian aid channel, NORAD and the Ministry of Foreign Affairs with a staff of about 10 people supported more than 1,000 individual projects carried out by about 100 Norwegian NGOs in about 100 countries, and supported about 400 local NGOs in the developing countries.

17 In Holland, local counterpart organizations are supposed to present their needs to the Dutch Co-financing Organizations (CFO) each year, and then spend their block grants as they see fit. They have to produce an annual report on their activities. The main criterion when CFOs allocate money is the quality of the recipient institution. In Denmark, under a similar system, official aid is disbursed in block grants to four main NGOs deemed by DANIDA to have the best expertise. One programme analysis is carried out every year by DANIDA, but DANIDA staff acknowledge that NGOs are mostly self-evaluating (Keen, 1994). In Sweden, SIDA gives two-year block grants to Swedish NGOs without needing to see project applications, and expects a report from NGOs on each project activity every year. Again, while SIDA has undertaken capacity studies of the bigger Swedish NGOs, evaluation of projects is largely a matter of self-evaluation. In Britain, five of the largest NGOs receive block grants from the government. Projects funded from these grants must have at least 55% private funding, but the agencies can choose how the block grants are spent. In Canada, CIDA funds both NGO projects and programmes, providing up to 75% of the funding.

18 There are, of course, important exceptions to this rule. Norwegian Church Aid has worked in Equatoria, Southern Sudan since 1972, and would like to keep the region as a core area in its development work; Redd Barna, Norway, has been involved since 1969 in the Armauer Hansen Institute in Addis Ababa; and the mission organizations may have worked in the same areas for decades, if not a century.

19 Keen (1994) relates the following story: 'Only half joking, one experienced international NGO worker said, "If we get them [local partners] to be independent, they can approach the ambassador themselves. We don't want that to develop."'

20 The summary of evaluations under the Dutch Co-financing Programme found that organizations tended to take over-hasty action. The reasons most often given to the researchers in this evaluation were the urgency of the problem being addressed, pressure from the target population, and pressure to make expenditure quickly (Wils, 1991: 40). The report talked about 'a tendency to adopt an "activist" and anti-intellectual attitude' (Wils, 1991, summary, quoted in Keen, 1994).

21 The Oxfam *Field Directors' Handbook* notes: '... evaluations have frequently resulted in the postponement of important decisions, yet these decisions have usually been made with little regard for the results of the evaluation' (quoted in Burnell, 1991: 98).

22 The evaluation carried out by the Overseas Development Institute of interventions funded by British NGOs made few specific criticisms of the role of international NGOs, even though many important shortcomings in the assistance provided were detected (Riddell and Robinson, 1995). The basic NGO language and the narrow NGO focus were reproduced. A Dutch study of bilateral development assistance, entitled *Rationality or Ritual*, raised the question of why evaluations had been allowed to be so unsatisfactory for so long.

23 An assessment of the evaluation procedures of British NGOs observed: 'The majority of NGOs do not carry out any evaluations beyond normal office procedures of project report-back and financial audit. Evaluation is probably most advanced within Oxfam, the biggest British NGO, which has a separate unit for research and evaluation, and Christian Aid. But even here, no common framework, guidelines or procedures for evaluating projects or programmes have yet been adopted. While Oxfam, Christian Aid and most of the larger NGOs have carried out or commissioned evaluations of particular projects (usually their bigger ones), there has been no uniformity of method, and in almost all cases the results have remained confidential to the organisation. In short, evaluation has tended to be discrete and mostly marginal to the cycle of project proposal and acceptance' (Riddell, 1990: 6). In Tvedt ,1993, there is a list of all evaluations of NGOs and NGO projects in Norway. These empirical data demonstrate the narrow focus that has characterized NGO evaluations.

24 Many general reports and studies acknowledge the absence of good baseline data or control groups regarding analysis of NGO assistance (see, for example, COWI, 1992: 14; Riddell, 1990: 8).

25 Commenting on his study of CFO emergency relief self-evaluations, de Klerk observes: 'It is very difficult to get a picture of the quality of the work. They [the CFOs] have no interest in showing the weaknesses of the operations... Out of 30–40 evaluations, none came up with a predominantly negative assessment' (interview with Ton de Klerk, in Keen, 1994).

5

How to Analyse an NGO Scene-III: The Norwegian Sub-System

NGOs in development aid have often been analysed without regard to the historical and societal background of the different NGO actors and types of NGO channel. This book, on the one hand, argues that it is fruitful to analyse the individual NGOs as part of an international social system of established structures of power, language and resource transfers. On the other hand, the need for paying due regard to national differences and national histories in the NGO system is emphasized. The voluminous literature on the impact assessments of Northern NGOs, which tends to treat them as if their activities can be understood unrelated to international trends and to the character and political aims of the donor states, the particular state–society relations in the home countries, and national public opinion regarding aid is therefore not very useful. This chapter aims to show that, in order to understand the constraints and opportunities of Northern NGOs, it is useful to give proper attention to the particular political-ideological environment and historical-institutional context that sustain and frame their activities. The terms 'Northern' and 'Southern' NGOs may in themselves be regarded as ideological constructs, serving important political and organizational agendas, while at the same time covering up important internal differences within both the North and the South.

It is necessary, therefore, to study not only the international ideological and political trends which form the NGO channel globally and in each particular country, but also its history in the different countries, especially when it comes to state–society relationships and how these factors interact. The focus here will be not so much on broad cultural structures or deep-seated national traditions, as on the concrete history of the aid channel itself. This analytical approach is based on the theory that the NGO field is most fruitfully explained as a product of international aid trends and aid rhetoric, national traditions regarding voluntary work and state/society relations and the special challenges and tasks inherent in the aid activity itself.

Typologies of NGO–state relations

As discussed in previous chapters, the concepts of the third sector (often referred to as the 'charitable sector', the 'non-profit sector', the 'voluntary sector' or the 'independent sector') and the public sector have often been used profitably in descriptions and analyses of NGOs in Western welfare states. Based on empirical data and reconstructions of the history of NGOs in aid already presented, these new concepts are not thought to be particularly helpful in understanding the aid arena. Nor are the terms 'civil society' or 'civil society organizations', on the one hand, and 'the state' or 'big government', on the other thought to be particularly fruitful. Development aid has in many cases been a project where states have used NGOs to further foreign policy interests in other countries and is in general more and more becoming a project in which donor governments and donor NGOs collaborate in changing other societies. The focus here is therefore on the NGO channel – seen as a distinct organizational field – in which the links between the state and the NGOs, between the NGOs and the public and between the organizations and the beneficiaries have been of a special character.

For the purpose of this analysis the state is defined here as more than the government but less than what in the literature is called the public sector. It is defined as the continuous administrative and legal systems that attempt to structure the relationships between NGOs and public authority within the development aid field. This state has established structures that affect many crucial relationships also within the organizations and the character of the organizational landscape. It is seen as important not to limit the study to a set of formal organizations and rules, because of the special characteristics of the aid project. The state institutions are also normative orders that enable and create behaviour motivated by moral ideas, and state policies in this field should also be understood in terms of fundamental cognitive structures shared by the channel as a whole.

Some analytical models

Gidron, *et al.* 1992 discuss one model which has been used to highlight aspects of government/NGO relations in welfare states. Central to it is a distinction between two sets of activities that are involved in producing social services: first, the financing and authorizing of services; and second, the actual delivery of them. They suggest four typologies of government-NGO relations:

a) *Government dominant model.* Here the government plays the dominant role in *both* the financing and delivery. The tax system is used to raise funds for the services, and government employees deliver these services.

b) *Third-sector dominant model.* This is the opposite extreme; voluntary organizations play the dominant role in both the financing and delivery of services. It prevails where opposition to government involvement in social welfare provision is strong for either ideological or sectarian reasons, or where the need for such services has not yet been widely accepted.

c) *Dual model.* In between these two extremes are two hybrid models, referred to as the 'dual or parallel track' models. Here non-profit organizations supplement the services provided by the state, delivering the same kinds of services, but to clients not reached by the state, or alternatively filling needs not met by the state.

d) *Collaborative model.* Here the two sectors work together rather than separately.

The non-profit bodies can function as agents of government programmes – the 'collaborative-vendor' model – or alternatively, they can retain a considerable amount of autonomy and direction – the 'collaborative-partnership' model.

This model of state and third sector organizations is critical of the dichotomization between society and the state or between the third and the first sector. Research has shown that, despite present rhetoric and the perspectives inherent in the new development paradigm, the collaborative model is most common in Western welfare states (Kramer, 1981; Salamon, 1981).[1] Previous chapters have shown that development NGOs in most OECD countries are very dependent on the state for financial support, and there is nearness between the state and the organizations in both development aid and emergency assistance.[2] In many donor countries the development field can safely be described as a collaborative system, although power relations and the degree of integration between the partners vary from country to country. The content and character of the collaboration change over time, however, (in the first years of NGO support states generally regarded the NGOs as unimportant channels for aid, whereas official policies in the early 1990s treated them as crucial implementing actors in both aid and emergencies) and from issue to issue.

How can one study this process of integration and collaboration? One model has been proposed by Kuhnle and Selle (1992). The first dimension relates to how near organizations are to the state with respect to the scope, frequency and ease of communication and contact. Organizations may be near and hence integrated with the state, or distant and hence separated from it. Political traditions and culture determine how great the ideological distance between state and voluntary organizations can be and close contact still be maintained (ibid:26). In a 'state-friendly society', the distance can be great, but still the likelihood of adaptation and integration over time is great. Ideological distance does not preclude nearness in terms of communication and contact; the extent of communication may also simply be dependent on the size of the country and the population. Consequently 'physical nearness does not imply ideological nearness' (ibid.: 27) and vice versa. This model highlights important variables influencing the type of collaboration or conflict that exists and includes power relations at the same time as the NGO-state dichotomy is evaded.[3] Lorentzen has distinguished between four forms of integration which are useful in this context (Lorentzen, 1993:71): normative, economic, professional and administrative. They comprise different steering instruments available to states in regulating NGO integration, which can be either broad frameworks of mutual understanding or more specific agreements. In addition to these forms of integration, this study has included another form, which is of particular interest in the development aid field – political integration.

In the rest of this chapter a national NGO system will be analysed, aiming at a description of how such a system may develop in this particular field, while at the same time paying attention to the importance of wider national and international contexts.

The Norwegian sub-system

The analysis will focus on the Norwegian field. What are the traditions regarding roles and the relation between state and organizations in Norway in general? Two factors have been of special importance: (i) voluntary organizations are a common feature of Norwegian social and political life, and most Norwegians belong to several organizations; (ii) there is a close relationship between the voluntary organizations and the state. The history of organizations working on the home front has been described as marked by 'shifting forms of interplay, mutual influence and cooperation between the public and the voluntary organizations for the common good.' (NOU, 1988:19). It is difficult to speak of a 'golden age' where voluntary organizations have been entirely autonomous and independent. The connections have been those of co-operation and integration, rather than conflicts and struggles between what in the present aid terminology is conceptualized as civil society *vis-à-vis* the state. The voluntary organizations have been an important force behind the ideological and organizational changes leading to increased public responsibility for the welfare sector (Kuhnle and Selle, 1990:182). They have generally taken little interest in the problem of autonomy and independence from the state, because, as it is argued, the two sides have largely agreed on the main goals. Since World War II, the co-operative relations have been strengthened and both parties have seen this as based on mutual goals. Rarely has the relationship been seen as based on a purely hierarchical structure of command, where the civil society establishes organizations in order to defend itself against the state. Rather, the development has been towards a stronger public involvement in the activities of the organizations. Especially since the 1960s and 1970s, the growing state support has been of decisive importance for the existence and development of many organizations (NOU, 1988:187). There are, of course, many reasons for this strongly collaborative model, some of which can be mentioned here. The strong influence exerted by the Social Democratic political movement on the development of the welfare state is important, since co-operation rather than conflict between state and society was a central element in their political programme. Moreover, being situated in a long and sparsely populated country with a relatively egalitarian socio-economic structure, the Norwegian NGOs have had a weaker basis for adequate and permanent private subsidies than has been the case in other donor countries.

What about the particular history of the development aid field? The present study has shown that there are important similarities between this history and the history of the third sector as such, but that there are interesting differences as well. The tendency towards collaboration and integration seems to have been even stronger in the development field than has generally been the case. At the same time, however, the organizations enjoy autonomy and independence to an unusual extent in certain areas, and the state, especially in some instances of emergency assistance, has become virtually dependent upon them. It was found that the field is clearly marked by collaboration between state and NGOs. But it will also be shown that the nearness between them has not been replicated in relations between Norwegian NGOs and NORAD in developing countries, nor in the Norwegian NGOs' policy *vis-à-vis* the state in the countries where they work. An analysis that limits itself to formal institutions and general national traditions is insufficient, since the field's development clearly shows that the state's willingness to use and support NGOs has at the same time restricted its own autonomy and created a form of mutual dependence.[4]

Political integration

Politically as well, relations between the NGOs and the government and state have been close. Compared with many other donor nations, Norwegian aid has been marginally influenced by national or economic self-interest.[5] This can best be explained by the fact that Norway as a state has had relatively marginal economic and political interests in the developing world. Aid has, in general, been given with relatively few economic strings and political conditionalities. Historically, Norway has also striven to avoid having its aid become entangled in the internal politics of recipient countries, thus contrasting with the aid policies of the US, France and the UK. The big powers have for a long time devoted large sums of money (also channelled through NGOs, especially in the US) to supporting organizations and groups which could further the donor state's economic or political interests. The point here is not whether this Norwegian policy has been productive in promoting development or the extent to which there have been gaps between rhetoric and reality or between official justifications and actual policy, but that the political and economic context of the channel has been different from that of many other donor nations, and that the state and most of the organizations have shared many of the same views regarding aid and its profile. This does not mean that a Norwegian NGO is more independent of political constraints than NGOs in many other countries, but that the structural environment of the channel as a whole has created other opportunities and constraints. Nor does it imply that Norwegian aid has not also been motivated by cultural, political and economic self-interest. What is underlined is that, in a historical and comparative perspective, the channel's fundamental legitimation has been altruistic and that the state and the NGOs have in many respects shared this altruistic motivation.

The Norwegian Government has supported mission and solidarity organizations as well as other types of organization without having clear or specific foreign policy objectives. Its aid via NGOs has thus defied traditional realist definitions of foreign policy. The state has funded the projects of important organizations in Norway, like the Norwegian Trades Unions, Norwegian Church Aid, the Norwegian Association for the Disabled, etc., and very marginal organizations, like Mary's Friends, without looking for relative gains internationally, while support nationally has been more important. Up to the early 1990s the funding of the channel has not been linked to such political interests, although the whole system, of course, reflects an intention to export Western values, social democratic ideas or different types of Christian morality. This Norwegian 'naïvety' has increasingly come under attack in Norway; politicians are arguing that aid should also serve Norwegian business interests and help to strengthen Norway's global image. Recently, the state has contracted NGOs, not to further Norwegian interests in a narrow sense, but to further, as it has been said, Norway's international standing, to make it a superpower as a proponent of democracy and human rights.

In this field the NGOs and the state have shared a basic consensus about objec-tives. People from the NGOs have taken leading jobs in the state administration and vice versa. There has been policy dialogue with NORAD at the top levels, and some of the most important NGOs have discussed foreign policy issues with the Ministry of Foreign Affairs for years in the Catastrophe Committee (Katastrofeutvalget). The whole period has been characterized by a close and consensual relationship between the state and the organizations. Not only that, the state has mobilized Norwegian voluntary organizations to become involved in aid, by establishing strong incentives for organizations taking up work in developing countries. Before the aid era in Norwegian foreign policy, mission organizations and also a few secular organizations worked in developing countries, but without any form of support from the state. Since the establishment of Norwegian Development Aid in 1962 the state has steadily become a more and more important supporter of the NGOs working in aid, including the mission organizations. About 30 years later, in 1991, one in four of the most active NGOs received more than 80 per cent of their aid budget from the state. While development aid was something of a state monopoly in the 1960s, parts of it have become 'privatized' in the 1990s, in general as a result of deliberate state policies.

While organizations in other arenas were often established because of dissatisfaction with public policies and in opposition to the state, the NGOs in aid became active as aid organizations partly because they supported the state's broad aims. The political and administrative leadership of aid and the aid lobby in Parliament have historically been quite strongly influenced by aid altruism, because government aid in Norway, especially in the 1970s and the 1980s, has to a large extent been an arena monopolized by the 'good-hearted' politicians. Political and NGO leaders have basically shared the same goals of poverty-oriented aid, the focus on women, on sustainable development, etc. Although there may have been disagreements, there has been no Margaret Thatcher to poison the relationship, as happened in the UK in the 1980s. The organizations have also been legally free to take up political issues in opposition to the government, without jeopardizing their standing. Since the Norwegian state is a small state, without a colonial past, it has enjoyed a relatively good reputation in the international NGO community, and Norwegian aid organizations have felt less need to distance themselves from the state in their development work. And perhaps most importantly, the state and the organizations have for different reasons experienced the collaboration as positive, which again has reinforced further co-operation. These aspects have helped to shape the state-NGO relationship, and may provide a background for understanding the particular features of the Norwegian NGO system.

The Norwegian state has no capacity to control and follow up what the NGOs do in the field. Norwegian organizations are working in about 100 countries, while the state works with ten main co-operative countries in government-to-government aid. In some countries this support is without relevance to a foreign policy perspective. NGOs have historically received state support for starting up NGO projects, without the state attempting to direct their activities to certain geographical areas or to certain politically prioritized issues, except in broad terms: the state has, for example, initiated AIDS programmes, and earmarked funds for projects aiming at protecting the environment, thus indirectly affecting the profile of NGO work. This is partly because the state has had no such priority list and partly because the NGOs have started work as a result of traditional links (mission organizations) or more accidental encounters at conferences, meetings, etc. In 1991, for example, there were 22 countries where only one Norwegian NGO was working. This geographical profile reflects that the NGO channel has been seen by Parliament as a global channel, as opposed to government-to-government aid which has been concentrated in the past on a few selected countries.

In the main co-operating countries the number of organizations and projects makes the question of co-ordination and integration an obvious political-administrative issue. For example, in 1991 NORAD supported 12 Norwegian NGOs working in Bangladesh, 18 in Nicaragua, 12 in Ethiopia and 16 in Zimbabwe (NORAD, 1993). They were not all implementing organizations, but the numbers are an indication of the level of activity. The support amounted to about NOK 200m in that year alone. In addition, there were the organizations' own funds. In parts of Ethiopia, Bangladesh and Zimbabwe, NGOs supported by the Norwegian state have been important local, regional or national actors, but without having to relate to an overarching Norwegian policy in the area. In Bangladesh, Ethiopia, Nicaragua and Zimbabwe Norwegian NGOs support or co-operate with more than 50 local NGOs, also financed by NORAD (see Tvedt, 1995c). This means that in these four countries about 100 organizations have been working with money from the Norwegian state, but basically uncoordinated policy-wise.

From being a clearly government-dominated field in the 1960s, the aid field in Norway has evolved close to what we noted above as a collaborative model. This model has been initiated, and for long controlled, by the state. The emergence of strong NGOs and conflicting state agendas has helped to slow the process of isomorphism, although the organizations have gradually adopted organizational mechanisms propagated by the state. Governments and the Storting have regarded the NGO channel as of varying importance, but until the early 1990s basically as something apart from Norwegian aid in general. It was felt that the NGOs should be free to work wherever they would and within the sector they preferred, so long as they fulfilled the administrative requirements.

Report to the Storting No. 51 (1991–2) changed all this. What was seen as a fragmentation of Norwegian aid ought to be reduced. Norway was supporting projects to the same country, via NORAD, different UN systems and NGOs, without any efforts at co-ordination. Or NORAD and the Ministry of Foreign Affairs were supporting the same international organizations, without knowing that five different government departments had funded the same organization, while some organizations greedily exploited this lack of co-ordination.[6] Complementarity and even co-ordination between NGOs and NORAD were suggested. On the other hand, the Storting has laid down policy that underlines the autonomy of Norwegian NGOs, and the policy that all NGOs should be treated in the same way by NORAD has not been changed. In the last few years NORAD has been caught between these two policy signals and a gradually stronger NGO community. For the Foreign Ministry co-ordination of NGOs has not been the most important issue, but rather the contracting of individual NGOs for its shifting and immediate policy initiatives.

An analysis of the programme aims, project profiles and goals of all the Norwegian NGOs (see NORAD, 1993), shows the proximity in aims and project profiles between the NGOs and NORAD (see Tvedt et al., 1993). They have both given assistance to more or less the same sectors, although the NGOs naturally have shown less interest in industry, banking, etc. But this 'sameness' does not imply that there is co-ordination or complementarity, only a basic sharing of development aims. There have been few concerted efforts at creating an overall Norwegian profile and coherence of the assistance in a particular country (except in the Middle East and Gaza, following the 1993 Peace Agreement). In spite of the policy formulated in the Report to the Storting, the role of the NGO Division in NORAD became basically restricted to assessments of what have been termed 'quality criteria', i.e. securing what is defined as the efficiency and sustainability of NGO work. The NGO Division has time and again felt the need to distance itself from the government's ideas about co-ordination and closer co-operation, in order to reduce fear and distrust in the NGO community. Even hints at greater co-ordination have met with strong opposition from vocal NGOs. By effective lobbying, questions have been put to the Minister for Development Co-operation in the Storting. The signals of co-ordination given in Report No. 51 have in practice been reduced to a dialogue about experiences, to co-operation in the main co-operating countries where common interests are identified, and to NORAD contracting some organizations for specific projects. The policy has been implemented via discussions on general issues, such as overall aid profile, reporting systems, etc, the stated purpose being to involve the NGOs more actively in the discussions and debates on Norwegian development policy in general and the aid to individual countries in particular.

NORAD has not had the power or the capacity to achieve co-ordination, partly because of its own organizational set-up and partly because of historical legacies and resistance from NGOs. The history of NGO activities will tend to hamper co-ordination and complementarity. The present NGO profile was basically laid down when NGO activities were influenced by the strategy proposed in Report to the Storting No. 36 (1984–5), which gave little, if any, attention to co-ordination with either Norwegian state policy or the policy of the recipient governments. For the biggest NGOs NORAD has gradually become a less important partner. As they become increasingly involved in emergency aid and are supported by other and perhaps richer donors than NORAD, they will show less inclination to co-ordinate with NORAD policies, at least in situations where funds are more easily available elsewhere. At the same time the relationship is, as noted above, very close because of a fundamental consensus regarding development aims and strategies between the state and the NGOs.

The NGO Division has developed a method that might stimulate closer co-ordination in the long run, without having to decide on overall aims and strategies. It has stated that additional allocations will in general be used for priority areas. It has also established a system whereby NGOs, by identifying tasks of common interest with NORAD, can be supported more generously than is normally the case.[7] If this system of 'invitations' becomes a success, there will be fewer funds for other areas, and consequently a co-ordination of activities will take place over time.

Normative integration

The most interesting example of normative integration may well be the history of the so-called 'neutrality paragraph'. The formal, legal norms of integration are reflected in guidelines on administrative matters, finance, monitoring and control as they have been formulated in NORAD and the Ministry of Foreign Affairs. Normative integration is also influenced by, and reflected in, a society's general view on state-society relations, and more specifically, its perception of aid and how NGOs and the state should operate or co-operate. The following is based on an empirical study of the history of the neutrality paragraph (see Hødnebø in Tvedt 1993a; Tvedt, 1992), and on analysis of European (EUROBAROMETER) and Norwegian opinion polls about attitudes to development aid.

Donor motivations and perceptions of the NGO channel

The legitimacy of the Norwegian NGO channel rests on its standing in the opinion of the public, both as taxpayers and as private donors. These attitudes should not be overlooked, since they are part of the political-ideological context in which the state-NGO relationship has developed. What is the political and ideological backing of Norwegian NGOs among the Norwegian population? Do they expect them to act as the openers of doors for Norwegian political or economic interests, are they conceived as instruments in furthering particular political agendas, or are they primarily viewed as altruistically oriented organizations?

In the formative years of Norwegian aid, opinion polls showed that around 40 per cent of the public supported aid because of the moral 'duty to assist', while almost none mentioned the motivation of it being 'positive for Norway' (in 1974 and 1977 none answered in this way) (Bjørnøy, 1988: 13). The fact that Norway has often contributed more to aid activities than any other nation, and has given it more or less unconditionally, has been an important element in Norwegian identity management and production. This altruistic attitude has dominated the whole aid epoch.[8] In 1993, for example, 66 per cent were of the opinion that developing countries receiving aid from Norway should be allowed to buy their products wherever they wanted, even if this would harm Norwegian firms (Vaage, 1993:24). These ideas partly reflect and have partly reproduced a system in which Norwegian NGOs have had very weak – almost non-existent – connections with the for-profit sector, unlike the situation in some other countries.

The NGOs emerged in Norway as one of the most important and most visible organizers of altruism. Norwegian Church Aid, Redd Barna, the Norwegian Red Cross, etc. have become national symbols of 'good-heartedness'. The work of the organizations overseas is usually mentioned by the King and the Prime Minister in their addresses to the nation every New Year. Their leaders might broadcast to the nation on moral issues on the same days, or they might star in prime-time entertainment programmes and talkshows, speaking about the need to help. Every autumn they gather the nation in front of the TV-screen in a national campaigning day for unconditional aid to poor people in the Third World. The NGOs represent a belief that it is not only possible, but also preferable, to help other people without expectation of reciprocity. Dominant theories about the economic man or the interest-maximizing actor ('If you scratch my back I will scratch yours') are therefore not very useful to apprehending how the channel has been perceived and understood. Reciprocity and reward have not been implied in the vision of this relationship. One important reason for the channel's high standing in the public view is probably precisely this image of the selfless, poverty-eradicating and efficient 'do-gooder'. Contrasted with the realism and cynicism that affect other parts of the public discourse in Norway, the channel symbolizes a kind of Norwegian naïvety. These visions of the NGOs have made collaboration with, and financial support from, what has been regarded as a benevolent, small and well-intended state administration less questionable than co-operation with private business, but also more necessary, since other types of funds have either been non-existent or unacceptable.

Some NGOs have been supported by particular sections of the population and have involved themselves in aid primarily to strengthen a value-sharing community. Missionary organizations have as an overall, strategic goal to expand 'the community of believers'. The Norwegian Trades Union supports the build-up of unions in other countries to strengthen the cause of workers internationally. Norwegian Church Aid works primarily through local Lutheran churches, although its ecumenical strategy encourages work with other groups as well. The search for like-minded partners in what is called 'development partnership' has an important consequence; it will gradually strengthen this 'community-motivation', away from donor altruism towards reciprocity. But these NGOs also contribute to what is regarded as the needs satisfaction of others, without insisting on the satisfaction of the wants of their own members, and are in this sense influenced by altruistic behaviour as it is usually defined. They may have counted on support from their own community, but as aid activities have increased and the number of organizations has grown, the competition in the aid market has hardened and growing public support has therefore become an organizational necessity – even a question of organizational survival – for many.

What is focused on here is the fact that the Norwegian NGO channel has primarily been altruistically legitimated by the public, governments and NGOs themselves, and the impact this has had on the system as such. The channel cannot be explained as the result of the state's strategic interests in developing countries or as a reflection of a theoretical contractual relationship between egoists. It is best understood as the expression of a wish to help the poor and suppressed, primarily because people feel sympathy for 'the other', and as the reflection of a belief that Christian, or social democratic Norwegian values encourage development. There is no evidence to substantiate the argument that reciprocity has been a predominantly calculated expectation. It might be useful in this context to distinguish between three types of motivation, although some will argue that actions are always motivated by rational value maximation. For example, when people give aid without apparently expecting to get anything back in material or status gain, they none the less maximize values; what they 'earn' is the excitement of giving. This theory about general human behaviour is not very helpful in explaining what actually are different aid policies in different countries and changing aid policies in the same countries and in the same organizations and among organizations. Motives and intentions are mixed. As shown elsewhere, many organizations gradually become as much concerned with their own growth and their own standing and prestige in society as with helping the poor. None the less this chapter will suggest 'altruistic intentions', the intention to strengthen the 'community of believers' and the intentions 'to maximize own gains', and that the popular support for the channel has been related to the first and second types, while actors within the channel have moved among all three categories. It will also suggest that, combined with the particular history of the Norwegian state and economy in developing countries, this has created unique frameworks for NGO-state relations in the aid arena and for the formulation of NGO strategies which should be of general interest for the understanding of the NGO channel.

Value-sharing organizations as value-neutral organizations

An important issue in the policy of the state and NORAD towards Norwegian NGOs has been the so-called neutrality paragraph (the same criteria should also apply, according to the regulations, to indigenous NGOs). Three factors are of importance. a) Aid has traditionally been regarded as a non-political affair in Norway; a precondition for receiving support was that the state (NORAD) was guaranteed that the NGO activities were politically, religiously and ideologically neutral. b) NORAD, and later the Ministry of Development Co-operation (from 1984), developed an aid culture during the 1970s and 1980s which rejected or was not interested in ideas of using aid as a political weapon linked to Norwegian interests. c) The organizations have portrayed themselves nationally and inter-nationally as humanitarian, non-political organizations. This does not mean that aid was not political or that decisions in NORAD were not taken that were openly political, or that organizations have not supported special groups, special religions and special policies. The important thing in this connection is that the ideal has been to disregard such 'realist' considerations, and that the rules of the NGO discourse have forced all actors to embrace neutrality, at least rhetorically.

The position and authority of the neutrality paragraph in Norwegian aid stems from the discussions between the state and the mission organizations in the 1960s. The government and the state explicitly did not want to support mission organizat-ions using state money for missionary purposes. They also wanted to broaden the support for Norwegian aid.[9] Both at the start of the first Norwegian official development aid in 1952 and at the establishment of Norsk Utviklingshjelp in 1962 it was explicitly stated by the Storting that international aid based on public money should be given according to the 'principles of neutrality' as adopted in the principles of the United Nations. These principles were discussed by the Storting in relation to the first guidelines for public support to private organizations. A paragraph on political and religious neutrality was included in its general guidelines for develop-ment aid:

> The Norwegian efforts must be undertaken on a general humanistic basis without being motivated by economic, political or religious special interests. (Recommendation to the Storting No. 75 1961–2).

These principles and this specific paragraph were subsequently carried into the special guidelines regulating the government's financial support to Norwegian organizations. Following political discussions and negotiations with the organizations the paragraph was formulated in the following way:

> The organization shall commit itself to work with the projects on a general humanistic basis without being motivated by economic, political or religious special interests.

This formulation was accepted by the NGOs. It was vague enough to conceal disagreements that existed between the missionary organizations and NORAD on this point. The support to mission organizations was initially confined to investment in physical structures, like hospitals, schools and other activities around their mission stations, and from 1966 to the salaries of personnel working at these stations, and was given on condition that the personnel were not acting as missionaries, but were technical personnel (doctors, nurses, teachers, etc).

In the new guidelines approved in 1971, the paragraph on neutrality was somewhat sharpened:

Support can only be given to schemes that benefit the local population without any discrimination of race, faith or opinions. Schemes which have as a primary aim the furthering of particular economic, political or religious special interests fall outside this kind of support.

When the general guidelines underwent major changes in 1977, 1983 and 1992, this paragraph remained unchanged. All these general guidelines, including the neutrality paragraph, were included as appendices in the separate contracts for every project, as signed by NORAD and the relevant organization.

In the new revision of these guidelines in 1994, the paragraph on neutrality has been changed. Now it simply reads that the Norwegian Government:

... supports activities that benefit the local population, irrespective of race, creed, sex or political convictions.[10]

The principle is important from many angles, but what is of interest here is that it asked or required organizations based on certain value orientations to comply with the neutral policy of the state bureaucracy. From the state's point of view it was a rational policy, and a necessary policy. In order to enter into a collaborative partnership with the state the mission organizations (and other organizations with strong value-sharing) were asked to sell out on their motivation for being involved in aid. This may, on the one hand, be interpreted as a 'thought-stopper', because it makes it more difficult to discover the role of the organizations as political agents; in other words, that Norwegian organizations, claiming to be neutral, are talking with several political tongues. On the other hand the neutrality principle may be seen as a significant signal, and to abandon or modernize it would entail difficulties greater than those now created, since it functions as a 'tread carefully' sign. Given the probability of ethnic, religious and national discord in several countries during the coming decade, this issue will become a basic question for all donor states.

Table 5.1
Financial support to NGOs from the Norwegian state, selected years, 1981–93 (NOK '000).

	1981	1986	1989	1990	1991	1993
NGO division (NORAD)	79,546	367,280	441,924	589,210	536,424	538,806
Humanitarian support (MFA)	125,317	333,188	426,155	378,231	504,342	651,547
Other grants	0	0	92,734	139,188	149,220	208,696
Total	204,863	700,468	960,734	1,106,629	1,189,986	1,399,049

Note: NGOs in this table are NGOs involved in aid and receiving support from the Norwegian state. The Norwegian state also supports Norwegian NGOs working only in Norway.
MFA = Ministry of Foreign Affairs.
Source: Dalseng 1992.

Table 5.2
Number of Norwegian NGOs with government support, selected years 1963–93

Year	No. of organizations	No. of projects
1963	7	
1975	20	
1981	54	98
1986	77	509
1991	98	1,058
1993	82	

Table 5.3
Number of Norwegian NGOs with state support according to size of grant, 1981, 1986, 1991 (NOK)

Size of grant	1981	1986	1991
Less than 100,000	11	14	20
100,000–500,000	18	14	19
500,000–1,000,000	6	13	8
1,000,000–10,000,000	16	24	31
More than 10,000,000	3	12	20
Total	54	77	98

Table 5.4
State support as percentage of total financial development aid for the Norwegian NGOs, 1990

Percentage	No. of organizations
More than 90	6
80 – 90	16
40 – 60	8
Less than 40	23

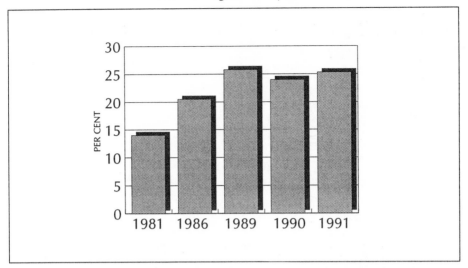

Figure 5.1
Grants as percentage of official Norwegian bilateral aid, selected years, 1981–93

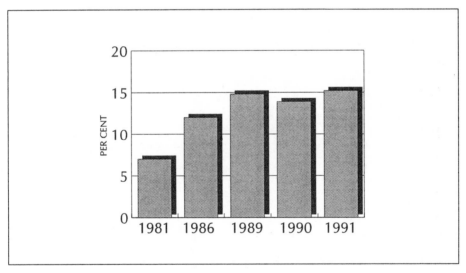

Figure 5.2
NGO grants as percentage of total Norwegian official aid, selected years, 1981–93

Table 5.5
Financial sources (budgeted) of selected Norwegian NGOs, 1992 (NOK '000)

Organization	Total development budget	Own funds	Government grants	International support	Other sources
Blue Cross in Norway	2,698	299	2,081	191	127
CARE Norway	40,000	6,211	40,000	750	2,000
Caritas Norway	16,115	2,606	13,850	–	–
FORUT, Campaign for Development and Solidarity	16,543	2,570	8,353	5,000	300
Latin American Solidarity Groups Norway (1991)	1,200	240	960	–	–
Mission Covenant Church of Norway	5,350	4,755	595	0	0
Norwegian Association for Mentally Retarded	6,804	2,432	4,372	–	–
Norwegian Bangladesh Association	800	800	0	0	0
Norwegian Bar Association	1,880	156	1,724	0	0
Norwegian Church Aid	299,556	100,285	182,175	42,250	2,500
Norwegian Committee for Afghanistan	15,000	800	14,900	500	1,000
Norwegian Confederation of Sports	2,050	410	1,743	–	–
Norwegian Council for Southern Africa	7,500	100	4,330	–	3,070
Norwegian Federation of Trade Unions	30,000	6,000	24,000	–	–
Norwegian Guide and Scout Association	2,128	503	1,625	–	–
Norwegian Himal-Asia Mission	27,993	1,705	25,524	0	0
Norwegian Housewives Association	1,880	956	852	–	52
Norwegian Lutheran Mission	25,498	10,798	14,700	–	–

Table 5.5, continued

Organization	Total development budget	Own funds	Government grants	International support	Other sources
Norwegian Missionary Alliance	32,841	19,755	14,804	–	3,372
Norwegian Missionary Society	10,000	139,283	10,100	0	6,800
Norwegian Nurses Association	2,900	430	2,090	280	100
Norwegian Red Cross	193,038	59,129	133,909	–	–
Norwegian Refugee Council	105,692	20,570	65,786	11,613	2,613
Norwegian Santal Mission	35,000	45,000	20,000	–	–
Norwegian Save the Children (1993)	277,000	114,000	173,000	–	–
Norwegian SAIH (1991)	22,019	1,093	19,486	–	3,680
Norwegian Union of Teachers	9,000	1,783	6,804	–	–
Royal Norwegian Society for Rural Development	16,856	3,289	13,567	–	–
Salvation Army - Norway	6,534	4,047	2,487	–	–
Strømme Memorial Foundation	46,271	50,010	16,306	–	6,830
Namibia Association of Norway	14,996	482	8,652	3,804	1,839
Norwegian National Health Association	2,350	470	1,880	–	–
Norwegian Heart and Lung Association	4,640	928	3,712	–	–
Baptist Union of Norway	1,690	1,510	180	–	–
Development Fund - Future in Our Hands	22,181	3,760	17,421	0	0

Note: The figures have been compiled based on the official documents of the organizations and a questionnaire sent to all the organizations (for methodological details see Tvedt *et al.*, 1993).
SAIH = Students' and Academics' International Assistance Fund.
– = not available.

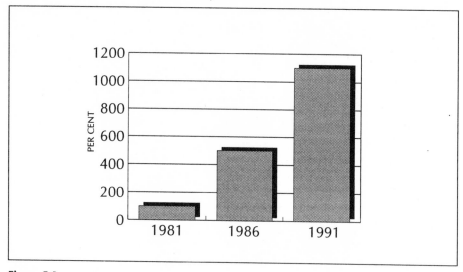

Figure 5.3
Number of Norwegian NGO projects receiving government grants, 1981, 1986, 1991

Economic integration

Economic measures are often used as an indicator of how the integration process has developed. Allocations from the state to NGOs are often expressed in terms of a percentage of their income. How the money is transferred is also important, since this will affect the degree of autonomy or integration. To study this issue historical data on state allocation to all Norwegian NGOs involved in aid have been reconstructed from the beginning of the system, in 1963. Data have also been collected on almost all Norwegian NGOs' own funds as compared with the total aid budget, and on all organizations in the four selected countries that receive support from the Norwegian state or Norwegian NGOs .

Table 5.6
Number of employees working with development aid in NGOs receiving support from the Norwegian state 1990/1991

No. of employees	No. of organizations
0	24
0–4[a]	31
5–9	13
More than 10	5

Professional and administrative integration

The state has increasingly underlined the need for professionalism as opposed to amateurism, in both administrative and financial matters, as well as in development thinking. Data collected on staff growth in all Norwegian and collaborating local NGOs, the number of volunteers, the development of planning instruments and a separate study on the learning ability of different types of organization (see Morvik, 1992, in Tvedt 1993a) show clearly that the big organizations in particular have increased their professional staff. Even so, 24 organizations still had no staff earmarked for this activity in 1990–91 (see Table 5.6).

Administrative integration focuses on the formalization and institutionalization of how state–NGO collaboration should be managed. It deals with reporting requirements, the character of the policy dialogue, auditing regulations, etc. A huge amount of empirical data has been collected and analysed on how this relationship has been managed in Norway and in the developing countries that have been selected for a closer study.

NORAD's guidelines for support to and co-operation with Norwegian NGOs provide information about goals and principles, the kind of requirements the organizations must fulfil and how the co-operation is to be organized. NORAD also draws up decision documents, with relatively clear criteria about the allocation of funds. NGOs must comply with a number of different criteria connected to organization and competence, including popular roots, economic strength, etc. They are also required to undertake evaluations of their work. Generally NORAD is able to support up to 80 per cent of budgeted costs, with the organizations providing at least 20 per cent. There are also detailed criteria for administrative support. Tvedt, 1992 describes and analyses these guidelines in detail. Here the focus will be on issues related to how the collaborative model functions.

The state considers that the work carried out by NGOs with public funds falls within its responsibility, and consequently that it has the right and the obligation to ensure that these funds are used according to the guidelines. NORAD has not been very efficient in assessing NGO work when it comes to aid policies; the information problems and the administrative set-up have tended to focus control functions on financial aspects, and not so much on the social effects of the funds used. Regarding NORAD the interesting question here is not whether the administrative guidelines are 'good' or 'bad' (from being rather liberal in the early period of NGO support, NORAD has now developed a system with few loop-holes), but how they interact with and affect overall NGO strategy and the process of isomorphism it has warned against.

Voluntary organizations in Norway, in general, are not subjected to the same strict rules and regulations regarding budget, economy, personnel policies, reporting systems as are the public institutions. Nor are they bound by the same institutional control mechanisms as the actors in the market have to comply with, such as stock market regulations, accountancy controls, public registration and reporting, etc. In this sense they fall between the state and the market. It is precisely this structural position that makes it difficult to control them and problematic to control them too much.

The increased emphasis on administrative professionalism has simplified co-operation between the parties. Obviously, the increased demand on the NGOs to report to the state has enhanced the state's control. It has also increased the workload of the NGOs. Professional NGO employees who are continuously held responsible by the state, but only rarely so by their own constituents, are likely to have their loyalties changed. The increased emphasis on administrative professionalism has reinforced the already considerable distance between the smaller and the larger NGOs. The large organizations are better prepared to meet the demands. Smaller NGOs, which NORAD has deliberately encouraged to take part in aid activities because they represent a contribution to the creation of a manifold organizational landscape, may emerge as the losers in this process, thus creating isomorphism by proxy.

Through its set of regulations, NORAD has developed a flexible system of co-operation which incorporates considerations of the varied competence, professionalism, etc. of NGOs. The system is not shaped so as to develop the various NGOs' special advantages. The system functions both as an encouragement and as a set of sanctions. Assuming that the NGOs' ambition is to 'climb the ladder', to increase their portfolios, there is a risk that the regulations will streamline them in their bid to please the donor. Increased emphasis on professionalism and goal attainment will, on the one hand, help NGOs improve their efficiency. On the other hand, if it leads their activities into forms that require clear, measurable aims – with development indicators that are easily formulated in budgets and reports, – this might be to go against the fundamental policy aims formulated by some NGOs and also by NORAD. It might lead to a situation where potentially useful initiatives might be rejected out of hand, because the character of the process makes it difficult to work with other than very open-ended goals.

Foreign policy and collaborative partnership

The most important development in the Norwegian NGO field during the last few years is connected with changes in the NGO policy of the Ministry of Foreign Affairs (MFA).[11] While NORAD has had quite close relations with Norwegian NGOs since the mid-1970s, the MFA's policy has changed from one of relative lack of interest to one of active consultation and co-operation. NORAD has underlined long-term development and political neutrality. The MFA focuses on emergencies and uses NGOs as instruments in foreign policy initiatives. In a comparative donor perspective, the MFA's priorities have implied bringing Norwegian NGO policy more in line with what has been a main feature of the channel internationally. In most donor countries development NGOs have acted, and partly emerged, as instruments of governments' foreign policy.

Foreign policy makers in most countries have, for long, regarded NGOs or voluntary organizations as potential instruments in conducting a foreign policy which the state cannot so easily perform. They can bypass the formal procedures and regulations which the established rules for state-to-state conduct have created. NGOs are also regarded as especially efficient in emergency situations; they act swiftly and can mobilize popular support for different initiatives. With a few important exceptions, voluntary organizations have for centuries more or less accommodated such government strategies or policies. Even before the aid era they played an important role in supporting European state policies in overseas colonial regions (the historical literature basically agrees on this role of British, Portuguese and French mission organizations).[12]

The US Government in particular, beginning around World War I, came to see the value of NGOs 'when it could not act officially to promote its interests abroad'. They were 'surrogates for US government interests in neutrality periods during the two world wars and in the Soviet Union in the early 1920s' (Smith, 1990:43). Their role lay in 'complementing foreign policy efforts of their home governments during wartime (particularly the United States in the first half of this century' (ibid.:27). There were, of course, exceptions to this general trend in the US, as in Europe, where, for example, the OXFAM Famine Relief Committee in Britain expressed open dissent against the policies of the British Government.

The US Government regarded aid as a political weapon in the Cold War and in dismantling the colonial system of the old European powers. It initiated the Organization for Economic Development and Co-operation (OECD, founded 1960) and the Development Assistance Committee (DAC) in 1961. It urged the other Western states to become more involved in aid. To increase public support for more aid and, more specifically, for the Development Decade declared by the UN General Assembly in 1961, voluntary organizations were regarded as important. Several governments started to give support to NGOs, and in 1963 a resolution was proposed in the UN by the United Kingdom and four other North Atlantic governments underlining that NGOs should be mobilized. After having established Norsk Utviklingshjelp (NORAD's predecessor), in 1962, the Norwegian Government channelled money to Norwegian NGOs the same year.

But while the former colonial powers were motivated by the wish to create a humanitarian image for themselves in the ex-colonial territories, getting a foot in the door economically in the developing world through private surrogates with no colonial heritage, and stimulating a greater domestic interest in international questions (Smith, 1990:109), the Norwegian policy was formulated in a different historical and political context. The policy was, of course, regarded as part and parcel of a Western strategy to halt communism and to promote democracy and social justice, i.e. to export neutral values, as it was said. The channel was established at the height of the Cold War, just after the shooting down of the U-2 plane over the Soviet Union and the Cuba missile crisis. For the government, and the NGOs, to think in these political terms was therefore so natural that it did not need to be underlined (later developments have shown that this US and Western strategy was one successful step in the effort to stop communism). But the Norwegian Government had neither a national image to remake nor national business interests to further. In this context the Ministry of Foreign Affairs was not very interested in what the NGOs were actually doing (so long as they were seen as strengthening public support for aid and not doing anything abroad that damaged Norwegian and allied interests).

Until the end of the 1980s the Norwegian Government and the MFA followed an *ad hoc* policy regarding using Norwegian NGOs for foreign policy purposes. Norwegian NGOs channelled money to groups fighting apartheid, but this did not constitute a policy; it was regarded as difficult but natural, in such and similar obviously just cases. Norwegian NGOs were involved in political activities; some worked closely with political organizations – in some cases political organizations dressed up as humanitarian or neutral NGOs – in Southern Africa, Nicaragua, Eritrea and Palestine. In quite a few situations they influenced Norwegian foreign policy in the Third World. (To exert influence of this type is easier in Norway than in countries where the Foreign Ministry also has to defend important domestic business and strategic interests in these countries.) The aim was generally limited to solidarity in support of particular groups. It was in the early 1990s that NGOs, with the MFA's support, first intervened directly in political processes.

This short historical summary shows that NGOs and foreign policy interests have been intermingled from the outset. Governments have used NGOs, and NGOs have used governments. Some differences between the Norwegian context and that of some other donor countries have been indicated. The importance and relevance of these differences will be discussed below.

Collaborative partnership in practice: the Horn of Africa

As shown in the following chapter, Norwegian Church Aid (NCA) played a very important role as the lead agency in the Emergency Relief Desk, operating across the border from the Sudan into rebel-held areas, during a crucial period in the wars between Eritrea and Ethiopia and in the internal rebellion against the Mengistu regime in Addis Ababa. During the 1980s NCA received part of the funding for this operation from the Ministry for Development Co-operation (DUH) (Emergency Division) and from the Ministry of Foreign Affairs (Second Political Division). The government's support was substantial. In the period 1984–9 emergency support to Ethiopia totalled more than NOK 391m of which NOK 124m came from the MFA and NOK 267m from the DUH. In addition to this NORAD provided about NOK 255m in development aid. More than half of this aid went to areas outside the control of the government in Addis Ababa. For instance, during the eight months 1 September 1989 to 10 May 1990 the Norwegian state gave NOK 131.8m to emergency activities in Eritrea and Ethiopia. Most of it, NOK 107.3m went to cross-border operations, while NOK 24.5m went to areas controlled by the government. Almost all this money was channelled through Norwegian NGOs, primarily NCA.

Within the general framework of a model of collaborative partnership, this section will discuss the role of the MFA and the extent to which it controlled developments or became the captive of the organizations rather than their becoming its instruments. The policy was obviously based on a collaborative model, but a study of the actual development of the operation shows that the NGO became, at least for important periods, the dominant partner, not because it had the money or the formal political instruments, but because it had the knowledge and the networks and recognized the potential power in being a risk-aversion channel for a foreign ministry. By comparison with the policy regarding the war in the Sudan, this point is highlighted from another angle. In the Sudan the Sudan People's Liberation Army (SPLA) had taken up arms against what it regarded as the illegitimate regime in Khartoum in 1983,[13] and since 1986 the Norwegian Government (the funding came from the Emergency Division and the Political Divisions) supported both Norwegian People's Aid (NPA), working in SPLA-controlled areas, and NCA, working on both sides, with annual allocations that made the Sudan the second most important country for the NGO channel.

A thorough presentation of these cases would have shown more clearly and in more detail that the main actors in shaping policy were the organizations themselves, to a large extent based on the relations which they had built up over time in regard to local and regional actors. To the extent that anybody had a clear vision of the complexity of the situation in which they were involved and what the outcome of these huge emergency operations could be, it was the NGOs and not the MFA which were calling the tune. The MFA did not have a clear-cut strategy regarding the two big issues: Eritrea's secession from Ethiopia and the civil war in the Sudan. Nor did it have a clear idea of the complicated context in which the NGOs were operating, and its humanitarian policy was so broad that the NGOs could manoeuvre within it. The main reason why Norway became politically involved in these conflict areas (and not in other areas to the same extent) was at the start not basic policy considerations or an assessment of these issues' general importance or importance for Norway, but mainly the fact that Norwegian NGOs were working there. During the 1980s, Ethiopia and the Sudan were the two countries that received most funds via the NGO channel, in some years close on 25 per cent of the entire budget (Dahlseng, 1992:41, in Tvedt 1993a).

MFA, NCA and the Eritrea question

Due to historical accidents, Norway and Norwegian foreign policy have twice played a very important role in the history of the Horn of Africa in general and in relations between Eritrea and Ethiopia in particular. In 1952 when the UN decided the future of Eritrea, Norway was a member of the Eritrean Commission and opted for unity with Ethiopia.[14] At that time the Norwegian Government was not collaborating with any Norwegian NGOs in the area and no Norwegian NGO had any impact on foreign policy issues there. The government acted without internal pressure, but under pressure from its allies in NATO. Thirty years later the Ministry of Foreign Affairs followed a very different policy, but without prior systematic discussions about the Norwegian attitude to Eritrean independence or strategic discussions about the new policy line. The actual policy and impact were to a large extent the result of reacting to initiatives from different Norwegian NGOs, especially NCA. The Norwegian Government's humanitarian support for the ERD, led by NCA, through an Implementing Agent, ERA, at the receiving end, led to boosting the standing and political and economic power of the guerrilla army, the EPLF, and also the TPLF in Tigray, Ethiopia.[15] This support was undoubtedly an important factor in the Eritreans' victory in their struggle for independence as it was for the TPLF's victory in Ethiopia (interviews with REST, Addis Ababa and ERRA, Asmara, February 1994). The requirements for a policy line were neglected, because nobody seemed to have had the time or the knowledge to assess the importance or the implications this support had for crucial regional developments.

The MFA gave financial and political support to an operation that was regarded by the Ethiopian Government as a violation of the country's territorial integrity and national sovereignty.[16] There can be no doubt that Norway did violate what was generally regarded as a ruling principle in state-to-state relations. The operation was none the less able to continue, because the Mengistu regime was very unpopular at the time, both with Western public opinion and with important Western governments. Moreover, it had neither the strength nor the capacity to control the inflow of food and aid, although in 1988 it threatened to bomb everybody who crossed the border from the Sudan. The Norwegian Government knew, of course, that the UN had to operate in agreement or following agreement with the government, and was thus constrained in its relief efforts. Norway also supported drought victims via the Joint Relief Partnership (also implemented by NCA), which opened a supply route within Ethiopia from the south to Wollo and the north. The Norwegian Government attempted to maintain its support to Ethiopia also, as a balancing act. Norway was well aware that the government in Addis Ababa knew about its policy, but did not want to make it an issue. The Norwegian Government was initially very careful about mentioning the support to the 'liberated areas', for fear that relations with the Ethiopian Government might deteriorate and, among other consequences, make the work of other NGOs in the country more difficult. It did not report this support to the UN system until 1990. The aim was restated again and again – humanitarian support to both parties in the war.[17] The Emergency Division justified this support on purely humanitarian grounds; the suffering was worst in Eritrea and Tigray, etc, and therefore it was natural that this area got most help.

The implementing partners of the Norwegian NGO, ERA and REST, were described as 'humanitarian organizations', although a more apt term would be the 'humanitarian arms of a political organization'. Since these were the only organizations available, in addition to being very efficient aid distributors, the MFAs humanitarian policy became a highly political policy by proxy, contrary to what was planned. By avoiding discussion on the local organizations' status and role in the wars, a political decision on the Ethiopian-Eritrean question could also be avoided, or at least postponed.[18] The strong pro-Eritrean opinion in Norway made it politically necessary to act, but it did not make it necessary to consider the overall regional impact of these actions. In discussions with the organizations, political issues were seldom mentioned. The state's role became more and more to assess the amount of money which was to be channelled, and not to assess the political implications of the support, since the collaborative model and earlier commitments made it very difficult to back out if anyone had so wished. After all, the local organizations, which were implementing Norwegian-supported projects on the ground and were outside effective control and monitoring mechanisms, were involved in war, and their priority was, of course, to win the war rather than to comply with some Norwegians' insistence that food and vehicles should be used for humanitarian purposes, only.

This short summary of the dramatic change in policy that had taken place since 1952, and the role of the ERD operation in creating new power relations in the Horn of Africa, can demonstrate the potential impact of NGO assistance in such situations. It can indicate the importance of emergency operations and how the use of an NGO channel may affect policies and define states' room to manoeuvre. It can also illustrate some of the problems a small state like Norway may have in the follow-up to this kind of policy, whether the constraints are competence or traditions. Norway was on the winning side; ERA and the EPLF came to power in Eritrea and REST and the TPLF came to power in Addis Ababa. The map had been changed, with Norwegian support, but not as a result of deliberate long-term policies, and without being followed up with either business investments or aid. The arguments put forward by Norwegian representatives in the UN Commission of 1952 may have been right or wrong. That is not what interests us here. What is interesting is that the MFA and the Emergency Division implemented a policy that had a directly opposite consequence. The issue had become a domestic policy one. The radical shift in actual policy in a geo-political area that for centuries has been regarded as strategically important, was not much reflected upon. The NGOs had not so much been contracted by the MFA: rather, they had contracted the MFA. NCA was an efficient lead agency of the ERD. It was also very efficient in mobilizing the Norwegian Government to support the ERD, which gave the ERD credibility. The MFA on its side had a channel through which it could do something to alleviate the consequences of drought and the war, but on the other side it had suddenly got a political instrument in its hands which it did not have a clear idea about how to use.

The Sudan

The Norwegian Ministry of Foreign Affairs faced related but different problems in the Southern Sudan and the handling of the 'humanitarian mandate' in that civil war. The international situation was also quite different. In the Southern Sudan it was clear that the UN Secretary General, de Cuellar, had personally in 1986 forbidden the UNHCR and the World Food Programme to co-operate with the Sudan People's Liberation Army. To support the Sudan Relief and Rehabilitation Association, the humanitarian arm of the SPLA, was therefore politically much more risky. After all, Eritrea had another status internationally (there were disagreements on whether it had the right to secede or not). The history of Norwegian NGO involvement also took on a different character; it was more high-profile and politicized.

At about the time the UN forbade co-operation with the SPLA/SRRA, Egil Hagen, an experienced Norwegian aid worker on assignment with Norwegian Peoples' Aid (NPA), left Nairobi with two lorries loaded with 50 tonnes of grain for the Southern Sudan and the SPLA-controlled areas. He took along a journalist from the Norwegian Broadcasting Corporation. The grain came from the European Community, but since WFP was not able to do anything with it, NPA and Hagen had taken on the job. NPA planned to apply for transport support from the Norwegian Ministry of Foreign Affairs, which at this time was not involved.

On the one hand, the Norwegian Government was positive about providing humanitarian relief to people in SPLA-controlled areas. On the other hand, it recognized the difficult diplomacy involved. In line with other countries Norway wanted to be careful. One factor which intervened in discussions was NCA's role in the Southern Sudan and its huge project there (see Chapter 7). A main problem, seen from the MFA's point of view, was that the NPA initiative and the media coverage would most probably increase pressure on it to act. It was important to avoid a situation in which the Ministry was forced to argue openly about what were regarded as touchy issues from a diplomatic point of view. By swiftly accepting the application, combined with a request that NPA should be very low-key regarding publication of the MFA's support, the problem could be solved. NCA on its side was highly critical of Hagen's activities and the support NPA got from the MFA, partly because it was seen as jeopardizing the working opportunities for all NGOs in the area, but also because Hagen was regarded as too liberal in ensuring that the aid was given to the needy and not to the SPLA. NPA's application had stated that Hagen would personally be responsible for transport and distribution. It turned out that he had left the grain in Narus and proceeded to Mogot together with the NRK journalist, who later made the whole story public in the Norwegian daily *Verdens Gang*. When Hagen got back to Nairobi, the EC withdrew their agreement with him, because of the publicity. 1,535 tonnes of grain would not be given to Hagen free of charge. The MFA had already given its verbal assent to supporting him. What could be done now? The conditions had changed with the EC's withdrawal of support.

The situation in the Southern Sudan went from bad to worse. Now NCA also had decided to start work on both sides, being aware that recent developments might make it an organization *persona non grata* in the Sudan. It wanted the Norwegian Government's support in this. It was following a different policy from its action in the ERD operation and from that of NPA. It was important that the government in Khartoum at least tacitly agreed, and NCA put more emphasis on donor control of food distribution than in Eritrea and Tigray. The Ministry of Foreign Affairs also funded NCA activities, and therefore ended up by supporting different Norwegian NGOs with different agendas and different attitudes to the government, the rebel movement and the relationship between development and emergency aid.

NPA had fewer constraints on its activities than NCA or the Norwegian Red Cross. (The Red Cross was working in the Red Sea hills in the east of the Sudan and had also initiated a project with the International Red Cross for bringing a boat down the Nile to transport food to Upper Nile province.) NPA had nothing to lose, it was working only in the SPLA-controlled areas and could therefore go into them with maximum publicity because it had no other commitments in the country. NPA and Hagen also publicly informed the SPLA that their co-operation depended on support from the Norwegian Government. When this 'diplomacy' became known to the Ministry of Foreign Affairs, it at first refused to give further support, while agreeing to pay some of the expenses that had already been incurred.

Gradually NPA's standing in the donor community improved. In 1987, it planned to develop as a liaison organization for other NGOs in the area. The Zürich group, a church-based organization, financed part of the feasibility study it undertook in the SPLA areas. The group consisted of more or less the same partners as those supporting the ERD. They wanted to use NPA, and NCA was thus, in spite of their public disagreements, a door-opener for NPA. In September 1987 the Ministry of Foreign Affairs proposed that the government should support the NPA's emergency work in the Southern Sudan to the tune of NOK 3.9m. It knew the matter was touchy, partly because some organizations had recently been expelled (ACROSS, the Lutheran World Federation and World Vision). The Foreign Minister finally decided that the issue should not be taken to the government, and made the decision himself to give NPA NOK 2m.

The Ministry of Foreign Affairs knew of course that the Sudan Government regarded support to the SRRA as support for the guerrilla army. If something were to happen, the Norwegian Government had no means of supporting the personnel in these organizations. The principal questions involved were discussed, but the already established relationship with NPA and the fact that the media already knew about its involvement restricted its freedom of action.

In the meantime NPA increasingly emerged as a broker for aid to the SPLA-controlled areas. At the same time it had become dependent on the SRRA, because its co-operation was a precondition for continued work there. In the agreement between the two, NPA was, for example, given the right to 'appoint a representative in Nairobi', but only 'with the prior approval of SRRA'. The aid also affected the development of the war itself. The food distribution centres became important military points. The SPLA advanced southwards, also because of the food aid from NPA.

In 1988 signals from Washington became clearer. The US attitude towards Khartoum hardened. The Americans had found out about NPA and its activities and argued that the NGO commitments remained modest, and could themselves be significantly expanded, reinforced or complemented through US support. NPA had become, by unorthodox means, a channel used by many donors to reach victims of war and drought in rebel-controlled areas. By pursuing (sometimes hesitantly and at other times actively) what was described and conceived as a policy of purely humanitarian assistance, the MFA had established a channel of great political importance. And again, by chance, the US Government came to its rescue, in the sense that the rules of the game had changed in such a way as to make it possible to avoid awkward decisions on the relationship between humanitarian aid and political interference.

From these cases it is, of course, impossible to draw any general conclusions about the usefulness of NGOs as an instrument in Norwegian foreign policy. From certain points of view, the emergency assistance was a success. From others it was not. What the examples basically show is that the NGOs' choice of policies tended, in important respects, to reflect their interests in the actual area.[19] These organizations cannot be compared with a foreign service, where people are stationed in one place for a few years – often among like-minded, cynical diplomats – as a step in a career within the system. NGO actors tend to become more involved politically and emotionally, and to be coloured by their location. Some organizations have their organizational identity based on such locations, and for them an important concern will be how to secure this identity in the longer run. To rely on such organizations for policy advice or implementation in difficult, but potentially influential, policy situations will imply both constraints and opportunities. The NGO actors may be knowledgeable and well-intentioned, but the organizational context has affected policies to an extent that should not be disregarded in a study of their role. The MFA, on its side, has its own limitations. The most important in this regard is that it had insufficient competence and capacity to follow events properly, and relied to a large extent on up-dated information from the leaders of NPA and NCA operations. Its main informants were often its instruments, but instruments with their own interests, sufficiently important to influence fundamental policy lines – certainly an interesting version of the collaborative model.

The NGO channel has provided the MFA with a number of instruments which can be operated on the side of its own bureaucracy. The NGOs have initiated and implemented MFA-supported projects that have not required the same political backing as if the government itself had put them in hand. They have carried out politically risky projects, and thus simultaneously functioned as a channel for 'risk-aversion' and for 'opportunity-realization'. The system has also been able to tap some of the considerable knowledge about political situations and conflicts that some NGO actors have acquired. And not least, the MFA has consciously tried to use NGOs as a channel for crisis prevention and peace promotion. While the MFA is making the big Norwegian NGOs bigger and thus more successful, and propagating the Norwegian model and the achievements of the 'big five' organizations *vis-à-vis* multilateral institutions and other donors, its control of what these NGOs do is bound to be undermined in the longer run. The organizations will become accountable to different donors and different governments, and will not necessarily feel most allegiance to the 'small state'. For example, between seven and nine per cent of NPA's budget for 1993 was financed by NORAD, about 30–40 per cent by the Ministry of Foreign Affairs, while USAID channelled more than double the amount of NORAD, and different UN organizations and a European network financed the rest. This change in funding profile has taken place in the last few years. Similar changes are taking place in the Norwegian Council for Refugees and to a lesser extent in Norwegian Church Aid (which was the first Norwegian NGO to take on UN contracts). It is a new departure, and perhaps signals a development in which what have been Norwegian voluntary organizations are gradually becoming international NGOs, operating in a global aid market and with less accountability to the Norwegian state.

The Norwegian Sub-system and Local Organizations

Relations between the Norwegian state and the Norwegian organizations have been analysed above. What is equally interesting in a comparative and historical perspective is Norway's direct support to organizations in developing countries. Donors and donor states have shown an increasing interest in direct funding of Southern NGOs. The big powers have always aimed at mobilizing friendly organizations in other countries. During the development aid era the Norwegian state also began for the first time to give such financial support, but with less clear policy objectives. The aim was simple: development.

Exact figures are difficult to establish, but, based on a compilation of official budgets and different 'windows' it is safe to conclude that during the last decade something around NOK 1 billion has been given by the Norwegian state directly to local organizations in Norway's main co-operating countries.[20] According to recorded transferrals about 11 per cent of total grants or NOK 154m was channelled to local or regional organizations in 1993. In 1979 the Resident Representatives were for the first time given the power to support local NGOs with up to NOK 0.05m, without prior consent from Oslo. In the same year the Country Office in Kenya was allowed to use NOK 0.15m in the same way. Gradually the amount was increased, and now they can hand out NOK 750,000 on this basis. In 1981 the total budget for direct support was NOK 1.5m, while it in 1993 it was more than NOK 89m.

This signifies a new foreign policy line for Norway. The Norwegian Government has never before channelled money directly to organizations in other countries. An empirical study can show how the Norwegian state actors have thought about and handled relations between a Western rich donor government, indigenous NGOs and governments and states in the Third World.

The data on how this policy has developed are scanty. The available literature suggests that other donor nations have no clearer an idea about what they are doing in this area, and that it is based on assumptions and beliefs. Here we will summarize some of the main findings from an empirical study of direct NORAD support to Bangladeshi and Zimbabwean organizations (see Tvedt, 1992:85–95).

Opinions of NORAD and the role of the government

From one point of view NORAD has contributed to what has been called an 'associational revolution'. In Bangladesh, Nicaragua and Zimbabwe it supports more than 100 organizations from its country offices and embassies. Whereas in 1987 it was the main funder of four organizations, by 1992 it was funding 15 organizations in these three countries, some of them very important organizations in a national context (see the survey of Norwegian-supported organizations in four selected countries, Tvedt, 1995).[23] The organizations that it has supported directly (ranging from BRAC in Bangladesh with its estimated one million members to small human rights institutions in Nicaragua) have by and large played an active role in development in the countries concerned, mobilizing millions of people, and bringing education and self-respect to poor people in remote areas. In some countries – as in Bangladesh – they have stirred public debates about fundamental development questions. In others – as in Nicaragua – they are important instruments in the struggle between government and opposition.

Support to NGOs has already had a far-reaching impact on many societies. It may not necessarily strengthen civil society, although that does of course happen. NORAD has supported opposition groups and what are most aptly called government bureaux. Its policy has strengthened some organizations, while disempowering others, both cases with regard to organizational talent, resources, and internal power relations. Disproportionate support to development NGOs, as in Zimbabwe and Bangladesh, may create, and has created, imbalances across the organizational landscape with, most probably, far-reaching historical consequences. NGOs have been given the role of representing such organizations in policy discussions at national and regional level, organizations that may have no real basis, apart from funds from abroad and dedicated employees with a sense of a mission. This kind of support has consequences no one can foresee today. It might strengthen democratic development, or create an enduring lack of accountability.

But to what extent is it useful to talk about NORAD furthering an 'associational revolution', a global movement with historical consequences which redefine relations between states and society? Based on empirical data, such an analysis may seem too hasty. It de-emphasizes this 'revolution's' dependence on foreign states' funds. The description presupposes, so to speak, that the states are financing their own global roll-back, since it is the states, including the Norwegian state, that keep the majority of the most important organizations going. The phenomenon should therefore be analysed within a perspective of organizational proliferation and growth, but also of dependency. While many states have for a long time been dependent on foreign aid, now also the societies themselves – or at least important actors in them –

are becoming dependent on the benevolence of donors. All except one of the organizations supported by NORAD in the four selected countries depended on foreign donors for more than 50 per cent of their funds, and it is safe to assume that the great majority of them were close to 100 per cent dependent on Northern charity.

The space available to NGOs is decided by foreign interests and not simply by the political will of the recipient governments.[25] It may also reflect, in some cases, the fact that some of these organizations provide an arena for a new type of strong man, with a personal or partial agenda rather than a people's agenda. The way organizations are supported, the 'closeness' of the system, the lack of organizations with a history and traditions in some of these countries, also create this kind of social impact.

NORAD is far from having accomplished the aim declared in Report to the Storting No. 51 (1991–2) that the organizations it supports should be rooted in society, etc. The Norwegian Government's policy is that organizations will contribute to democracy and development, but it is underlined that they must be rooted in society. In general, they have very few members and very few volunteers, and by and large they are organizations established by intellectuals for political, humanitarian or economic reasons, are more or less totally dependent on donors. Most of them are very recently established and few of the NORAD-supported NGOs are membership organizations. The organizational landscape varies according to the countries' histories, but the trend is for NORAD's focus on development-oriented NGOs to imply support for a special type of organization, one that consists more of development agencies than organizations as they are known in, for example, a Norwegian context. This is a type of organization that manages to attract the donor's interest and concerns when it comes to aid rhetoric, reporting capabilities, discussions on Logical Framework Analysis, etc. Such organizations will always represent only a certain section of the recipient society, and – strengthened by the profile of NORAD's 'windows' – this will be mainly the educated, English-speaking middle class. It is therefore unlikely that NORAD has managed to strengthen the organizations of the poor or the interests of the marginalized through its direct support: they do not knock on embassy doors in Dhaka or Managua.

In Bangladesh NORAD has been an active participant in the donor community and in the NGO community. In Zimbabwe it has played a more peripheral role; its policy has been more *ad hoc*, and the turnover of staff more frequent, etc. (this has, indeed, also been the case in Nicaragua). But whatever approach the NORAD staff have adopted, they have still been regarded as representatives of the Norwegian Government, with huge amounts of money in their pockets. This has produced, and reproduces a barrier to equity in relationships and mutual reciprocal communication. In the eyes of many people in the recipient society, a diplomat with access to funds so huge that he can in important ways change the organizational landscape in the country, has never been, and will never become, a partner with a local organization in development. He might become their patron and benefactor, but not a long-term partner in institution-building, etc.

NORAD's policy of NGO support is by NGOs generally regarded as risk-taking, supportive and progressive in many cases. NORAD has engaged in policy dialogue with some organizations, but with others there is little or no contact. NORAD staff have monitored NGOs mostly by means of interviews during the application process, audit statements and narrative reports provided by the NGOs, and a 'few fleeting visits' (Moyo, 1994) to some projects and NGO offices.

In most countries where NORAD has an office, the co-ordination with, and attention to, the NGO issue is not very visible. The policy has gone through three stages. The first phase was what can be called a 'responsive programme'. The Country Offices responded to applications from a number of NGOs, and in Zambia alone they at one time supported 130 projects. The support had no clear profile, the Country Offices had no possibility of visiting more than a fraction of the projects, and control of how the money was spent was almost non-existent. NORAD, Oslo, then initiated a second phase, where the emphasis was put on complementarity; the support was to be in line with Norway's overall aims with regard to assistance to the country concerned. NORAD asked for country plans, and if such plans were not forthcoming the Resident Representatives were denied the right to allocate money without prior acceptance from Oslo. The aim was to stimulate a development away from *ad hoc* project support to programme development. Now NORAD has entered phase III. The focus on country plans helped to reduce the 'post-box' function, but at the same time it isolated plans for NGO support from the general country strategic planning. The aim now is to try to integrate the country plans into the over-all strategy.

Structural features of the administrative set-up seem to have made this policy difficult to achieve. NGO support has generally (with some exceptions) been regarded as a thing apart. The administrative system, with a separate compartment for NGO matters, has, on the one hand, increased local NGOs' opportunity to acquire funds according to their own plans and priorities. It could perhaps have developed into a centre for strategy formulation on 'civil society'-state relations, but in general the offices have instead become a mixture of post-boxes for the *ad hoc* management of applications which are too many for one person to handle, and a more strategically oriented planning unit. The system has made it difficult for the Country Office to co-ordinate the overall country activities. The history of the support shows that it has been difficult to co-ordinate NGO support with sector programmes, not because of individual, personal factors, but because of this very administrative separation. The present NORAD policy of closer integration in Country Plans and Country Programmes has met with obstacles, also because of the profiles of past NGO-support schemes implemented in line with other policy guidelines (see, for instance, the policies in Report to the Storting No. 36 (1984–5) and Report No. 51 (1991–2). The support may be in line with sector priorities, but it does not have to be so. Support for women-oriented projects amounts to six per cent in Zimbabwe and 20 per cent in Bangladesh, and support for human rights and the environment to one per cent in Bangladesh, while the environment is supported with 17 per cent in Zimbabwe. In both countries the main support goes to urban-based middle-class organizations, and not to the poor and the marginal groups' organizations, as suggested in overall policy and country strategies.

As a state institution in another country, NORAD has generally been supporting organizations and projects that already have the support of the government. This is natural, since NORAD organizes state-to-state aid. Support for a stronger civil society will in reality (rhetoric is quite another matter) not be able to carry on, unless the recipient state agrees to some extent. This state-to-state link therefore puts limits on NORAD's role as a supporter of civil society. The profile of the support (along with that of other donor states) may therefore help to form an organizational landscape that is opportunistic; the organizations are closely linked to the state, but employ a rhetoric that in certain cases is close to anti-statism.

In some countries NORAD supports opposition groups and minority Lutheran churches, even where this runs contrary to the recipient government's policies. These organizations may be very efficient in development aid, and they may have weaker or stronger roots in the society. The point here is that this policy, with its potentially important diplomatic repercussions, has been handled by the person in charge of NGO support, often working quite isolated from the rest of the office, often a non-Norwegian and often with little diplomatic experience.

In all countries foreign states' support for national organizations is, of course, a touchy issue. It would have become a big issue in Norway if it turned out that the government of Islamic country X had supported, via its embassy in Oslo, an organization in Norway which was working to organize students in Troms or Oslo so that they could 'empower' themselves. Such support may be regarded as 'right' and important. That is not the issue here. The problem is that the Storting, the Norwegian public and the Foreign Ministry and NORAD have not discussed how to handle these diplomatic aspects of NGO support, and how the Norwegian way of doing things will impact on other countries' organizational landscape and state-society relations.

Notes

1 In many developing countries a version of the 'dual model' seems most appropriate, however, because the state has neither the financial nor the administrative capacity to produce the needed services. The donor comes in to fill at least some parts of the gap. The model introduces some useful concepts, but for understanding third-sector relations with states in developing countries it is too formalistic. It says nothing about how the NGOs and the rest of organizational field relate ideologically to the state and government. Neither does it deal with the power dimension, be it the power of the state or of the international NGO channel. It is also important that it does not capture the relation where external donor linkages might be more important than national traditions or styles in forming this relationship. If employed universally, the model therefore needs refinement, and a new typology should be added: the 'donor-dominant' model. The model will, moreover, tend to give too much emphasis to structural model characteristics and underplay the radical shifts in sector relations that may take place and have taken place in many developing countries in short periods of time. It captures neither the importance of the NGO channel in creating and forming what might develop into a third sector, nor indirectly (and sometimes directly) its relation to the state and government.

2 The British ODA has, for example, undertaken a series of joint evaluations by NGO personnel and staff of the official aid agencies. The same has been the case in many other donor countries. For instance in New Zealand and Norway, there are policy discussions on aid and the projects that should be supported in committees where there are people both from the state bureaucracies and from the NGOs.

3 It does not, however, capture the particular characteristics of the NGO channel and the role of NGOs in developing countries (this is natural, since the model is developed within a Western welfare context). Some NGOs may be distant from the national government but close to a donor government and vice versa, and what is 'distance' will vary extremely (the difference between the landscapes in Ethiopia and Bangladesh provides very different physical barriers, so that what appears to be very distant in Ethiopia is simply a reflection of canyons and ravines making

communication almost impossible in large areas, while 'nearness' in Bangladesh may express everyone living on a plain where 80% of the country is less than 10 metres above sea level.

4 It has been claimed that in the foreign policy area the Norwegian state faces less tension within the national decision-making system and is less likely to clash with other external political, strategic or economic interests, and that Norway has fewer and less complicated foreign policy objectives than many other countries (Egeland, 1988). Consequently it has both the potential for becoming an important humanitarian power and has a state with a higher degree of autonomy than most other donor states.

5 In 1963, when support to private organizations began, the government's intention and plan was that Norwegian business firms would become more important than NGOs. Norwegian firms were not interested, however, at that time, unlike Norwegian NGOs. In the last few years NORAD has made more efforts to support Norwegian firms. The total value of project applications was NOK 7.962 billion in 1994 as compared to NOK 3.338 in 1993, while by July 1994 NORAD had channelled NOK 142.6 million to 43 projects as investment and export support.

6 Documentation about country programme discussions for Bangladesh shows that Norwegian NGOs are barely mentioned at all by NORAD or the government. In the Country Programme discussions for 1991 to 1994 NORAD Dhaka, notes that 'the Representation has no regular contact with the Norwegian organisations' (NORAD Country Programme Bangladesh 1991–4, vol.2:37). Norwegian NGOs have operated in the same country without knowing of each other.

7 Interview with Gunnar Bøe, NORAD, Director, Office for Private Organizations, 5 October 1994.

8 In Norway, unlike many other big donor states, it is fruitful to use the term 'aid epoch'. The reason is that the aid relationship has dominated relations between Norwegians and people from Asia, Africa and Latin America in some decades after World War II. This part of the world has to a large extent been conceived through the lens of the 'giver-receiver' relationship (see Tvedt, l 990).

9 The way the paragraph was formulated reflected the thinking at the time; the ideas which Norway did promote were universal and therefore neutral. Of course, NGO aid like other Norwegian aid was the export of Western ideas with a dash of Norwegian social democratic and Protestant virtues. Ideologically, the neutrality paragraph rests on one fundamental assertion: that the ideas pursued by Norway and Norwegian NGOs are universal. In the guidelines for 1994 this is for the first time spelled out: 'Democracy and respect for human rights are universal values and among the basic tenets governing Norwegian involvement in development assistance.' In most countries dominating politicians and theorists now argue that the fight for human rights, for women's rights, etc. is a fight based on ideas developed within Western societies. Aid is therefore also the export of the 'American dream' or of Western concepts and notions.

10 Few projects fulfil these requirements, however. NORAD and Norwegian NGOs in Bangladesh are the main supporters of a number of Christian Lutheran organizations, because they are Christian and Lutheran. There are also a few examples of Norwegian missions intentionally giving support to Christians and not Muslims. In Orthodox Ethiopia money from the Norwegian state, channelled through Norwegian NGOs, has overshadowed all other donor funds in the South and South Western Synods of the Lutheran Church there. Fifteen out of 83 local organizations supported by NORAD are organizations with Christian long-term goals and with aims relating to the strengthening of Christianity also in their project goals (information gathered from the survey of all organizations receiving support from NORAD or Norwegian NGOs in four selected countries). There is no indication that this is a result of a deliberate state policy. Rather it reflects NORAD personnel's private affinities and networks.

11 This section on MFA policy is based on primary sources collected by archival studies in the Ministry of Foreign Affairs and the Ministry of Development Co-operation, documents from relevant organizations and interviews with officials in the MFA and leaders in Eritrea, Ethiopia, the SPLA in the Sudan and core people in the ERD operation.

12 The extent to which the home governments subsidized and supported the mission organizations varied, both among countries and in relation to specific organizations. The most famous example may be the Catholic missionaries sent from the Iberian peninsula to Central America, which restored legitimacy to the *conquistadors* for government support. In other areas also the mission organization paved the way (expanding Western cultural notions and values) and legitimized

colonialism, regarded as benevolent paternalism. In Africa, where most Norwegian NGOs work, they were frequently given government subsidies for their charitable work, while being allotted parts of the country where they were allowed to evangelize so as not to compete with mission organizations with other beliefs (the Southern Sudan under British rule can be a case in point). There were, of course, exceptions to this rule. The Norwegian mission organizations, many of whom today are also development NGOs, were not among the severest critics of Western colonialism, although they were not subsidized by a colonialist government.

13 For articles on the impact of the war, see Tvedt 1993b, and for a background study of the war, see Harir and Tvedt, 1994.

14 Norway was a member of the Eritrean Commission, appointed by the United Nations, in the early 1950s (other members were Burma, Guatemala, Pakistan and South Africa). This commission put forward proposals for future relationships between Eritrea and Ethiopia. Pakistan and Guatemala wanted Eritrea to become a sovereign state after a maximum of ten years. In the meantime it was to be administered by the United Nations. Norway's representative in the UN Commission was very clear: Eritrea should be under the Emperor and he opted for reunion. The delegation argued in support of the 'necessity for the political association of Eritrea with Ethiopia' and about the mutual benefit to 'both countries, by their complete and immediate union' (United Nations, General Assembly, UN Commission for Eritrea. Report of the Commission to the General Assembly, 10 June 1950, A/AC.34./3.201, Foreign Office Archive, 26.6.26. Eritrea-Commission Vol. II, 1 June–31 July 1950). The western part of Eritrea was to remain under British administration. Ethiopia wanted an intimate union between Eritrea and Ethiopia. Italy wanted maximum sovereignty for Eritrea, and was supported in this demand by the majority of Latin-American states. In the General Assembly debate the Norwegian proposal received support only from Liberia (and Ethiopia). Burma and South Africa proposed a federal solution, with the countries united under the crown in Addis Ababa. This was supported by the General Assembly. Finally a resolution proposed by Bolivia, Brazil, Canada, Denmark, Ecuador, Greece, Liberia, Mexico, Panama, Paraguay, Peru, Turkey and the US carried the day by a majority of 38 votes to 14. Norway had backed away from its commission member's proposal, and supported this motion which implied that Eritrea should be a self-governing area in union with Ethiopia under the sovereignty of the Ethiopian crown. Norway opted for a compromise, a federal solution behind which the British delegation played a leading role.

15 'The soldiers learnt to like the BP5', interview with ERRA, February 1994. BP5 are biscuits rich in nutrients made in Norway and provided by the ERD operation.

16 Addis Ababa also knew that the Norwegian Government was involved through NCA (Ethiopians working at the NCA office in Addis Ababa reported to the government all the time, without NCA and the Norwegian government knowing it.) This example is an indication that the MFA should have no illusions about the 'secrecy' of such operations.

17 The cross-border support was broadly in line with that of other big donor nations. From 1984 to 1986 US government gave $450m to famine victims in Ethiopia and about $50m in assistance to Eritrea and Tigray, across the border from Sudan, mostly handled by ERD.

18 The MFA was, however, put under increasing political pressure. The 2nd Scandinavian Conference on Eritrea in Oslo 15–16 March 1986 stated, for example, that Norway had a special responsibility because of its role in the first UN conference on the Eritrean question. Norway was asked to become a central country in the new diplomatic efforts.

19 NCA staff in Addis Ababa complained about NCA's cross-border operations. NCA thus had two heads in Ethiopia. This created internal conflicts between the Addis group and the ERD group. NCA-Addis was critical of the employment of foreign policy advisers, and complained that NCA had given up both its church profile and its control profile in relation to REST and ERA: 'They received half-page report after giving them US 30 million' (Odd Andersen, Resident Representative NCA, Addis Ababa in interview with author, May 1992).

20 Tvedt, 1992 presents a more detailed account of how a donor's discovery of Southern NGOs was turned into official aid policy, by giving an empirical analysis of the history of direct Norwegian support to local NGOs.

21 The material is primarily based on archival material on the two countries in NORAD, Oslo, and archival material at NORAD, Dhaka. In addition, a number of reports written by NORAD, Zimbabwe, are used.

22 Support to NGOs is given mainly from five budget lines, namely: Support to Local NGOs, Environmental Activities, Cultural Co-operation Support, AIDS, Grant and Women's Activities. The Government of Zimbabwe has requested the allocation of some bilateral funds for small- and medium-scale enterprises development; focusing on indigenous enterprise institutions. Whether these should be called NGOs is a question of definition.

23 Western embassies in Bangladesh and Ethiopia in 1992 and 1993 put pressure on the governments to reduce their control of the sector.

6

NGOs
& the 'Articles of Faith'

In spite of the extreme heterogeneity of the development NGOs in aid regarding value orientation, size, traditions, constituency and relation to the state, and despite the way in which their functioning is influenced by system mechanisms, different national traditions, international political and ideological trends, NGO literature, policy statements and a number of research reports have for more than a decade ascribed to all NGOs certain definite characteristics. Enormous quantities of paper have been used for such myths to be produced and reproduced, and a number of evaluation studies have been carried out, ritually confirming these basic assumptions while criticizing certain NGOs for not meeting these standards.

For more than fifteen years the main argument for the NGO channel in aid has been the NGOs' comparative advantage in relation to states. The growing role and importance of the NGOs have been justified by arguments emphasizing their flexibility, creativity and cost-effectiveness, including their ability to mobilize voluntarism. But to what extent have these assertions been substantiated by research findings? Is it perhaps just as appropriate to talk about NGOs' comparative disadvantage and philanthropic failure? And how useful are such neo-classical economic concepts when discussing NGOs in development? Since NGO studies have often been NGO propaganda by other means, research has tended to neglect the fundamental methodological problems involved in trying to answer such questions. The aim has often been not to understand the NGO channel as a social phenomenon, but to formulate nomothetic generalizations about the NGOs' advantages as compared with other institutions in society (especially the state). Here the aim is to discuss theoretical and methodological issues in analysing NGO achievements. The focus is especially on efforts at ascertaining the comparative advantages of NGOs as compared with states in development.

The question of comparative advantage

In 1982, at the beginning of the NGO decade, a list of what was called the NGO 'articles of faith' was drawn up (see Tendler, 1982: 3-7). In comparison with governments, NGOs claimed to be better at:

1 reaching the poor, i.e. targeting their assistance on chosen groups;

2 obtaining true meaningful participation of the intended beneficiaries;

3 achieving the correct relationship between development processes and outcomes;

4 working with the people and thus choosing the correct form of assistance for them, i.e., not being dominated by resources as the basis of the relationship;

5 being flexible and responsive to their work;

6 working with and strengthening local institutions;

7 achieving outcomes at less cost.

A decade and a half of experience later, these 'articles of faith' are still championed by NGO propagandists, but now they should rather be called a 'list of dogmas', representing a way of thinking about NGO activities which blurs analysis of both potentials and constraints, and which, interestingly, has been championed ever since Tendler showed that they could not be substantiated. An additional, newer list has, however, been put forward (see Fowler, 1988:8-9), which is an unclear mixture of organizational potentials and characteristics compared with those of state institutions:

• ability and preparedness to experiment with unorthodox ideas and practices;

• patience coupled with a strategic perspective;

• ability to undertake people-centred research;

• faster learning through, and application of, experience;

• better ability to articulate rural realities.

A last-ditch defence of the comparative advantage theory concentrates on the argument that NGOs are more innovative than public bureaucracies. Others mention their 'freedom from political manipulation' and that their work and projects are labour- rather than capital-intensive.

The notion of comparative advantage has become a focal point in the NGO discourse and popular and undisputed as it is, it seems to have been taken for granted. In the 1970s and early 1980s the concept was not part of 'everyone's' jargon. In the first two decades of NGO aid NGOs were supported mainly because they were regarded as useful supplements to state-to-state aid and a way of involving broader sections of the donor population in aid.[1] Only later were the role and potentials of NGOs formulated in general and legal language with comparative advantage as the core term, regarded as a general characteristic of NGOs as a group as compared with states, governments or markets, irrespective of time and place. Their assumed advantages have for years been a main argument in most donor countries when defining the distribution of roles between NGOs and the state in public aid budgets. The US Congress in 1973 talked about NGOs special ability to focus more directly on the needs of the poorest majority, but this did not amount to a general theory about states and organizations. In the late 1970s the US Government declared that NGOs had a comparative advantage, and in the early .1980s Congress required that from 12 to 16 per cent of USAID's annual budget should be channelled through NGOs working overseas (Smith, 1990:5).

What do we know?

The concept of comparative advantage raises a number of problems, both theoretically and empirically. Despite more than a decade of evaluations and reports of thousands of NGO projects, research has not been able to draw definite conclusions or to show empirically that NGOs possess these comparative advantages.

In 1982 an analysis was carried out of 75 NGO project evaluations in the files of the US Agency for International Development (Tendler, 1982). It concluded that the 'literature and knowledge is by and about PVO [NGO] organizations, not about the world and the problems in which the project is taking place; or about the general class of problems being dealt with and the experience in dealing with them', and that, based on the projects evaluated by USAID, it was not possible to argue that NGOs obtain more or better participation or are better able to target and work with the poor effectively. The NGO articles were therefore articles of faith.

Shortly afterwards a comparative study was undertaken of the performance of 150 projects involving membership and public service organizations in Africa, Asia and Latin America, selected in a 'random walk' through the literature (Esman and Uphoff, 1984:84). One of the authors argued that NGOs were 'more likely to adopt a favourable orientation towards and effective support of the actors in micro-development than are governments.' (Uphoff, 1987:14). In 1987 the OECD concluded that the limited evaluation work available so far 'tended to show that NGOs have a comparative advantage in addressing basic human needs at the grass-roots level' (OECD, 1987:104, quoted in Fowler, 1990). These studies cannot, however, be used in this manner as evidence for the very general and ambitious comparative advantage theory, because of non-comparable environments and contexts, the time factor, and because the unit of analysis is unclear. The 1993 *UNDP Human Development Report* noted what is still evident: there has been little systematic analysis of NGO impact, either by NGOs themselves or by independent organizations (UNDP, 1993:94).

A slogan of comparative advantage often used in fund-raising campaigns is that NGOs always reach the poor, or are particularly capable of helping the poorest among the poor. To this claim, UNDP replied that 'NGO interventions probably miss the poorest 5–10%' (ibid.: 96). The DANIDA/CASA study of Danish NGOs underlined the difficulties that NGOs had in reaching the very poorest groups, particularly where the emphasis of the project or programme was on mobilization of voluntarism or self-help (DANIDA/CASA, 1989:91–2). The studies by the Overseas Development Institute (ODI) of projects supported by British NGOs showed that most of the projects examined failed to reach the very poorest. Project mechanisms caused disproportionate benefits to accrue to those who had some education and access to some land or business, and to men rather than women (see Muir, 1992:109–12 for Zimbabwe and White 1991: 98 for Bangladesh). A recent study of Swedish NGOs has found that they have not been particularly successful either in fostering processes that generate wealth among the poor or in developing methods for service delivery that mobilize and redistribute existing resources (Riddel et.al 1995). And a worldwide review of research projects on animal-drawn agricultural equipment shows that NGOs have been no better and no worse than other (private or public) organizations (Starkey, 1987).

A study which attempted to analyse the NGO channel's overall impact concluded that in the countries studied – Chile, Brazil, Burkina Faso, Zimbabwe, India and Indonesia – NGOs were 'not a substantial social force' (Wils, 1991:32). On the other hand the present study shows that NGOs have played a very important political and socio-economic role in Ethiopia, in the Eritrean war of independence, in the Southern Sudan and in Bangladesh.

To assess critically the comparative advantage perspective is therefore not synonymous with denying NGO potential. Rather it is deemed necessary to criticize this dogma in order to achieve a more precise analysis of the potentials of types of NGO intervention in different contexts. It is, of course, possible to assess whether NGOs have succeeded in mobilizing people, achieving project targets and improving the standard of living of the target groups, as it is possible to do the same for state-to-state aid and government projects. But such studies cannot substantiate a claim about comparative advantages for a whole group of organizations *vis-à-vis* another equally multifaceted group of states. To compare NGOs and governments faces some of the general problems inherent in comparisons. The way it has been employed within this field is especially problematic. The thesis has a universal ambition; it claims that NGOs are 'better' than governments, disregarding the heterogeneity of NGOs and government in time and space. Since the middle of the 1980s the whole issue has become captured by a political-ideological debate about states *vis-à-vis* civil society, where the NGOs represent the alternative to the roll-back of the state.

The concept and the question of methodology

The main problem with most studies of comparative advantage in development aid is that major conceptual and methodological problems are neglected, and that the organizations are viewed as if they possess certain universal characteristics, whatever their history or the kind of relations they enter into with states and beneficiaries.

How can we assess comparative advantage? Fowler has argued: 'What does comparative advantage mean in organizational terms? We will take it to mean that an organization has traits or features which make it more suitable for achieving a particular purpose than an organization which has the same purpose but does not possess these traits or features' (Fowler, 1988:5). He wants to compare organizations with 'the same purposes', but to find out which organizations have the same purposes is not easy, partly because organizations do not have purposes (only leaders and individuals in the organization have them), partly because it is very difficult (if not impossible) to find out 'real intentions' as compared with rhetoric, conflicting strategies, etc. and partly because the questions presupposes that what is to be compared – voluntary agencies and states – have the same aims or purposes. Therefore, to show that a grassroots-oriented NGO in Chile under the Pinochet Government managed to achieve true and meaningful participation of the poor to a greater extent than the elitist government says nothing about comparative advantages in general, but only something about differences between a particular government and an NGO in a particular area at a special time in the country's history. To show that a Northern NGO is better at implementing projects among poor people than government agencies like ODA, SIDA, USAID or national governments, does not imply that general comparative advantage is evidenced or that the former assists the poor better in the long run than the latter.

NGOs and governments differ fundamentally, at least according to the rhetoric championed by supporters of the comparative advantage argument. Many NGOs are based on strong ideological orientations, be they political or religious. They are value-rational rather than means-rational (as state bureaucracies are said to be), to use Weber's terms. To compare them generally would therefore entail comparison of entities with different rationalities. In some cases NGOs and governments and NGOs and for-profit organizations have opposing goals for development and declared differences in target group orientation. In addition, NGOs as a group do not themselves have the same aims, the same degree of value-orientation or the same abilities and advantages, as is also the case with states and governments. NGOs are established to serve many interests, and not only the progressive ones, as is usually implied in NGO literature, a premise which is a precondition of the comparative advantage argument. For-profit organizations, on the other hand, have more similar aims: to make profits (at least in the long run). Thus they can be more meaningfully assessed according to comparative advantages and described in neo-classical economic terms. The faddish application of concepts of neo-classical welfare economics to the NGO channel should however be questioned.

The theory is also based on a very different, but functionalist argument: if each actor or institutional sector does what it can do best, then improvements in society will be optimal. By emptying the analytical language of national, organizational and political histories, power and distributive aspects, the main factor becomes one of comparative advantage: for governments the primary relationship is one of control, whilst for NGOs it is one of voluntarism. An important feature of this comparative advantage *vis-à-vis* the state is the 'different way that NGOs can relate to the intended beneficiaries, and their freedom in organizing themselves' (Fowler, 1988:1). Relations between governments and citizens are said to be based on control and authority, while NGOs are able to form unambivalent relationships with their clients free from any control orientation. NGOs have the 'potential to adopt an unequivocal, unambivalent position of support, mutual trust and equality of interest with the intended beneficiaries; dominance and control need not lurk in their shadow.' For governments, the 'hierarchical structure of bureaucracy may be suitable for the maintenance of a stable state in a stable environment, but it is much less suitable for development and change in situations of unpredictable futures.' NGOs are said to be free 'to design their organizations in ways which are optimal for the situations and development tasks they themselves select while demands on governments lead to hierarchical bureaucratic structures which rely on uniformity, standardization and rigidity' (ibid.:10). Based on such descriptive stereotypes, comparative advantage cannot be measured, because the ascribed advantages are identical to the given institutional descriptions. The whole argument turns out to be a tautology.

How is it at all possible to substantiate the argument that NGOs are better than governments? Let us assume that all development NGOs are identical (have the same aims, the same attributes, etc.) and all states are similarly identical. The theory can be tested only when the performance of the different organizations being compared takes place under identical or at least reasonably identical conditions. Methodologically this is problematic. NGOs and governments have extremely different types of instruments to influence actions and impacts. Governments, for example, can use such instruments as taxes, legislation, the national media, prisons, etc. NGOs will usually control fewer instruments, and their performance and implementation are based on more particularistic perspectives and approaches than those of governments. The government can, for example, change the tax system or the curriculum of primary schools with immediate and important (positive or negative) consequences for all the poor people in a country, while the NGOs with all their combined efforts can never reach more than a fraction of the people. On the other hand, governments can have a number of planning and experimentation units without producing structures for innovation, while NGOs may well be able and willing to experiment. Even in relatively similar situations and in cases where a state and an NGO appear to have some of the same aims, it is difficult to draw clear conclusions.[2] In the late 1980s the actors within the Norwegian NGO system, whether NORAD or the NGOs, shared many of the same values regarding support to the poor, flexibility in approaches, etc. This makes assessment of comparative advantages on an institutional level more relevant and fruitful.

The history of aid to Kenyan organizations after the diplomatic breach between Kenya and Norway in 1990 is interesting in relation to a question of a different order: can NGOs be used as a flexible channel for governments in touchy political situations? When Kenya broke off diplomatic relations on 22 October 1990, NORAD was given one week to pack up and leave. All state-to-state co-operation was terminated, but the Norwegian NGOs were allowed to stay on. A decision was then taken to allow for the continuation of NORAD support to some Kenyan NGOs, but via a Norwegian NGO. These Kenyan NGOs were NGOs that had just signed three to five year contracts with NORAD, and whose work would have been seriously hampered if NORAD funds had suddenly stopped.

NORAD's problem was simple: how to minimize the negative impact on Kenyan NGOs if all Norwegian financial support were suddenly to be cut off? To hand the support over to a Norwegian NGO which was continuing to work in Kenya was regarded as a flexible way of securing continued assistance to Kenyan NGOs. As an important part of this assistance was support for democratization and popular groups that advocated certain interests in the civil society, the Norwegian Foreign Office had no objections to such a policy. The NORAD support of NOK 15m in 1990 was reduced to 5.6m. Support was given to 12 Kenyan NGOs, plus follow-up and payment of 10 per cent retention money to 32 other projects. Norwegian Church Aid, as a result of negotiations with NORAD in November 1990, was willing to serve as the contractor for NORAD.

At first NCA had hesitated. It was initially reluctant to play such a role for the Norwegian Government. The NCA Board agreed that their Nairobi office could function as a mail-box between the Kenyan NGOs and NORAD, but on two conditions. This function should not harm any of the other NCA activities in Kenya. This was important to NCA, since its regional office for East Africa was in Nairobi. Secondly, the role of contractor for NORAD should in no way alter NCA's aid profile. The organization immediately approached the Kenyan Government, and was assured that it would be allowed to continue to work in Kenya, and to take over the NGO portfolio of NORAD. NCA soon took several initiatives. In a joint seminar with the 12 Kenyan NGOs, it presented itself and its profile as a

Christian aid organization, different from NORAD in orientation and rationale, but at least in the short run this had no noticeable impact on the profile of its activity. During 1991 it was evident that both the 12 NGOs and NCA found the situation satisfactory, as probably did the two governments. A flexible solution had been found in a diplomatically and politically difficult situation.

One reason why this shift was managed so smoothly was that the development strategies and project aims of NORAD and NCA were quite similar, though not identical. Support for institution-building, welfare and advocacy organizations, poor and marginalized groups, etc. was a goal shared by both. The Norwegian aid system at this time shared many of the same project values. A review of the aid profiles and activities of NORAD and NCA in Kenya regarding their support to NGOs shows that they both supported projects within six of the same sectors, while NCA also worked with refugees and displaced people and for institution-building within organizations (see Hødnebø et. al., 1993). It is interesting – and says much about the channel or the 'NGO thing' – that NORAD and NCA more or less did the same thing in Kenya.

The strategies and aid policies of the two Northern institutions can be compared in this situation.[3] The NORAD policy for support to Kenyan NGOs was formulated in 1985 and revised in 1988 building upon Report to the Storting No. 36 (1984–5) to the Storting. NCA based its policy for Kenya on its regional objectives for East Africa, building on its strategy document: 'NCA towards the year 2000'. Three years after NCA had taken over responsibility for this NGO support, it was supporting work in four of the same sectors as NORAD (education, income generation and small-scale enterprise, environmental conservation and human rights and democratization). While NORAD had supported work in the health and social sectors, NCA had withdrawn support from these sectors and prioritized emergency relief, rehabilitation of refugees, facilitation of the peace process (NCA was active in supporting peace negotiations in the Sudan) and organizational support and development. The difference between the two organizations was less than this over-view indicates. The training component in many NORAD-supported programmes was extensive, and could be categorized as organizational support, and NCA's support for slum projects and children's homes could be described as social welfare. Both organizations channelled extensive support to church organizations and NGOs working on behalf of marginalized groups. NORAD supported many *ad hoc* initiatives, such as building of schools, hospitals and other physical constructions, whereas NCA, in addition to relief and refugees, worked more with people and institutions (training programmes, etc.). All in all, the sector policies of the two were quite similar and the flexibility and profile in funding patterns did not vary very much, although NCA gave more emphasis to institution- and capacity-building (this latter difference might be explained by a similar shift in emphasis in Norwegian aid policy after 1989–90).

This example does not show that NGOs and public donors or Norwegian NGOs and NORAD have similar characteristics. It simply illustrates that an NGO and a state, under certain conditions, can carry out more or less identical projects in more or less the same way, although in different political contexts, and thus that the differences are less general and less clear-cut than the prevailing wisdom would indicate.

Comparative disadvantage

It has been argued that the main task of the non-profit sector (or NGOs, which we focus on here, as distinct from the third-sector notion as such) is to provide the public sector with unique opportunities to get rid of insoluble problems which may prove politically risky. In the context of NGOs as a channel for development aid, these insoluble problems may be poverty alleviation or assistance in areas of political conflict, for example. In this perspective NGOs serve as a risk-reduction channel for the state and the for-profit sector, and not as efficient, flexible and grassroots-oriented providers of services. The cynical version of this theory would be that NGOs are swarming the world, creating the impression that something is being done about poverty, injustice, the environment, etc., while most basic relations continue exactly as before. A 'leftist' version of the same theory (argued, for example, by Marxist-oriented political groups in Bangladesh) is that the NGOs are 'opportunistic' organizations with narrow political roles and aims, which are diverting and fragmenting the struggle of the poor classes. An analysis of Brazilian NGOs describes them as follows: 'NGOs established by a worried bourgeoisie which hopes to disarm what it considers a "social bomb" threatening to explode and destroy Brazil's capitalist system; and another group of NGOs which began to emerge recently and which is tied to right-wing Protestant sects and movements inside and outside Brazil' (Wils, 1991:9).

Based on his research into mismanagement in the third sector in Western states, Seibel has emphasized a paradoxical phenomenon: that organizations survive 'despite organizational failure'. He argues that non-profit organizations can survive, even in the long run, 'despite a substantial lack of organizational learning and responsiveness' and they 'survive not *despite* but *because of* their notorious lack of efficiency and responsiveness' (Seibel 1990:107). The particular function of NGOs is 'to cope with the political risks of organizational efficiency and responsiveness in a democratic society' (ibid.:108). They are not inevitably inefficient and irresponsive, but they exhibit a broader range of inefficiency than for-profit organizations and public bureaucracies. They are able to exist and thrive because they represent a de-modernized area in a modern, means-rational, organizational culture, in other words, they represent an alternative because they are less efficient. Seibel argues that non-profit organizations exist because there are functional necessities *other* than organizational responsiveness and efficiency. If this had not been the case, their long-term organizational behaviour would, because of requirements of efficiency and responsiveness, have become similar to that of for-profit organizations and public bureaucracies. This means that only to the extent that organizations manage to maintain their comparative disadvantage, can they hope to exist as something distinguishable from state or market actors. In the context of development aid the argument will be: NGOs will become more and more like public donor agencies or types of consultancy firms in the long run, if they do not strengthen their compara-tive disadvantages, i.e. their value commitment, for example, a commitment that may make them less efficient and less competitive in a comparative perspective.

Governments cannot be always responsive to people's demands and needs, because this may inhibit the continued existence of democratic government and public administration. No responsible government, whether in Norway or in Bangladesh or Ethiopia can, for example, accept all the people's demands. On the other hand, this lack of responsiveness cannot go too far. They cannot reject all demands by showing them to be against the universal or overall interest of the country. That would endanger the legitimacy of the political system. In this perspective, organizations can be seen as a solution to a real dilemma: NGOs compensate for market failure in helping the victims of structural adjustment programmes, but, unlike governments, they also provide a structural irresponsiveness and inefficiency. Organizations can function as a *cordon sanitaire*, Seibel argues: they are both a disguise (of the real problem) and a buffer (between people and government), but they cannot solve the initial problem. They help to segregate a social problem from the government's responsibility and install what has been called a 'a tyranny of structurelessness' (ibid.:115). An illusion is created: a lot of activity is going on even if hardly anything of importance happens for the population at large. In this way, NGOs may in a broader perspective be seen, not as representatives of the civil society against the state, but as a means by which the *status quo* is maintained. Within the same perspective, but in a broader context, it is possible to regard them as being primarily producers of ideology and images of the world, and it is as such actors that we all need them.

Salamon has also stood the comparative advantage theory on its head. He talks about the 'voluntary failure' theory instead. Rather than viewing the voluntary sector as a 'residual line of defense for the provision of collective goods that governments will not supply', this theory views the non-profit sector as 'the first line of defense'. (Salamon, 1990:230). It is argued that the voluntary organizations have certain inherent limitations in responding to social needs. One of these is called 'philanthropic insufficiency' (i.e. that resources are often not available where the needs are greatest), 'philanthropic particularism', (or as Salamon puts it: 'the fact that private charities tend to focus on particular problems or groups of individuals, creating gaps in coverage and the potential for considerable duplication'), 'philanthropic paternalism' (i.e. can at best establish aid as a privilege, but not as a right) and finally 'philanthropic amateurism', (i.e. that voluntary aid is frequently too uneven and volatile to establish the professional forms of care that are often needed) (ibid.).

General theories about development NGOs' comparative disadvantages can also be easily falsified on the same conceptual and methodological grounds as the opposite theory. There are a great many organizations, Islamic organizations, trade unions, etc. that have played important roles in both social and political processes, financed at least partly via donors' NGO budgets. NGOs in the aid channel take on other roles and have developed other relations with the public and the beneficiaries since governments, UN organizations and donors have contracted out projects to them. Aid is a form of philanthropic paternalism, whether implemented by governments, the UN or NGOs. Amateurism is not necessarily more widespread in big NGOs like OXFAM, Redd Barna, CARE and Norwegian Church Aid, than in UN organizations or in SIDA, CIDA, ODA or NORAD. The question of philanthropic insufficiency is as relevant to public as it is to private aid. The differences between governments and NGOs in aid are thus different from those in Western welfare societies, since the problem of, for example, setting priorities based on a democratic political process would be very much the same for a donor government, a UN operation or an NGO.

Instead of maintaining an analytical approach which analyses NGO potentials in terms of economic functionalist language, the focus should be on different types of state–NGO relations and different types of aid contexts so as to get a clearer understanding of the way this channel functions.

The question of flexibility and creativity

As discussed above, it is not particularly fruitful to compare NGOs with governments, or the 'NGO-group' with the 'government group' at a general level. Governments are as heterogeneous in structure, aims and powers as are NGOs. It is impossible to establish conditions which methodologically make such comparisons worth while. The focus here is rather on the situations in which NGOs might be especially flexible and efficient. To what extent will the NGOs legal standing as non-governmental organizations affect their *potential* flexibility in situations where governments face particular legal or political constraints? And to what extent will NGOs value orientations affect their flexibility in reaching development objectives? NGO literature ascribes many good attributes and deeds to NGOs, but shows little self-reflection when it comes to the comparison and interconnections between these deeds. Voluntarism, effectiveness, responsiveness and democratic structures may not always coincide with flexibility, and the concept of flexibility itself is ambiguous. Here we discuss types of flexibility and how NGO roles may be studied in relation to three main issues regarding this question: flexibility and value-oriented organizations, flexibility and micro-developments and flexibility in political conflict situations.

Types of organization and the question of flexibility

In general it is impossible to say anything definite about NGOs as a group with regard to flexibility. Such general statements ignore completely the challenges put by the Swiss social scientist, Robert Michels, for example. In 1915 Michel published *Political Parties* in which he argued that he 'who says organizations says oligarchy', and that all organizations would become dominated by a self-perpetuating and self-serving leadership. In the sociological tradition this has become known as the 'the iron law of oligarchy'. This law may be questioned, but everybody who knows even a little about the history of development NGOs can come up with examples to demonstrate that the flexible organization of yesterday may well become the rigid organization of today, depending on leadership, individual actors, financial situation, etc., etc. Flexibility of an organization will develop over time.

Flexibility may also vary with size. In Norway the organizational landscape shows great varieties. There are five large NGOs (according to aid budgets in 1992). In 1993 four of them received more than NOK 100m from the state, Norwegian Church Aid: NOK 299m; Save the Children Fund: NOK 277m; Norwegian Red Cross: NOK 193m; and Norwegian People's Aid: NOK 161m, and the five largest received 56.4 per cent of the total as compared with less than 50 per cent during the

1980s (47.5 per cent in 1981, 50 per cent in 1986 and 48.8 per cent in 1991). Twenty organizations received less than NOK 0.1m in 1991 and 19 between NOK 0.1 and 0.5m, while the 22 biggest received 90 per cent of the funds the same year (for more details, see Tvedt, 1995e). Moreover, some organizations are working only in developing countries, some organizations that continue to work primarily on issues in Norway have established development departments, while about 40 organizations are involved in aid without having any salaried staff at all. Some work in more than 30 countries, while the majority have a small project in only one country. To talk about NGOs and flexibility in general against such a background is not very meaningful, especially since funds and number of employees are not only a mechanical reflection of size, but also mirror activity profile, and relations with the state, the Ministry of Foreign Affairs, government in the developing country, membership and beneficiaries.

A similar heterogeneity is found in developing countries. In Bangladesh the largest NGO is BRAC, which in 1993 had 12,000 on the payroll, about 1.1 million members and a yearly budget of about US$30m, while the number of organizations in the country was estimated at about 16,000, the great majority of them receiving no public funds at all. In Zimbabwe in 1990 there were more than 800 registered organizations, but only 20 had a financial turnover of more than Z$ 1m. 50 NGOs employed more than 20 staff. ORAP claimed to have more than 10,000 member organizations (de Graaf et al., 1991; Moyo, 1994). Only a few of these NGOs were connected to the aid channel, however. The Orthodox Church registered as an Ethiopian NGO after establishing a Church Development and Inter-Church Aid Department in 1972 to 'perform the church's historical duties, social welfare activities and act as a catalyst to development', the main priority being to involve the Church in the economic, social and cultural development of society. According to its own statistics, it has over 30 million members, over 25,000 parish churches and 400,000 clergy. Coptic Christianity has been the state religion since around 350 AD. The Church has been, and is, a hierarchical organization which can be compared to a pyramid with an increasing number of people at the lower levels. At the other extreme there are very weak, one-man (or one-woman) organizations among the 150 or so other Ethiopian NGOs registered by the government in 1992.

The degree of flexibility and need for flexibility may vary with size, organizational set-up and degree of bureaucratic professionalism, etc. The more successful (or the more 'scaling-up', as the present jargon puts it) an NGO is, the less flexible it is likely to become. On the other hand, large NGOs, like BRAC and Norwegian Church Aid, may be more flexible than smaller organizations when it comes to ability to change and experiment, both of which presuppose more financial resources and a stronger backbone to cope with failures. Thus one could argue that the combination of financial strength with a non-governmental status could constitute an environment conducive to flexibility in this sense of the word. In this context 'scaling up' is not a threat to innovation, but its prerequisite.

Flexibility may vary with activity profile. Many of the big organizations are multi-sectoral, and over the years they have shown great willingness to shift from one sector to another and from one activity – and also one slogan – to another. Many of the big organizations therefore have a project portfolio that is very multi-faceted and partly reflects the fads and fashions of the past. Most observers have noted the rapidity and flexibility with which organizations adjust their public image. Redd Barna, Norway, for example, has renamed previous projects in Ethiopia from 'Rural Development Projects' to 'Child Centred Rural Development Projects' in line with what other organizations have done in other countries in order to adjust to shifting priorities in the organization and shifting focus in the donor community. This shift may be genuine, but it always takes much longer to change projects on the ground. Organizations have tended to take on the most popular slogans of the day. Whether this is flexibility or reflects a split personality (organizations are not only jacks of all trades, but act as if they were both Dr Jekyll and Mr Hyde as well) is open to question and research. The degree of flexibility in one area is affected by the organization's activities in other fields. A weak NGO, dependent on a good image and happy beneficiaries, may try to exert as much control and dominance over the beneficiaries as a state institution in the quest for organizational survival.

Other organizations are working only within one narrow area and with special target groups. This is the rule rather than the exception among almost all the Norwegian organizations which have only a small input in development aid. Many of these are interest organizations for special groups or professions in Norway: the Norwegian Association of the Disabled; the Norwegian Association of the Blind and Partially Sighted; the Norwegian Union of Teachers; the Norwegian Nurses Association; the Support-committee for Children in Need of Aid in Chile, etc. Some international examples are: World Wildlife Fund; the International Consumers' Organization; the World Council of Indigenous People; the International Tropical Timber Organization; the International Confederation of Sea Fisherworkers, etc. These organizations naturally tend to be rigid in taking up responsibilities outside their special domain or mission. On the other hand, the same organizations may show impressive creativity and flexibility in achieving their more easily defined aims. Rigidity of aim may relate positively with flexibility in implementation, and vice versa.

Flexibility may vary with organizational structure. NGOs that are one-man institutions (as is the case with many of the new NGOs in the developing countries) or led by charismatic leaders (like BRAC or the Green Belt Movement in Kenya) will tend to be more responsive to external changes than membership organizations with democratically elected boards, etc. In some cases flexibility and membership democratic organizations are opposites, while in other cases they may coincide. The apparent rigidity or reluctance of Redd Barna as compared with Norwegian People's Aid in taking up new assignments proposed by the Norwegian Government and other donors outside their traditional work profile partly reflects the fact that the former is an organization with a board and a number of local groups, while Norwegian People's Aid is to a larger extent led by professionals.

Flexibility may vary with value orientations and traditions. Brown and Korten argue that what characterizes NGOs is the fact that they are organizations with shared values. Let us assume that this is generally the case. Some NGOs are organizations with values that they may share with public donors. This has been the case in Norway and in many other donor countries where representatives of the organizations and the state have jointly formulated NGO policy and decided what projects should be approved. Other organizations share values that to them are much more important than the official aid agenda or the particular aid projects. Mission organizations and organizations primarily working in aid in order to spread some kind of message, be it religious, political or ideological, are organized around values that will generally regard aid as a means to an end. These organizations may be extremely inflexible regarding these overarching questions, but very flexible in ways of achieving their main ideological or religious goal. In such connections, the voluntarism or the energy fostered by strong convictions – conventionally described as sources of NGO innovation and NGO flexibility – might be their Achilles heel when it comes to flexibility in adjusting aims, working methods, etc. in aid projects. To show how this conflict between two positive values attributed to the NGOs has affected project performance and strategic orientations in a particular historical context, a case study of a project of a mission organization involved in aid is presented below.

A case study: the Norwegian Lutheran Mission – mission and aid

The example is the Norwegian Lutheran Mission (NLM) and its work in southern Ethiopia. Other organizations, both mission and secular, could have been chosen. But few secular organizations with similar traditions and strengths can be found.[4]

The NLM is a mission organization which is also a development NGO. Its development projects have been financed from the Norwegian aid budget since 1963. Mission organizations often constitute an important part of the NGO landscape in both donor and developing countries. It is therefore important to study them, and also because NGO literature deals mostly with secular organizations, such as OXFAM, CARE, Save the Children, Médicíns sans Frontières, etc., and with some religious organizations, such as Norwegian Church Aid, Christian Aid, NOVIB in the Netherlands, but only rarely with mission organizations. This narrow perspective reduces the heterogeneity of the field, and makes it less easy to analyse the impact of NGOs in a longer historical perspective.

THE NLM IN ETHIOPIA

The NLM was established in 1891 and was working in China up to 1948. It was invited to Ethiopia by a Swedish mission organization. Following a decision at the NLM General Assembly in 1946, a delegation visited Ethiopia and were given an audience by the Emperor, Haile Selassie. He asked them to start work in the then provinces of Sidamo and Gemu Gofa, which have been their area of concentration ever since. Ethiopia is the most important mission field for the NLM.[5] In 1993 a total of 110 missionaries were attached to 24 mission stations serving 1,356 organized parishes, 1,800 women's and youth groups, 16 primary schools, 624 literacy schools, 2 schools for health assistance, 1 school for homecrafts, 1 theological seminary, 1 orphanage, several Bible schools, 1 youth polytechnic and 3 hospitals.[6] The permanent secretariat in Ethiopia was manned by a staff of five: mission secretary, project consultant, economic secretary, secretary and accountant.

The total budget of NLM projects in Ethiopia in 1993 amounted to NOK 10.2m, of which 80 per cent or NOK 8.2m came from NORAD. This included invest-ments and running costs for three health projects in cooperation with the Ministry of Health and nine health and emergency preparedness projects together with the Ethiopian Evangelical Church, Mekane Yesus (EECMY).[7] Project administration at the NLM secretariat in Ethiopia was covered by NOK 365.000 as part of total NOK

10.2m project costs and under the 80 to 20 per cent NORAD and NLM arrangement. In addition, NORAD paid five per cent (NOK 513,200) of headquarters administration costs.[8]

MISSION, LOCAL CHURCH AND CHARITABLE WORK

How has the NLM's relationship with its local partners and nationalization developed? The NLM's policy regarding evangelization and development work, and its relation to what in modern secular development language is called a 'local organization' or 'partner', have a long and well-documented history. The present analysis focuses on what has been a major problem in the history of the NLM (and other missions, but the problem takes on different aspects from organization to organization and depending on which country they work in): the problem of nationalization. While this is a term used in aid and belongs to the development aid era, in missionary terms it is closely related to the question of the relationship between the local church and the mission organizations. An early study from the middle of the last century, Peter Beverhauss: *Die Selbständigkeit der jungen Kirchen als missionarisches Problem* gets to the crux of the matter. The question involves fundamental aspects of both mission strategy and development strategy and can bring to the fore constraints of flexibility in organizations with strongly shared values.

Scandinavian missions have played a leading role in spreading Lutheran Christianity to Ethiopia. In 1866 the first Swedish missionaries arrived in Massawa. A mission was established in Eritrea and started work in Jimma. In 1904 Karl Cerderquist arrived in Addis Ababa as the first Swedish missionary. The Swedish mission, Bible True Friends, started work officially in Ethiopia in 1921, although a missionary family had already worked in Adwa for some years before that date. The first missionaries of the NLM came to the country in 1948. In their assigned area they were allowed to work among 'unreached people' but, according to the regulations, only to undertake development work and not to evangelize. The Emperor's decree of 1944 on establishment of missions ruled that mission activities in so-called 'closed areas', i.e. areas where the Ethiopian Orthodox Church was dominant, had to be confined to medical and non-denominational educational work. The missions were therefore obliged from the very beginning to concentrate on what were then called 'charitable activities', such as running schools and hospitals. The more modern holistic approach was not yet internalized in strategic terms.

The NLM was not primarily interested in development projects as such. Its main concerns were, of course, church-related. Should a church be established or not, and if it should, how should it function and what should the NLM's role be? The NLM supported the establishment of independent Lutheran congregations instead of working through the Ethiopian Orthodox Church (EOC).[9] It followed a proclamatory mission policy. Just a few days after the close of the first NLM missionary conference in 1950, the EOC bishop at Yirga Alem warned the faithful against the NLM. In his judgement its missionaries were 'lions and poisonous snakes' who planned to harvest the fruits of EOC efforts.[11] He later complained to the Emperor that the NLM perverted the people and that he therefore could not return to Sidamo as long as the mission remained in the province.[11]

These external pressures changed the mission's policies in regard to what in today's aid language would be called 'competence building' or 'local participation'. In the 1950s it was still rare to give leading positions in mission work to 'local boys'; the colonial impact on Western missions was clearly felt. In Sidamo the NLM gradually had to give leadership positions to young Ethiopian converts. Because of EOC pressure the missionaries were forced to concentrate on leadership training, rather than on direct evangelism (or, as it would now be called, 'direct implementation of projects to target groups').[12] This pressure also convinced those NLM missionaries who did not favour co-operation with other Protestant groups that there was a need for evangelical believers in Ethiopia to build an organization through which they could approach the government. This development was important for the establishment of the new church.

The NLM's policy reflected religious disagreement and different organizational agendas. The NLM emphasised the role of the laity and had (as it still has) a very critical attitude towards clericalism. NLM policy in the home country concerning co-operation with the Church of Norway was another factor: since it did not favour such co-operation and the ecumenical idea in Norway, why should it co-operate with other Lutheran missions in Ethiopia? It was critical of the establishment of the World Council of Churches (WCC) in 1948, on the grounds that its basis of belief did not 'clearly express that Scripture alone should be the organizational basis', especially expressed in 'the work of the so-called dialogue programme' (NLM, 1991:18). Then as today, the NLM dissociated itself from the WCC, regretting that Norway was a member and advising its co-operating churches to remain outside the organization. It was, and is, also highly critical of the Lutheran World Federation (where, for example, Norwegian Church Aid is a prominent member), because it has not 'portrayed a genuine Lutheran understanding of the Biblical message', especially on the vital question of the relationship to non-Christian religions. It therefore also advised the co-operating churches not to belong to the LWF (ibid.:19). The NLM could not choose 'partners' or co-operating institutions without regard to their interpretation of the Bible. After having worked more than 60 years in China, the NLM was now for the first time being asked to accept co-operation with another Lutheran mission on more than a purely theoretical issue.

This reluctance was noted by contemporary missionaries. Missionaries from other countries could write: 'Traditionally, Norwegians and Swedes distrust each other and historically, because of the last World War, Norwegians and Germans find it difficult to forget the old bitterness' (Bakke, 1987:162). Others said: 'I see this on (sic) the background and my knowledge of my own people who are, I believe, the hardest group to work with when it comes to all kinds of cooperation. The theological and psychological temperament of the Norwegians sometimes necessitates making haste slowly.'[14] The NLM Home Board discussed the issue, but were not willing to support co-operation. The General Secretary was sent to a missionary conference in Ethiopia and came to the conclusion: 'I believe we may work better and more peacefully by not joining. We shall try to be faithful towards our own convictions (sic) and at the same time respect the opinion of others'.[15] The vote taken at the conference still showed a small majority against such co-operation, but in 1960 it was overruled by the NLM Home Board.

Due to its long traditions and its interpretation of the Bible, the NLM could not be flexible in its attitude to building up the church, or a 'local partner', according to

NGO-speak. It disagreed internally and regarded it as unnatural to co-operate with people who did not agree with its views on what were regarded as fundamental religious matters. Gradually it accommodated to new realities, and started to involve itself actively in building up the new church. It also took on more development work, both as a way of preaching the Gospel and also as a means of securing working permits in order to do evangelical work. A classical discussion in the history of missions started very soon: should the new, weak EECMY church, established in 1959, be burdened with development tasks?[16]

The NLM held that it was important not to give it responsibility for institutions and programmes which were not really necessary. The foreign missions were under an obligation to run educational and medical institutions. However, this was not the case for a national church, and the EECMY could follow a policy of 'selective integration'. The NLM, on the other hand, had to take on development projects – whether it wanted to or not, and whether it felt it had the capacity or competence – in order to be allowed to stay and implement its real mission.

And could the NLM continue its mission in Ethiopia after a national church was established? This was a political question *vis-à-vis* the Ethiopian Government and the EECMY, but primarily an economic question at home. To continue its work, the NLM was dependent on funds from Norway, obtained through appeals. In order to be able to persuade the mission people, it argued that it was crucial to have missionaries in the field. The NLM and its leaders therefore fought with the EECMY over the right of the mission organization to remain in Ethiopia. The strategic question was how to maintain a mission organization in the field when responsibility had been transferred to the national church? The mission was to be a partner of the EECMY, not integrated with it. As a partner, it could work in and through the EECMY, and at the same time appeal as before to its supporting groups (Sæverås, 1974:155). It was also important to maintain its position in relation to other mission organizations that had competing religious messages. The conflict with the Norwegian Missionary Society (NMS) in 1968 illustrates this. The NLM was against the NMS's plans to become involved in Ethiopia, partly because, according to the NMS, it interpreted this as an attempt to capture the many mission friends in Norway who supported work in the country (Kjosavik, 1992:130–1). The NLM's working areas were also restricted for religious reasons; it had to refuse to work in some other areas in the West Synod, for example, because liturgical and church arrangements in the EECMY had been influenced by Swedish and American church traditions (ibid.:131).

Finally, in which direction should the new church develop? The NLM advocated that the EECMY should not become a church with priests, and if it had priests, women priests should not be ordained. To the NLM it was, of course, important that the EECMY should not join the LWF and such networking institutions. Norwegian Church Aid on the other hand, also supported financially by NORAD, has strongly urged the EECMY to take an active part in the LWF and has also, at least unofficially, supported the ordination of women priests. Religious divisions in Norway are thus exported to the EECMY, paid for by the Norwegian state. An Ethiopian minority Lutheran Church has been built up to a large extent with money from the Norwegian state and under official guidelines that have strongly underlined that projects shall not be motivated or serve partial economic, political or religious interests. For the NLM to hand over its projects to its local partner involves questions not only of project sustainability, but of fundamental religious importance.

The NLM, NORAD and Sidamo Hospital

In 1963 the NLM signed the first agreement with Norsk Utviklingshjelp (later NORAD), regarding support for the Sidamo Regional Hospital in Yirga Alem in southern Ethiopia. The NLM has had several other projects in the south of Ethiopia, but the following review will limit itself to a short account of those aspects of the hospital project which have relevance for the flexibility – value orientation issue. This hospital is famous in Ethiopia, and is considered to be one of the best, if not the best, in the whole country. The cost, in comparison with similar hospitals elsewhere, is very low. The expatriates working there are missionaries on salaries far below those of other expatriates in Ethiopia, so, compared with other NGOs, the NLM is mobilizing voluntarism and idealism. Everyone who visits the place seems to be impressed by what the NLM and the Ethiopian staff manage to do with relatively modest budgets; it shines, like Albert Schweitzer's hospital, in the jungle.[17] The following is not an assessment of the project as a development project in a narrow, conventional sense. It is an analysis of how the relation between mission and development aid has been handled in the development aid era,[18] and how different and competing agendas affect organizational flexibility in achieving localization or nationalization goals in development aid.

Under the contract the NLM committed itself to undertake the project on a general humanitarian basis, without being motivated by economic, political or religious party interests.[19] The Norwegian state made it very clear that, in return for its support, the NLM should not carry out religious activities. From the outset the exact interpretation of this paragraph was a matter of confusion. In the same contract it was stated: 'The economic responsibility for the management of the hospital will be specified in a contract between the Ethiopian state and Norsk Luthersk Misjonssamband, and is not the concern of Norsk Utviklingshjelp.' In other words, the Norwegian state made it very clear in 1963 that it was not prepared to support the running costs of the hospital. By 1994, more than 30 years later, tens of millions of Norwegian kroner had been transferred to the project, and the Norwegian state is still financing expatriate salaries, anti-TB programmes, etc. and the hospital is still run by the mission, but in co-operation with the Ethiopian Ministry of Health.

NATIONALIZATION OF THE HOSPITAL

What has happened in the meantime and why is the hospital not yet nationalized, or why is the EECMY not responsible for the project? There are, of course, a number of reasons for this situation. In general the hospital has been functioning very well. The mission, and many Ethiopians, have feared that, if the NLM were to withdraw, the level of services would deteriorate. Because of war and general poverty, the state has been unable to take it over and maintain established standards. The government has therefore been sceptical about a handover. Many in the EECMY have felt that the church's commitments are heavy enough, without taking on the burden of running the hospital. Recurrent administrative shake-ups at the regional level (the overthrow of the Emperor, the war situation, the overthrow of Mengistu, the ethnification of regional and local politics after 1991, etc.), have made it difficult to find state institutions capable of taking, or willing to take it over.

Here a different aspect will be focused on: how the mission agenda itself has affected NLM development policies and choices. Other mission organizations face similar problems in many countries. Fundamentally these reflect conflicts over goals: the mission's mission agenda and its externally defined development agenda, or, as it is called in the internal language of mission organizations, projects run with 'alien money'. The point here is not to discuss whether mission organizations are 'bad' or 'good' NGOs, nor whether donor countries ought to support organizations that use development funds as a shield to protect the execution of missionary activities. The task is to show how organizational values may breed inflexibility in relation to development aims. One analytical starting point can be a comparison of the language of the NLM's *Statement on Mission* of 1991 and its *Strategy Document on NLM's Project Work Abroad* of 1988.

NLM GOALS: MISSION AND DEVELOPMENT

It may be useful first to refer to some central mission goals of the NLM, as approved by the General Assembly in 1991, in order to highlight the importance of its main agenda:

> Sending mission: Mission is no more a human invention than the Gospel itself. It has its starting point and mandate in Jesus' own words to us. The great commission, as it is given to us at the end of all four Gospels and in the beginning of Acts, is a call to all believers to proclaim the Gospel so that new people can become disciples of Jesus. The preaching of the word of God and the witnessing for Jesus are the main concern of the mission, because it is only the good news about him which can give salvation to sinners.
>
> NLM therefore wants to be an instrument for fulfilling the great commission in the world of today. We wish to be available to persons who are called by God and suited for missionary service, to train them and send them with the word of God to those parts of the world where it is little known. We want to be a sending mission, because our most important resource in mission are people who have a living testimony about Christ.
>
> We want to serve the whole person: In John 20:21 Jesus gives his commission in a wider sense than elsewhere. 'As the Father has sent me, I am sending you'. Jesus' ministry included both preaching and caring for the welfare of the people. He both taught and helped the sick and needy.
>
> The disciples should serve in the same way. In the word of God there is no contradiction between serving with the Gospel and doing the deeds of Christ's hands among people in social distress. It is therefore an important goal for us as a mission to meet different types of human need with adequate help. Jesus asked us to do so. (NLM, *Statement on Mission*, 1991.)

The main aim of their project work is also spreading God's word. Diaconia is not primarily based on mission tactical arguments, it is said, because for a Christian it is 'impossible to live in a society where the suffering is great, without trying to help as long as resources are available' (*Strategy Document*, 1988). The most striking thing about this document, as compared with the *Statement on Mission,* is its language. While the *Statement* uses an expressive language, highlighting the convictions and seriousness of NLM commitments, the aid document is written in imprecise NGO-speak. Its project criteria are:

- projects that support the poorest, the weakest and the most oppressed
- local needs and conditions
- priorities set by the local population
- need to be adapted to public plans
- the resources of the organization and its partners
- projects with an educational profile

On partnership in development aid, the *Strategy Document* states that:

> The main co-operation partners of the mission are local churches and synods. Where such do not exist, the mission wants to work for the establishment of church societies built on local congregations. In those cases where there is a church co-partner, the other types of co-operations are organized through the church organization and not directly with NLM.

It thus refers to the local partners as if their religious convictions are unimportant, with no trace of its opposition to the ecumenical movement and church networks like the LWF and WCC. The impression is that the NLM is a development aid organization, religious yes, but that this is not the main point. The document does not reflect problems related to encounters with local cultures, dialogue, etc. The emphasis is straightforward: preaching its version of Christianity is the best way to create development. This way of handling concepts creates a notion of uniformity (on the surface, i.e. in the documents circulating within the aid channel), whereas the realities on the ground are ambiguous and contradictory. As a mission organization bred within the Norwegian lay movement the NLM has several objections to any co-operation with churches of a high-church type or with powerful hierarchies. Its interest and agenda are rather to maintain and continue its mission within a lay structure, and neither to co-operate with strong formal church structures nor to nationalize, if its fundamental convictions about the message of Christ are not secured. Thus co-operation with a local partner, organizational support or institution building becomes difficult and leads to ambiguous strategies that conflict with the fundamental goal of the mission. When such concepts are used so readily by the organization in its official development document (as demanded by NORAD), this should be interpreted, against the background of its mission strategy, as a rhetorical device.

NLM, VALUE DILEMMAS AND NATIONALIZATION

How have contradictions between mission strategy and development policies, between NORAD's emphasis on religious neutrality and nationalization and the NLM's aim of evangelization and a continued missionary presence, been solved concretely in relation to this project? These dilemmas were already brought into the open in 1972, when the EECMY, the NLM's co-operating partner and 'offspring', became famous within the world missionary movement by issuing a religious statement attacking the separation between development and evangelization in Western churches. The EECMY urged the NLM and other missionary and religious organizations to implement a holistic approach; i.e. not to separate the two and prioritize evangelization. For the NLM, which is not registered with the Ethiopian authorities and is allowed to work there only as employees of this same EECMY, this has created permanent and deep conflicts of orientation. Even more so, since it had signed contracts with NORAD that formally and legally demanded that such a separation should be maintained in NORAD-supported projects.

What was the background to the EECMY's appeal? The EECMY soon took over some of the projects the NLM had started and also projects initiated by other donors. All the health work of the NLM, except the running of two hospitals, became the responsibility of the South Ethiopian Synod of the EECMY in 1971. The administration of these institutions and programmes made it necessary for the EECMY to establish development departments at both church and synod level.[20] The church discovered that money for development work was not a big problem; support was coming from abroad. This sharpened the conflict between evangelization and development work: it was easy to obtain funds for development schemes, but not so simple to get help for other church activities – an imbalance which had been pointed out earlier by the Norwegian missionaries. It was said that the medical and educational work had become a means to an end, 'baits by which the unsuspecting and the suspecting are caught'.[21] An employee at the Sidamo Hospital wrote a memorandum to the LWF complaining about the tendency to 'count charity work as a footstep for the real mission work which is preaching the gospel to the baptized'[22] and suggesting that 'an inquiry be done inside the Lutheran missions in order to make out the relative share in their missionary programs occupied by medicine and welfare, education and evangelism'.[23] The huge input of development aid resulted in a new demand for technical personnel in all fields. Such people were not easy to find, and it became necessary to offer them higher salaries. Living conditions and benefits above the norm were the inevitable results. An imbalance between evangelism and development became increasingly visible. The problem was raised at the Seventh General Assembly of the EECMY in 1971, where it was agreed to approach the donor agencies through the LWF to ask them to reconsider their criteria for aid and include direct support of congregational work, leadership training and church buildings. This initial request was followed up by the now famous EECMY letter, On the Interrelation between Proclamation of the Gospel and Human Development. This accused the missions and the Western churches of distorting the churches' aim to serve the whole person. It emphasized that evangelism and development were not two separate activities but one. Development activities without the evangelistic aspect meant accepting that man can be treated in parts. On the other hand, evangelism is development work, because the preaching leads to improved living conditions. True development takes place only when a person is renewed in 'his inner man'.

How did the NLM operate in this context? How could it balance, not only between the two principles, but between the two partners, EECMY and NORAD, both requiring that it should work in line with their expectations? As already noted, NLM missionaries had already, even before the contract with NORAD was signed, questioned the tendency to separate evangelization from development work. The initiative of the Home Board to co-operate with NORAD, based on overall assessments of strategy, funds and expansion, threatened to widen the conflict. The EECMY letter was written against a background where amounts for evangelism did not increase, while there seemed to be no problem with grants for development schemes. Many argued that the best way to develop an area was to channel funds through the church. The development aid available made it possible for synod leaders to direct funds to their own area and their own people; a number of new jobs were created. The growth of the church was partly a result of growth in development budgets, job opportunities, the power to allocate resources locally, etc. Many interpreted the fact that the EECMY and missionaries from the NLM were allowed to operate under the Mengistu regime, partly as the result of their being involved heavily in development activities.[24]

In 1971 EECMY leaders did question why the NLM preferred to keep the contracts concerning the running of the government hospital in the south in its name. The NLM argued that the contracts had been made between the government and the mission and could not easily be transferred to an Ethiopian church. It also argued that these institutions would be far too heavy a burden for the EECMY, requiring as they did highly qualified personnel and large financial contributions, which the EECMY did not have. In the opinion of the NLM these institutions would serve the people and the church best if they remained as projects under direct mission control and influence. The NLM also pointed to its special relationship with NORAD, which had invested heavily in these institutions and was, it said, 'in the process of accepting responsibility for an increased number of positions' (Bakke, 1987:224–5, footnote 7). As a mission history summarizes: it was not 'difficult to raise funds for that kind of work'. Information about such institutions convinced possible donors that the mission 'was not only preaching'. The different development activities were regarded by the missions as useful also for their position in relation to the Ethiopian Government. Schools, hospitals and clinics were no doubt popular services [25] (Bakke, 1987:123). The hospital has therefore been important from many aspects: it has served tens of thousands of Ethiopians for a comparatively modest sum of money; it has been a central element in the NLM mission strategy in Ethiopia and most probably has been an important factor behind the build-up of a large, quite efficient and development-oriented Lutheran minority church in Ethiopia.

Put under continued pressure from NORAD in the late 1980s – the Office for Private Organizations incessantly rammed home the need for nationalization, without showing much knowledge or interest in the particular histories and role dilemmas of mission organizations and their local partners – the NLM was forced to put forward a ten-year nationalization plan for the Sidamo Hospital (and for the Arba Minch Hospital) in 1988. Since then a number of evaluations, reports, discussions, internal seminars and open conferences have taken place internationally and with NORAD where this issue has been at the top of the agenda.

Some of the discussions with NORAD were based on the premise that all the NGO actors favoured nationalization (also that other NGOs would find it hard to make themselves redundant). Reluctance was generally explained sociologically or psychologically (a general fear of change, a fear of losing the mission identity, etc.) or historically (it takes time to adjust to new challenges, etc.). These arguments are all relevant, but any analysis of the problem that fails to focus on how the organization interprets missionary work or the diaconal project, elements that are crucial to its existence and self-understanding, and how these relate to existing NORAD guidelines and policies, will blur the issues.

The NLM could not implement the EECMY doctrine because of its link with NORAD, although it shared their values in this respect. The NLM has received money to undertake development work, separated from evangelization, but at the same time they have been employed as missionaries in a church that preaches a holistic approach. The NLM could not give the hospital to the church, because that would have threatened its own presence and undermined its own agenda (An EECMY distancing itself from parts of the NLM teachings implies that the NLM has not finished its job. In addition, there are still a number of 'unreached' people in the country.) Although both the EECMY and NORAD wanted nationalization, the NLM did not, but on grounds that could not easily be discussed. (This does not mean that there were not a number of other reasons for not nationalizing the hospital in this context, reasons partly neglected in both the EECMY's and NORAD's arguments. See above.) The NLM could not continue as before, because of opposition from the EECMY and other donors' influence on the EECMY, but primarily because NORAD threatened to end its support if nationalization did not take place or was not seriously considered. The NLM leadership was not interested in an end to this support, which was regarded as an important financial asset.[26] In addition, a survey undertaken by the NLM in 1972–73 supported the 'developmentalists' within the organization; the literacy schools were said to have a markedly positive influence on church attendance and church collections. Later, while other missions (like the American Sudan Mission) were expelled from Ethiopia, the NLM was able to continue more or less as before, even maintaining its beautiful camp at Awasa, aid as a political guarantee was underlined.[27] Undoubtedly, development programmes have been furthering the authority of both the EECMY and the mission, and have enabled pastors and evangelists to operate. The imbalance in funds between development and evangelization work has increased, notably in the late 1980s and beginning of the 1990s, as NCA and other European NGOs have increased their support to the church. In this situation the NLM becomes even more important as a bridge between those who put most emphasis on evangelization and the European church-related organizations that are regarded by the EECMY almost as secular organizations. In the mid-1980s NCA was criticized by the EECMY for being too secular in its orientation and work.) Seen from the EECMY's point of view, the NLM was an organization on 'the right side', but at the same time, and from NORAD's point of view, it should act according to the neutrality regulations of the Norwegian state, including the issue of religion.

To sum up: the NLM is a value-oriented organization, like other mission organizations and many other (although not all) development NGOs. This value-orientation may be conducive to flexibility and efficiency in some areas, but it may also hinder efficiency and flexibility in certain areas. The NLM's project history defies broad statements about voluntary failure, that NGOs are notoriously inefficient, that they always express voluntary amateurism, etc. Instead of making mechanical generalized statements about the relationships between value orientation and flexibility or voluntarism and the ability to adapt to local sentiments, it is important to develop a conceptual framework and an analytical approach that can fruitfully analyse these relationships. We have focused here on the conflicting zones of value orientations, because the Norwegian state also promotes values in its use of NGOs. In this relationship, questions of values and flexibility are expressed, and factors of autonomy and independence intervene. Nationalization processes and changes in organizational value orientations can be, and have been, set in motion because of internal conditions in the organization (changes of opinion, lack of educated missionaries) and relations with the national church (changing ideas and capacities). But this can also happen because of external pressure. Perhaps one of the most important impacts of NORAD's support for Norwegian NGOs is precisely that the character of the resource transfer and the political demands linked with it, have forced mission organizations to rethink their role in the present-day mission field. After all, the European missions' difficulties in establishing relations of equality and reciprocity with new churches are not new.

Flexibility and micro-development

It has been argued that NGOs' main advantage is their flexibility in micro-development situations which require extensive and intimate contacts with the intended beneficiaries. It is asserted that as a group they have features which make them more appropriate than governments in this regard. Fowler has described micro-development situations as follows: activities which require control based on micro-social relations; new types of activities which stand or fall on the basis of community inputs and support; activities which require specific local adaptations and applications of general improvements in technology; experiments or research which require significant inputs from the intended beneficiaries for them to be relevant, or where natural conditions are desired and/or controlled conditions are not possible; and activities which stimulate learning, adaptation and sharing of knowledge and comparative experience.

It is likely that a group of experienced development NGOs or local organizations with local knowledge will be able to do this kind of work better than most government bureaucracies can. There are a number of studies showing that organizations are good at such things, although they do not necessarily meet the expectations of NGO propaganda.

There are a number of cases where NGOs, with a dedicated staff, willing to live 'in the bush' or in remote rural areas, with local knowledge, etc., have been able to carry out good projects in this area. A famous model can be BRAC in Bangladesh. Although the success rate may be exaggerated and the benefits of such schemes will be reduced if all NGOs initiate such projects targeting the rural poor, such activities may demonstrate that NGOs have potential not shared by government bureaucracies.

BRAC's Non-Formal Primary Education (NFPE) programme was running about 20,000 schools in 1993. Girls were prioritized because they were the most underprivileged among rural children. All the schools had high attendance rates. The reported drop-out rate was only three per cent as compared with 80 per cent in government schools. BRAC schools were different in the structure of the curriculum and the flexibility of the teaching system. Schools were in general located in rural areas. The classes met for three hours a day, the time being decided upon by both parents and teachers so as to fit in with seasonal work, etc. The teachers were recruited locally and the students were not required to sit formal examinations as is usual in government-run schools. Instead, the children's progress was measured by means of continuous assessment by the teacher. According to BRAC, the NFPE programme was not an alternative or a substitute for public education. It was intended to be complementary and supplementary, with the aim of dealing with drop-outs and non-starters. When the primary school system can cope more effectively with them, BRAC considers its job to be done. A number of countries and NGOs have shown interest in this programme, and are contemplating replicating it.

An example from Kenya may also show NGO potential.[28] The Kenyan NGO, Partnership for Productivity Service Foundation (PFP) is one of the oldest in this field, dating back to before the more generally known take-off of this type of schemes in Asia, to the Quaker settlements in western Kenya in the 1940s. It still has a 'Quaker spirit' – a simple, self-reliant way of living. The PFP is currently operating all over East and Southern Africa. In Kenya it conducts a number of small-scale projects in about 40 per cent of the districts, especially in the north and west. NORAD started co-operating with PFP in 1989 with the Bungoma Farmers Small Enterprise Development Project, a five-year plan with annual budgets of Ksh.2m. The aims and objectives to a large degree matched Norwegian development policy: to assist poor rural groups, such as women, young people and poor farmers with training and credit, to create employment and to develop agriculture in remote areas. The activities comprised training in business management and the administration of loan schemes. Loans were given to groups of 20 to 25 members. The original plan was to reach 30 such groups, but a total of 87 was brought into the programme. The groups were mutually responsible for the loans. Leaders were elected every year and were always women. Credit was given to groups on a 30-month basis at a rate of 18 per cent a year. Individual activity has been in small business, one-cow dairies, selling maize, handicrafts, small workshops, etc. The Lurare Women's Group, Malakasi received a loan of Ksh 10,000 in 1989 and made a profit of Ksh 23,900 after repayment. In 1990 the profit had increased to Ksh 33,900. Later that year the group received an additional loan of Ksh 60,000, transferred the total savings to its own revolving loan scheme and so, in 1991, became more or less self-reliant.

Answers to the question why the project and the individual groups were so successful, dealt with the following points: very good and proper training by the PFP staff who knew the area and the trade; good follow-up by the PFP; sound accounting practices; flexibility in credit and activity; small, self-ruled groups with elected leaders; obvious, direct benefits for all participants.

Flexibility was possible because the groups were small and the NGO had a good knowledge of the area and its population. At the same time, it had the financial security of a five-year plan in co-operation with NORAD. Neither the Kenyan central government, the district authority or the banks were able to provide such a low interest rate for loans, and certainly not the training component.

Flexibility and politics

There is one area which in the past has received little attention in research on NGOs: their flexibility as instruments for governments, especially in cross-border operations and in societies where the donor state for various reasons is not able to work. From one point of view, this flexibility can be described as the 'magic' of the

NGO channel. The advantage is related not so much to traditional positive attributes such as grassroots orientation, voluntarism, etc., as to one structural feature: they are not a part of the state apparatus of the donor communities. This is an advantage which can be used by governments supporting political opposition groups and by internal political movements in need of external support. It can also be used for humanitarian purposes in areas where the UN or the state system cannot work. In this case it is possible to talk about NGOs as a group, because they share this formal, legal quality. Their potential as actors will, however, vary, of course, according to size, experience, political position, local contacts, etc. Since they are working on contract for governments or donor consortia, the questions of philanthrophic failure (insufficiency, particularism, paternalism, etc.) take on a different character. The analytical question is not one of comparative advantage, but of the usefulness of NGOs as instruments for state interests, and how these interests are articulated and handled by both the NGOs and the state.

A case study: NCA and the Emergency Relief Desk (ERD) operation[29]

This relief operation, from the Sudan into Eritrea and later to Tigray, was one of the biggest cross-border operations in the history of aid.[30] In 1991 the total budget amounted to NOK 1 billion, and the whole operation involved complex issues of neutrality and diplomacy. It was, of course, also the biggest operation in which a Norwegian NGO – Norwegian Church Aid (NCA) – had ever been involved. It is an example of the potential political importance of humanitarian intervention; in this case a Norwegian NGO, supported by the Norwegian Government and other donors, had an important impact on the outcome of the war in Ethiopia and Eritrea and on the power relations in Ethiopia after the fall of Mengistu.

The background to the ERD operation was simple: it had proved very difficult if not impossible to assist the victims of war and drought in the areas controlled by the Eritrean Liberation Front (ELF) and the Eritrean People's Liberation Front (EPLF). They could not be reached from Ethiopian ports or roads, because of Ethiopian government policy. One of the few options available was cross-border support from the Sudan. The ERD therefore emerged as a response to humanitarian needs in Eritrea. From the very first day it was involved in what was regarded by the Ethiopian Government as illegal operations, and which was also problematic in relation to international law and conventions. It is the flexibility of the NGO channel in this highly complicated political and diplomatic situation that will be emphasized here.

Since many studies on NGOs have focused on the implementation of micro-projects or social service projects, their potential political importance is often underestimated. In this case the NGOs played a very important political role. They gave the ERA (Eritrean Relief Agency) and REST (Relief Emergency Society of Eritrea) international legitimacy. And more important – the way their aid was distributed affected in crucial ways the emerging power balance in Ethiopia. The total value of food donations between 1981 and 1991 was US$ 216.5m (see Tvedt, 1995: Table 3.13 and Figures 3.1–3.5). Support for transport in the same period amounted to US$116m. The ERD distributed on average about 60,000 tons of food every year during the period. Transport was carried out by the ERA, REST and the Oromo

Relief Association (ORA). From scratch the transport fleet reached 400 for ERA, 250 for REST and less than 10 for the ORA in 1991. Up to 1985 the ERD was responsible for about two-thirds of the food deliveries to Eritrea and Tigray; thereafter it stabilized at around 40-50 per cent. The ERA was given aid to a value of about US$ 200m, REST about US$ 150m and the ORA under US$ 10m. This aid profile must have had important consequences for the outcome of the wars and rebellions, especially since it was the political fronts that were in real charge and control of its distribution. Food is power, not only when it is denied, but also when it is given.

HISTORY AND THE ROLE OF NCA

The initiative for cross-border assistance was taken by the Protestant Scandinavian organizations, Swedish Church Relief (SCR) and Norwegian Church Aid,[31] after the Sudan Council of Churches (SCC) had agreed to channel aid into Eritrea from Christian organizations in Europe. Between 1977 and 1982 they were the only organizations involved in these operations, and they supplied almost all the relief assistance reaching Eritrea and Tigray from international agencies. In 1977 an Eritrean desk was established in the SCC, channelling aid to the humanitarian wing of the Muslim-dominated ELF. In September 1977, the other guerrilla movement, the EPLF, contacted NCA, inviting it to work in Eritrea, and in 1978 it was established in Khartoum to take on this task. In 1979 it became clear that the World Council of Churches (WCC) and the Lutheran World Federation (LWF) were unwilling to become involved in Eritrea (Duffield and Prendergast, 1993). NCA decided to go it alone. A few other Protestant agencies also became involved,[32] and negotiations to establish a co-ordinating group began in 1980. The agreement – between the SCC and NCA – to form the Emergency Relief Desk (ERD) was signed in Khartoum on 21 February 1981. This agreement, by establishing an ecumenical instrument, made it possible to approach other church affiliated agencies. In 1984, when negotiations concerning the reorganization of the ERD began, other member organizations first began to meet on a formal basis. It had been, and still was, NCA and the ERD Executive Secretary (an employee of NCA) who effectively ran the operation. In the period 1981–91 NCA – with support from the Norwegian state – supplied about 20 per cent of all cash donations to the ERD.

How did the ERD see itself in this period? It described itself as non-political and having a strictly humanitarian mission. It co-operated with the indigenous 'humanitarian organizations ... on an equal basis.' In the beginning, assistance to the ERA (the EPLF's humanitarian arm) and the ERCCS (the ELF's humanitarian arm) was divided equally. In relation to the ERA and REST (the humanitarian arm of the Tigrayan People's Liberation Front), however, equality was not achieved, although in some years the support could be more or less equal (food donations in 1988 and 1990). In the 1980s some aid was also sent to Oromo areas, channelled through the ORA (the humanitarian arm of the Oromo Liberation Front). In 1982 NCA and the ERD regarded the ELF and ERCCS as having been crushed after internal fights with the EPLF, and after 10,000 of them had been put in a camp near Kassala, in eastern Sudan. Whatever happened politically, however, the local partners were consistently described as humanitarian implementing agencies and it was only at the end of the war that they were described in NCA documents as humanitarian arms of the liberation movements.

The role of the ERD was to be a logistical and monitoring organization. It received requests for assistance from the ERA and the ERCCS and later REST and the ORA, in ERD-speak called 'implementing agencies'. Its role was to verify need assessments through field visits, pass on requests to member agencies, arrange procurement in the Sudan when necessary, clear shipments, receive distribution reports, and so on. In other words, it was an ecumenical institution organized to channel relief assistance in kind to the local implementing partners, and was also responsible for securing its legitimate distribution and providing information about the operations to its members.

The problem of neutrality and humanitarian aid

From 1981 the Norwegian Government, under pressure from a vocal public which was pro-Eritrean, assisted on a humanitarian basis in what was described as a humanitarian effort through the ERD. In 1982, support from the British Government, via Christian Aid, was made possible by stressing humanitarianism and neutrality, as was the case with the Dutch and US Governments. Western governments opposed the regime in Addis Ababa, and wanted it to fall, as was evidenced during the drought in 1984–5. They were willing to use food as a weapon, as was Mengistu. Since the ERD operation involved cross-border support to opponents of an internationally recognized regime, they needed a neutral screen behind which to act. The ERD, presented as an accountable ecumenical body, became this neutral shield. It demonstrated its flexibility on this issue, especially with regard to donor support for Tigray, which did not develop until the mid-1980s. At this time, with the increasing involvement of USAID and the European Community, the neutral screen was even more essential. In the autumn of 1984 NCA went to New York with representatives from the ERA and REST to secure this support.

The ERD's international credibility as a humanitarian agency rested on its non-political image as a neutral humanitarian consortium. Because it worked only on one side of the conflict and, moreover, collaborated with relief associations established by the liberation fronts, this required rhetorical skills or 'voluntary blue-eyedness' – or a combination of both. The solution was to describe the ERA and REST as neutral humanitarian organizations or as implementing agencies (IAs). They were, however, clearly part of the liberation fronts. They depended on the support of their respective civilian administrations, and could have implemented little on their own. The IAs themselves were very clear on this issue, and also asked NCA and the others to come out more in the open and take sides in the conflict.[33] By describing IAs as neutral, however, the ERD, as a consortium of agencies with different agendas, was able to continue its role. Some ERD members had long-standing relations with Ethiopian church agencies which were critical of what they regarded as illegal activities in support of rebel groups.

The ERA and REST were portrayed by the ERD as having similar aims, i.e. humanitarian relief in drought- and war-affected areas. REST approached the Sudan Council of Churches and Swedish Church Relief in February 1981, shortly before the establishment of the ERD. The TPLF was not fighting for independence, but for a de-centralized Ethiopian state; support for REST was therefore regarded by many as more sensitive. The ELF was seen as having a more or less legitimate territorial claim, while the TPLF represented a direct challenge to the integrity of the Ethiopian state. By supporting the TPLF, the ERD upset some of its Christian member organizations, but not the interests or strategic plans of the big donor states which wanted to undermine Mengistu and his ally, the Soviet Union.

Such an arrangement was fragile, since the ERD's neutrality was constrained by the nature of the operation. A combination of war, areas of drought and transport problems meant that it was able to work only on one side of the conflict even if it had preferred to be impartial. Being confined to one side heightened the tension between neutrality and involvement in forwarding the viewpoints of that side. By the mid-1980s, while the ERD's collective neutrality was confirmed, the individual members had started to support their cause in public. The contradiction between neutrality and involvement continued to influence the discussion in the ERD.

Neither the ERD nor NCA complied with the prevailing ideas about state sovereignty. Cross-border relief operations, according to these regulations for relations among states, were illegal. This was a main reason why governments could not be openly involved, and why many NGOs also refused to take part, and why, if they did, their personnel were segregated from the ordinary work of these same organizations (Duffield and Prendergast, 1993). The ERD defined itself in terms of meeting humanitarian need 'in parts of Ethiopia which are not accessible from areas controlled by the Government of Ethiopia'. It strengthened its diplomatic position with regard to a behind-the-scenes peace role which its members, on occasion, were able to play on behalf of the liberation fronts. In addition, its attempts to maintain a political distance allowed it to mediate the political differences which distinguished the fronts and their respective relief associations. From the mid-1980s, however, with support from USAID and the European Community for the ERD operation in addition to the international discussions about relations between state and society, state sovereignity, humanitarian interventions, etc., the situation began to change. Western humanitarian policy has been increasingly influenced by a new interpretation of, and approach to, the principle of state sovereignty. There has been a clear change in the way sovereignty (as applicable in the developing countries) is regarded in the West. In a longer historical perspective, did the ERD express this shift and herald the age of the new 'humanitarian interventionism'? NCA stated that it gave priority to the humanitarian mandate, while organizations like the LWF and WCC were more reluctant, partly because of their official links with the Ethiopian churches, but also because they partly disagreed about the disintegration of Ethiopia.

At the time the ERD's criteria were described and partly believed to be depoliticized by some of the ERD partners themselves. This is a good example of one of the analytical implications of perspectives framed by humanitarianism and good intentions. As a means of informing policy, these perspectives disregarded and failed to understand the complex realities in the Horn of Africa; no comprehensive analysis was therefore produced of either the emergency situation or the important political role played by NCA and the Norwegian state. Defining the ERA and REST simply as 'IAs' produced a neutral image of the international agency, which resulted in a superficial and very naïve view of the political dynamics in Eritrea and Tigray, and the political exploitation of their emergency operation.

This cross-border operation illustrates how NGOs can act in situations where governments, because of legal and diplomatic constraints, cannot. Their lack of accountability also makes them more flexible when it comes to being involved in matters which are not always easily defensible in public. In addition, the knowledge gap in most donor countries between what organizations are actually involved in and what the public (or politicians) understand, is so great that it creates considerable room for manoeuvre. NCA had no staff in the area to control the distribution of food or the use of lorries. It was accused again and again of taking sides in a war, but responded always with the humanitarian mandate, as it still does. The operation was summed up as being based on 'real local participation'.[34]

With hindsight, NCA has argued that politicians in the USA and Europe were of course aware of what was happening. Food deliveries from the US reflected, of course, political moods and foreign policy interests in Washington more than needs in the field. NCA gambled with its position in the Sudan in 1989 by taking over the entire responsibility for the operation. Lutheran World Relief acted as the middleman for USAID, while Dutch Interchurch Aid and Christian Aid played the same role vis-à-vis the EEC. This interpretation puts the whole ERD operation in a new light. The big powers wanted to support anti-Mengistu forces. They discovered the ERD, and saw clearly that it was not a neutral, humanitarian church consortium but a partisan in the war. The neutral screen of the ERD was believed by nobody, apart from some of the ERD participants and public opinion in Norway, and, also perhaps, those people in the Norwegian Foreign Ministry in charge of emergency assistance at the time. It has been argued that theories of national sovereignty need no modification in the light of the functions that inter-national charities perform (Smith, 1990:25). In general this is the case. The ERD operation and similar operations in the Sudan and Rwanda violated, on behalf of other states, state interests or state integrity, and disregarded prevailing and legal instruments at the international arena.

To sum up: NGOs in development do not function in any specific way. They do not have important common characteristics or potentials, apart from three: they receive money from public donors, they are formally independent and they are non-profit distributing. Their roles in societies vary tremendously, however. It is therefore more useful to analyse how different organizations have played and are playing different social, political and cultural roles in different contexts, than to try to summarize general characteristics. NGOs have played important roles in social and political transformation where they have become actors within wider social-political movements. In some cases they have been instrumental in spreading the ideology of self-reliance, the interests of minority groups, etc. In other cases they have been marginal and, by and large, play a modest role as gap-fillers in different societies' social sectors.

NGOs do not have the general comparative advantages the NGO language and official documents ascribe to them. This term, taken from neo-classical economic theory, is not useful in the aid context and blurs empirical understanding and assessment. NGOs might have important potential for supporting development and democracy in some cases, as has been shown, partly because of their value orientat-ions, but be inflexible in other situations, also partly because of these same values.

Contradictions between organizations' value orientation and donors' policies have been little discussed in NGO literature, partly because most reports have embraced the NGO mission uncritically and adopted hegemonic NGO-speak when describing their activities. This conceived unity is one reason why it has been possible to talk about the comparative advantages of NGOs, as if they are more or less the same type of organizations or, at least, similar enough to be compared in this way. In the literature value orientation and flexibility, grassroots orientation, etc. have in general been described as being compatible, while things might be quite opposite in the real world . On the other hand, the idealism of many NGO employees may make them flexible and willing to work 'in the bush', among the poor, etc. No doubt NGOs have been very flexible in working in conflict situations, in the sense that they have been doing a lot of things which governments and the UN cannot even contemplate.

Development NGOs and the question of accountability

The problem of accountability is difficult because the present popularity of the word is surpassed only by the lack of agreement about its meaning. In a recent state-of-the-art paper on NGOs and accountability, it has been described as 'mechanisms by which the agencies concerned can be held responsible for their actions, and whether they fulfill the agreements and conditions they enter into, including adherence to the values and principles for which they stand' (Edwards and Hulme, 1996). It is analytically useful to distinguish between three forms of accountability; a) explanatory accountability – being required to give an account; b) accountability with sanctions; the right to require an account and to impose sanctions and c) responsive accountability – the views of those accounted to must be taken into account (see Leat, 1990:144).

These types of accountability are more complex for the NGO channel in aid, because of the large number of participants, than is the case for organizations working in Western welfare states or for those outside the aid channel. A development NGO may often have many and very different donors, and different co-operating partners work with or in opposition to different states and governments. In addition, there is an unusually great geographical and communicational distance between beneficiaries and the organization involved. International NGOs may get support from their own governments, but since many of them also work in many different sectors they can get support from many different government departments. Norwegian Church Aid, for example, did in the early 1990s get money from ten chapters in the Norwegian state budget. In addition, they can receive money from other bilateral donors, for example from the UN system and from international network organizations and also from other governments with different agendas. An NGO working in a developing country might, in addition to getting funds from different foreign governments, also get support (in cash or in personnel, etc.) from the national and local governments, and from a number of international NGOs which again receive funds from a number of bilateral and multilateral donors. Beneficiaries contribute voluntary labour, small amounts of cash (a means of strengthening their involvement in projects) and political legitimacy. Members of organizations or the public in the home country give money to support NGOs. All these actors may be involved in one and the same project. This kaleidoscopic scene creates unusually complicated accountability mechanisms.

The problem of accountability has always been part of the NGO scene, although aid documents show that it was not so much discussed in the 1970s and 1980s because NGOs' working methods and roles were more limited in scope. Basically the accountability issue reflects a development NGO's intermediate position between the state and the population or target group, and it has therefore not changed in character, only surfaced and become more complicated because of increased funds and the increase in the number of actors. The question is: to whom are the local NGOs or the Northern NGOs accountable? To the beneficiaries, to the members, to the Board, to the public, or to the funder(s)? Or to all of them, indiscriminately? To ask who is actually accountable to whom, beneath the rhetorical level of equality and partnership, is to address the real balance of power within the system.

The whole channel can be seen as a transmission belt where different levels are receiving funds from above in exchange for some kind of accountability. How these funds and knowledge are distributed influences what type of accountability is most important in general and in connection with the individual programme or project. The donor states control the lion's share of resources, and possess the most efficient means to require and acquire knowledge of NGO activities by means of institutionalized reporting and accounting. NGOs that are intermediaries for funds to national NGOs will tend to institutionalize similar types of accountability – and control mechanisms – with their partner. National NGOs receiving money from foreign donors, the national state or international NGOs, may also channel money to ad hoc groups or smaller NGOs.[35] Due to the number of levels and funders, this creates a complicated system, encompassing state borders, economic and social sectors, and widely different legal systems or formal accountability mechanisms. The strong ideological emphasis on alternative accountability mechanisms, 'people's participation', 'putting the last first', 'partnership', etc., and the conviction of many NGOs that the marginalized groups should define what ought to be done and the NGOs should only provide, express important alternatives to more conventional, authoritarian accountability thinking, but they may blur how accountability is also linked to resource transfer in this aid system.

Resource transfers and accountability

Official donors are in a position to enforce accountability and to sanction organizational behaviour. It is natural that when a government gives money to an organization it will demand a certain level of influence about what actions are taken and in which ways. The recipients of NGO assistance do not have the same leverage on actual NGO performance. There are, however, exceptions to this rule. In some cases the donors have become so dependent on local partners that the latter in reality exert considerable power on the donors. Recipients whom donors compete to support, like REST and the ERA in Tigray and Eritrea or BRAC in Bangladesh, have had sanctionary possibilities, and, at least in some instances, have been in a position to deny donors responsive or explanatory accountability, by threatening to go to other donors. But in most cases when the target groups are, for instance, poor women's associations, landless farmers, illiterate young people, their only available sanction is to refuse to participate. They can penalize the action, but not the organization as such, since the NGO can move to another country or another place. International development NGOs have more 'exit-options' regarding downwards accountability in the system than national NGOs working in their home countries. This general imbalance of power shapes the structure of the accountability system within the NGO channel. In a situation where there is only one main donor and a private donor market which seems to be drying out, the pressure of competition on organizational decision-making will increase. The greater the degree of similarity of goals and tasks between the organizations, the greater the level of competition that is likely to occur among them. Organizations will in a given environment, of course, respond to the demands of groups that control the most critical resources (Saxon-Harrold, 1990:128). Moreover, focus on fiscal accountability is easier to deal with than programme or aim-measuring accountability, especially since development aid is an arena where the public and the donors have insufficient knowledge or interest to assess social impact. The imbalance between policy and media concern about aid money that cannot be accounted for, the effort at strengthening financial reporting systems, and the lack of interest in the development impact of NGOs, can all be seen as a reflection of these relations.

The discussion about accountability in the NGO community often presupposes that everybody favours improved accountability. This is an untenable assumption. When donors at different levels delegate resources and power to NGOs certain activities can be protected from political interference (this has been called the 'buffer theory'). Another theory is the 'escape theory': that by transferring tasks to NGOs the known weaknesses of government departments can be evaded, and by reducing accountability one can escape from the financial controls and checks of Parliament, and the regulation and salary scales of the bureaucracy (adapted from Smith and Hague, 1971, quoted in Leat 1990:144). A further theory can be added – the 'PR-theory': NGO successes can be used to further governments' reputations, while their failures can be written off as private failures, outside government responsibilities. Donors do not necessarily always want accountability systems without loop-holes. The 'magic' of the channel seen from a donor's political point of view is precisely this: the channel is a great asset when they succeed, but can be dropped when they fail.

To what extent are organizations accountable to governments in the country where they work? Many governments try to increase their control over the NGO channel by requiring different types of accountability from organizations receiving external support. The arguments are economic as well as political: since in most countries such organizations have the right to duty-free imports, for example, and are thus subsidized by governments, these governments feel entitled to demand accountability. However, many organizations are opposed to this kind of account- ability, which is often described as undue state interference, and is said to divert their responsibility from the target groups. In many countries there have been open political confrontations between the state administration and the NGO community related to this issue (for example, in Ethiopia in 1992 and 1993, when the govern- ment worked on a code of conduct for NGOs and required each NGO to be accountable to certain Ethiopian authorities; also in Bangladesh, especially in

1992).[36] It seems that international NGOs are accepting accountability and govern-ment control from their home governments to quite a different extent from those of the countries where they operate, partly because that control is pursued within what in many cases can be called a collaborative partnership. There has developed a culture in some NGOs of expecting more 'freedom', i.e. more room for manoeuvre, in developing countries than at home. State interference is criticised in developing countries, while many of them at the same time work closely with, or are totally dependent upon, the state in their home country. Interviews undertaken during this study suggest that it is precisely this freedom from bureaucratic regulations that is one of the most important attractions for NGO actors in the field.

Accountability and organizational behaviour

In general, institutions will tend to opt for separation of control over policy from control of resources. This is a marked feature of the NGO channel. In most donor countries Parliament decides the overall political guidelines, but has little possibility of controlling how the money allocated is used; be it in 'far-away places' like Torit in the Southern Sudan, Arba Minch in southern Ethiopia, Sylhet in northern Bangladesh or Rushinga in Zimbabwe. Northern NGOs prefer independence and autonomy in management and policy-making in relation to the donor state. Southern NGOs have the same preference in relation to Northern NGOs. The argument in favour of such independence is often that he who knows best should also have the power to decide what is best.

The form of accountability is linked to the form of resource transfer. A strategy pursued by both NGOs in developing countries and Northern NGOs is to diversify the control over the resources they receive, in such a way that the influence of any one donor is marginalized. Because of similar situations, national NGOs have an ambiguous attitude to donor consortia. Many organizations regard it as better to have a consortium of donors than only one donor, because the latter relationship will often be experienced as a form of paternalism and will lead to undue pressure for upward accountability. Nevertheless, consortia that become too effective, or which enable the different donors to agree, or to 'gang up' as it might be put by NGOs, aggravate this problem and NGOs therefore tend to dislike them. Accountability is thus not a relation that everybody supports at all times or in all situations, as current NGO myths imply.

In NGO literature it has been argued that accountability is related to the question of making NGOs more effective – i.e. the more accountable, the more efficient. Improved accountability may increase efficiency, but it can also increase in-efficiency. The theory that the two reinforce each other has been disproved. To show strong accountability towards external donors might counteract both efficiency and, not least, legitimacy. Especially in countries where there are political and ideological conflicts, an NGO that is seen to be over-concerned with pleasing (being accountable to) foreign donors, often faces a problem of local or national legitimacy. On the other hand, to demonstrate excessive accountability to poor women's groups or landless farmers might jeopardize financial support and work permits. Accountability and legitimacy are related, but should not be intermingled. Organizations may have great legitimacy and precisely for that reason be subject to few and weak accountability arrangements. This is a feature of development NGOs, especially those working in countries other than their home country. Legitimacy can be based on media legitimacy, elite legitimacy, church legitimacy, etc., and does not have to rest on either accountability to or legitimacy among recipients.

There is, of course, also a problem with accountability within NGOs. This problem might be less in non-democratic organizations or in organizations led by charismatic individuals. Membership organizations do not experience fewer accountability problems than non-membership organizations. In Northern NGOs, with expanding activities and a growing professional aid staff, involved in areas far away from where the members live and in activities they do not know very much about, the members or the Home Board will, because of this unequal access to knowledge, be marginalized within accountability flows. In some organizations a gap has developed between formal responsibility for overall management and policy and actual responsibility for policy implementation. Professionals in an NGO will consider that they know best and will gradually know best more and more. An experienced implementor, with no formal authority in the elected bodies, will thus tend to become central in deciding the organization's profile and policies.

Accountability and target groups

It has been argued that the implicit contract between NGOs and recipients is a fundamental basis for accountability mechanisms. But how real is the premise that such a contract exists? It is possible to develop a relationship that resembles a contract during the programme-period, but where recipients (as contract-holders) have no effective sanctions while the organizations have many options. To withdraw participation or voluntarism is a weak threat or sanction. The non-existence of contracts can be demonstrated in many ways. When an NGO withdraws from a project (which happens all the time), this is often justified by overall arguments about more pressing needs and the necessity for priorities, etc. An NGO often has greater freedom to manoeuvre in this manner than do governments, because there is no contractual relationship between NGOs and recipients.

NGO rhetoric asserts that NGOs do not work for but with others. This represents a reaction to attitudes of paternalism inherent in other organizations. The partner is the one who defines the problem while the NGO only provides the means of solving it. Let us assume that this is what is happening in the field, and that a policy of 'putting the last first' has succeeded. The project may have been improved, the target groups may have become more involved, but at the same time this may well increase accountability problems. Why should poor women in Wolata, Ethiopia or in Rushinga, Zimbabwe, bother about writing quarterly reports on project aims and results, so long as the project has established schools, latrines, etc., if that was what they wanted? The more a project is geared towards the target group, and adapts to every changing local circumstances, the more difficult it will be to be accountable upwards in the way the system expects. The legitimacy of the channel is partly based on ideas about recipient and constituency accountability. It rests upon the idea that the target groups have the same will, or one voice. Such a myth blurs the fact that in this context organizations are accountable to segmented and overlapping constituencies, and that some levels have more sanctionary power and knowledge than others.

The target groups in aid are victims of what can be called the imbalance of knowledge structures within the NGO system. Their knowledge and ideas in relation to a project have very little chance of reaching those in the donor country who are funding the project. They might receive a visitor now and then, but most people would tend to think that they know what they have and not what they might have had. Criticism of projects will therefore tend to be muted, also because the projects often represent enormous resource transfers in local terms. This imbalance is, of course, not solely created by the aid relation, but the aid relation is an expression of it.

Multiple accountability or institutionalized irresponsibility?

An organization might formally and rhetorically be accountable to a number of institutions and groups. Most models of accountability reduce this complexity and do not cater for the particularities of development aid, the great number of donors or their different characteristics and requirements. What happens when conflicting demands or conflicts of accountability arise? What comes first – in the end? It is reasonable to assume that choices are influenced by expectations and the seriousness of the potential sanctions. The different types of sanction the different groups in the international or national sub-system have at their disposal become important. It has been suggested that a general hierarchy of such groups exists to which organizations have to relate. Empirical data suggest, rather, a number of different hierarchies which change internally in the system all the time, related to the different political and resource needs and environments of different types of organizations.

The problem, therefore, is twofold. Rhetoric tends to promise more than it can deliver. This is the role of rhetoric everywhere, so the point here is how to assess the implications for this field. At the end of the day the organizations and those funding them cannot escape the question: 'Which group comes first?' NGO-speak suggests that it is the target group. The target groups and their opinions cannot be ignored always and in the long run, because lack of participation might affect the general legitimacy of the organization in the funding country, but they can be and often are ignored in the short run. When conflicts over accountability arise, it becomes primarily a question of being accountable to those who can exert most power over the organization. This is often, but not always, the donor. In general, withdrawal of financial support is more important than withdrawal of popular support from the target group; it is possible to survive the latter, but the withdrawal of financial support is more difficult to overcome. This does not imply that it is impossible to show voluntary accountability to selected target groups, based on organizational ideologies and values. But in a situation in which the organizations develop economic dependence on one donor, they will tend to play second fiddle over time. The amount and type of resource transfers, i.e. the imbalance of economic weight and the lack of reciprocity between the different actors, especially between the NGO and the target group, must affect the way accountability is handled.

In development aid the growing attention given to accountability issues could be interpreted from another angle. Because of physical and communicative distance and inequality in resources between the donor, the NGO and the recipient, the way the issue has been discussed may act as a cover-up. Multiple accountability, which for many has become a favourite slogan, is, practically speaking, impossible. It might therefore maintain existing roles between recipients, public donors and the organizations and their members. Since nobody is accountable to anybody in particular, but slightly accountable to everybody, one ends up being really accountable to nobody. Instead of somewhat uncritically embracing new slogans, empirical research on how accountability is tackled within the NGO channel needs to be carried out.

Notes

1 See, for example, the Norwegian state's justification for 'bringing the NGOs in' at the beginning of the 1960s (debate in the Storting, 8 February 1962; Hødnebø, 1992: 4–8; Tvedt, 1992: 24). The arguments were in this respect similar to those in other donor countries (Smith, 1990). Some of the mission organizations, however, underlined what they considered to be their comparative advantage; their experience in non-European countries since the middle of the nineteenth century. The Norwegian state acknowledged this background, but did not consider. it on balance an advantage. Some of the bigger donors, like the US and the former colonial powers such as Britain and France, also regarded NGOs as important and supplementing political instruments and informants from the very beginning of the aid era (e.g. the Eisenhower Administration and CARE in Egypt during the Suez crisis in 1955–6, and the British government and mission organizations in many countries).

2 An example: the Norwegian state (through NORAD) and a Norwegian NGO (Norwegian Church Aid, Sudan Programme) both implemented two integrated rural development projects in two remote and poor districts of Kenya and the Sudan from the early 1970s to the middle to late 1980s, and thus initiated comparable social processes. NORAD's district development programme in Turkana lasted from 1971 to 1990 (NORAD terminated its direct involvement in 1990 after the Kenyan Government asked the Norwegian Embassy to leave the country) and can be compared with Norwegian Church Aid's programme in the Southern Sudan, Torit District, from 1972 to 1985/86, when NCA had to terminate their programme due to the civil war in the area. Such a comparison would produce interesting similarities and differences about these different institutions in this particular context, but, most probably, not a general conclusion arguing that one group was more efficient or effective than the other. Studies undertaken of the Turkana project and the analysis of the NCA project in this book do not support the dominating characterizations. Philanthropic amateurism, value-orientation as against rule-orientation, particularism as against universalism in approaches to social service deliveries, etc. seem to have been as important in the NORAD project as in the NCA programme (see for example Harden, 1993, and his chapter on NORAD in Turkana, which aptly, in our context, is called 'Good intentions', pp. 177–217).

3 The data for this analysis are built on the evaluation report, Hødnebø, 1993.

4 The following is based on doctoral dissertations written on the history of the mission: Sæverås, O. *On Church Mission Relations in Ethiopia 1994–1969 – with special Reference to the Ethiopian Evangelical Church Mekane Yesus* (EECMY) *and the Lutheran Mission* (Oslo: Lunde forlag, no date) and Bakke, J. *Christian Ministry Patterns and Functions within the Ethiopian Evangelical Church Mekane Yesus,* Oslo Solum, 1987. Interviews were conducted with personnel working for the mission both in southern Ethiopia (in February 1994) and with their Secretariat in Addis Ababa in May 1992 and February 1994. The information is corroborated with archival documentation at NORAD, Oslo, on the work of the organization and is finally based on data collected in relation to the preparation for a meeting with all the Norwegian organizations working in Ethiopia held in Oslo on 7 January 1994, as part of the present study.

5 In 1993 NLM was engaged in 11 countries. The total number of members in Norway is 4,000. Additional financial support is collected from allied organizations in four other Nordic countries and the Internal Mission in Norway. NLM has 1,400 staff and fellow representatives in Norway, but only one full-time and one part-time permanent staff working with development aid at the secretariat in Oslo.

6 Norwegian Lutheran Mission, 'School and Mission' (in Norwegian), Oslo: NLM, 1988.

7 Projects are defined here according to budgeting in co-operation with NORAD, and not as they appear 'on the ground' in Ethiopia. Thus NLM operated with many more operational units within the system.

8 NLM apparently had no problem in fulfilling its own share in relation to NORAD. In 1992 more than NOK 2.3m was contributed by 38,816 individuals, under six different categories: (NLM, 1993) (Bistandsnemda's comment on NLM in Ethiopia).

Spring/Autumn gift	8,281,000	Fair adoption	2,823,000
Regular offerings	1,862,000	Social projects	4,011,000
Evangelical projects	2,971,000	Other collections	3,183,000

9 NLM: Minutes of Missionary Conference Ethiopia, January 1950, quoted in Bakke, 1987.

10 NLM: Yirga Alem logbook 19 January 1950, quoted in Bakke, 1987.

11 NLM: Yirga Alem logbook May 1950, quoted in Bakke, 1987.

12 NLM: Minutes of Missionary Conference Ethiopia, January 1956, quoted in Bakke, 1987.

13 Bauerochse (GHM) referred to this when he stated that the Norwegians were always quick to say: 'If we can do as we like then we had better leave the whole work.' SEM/AA: Bauerouchse to Arén, 8 July 1957, quoted in Bakke, 1987:162.

14 LWF: Aske to Schaefer, 16 April 1958, quoted in Bakke, 1987:164.

15 NLM: Minutes of Missionary Conference Ethiopia December 1959, quoted in Bakke, 1987: 164.

16 EECMY was used as the name in the first documents about the new church, but was not allowed, since there should be only one Ethiopian church, the Orthodox Church. After the revolution and the overthrow of the Emperor in 1974 the position of this church was weakened and it lost its role as the state church. EECMY again became the church's name, this time officially. It is used throughout this section.

17 For Norwegians it may also be emotionally important that King Olav initiated the work on the hospital in 1966, and, for the local people, that the Emperor also visited it the year after.

18 There are a number of studies of missions under colonial rule, but, as far as I know, almost none about missions and the development aid era.

19 Contract between NLM and Norsk Utviklingshjelp, 14 December 1963, NORAD Archives.

20 In 1992 the Development Department had the following sections: appropriate technology, building, child care council, education and training, medical, micro hydro power, relief, urban and rural development, and water development (see EECMY, *Annual Report of Development Department*, 1992, Addis Ababa: EECMY).

21 Schaefer, Field report 1, 10 November 1957, quoted in Bakke, 1987.

22 LWF: Tausjø to Florin, July 1962, quoted in Bakke, 1987.

23 LWF: Magerøy to Sovik, 18 May 1962, quoted in Bakke, 1987.

24 The leader of the NLM in Ethiopia was also the Norwegian consul there during the years of the White and Red Terror.

25 Sæverås, 1974:153.

26 The support of staff at the hospital was established by NORAD from 1966 and covered 50% of a stipulated cost per post. This support was hardly used by any organization until 1972, when it was stipulated at NOK 6,000 a year. From then on this kind of financial support became the type most used by the mission organizations until NORAD revised its regulations in 1988. This support to staff underwent a major revision again in 1974, when the rate was upgraded to NOK 35,000 a year, including an unspecified coverage of other living expenses and indirect expenses, such as travelling, transport, lodging, etc. The average level used for technical personnel by the missions was NOK 36,300 at the time, so almost 100% coverage of this type of missionary personnel was gained by these organizations. The rate was gradually upgraded every other year, and reached NOK 100,000 for single people and 150,000 for families in 1991. In 1977 a new type of operational support was introduced: coverage of 80% of total operational support to projects, but on condition that all expenses were specified. This type of support was

immediately used by all NGO development agencies. Most missions, however, NLM included, chose, on the other hand, to continue with the old system of staff support (until 1988). The reason for this must be that, with their salaries lower than the average, they obtained 100% coverage of some of their staff salaries and expenses – which constituted 85% of their total aid budget.

27 In a speech just after he took power in 1977 Mengistu declared that missionaries were CIA agents in disguise. At the beginning of March, Radio Evangelists Røst, was nationalized, and changed its name to Radio Revolusjonære Ethiopias Røst. The Red Terror was launched to fight the White Terror. American and Finnish missionaries in Djmma in southern Ethiopia, for example, were asked to leave the country within 24 hours at Easter 1977.

28 Based on the evaluation report by Hødnebø et al. 1993, and prepared for Norwegian Church Aid and NORAD. The focus was on what happened to the development projects and programmes undertaken by Kenyan NGOs and supported by NORAD, after the diplomatic breach with Kenya in 1990.

29 This section is based on Duffield and Prendergast, 1993, archival studies in NCA archives in Oslo and Asmara, archival studies in the archive of the Norwegian Foreign Ministry, Oslo, and interviews with many of the leaders of the ERD and of NCA in the periods studied (Khartoum 1983, Nairobi 1987, Addis Ababa 1992 and 1994, Nairobi 1992 and 1994 and at NCA Head-quarters, Oslo).

30 Interview with Gunnar Bøe, 22 September 1994.

31 There were many reasons for this. Swedish missionaries had been active in Eritrea since the middle of the nineteenth century. Escalating fighting in the mid 1970s weakened these historical links. Relief work was one way of maintaining this contact. Generally, opinion in the Scandinavian countries was very pro-Eritrea during the war. The NCA's Sudan Programme's first and influential director, Øystein Stabrun, had also visited war- and famine-affected Eritrea, and was positive about NCA support.

32 These included Brot für Die Welt (BFW), Christian Aid (CA), Dutch Interchurch (DIA) and the Interchurch Co-ordination Committee for Development Projects (ICCO). Lutheran World Relief (LWR) made its first bilateral grant to REST in 1980.

33 In 1979, for example, the General Secretary of the EPLF visited Norway where he tried to persuade NCA to display political solidarity. NCA replied that, in order to boost humanitarian assistance, Western agencies had to show impartiality and a low political profile. The ERA and REST were appreciative of the material support provided by the ERD, but again and again they criticized its lack of advocacy.

34 Case 123/93 Steering Committee Meeting, 26 November 1993, NCA, Oslo (in Norwegian).

35 Some argue that the problem of accountability stems from the hierarchic structure of a particular NGO. This analysis emphasizes the less important aspects, and its corollary tends to suggest solutions that will cover up the inherent problem of the channel. One natural proposal within this perspective is to support smaller community-based organizations, but this will not reduce the problem – only change some of its mechanisms (see Edwards and Hulme, 1994).

36 Official donor agencies claim that their accountability and legitimacy derive from entering into formal agreements with governments. These legal contracts specify what each party will do. In some cases Northern NGOs enter into similar arrangements.

7 NGOs at 'the End of History'

In the mid-1990s what has been termed 'civil society' and NGOs are at the centre of the development debate, while both were marginal or non-existent terms when development aid started. The aid system was established at the height of the anti-colonialist movement, in a very different ideological context. At that time there was an unprecedented promotion of the cause of the state: the European nation-building project was globalized, the prevailing development theories were state-centred and for the first time a global institution was established – the state-centred UN system. Influenced by the fall of the Soviet empire, the crisis of the welfare state in the West, and fundamental questions about the legitimacy of many existing state structures, theories have recently been formulated that express an assault on the state and a promotion of the civil society. Just as from the 1950s social scientists from all disciplines became 'state activists' (Migdal, 1988:11), so now social scientists from most disciplines seem to be discontented with only analysing civil society and have become civil society activists.

This chapter will identify some important features of this new paradigm, compare it with other ideas about civil society and the role of NGOs, and analyse the formulation of a donor country's policy on NGOs (the Norwegian policy). The aim is to understand how the NGO-'civil society'-state relationship is conceptualized in aid, in an historical period which influential political forces have termed the 'end of history', (see Fukuyama, 1992) while others argue that instead of a 'New World Order' there will be a long period of clashes between civilizations (see Huntington, 1993).

The 'New Paradigm'

Historically the need for NGOs in development has been argued in different ways. In the 1960s, when the NGO channel was established in most donor countries, NGOs were regarded as marginal actors complementing state-to-state aid. Their main task was to secure and deepen national support for aid in the donor countries (Smith, 1990; Tvedt, 1992). At the beginning of the NGO decade, NGOs were primarily described as places where people learn through praxis about society and how to organize, commonly equated with grassroots movements, often populist or leftist in orientation. From the early 1980s, documents on NGOs in development focused on micro-level development and the need for empowerment of marginal groups. The thinking centred around loose concepts like the strengthening of local capacities, grassroots participation and mobilization (see, for example, OECD, 1983), with no clear idea determining at what social level and to what extent this grassroots mobilization would be effective for societal development at large. Emphasis was often put on specific, marginalized target groups, local economic self-sufficiency and projects aiming at the mobilization of popular organizations like producers' societies, co-operatives, self-help groups, etc., possibly supported by foreign donors or implemented by Northern NGOs. The more politicized version aimed at de-linking rural producers from the capitalist world market, by mobilizing and organizing the local people for self-sufficiency. But up to the late 1980s very few, if any, argued that the NGOs, as a distinct institutional and social category, should have a role of their own to play in societal development.

In the 1980s the discussions about the crisis of the welfare state in the West led to more interest in the private and third sectors generally. In Britain under Thatcher and in the US under Reagan the role of the state as such was at the heart of the ideological agenda: big government was bad government. Thatcher's slogan was 'against a paternalistic state and a dependent people' (Lowe, 1993:3 cited in Seip, 1994:382). The logic of the market was evoked in the name of individual freedom as an alternative to public systems, and in the name of competition as a method and a technique to make the public system more efficient. In Norway the criticism was generally less ideological and more pragmatic; the welfare state required more funds than the people, or society could afford. In all welfare states it became common to argue that a strong, expanding state created passive, recipient-oriented citizens. Others saw the problem as a question of community relations; the emphasis should be put on encouraging mutual, moral obligations within smaller social networks rather than on the individual's legal demands and rights vis-à-vis the state. The growth of state administration and its interventions represented an oppressive force, contributing to an erosion of the local community network and its in-built support mechanisms.

Two factors have been of special importance in placing these viewponts at the core of the international development debate in the 1990s. The collapse of the state-led, one-party systems and economies of Eastern Europe changed the way civil society and the NGOs' potentials were conceptualized and described, not only in Moscow and Prague but all over the world. 'The roll-back of the state' became overnight almost a universal slogan. Within this perspective, NGOs could now be regarded as important actors within an alternative model of development. They were no longer simply gap-fillers in service delivery programmes; they represented important elements in a new development paradigm, focusing on civil society, market mechanisms, etc. Secondly, the restructuring policies of the World Bank and other influential donor institutions led to a planned reduction in the role of the state and increased space for NGOs, but here not so much as representatives of civil society, but rather as service delivery agents, paid by the same donors. The combination of this political factor (the collapse of the Communist bloc) and the economic factor (the World Bank's structural adjustment programmes) has stimulated an unprecedented growth in the NGO channel worldwide in most countries. The triumphalism of adherents of the neo-liberal paradigm and the enhanced power exercised by governments and agencies associated with it over recent years, may not as yet have created a 'New World Order', but it has helped to establish a new political and ideological agenda. The Western model has not only triumphed, it is said, but it has proved to be the end station of a universal and directional history (Fukuyama, 1992). Economic integration and modern science have had uniform effects on all societies that have experienced them, Fukuyama argues, and consequently there is a growing uniformity of modern societies. Utopia is here, he says, because history has finally shown that there is no better way to organize society than the liberal democratic system established (with all its faults) in the West.[1] Based on an understanding of 'recognition' (Hegel's point) as the motor of history, this allows a reinterpretation also of democracy. For democracy to work, Fukuyama argues,

> citizens need to develop an irrational pride in their own democratic institutions, and must also develop what Tocqueville called 'the art of associating', which rests on prideful attachment to small communities. These communities are frequently based on religion, ethnicity, or other forms of recognition that fall short of the universal recognition on which the liberal state is based (ibid.:xix).

In this perspective NGOs may be seen not only as important symbols of what constitutes history's end station, but development NGOs may also be regarded as this model's heralds in societies that not yet have reached this final stage in human history.

This new development paradigm is an amalgam term describing a particular set of discursive propositions and policy recommendations. It is far from being a homogeneous entity, and whereas Fukuyama discusses the general model (market economy, liberal democracy and the 'weakness of strong states'), this paradigm aims at producing more space for civil society and a deliberate roll-back of the state. It is supported by leading policy-makers in many donor states and strongly backed by influential international (and many big national) NGOs. Although intellectual roots and inspirations, aims and emphases may vary, a broad consensus seems to have emerged that former development strategies seriously downplayed historical experiences about the real and potential role of what is now generally termed 'civil society' and the organizations therein. The term 'new' implies the re-emergence or re-articulation of a different blend of development strategies, one, in fact, that in conventional parlance has made the celebration of the civil society and market mechanisms a central and distinctive feature. It suggests a far-reaching redefinition of relationships between state, society and external actors at a macro-political level. It is influenced by the new neo-liberalist ideology – the idea of the 'minimum state', reductions in the tasks of the state and strengthening of the private sector through households, markets or voluntary organizations (Mishra, 1989). The new paradigm has an economic dimension (reliance on markets and private sector initiatives) and a political dimension. Democratization is equated with strengthening civil society, and reducing the role of the state. While in the early 1980s support to NGOs was often based on ideas that the state was too weak or too bureaucratized to mean anything to the poor, or that it was controlled by anti-popular forces, the new paradigm regards the relation between state and civil society as a zero-sum game. Former development strategies are rejected because, it is said, they regarded the state as the origin and cause of progress, while society, when thought of at all, was considered either an obstacle to or an object of development. The policy for NGOs within this perspective is part of an agenda that includes monetarism, supply-side economics, economic neo-liberalism and the public choice approach to economic analysis. It changes the boundaries of what is considered the legitimate extent of direct state involvement in both economy and social service provisions.[2]

The NGOs' role is thus to substitute for the state in key aspects of societal development. It is a paradigm of competition and struggle between society and the state, carrying a major assault on the concept of the state itself and a widespread call for its roll-back. Aid should be geared towards civil society, defined as those uncoerced human groups and relational networks of consensual association and empowerment that enable society to exist independently of the state. NGOs are thus given a crucial role in creating a more just and democratic development. The paradigm has rarely made clear how NGOs and governments (and especially the former) are supposed to contribute to democratization. The theory with its universal ambitions is given authority by pointing to historical experiences in the West, where voluntary associations have played a formative role and represented a counterweight to the accumulation of excessive power by a political executive. This is the opposite of what is described as the norm in developing countries, where the sequence of institution-building has departed from the checks and balances model in the West.[3] Development and democracy are therefore dependent on building up a strong civil society with strong organizations, now represented by development NGOs.

Within the perspective of the new paradigm the growth of the NGO channel is interpreted as a verification of the theory. Within the aid system the NGOs represent one of the most important political-ideological symbols and also forces in the reappraisal of the role of states and governments. Their very existence and proliferation are used as an argument in this global political-ideological struggle, and thus also indirectly affect state-society relations in fundamental ways in many developing countries. This is so because the relationship between civil society and the state or between NGOs and state-to-state aid, is part of a debate that evokes basic ideological and political questions. It is interesting that very few NGOs, even those with a different, more state-friendly, value orientation, take part in this debate which in many areas has become a neo-liberalist monologue.

Civil society and NGOs

To support and strengthen civil society has become a declared aim of most donors. Most often the connotations in aid documents seem to be the realization of human rights, good governance, privatization or deregulation, participation, empowerment and public sector reform. It has become a core term in NGO literature over the last few years and has become synonymous with positive and compatible values and ideas.

The aid discourse on civil society is greatly influenced by Western political thought and by prevailing interpretations of recent Western experiences. The core terms, state, civil society, market, democracy, human rights, are in general used vaguely, but as if they carry a clear and universal meaning. This seems to have contributed to a situation in which everybody shares the same rhetoric, but without really agreeing about how to act. Norwegian NGOs may be a case in point: many of them have a traditional value orientation and profile that are very different from those of the neo-liberal paradigm, but they are still employing more or less the same NGO-language, and although their practice may be different they have not voiced opposition to the prevailing rhetoric. The character of the new paradigm's implicit definition of civil society and its relations to the state may become clearer if compared with other descriptions and definitions. UNDP has put forward a definition of civil society which, on a general level, reflects the influence of the new paradigm, but which distances itself from the most idealized and harmonized versions:

> Simply stated, civil society is, together with state and market, one of the three 'spheres' that interface in the making of democratic societies. Civil society is the sphere in which social movements become organized. The organizations of civil society, which represent many diverse and sometimes contradictory social interests are shaped to fit their social base, constituency, thematic orientations (e.g. environment, gender, human rights) and types of activity. They include church related groups, trade unions, cooperatives, service organizations, community groups and youth organizations, as well as academic institutions and others. (UNDP, 1993:1)

Before analysing this definition, it may be useful first to compare it with others. The German philosopher Hegel drew a famous distinction between state and civil society in 1821, in his book *Philosophy of Right*. Civil society (*bürgerliche Gesellschaft*) was regarded as a stage in the dialectical development from the family to the state 'which contradicted the kind of ethical life found in the human micro-community in order to be itself contradicted and overcome (i.e. cancelled and preserved, *aufgehoben*) by the macro-community of the politically independent, sovereign nation'.[4] Civil society represented a stage in the development of a metaphysical idea, where the state was the final end station of human development. Its role was to educate the community in moral norms, and in this way establish a basis for the ethics of the state and for the state's final victory.[5]

The term was reformulated by Marx, who made it (the bourgeois society), and not the state, the arena for political life and the source of political change, not against the state, but in order to take over the state. The civic organizations would disappear after the revolution of the proletariat, as would the bourgeois society itself. The organizations were primarily regarded as reflections of economic interests, and had therefore little or no independent, intrinsic value. While Marx had a more reductionistic view than Hegel, both of them, like the present notions, excluded national, historical or cultural characteristics from the notion of civil society.

One of the most influential theories on civil society was formulated by the Italian Marxist Antonio Gramsci whose revolutionary strategy relied on the concept of such an entity. He argued that in Italy and other Western European countries the working class under communist leadership had a better chance of gaining hegemony within civil society than within the national or political arena and that, when they had achieved this, they could then conquer the political power of the state. For him civil society was not identical to bourgeois society; its organizations had a relative autonomy, in relation to both the state and the market.

During the 1970s, French neo-Marxists put forward another view, arguing that both market and state were totalitarian systems (Cohen and Ararto 1992). This view, in this aspect related to traditional anarchism, regarded the intrusive and oppressive role of the state as being related not to who governed the state, but to the institution as such. In order to strengthen and develop independent social activity the role of the state should be curtailed. In Germany, Jürgen Habermas talked about the state as a colonizer of the 'lifeworld'. The legitimacy of the state was thus questioned from many corners and in many social fields.

Another, and more recent, theory of the role of civil society is represented by the new communitarianism. In 1993 Amitai Etzioni published *The Spirit of Community*. Here he put forward a programme for turning communitarianism into a political movement, placed between what he describes as the authoritarian, extreme right and the civil rights activists on the left. This intermediate position was expressed in the slogan: 'Free individuals require a community'. In 1988 Etzioni had published *The Moral Dimension*, in which he criticized the economic model of the rational, interest-maximizing individual, the right-based welfare-state policies and the erosion of local social networks. In order to counteract a development bringing increased criminality, social unrest and poverty, the way out was seen as a combination of increased local social responsibility and public resources, or the propagation of the 'I and We' view or the responsive community, which would give full status to both individuals and their shared union (Etzioni, 1988:8). Society was seen neither as a constraint nor as an opportunity; it was described as 'us' (ibid.:9). With Bill Clinton's victory in the US in 1992 the communitarian movement acquired increased importance. Both Vice-President Al Gore and the First Lady Hillary Clinton declared themselves to be communitarianists, viewing individuals as members of social collectives rather than as free-standing beings, as in the neo-classical paradigm. In Britain a similar trend is detectable. The new leader of the Labour Party, Tony Blair, is strongly influenced by the same communitarian movement: the free individual should be supported by a strong social network. Hence the slogan of social solidarity, instead of 'class', 'black', 'women's' solidarity, on the one hand, and the stark individualism and market liberalism of the Conservative Party, on the other.

The term 'civil society' has a much more marginal history than concepts such as 'state', 'class', 'public sector', 'private sector', etc. The *Fontana Dictionary of Political Thought* of the late 1970s had no entry for 'civil society', which can indicate how new the term is in research and mainstream policy discussions. In Norway the concept of civil society, let alone the anti-state connotations it carries within the prevailing aid rhetoric, has not been a part of the political or scientific vocabulary, until the last few years. The organizations have worked with the state rather than against it. As in Scandinavia as a whole, their goal has mainly been to increase the responsibility of the state, not to replace or supplement it on a permanent basis within a zero-sum game. Even the organizations opposing the state, such as the early labour movement of the 1850s and the stronger, syndicalistic trade-union movement before and after World War I, did not wish to limit its role, but rather to increase it, preferably by taking it over. They have been more interested in furthering basically shared goals than in distancing themselves from the state.[6] Thus, the idea that there is a civil society in need of defence – against the state – has not been prominent in Norway. The organizations have generally come to expect public support, and the state has naturally assumed this role. This state benevolence has prevailed ever since the establishment of the Royal Norwegian Society for Rural Development at the beginning of the nineteenth century. The Norwegian form of social and political integration has shaped the third sector, characterized as a state-oriented sector. The implied dichotomy of state versus society, which dominates the current aid debate, has played a marginal role in Norway's history. This contrast between traditional Norwegian political vocabulary and the extent to which Norwegian NGO aid in the 1990s is influenced by this concept and its implicit connotations, can indicate the speed with which the term has conquered a central position in a universalized NGO-speak.

The UNDP definition, quoted above, is clearly influenced by the American-Western tradition. It draws attention to the idea that civil society consists of a broad range of organizations. It is therefore opposed to some of the rhetoric of the new paradigm. It indicates that civil society is not uniform. It can be regarded as a social space where interests and ideologies confront each other: religion against religion, ethnic group against ethnic group, capitalist against workers, etc. UNDP says that the organizations 'sometimes' represent 'contradictory social interests'. Others would argue that it is safe to assert that there always are contradictory interests in society, but that the degree of conflict will vary. Civil society organizations are implicitly defined by UNDP as organizations caring for 'the environment, gender, human rights'. But what about organizations of racists, authoritarians, funda-mentalists and male chauvinistic interests and groups? They are, of course, also a part of civil society. It is therefore possible to argue that to strengthen civil society is never in itself identical with strengthening 'positive' or 'progressive' values. Its overall role and distinct historical impact depend on particular circumstances.

The rhetoric about civil society assumes that to strengthen it means to improve democracy, the freedom of the individual and also the 'popular will'. This theory has not been universally substantiated. The strength of civil society might increase in an implicit zero-sum game, if the state is also weakened. The sphere where the state does not function may be enlarged, but there is no evidence to suggest that this automatically strengthens civil society. This has been demonstrated in many developing countries as a result of the structural adjustment policies of the 1980s. To strengthen civil society might mean that some groups are strengthened, often at the expense of others. If some groups become very strong compared with other groups (for example, if development NGOs emerge as a much stronger force than traditional trade unions, left-wing parties, mobilizing landless farmers, etc.) some people would argue that the potential for their having an impact on government policies on crucial issues is reduced. This also implies that whether a particular strengthening of civil society is seen as good or bad depends on the observer's value orientations.

In important parts of the NGO world the term has signified progressive, positive, unified, democratic ideas and interests. There are many examples showing that strengthening NGOs has weakened civil society. The special character of international NGOs and the international NGO channel and its resource transfers, may create artificial organizations or fundamentally affect the balance between internal forces in the society unintentionally (see Tvedt, 1994b). Stronger NGOs may have emerged not as a result of a stronger civil society, but because of the vacuum left by a weaker rolled-back state and the funds provided by stronger external donor states.

The strength of the new paradigm and the weakness (if not the demise) of alternative development thinking have created a situation where the former's slogans have conquered the NGO world. But how useful is this term in parts of Africa, or in Afghanistan or Bombay or Calcutta? Is it fruitful in Zimbabwe and Liberia, but not in the Sudan or Rwanda? And what is the actual impact of the international and local NGOs on particular state-society relations? To what extent will the NGO channel's character as an international social system affect civil society in different countries? Research on what NGOs have actually achieved, how they have functioned and how they have affected developments in the developing countries has been very scarce indeed, not least because the field has been so cluttered with ideologies ever since it emerged as a force at the beginning of the 1980s.

A state-centred theory

A very different theory from that of the new paradigm, a state-centred theory, will be presented below. This is done not to present an alternative strategy, but as a way of getting a clearer understanding of the ideological character of the new paradigm. According to this perspective, the main problem in developing countries in general is weak states rather than weak societies, in other words, the emergence of stronger states is a precondition for functioning civil societies. This means that state-centred theories may well agree with Fukuyama about the directional, universal trend of history and its end station, but underline that at certain stages in this development strong states are necessary (and thus disagree with the new development paradigm) to bring societies on to the universal path.

The image of the strong state in developing countries is a fundamental premise for the new development paradigm in aid. The idea in large part derives, to the extent that it is based on empirical observation, from the rapid expansion of the state organization in Latin America, Asia, and Africa during the past generation. In this period, leaders in many countries set out to build a nation state by trying to offer viable strategies to the populace at large and win people and ethnic groups over to the state's rules.[7] The state-building elite in some places took over the colonial administrative system, enlarged it and built up impressive military power. One should not, however, equate a growing state apparatus and ability to get rid of opposition with state predominance or state power.[9] This type of politics has been characterized as patron-client politics, which has had devastating effects on institution-building. Since most theories agree that institutions are a key to increased political participation, it is a problem that many countries, especially in sub-Saharan Africa, have relatively few effective institutional linkages between rural, low-income farmers and the city elite. Another school of thought has argued that the elite is unable to construct institutional arrangements that can induce support and reinforce rational behaviour, and that it is this inability that has led to authoritarian politics, which Organsky (1965) has called 'syncratic politics'. This policy is seen as counterproductive in strengthening the state, creating development or building up the society. The new paradigm has not seriously addressed an alternative image, especially relevant in Africa: that of vanishing structures of statehood. Some have virtually collapsed, while others are mutating into local power centres.

As there are different notions of civil society and its potential role, there are, of course, also different ideas about how to define a state and the role of states. The new paradigm, as a development strategy, is basically a product of recent ideological trends and experiences in Western welfare states. There the history of state-society relations has in important respects taken on a different aspect from that in many (far from all) developing countries. Not least, the omnipresence of a strong state is much more visible and real than in large parts of the so-called developing world, especially in some of the countries where Western donors support NGOs. Simply to aim at repeating the sequence of, or at copying the relationship between, state and society in the West may be counterproductive, or it may be conducive to development. It is difficult to tell in advance, but in general NGOs will have to learn how to develop new combinations of policies from a detailed analysis of the many facets of European experience and experience in the developing countries.

State-centred theories will emphasize that most states in, for example, sub-Saharan Africa are still in the state-building phase. This is based on the argument that a main problem in securing development and democracy in the long run is that states manage to take control. Where states are at loggerheads with ethnic groups, kinships, particularistically oriented organizations, strong men or localized sentiments, neither living standards nor civil society can improve in the long run.

States differ, as do, of course, NGOs and third sectors or civil societies. They represent different elite interests and economic and political interests. This perspective is, however, less interested in the character of the state or the question of the autonomy of the state, than in the strength of the state, seen as a continuum in which states vary in their ability to enforce the rules of the game. States' social control has been described as the 'ability to appropriate resources for particular purposes and to regulate people's daily behaviour' ((Migdal, 1988:261). Without a tremendous concentration of social control, strong states cannot develop, Migdal argues. The following is a brief summary of his theory.

Migdal argues that the rapid extension of the world market from the late 1850s to the end of World War I led to a fundamental penetration of the world economy into all parts of society, This eroded existing foundations of social control. Migdal says that several factors worked against the creation of conditions for the emergence of strong states in the non–European world.[9] In Latin America and in societies that escaped formal colonial rule altogether, the alliance of European merchants and indigenous strong men limited the ability of state leaders to concentrate social control. Key players in the expanding world economy channelled resources into societies selectively, allowing for the strengthening of 'caciques, effendis, caudillos, landlords, kulak-type rich peasants, moneylenders', and others. By means of credit, access to land and water, protection, bullying, and numerous other means, strong men were able to hinder efficient state control across societies, and the existing survival strategies were able to be maintained. British colonial policies favoured in many places the emergence of new or renewed strong men, and often led to the re-establishment of fragmented control. State rulers have thereafter faced the legacy of such fragmented social control which has continued to constrain state-building efforts. Once established, Migdal argues, 'a fragmented distribution of social control has been difficult to transform. State leaders could not easily dismiss conflicting sets of rules in society. Their central problem has been in political mobilization of the population' (Migdal, 1988:263).

States and strong men

The effects of society on the state – that is, 'the impact of fragmented social control and the consequent ruler's dilemma on political style and state preferences in distributing resources have been monumental' (Migdal, 1988:264). Fragmentation of social control and the difficulties in political mobilization have led to a pathological style at 'the apex of the state'. It is this feature that has led to 'the politics of survival' characterizing many elite groups in societies with weak states (ibid.). Leaders in such states have destroyed the very apparatus of the state that could have achieved the goal of mobilization. They have used a variety of techniques to deal with major power centres in society, including co-optation and allocation of huge amounts of state resources to such centres.

At times state leaders have allowed power centres to grow, inside or outside the state organization, because they have felt they could not do without the services these centres provide (for example, as Migdal mentions, security and wealth from industrial production, or, in our context, strong NGOs providing necessary services). The risks to the leaders have not been reduced, however, since allowing them to grow may, in the case of NGOs, imply furnishing others with a political platform. Such centres outside the state may and often do, supply more highly valued services than does the state. The dilemma of the state leaders thus remains, resulting in vacillation and unpredictability in state policy toward powerful agencies and organizations inside and outside the state. State leaders have accommodated power centres, but they have also developed trade-offs with less powerful strong men. In exchange for resources and minimal interference, strong men have ensured a 'modicum of social stability'. The strong men of the NGO world do not depend on state resources, since they usually get funds from abroad. Due to the character of the resource transfer, they are not obliged to accommodate state leaders (although they often do), and due to their level of activities and support (from foreign donors, embassies, the UN system and the local people) they can capture lower levels of the state. Most NGOs do not have enough power to represent a serious form of fragmented social control. But as a group – or better, when conceived as the collective agent for the new paradigm – they often possess such power, which might make the strengthening of state power difficult, especially in societies where the state is not able, in spite of its apparent omnipresence, to make operative rules of the game for people in the society.

NGOs and the 'clash of civilizations'

Most observers agree that world politics has entered a new stage since 1989. The visions of this phase are described as representing 'the end of history', the return of rivalries between nation states, or the revival of ethnic chauvinism and conflict. These visions will all have an impact on the NGO channel and on how the potential role of NGOs is understood. We briefly discussed above the implications of what its propagandists call the 'New Development Paradigm' for NGO policy and for the discourse on NGOs internationally. Below a very different theory will be presented, which will divert attention away from the state–society dichotomy, and the role of NGOs in redefining the role of the state, to culture and religion, where NGOs will be regarded as players or instruments in a conflict between civilizations.

This perspective was most clearly put forward in an article by Samuel Huntington in *Foreign Affairs*, in 1993. Whether his theory is useful or dangerous is not discussed here. The point is that the theory has been presented and therefore forms part of the context in which NGO policies are formulated. In the United States some influential people in the Christian Right movement have suggested that development aid should be an instrument in the fight against Islam. In Islamic countries many politicians and religious intellectuals have already assessed Western development aid in this perspective, no matter what the intentions of the donors or NGOs have been. Huntington argues that the clash of civilizations will come to dominate global politics, and therefore that the 'fault lines between civilisations will be the battle lines of the future' (Huntington, 1993: 22). He refutes the idea of a universal history, and argues that, instead of creating homogenization, economic integration processes enhance the consciousness of civilization. The unsecularization of the world, or the revival of religion, will provide the basis for this identity. The phrase 'the world community' glosses over this development, and is, according to Huntington, nothing other than the 'euphemistic collective noun (replacing the 'Free World') to give global legitimacy to actions reflecting the interests of the United States and other Western powers' (ibid.: 39). He argues against V.S.Naipaul, who has said that Western civilization is the 'universal' civilization that 'fits all men', by saying that Western cultural influence has permeated at a superficial level only, and that Western concepts 'differ fundamentally from those prevalent in other civilizations' (ibid.: 40). He lists seven to eight civilizations, but argues that the main conflict will be between the West and the Islamic civilization – as in the centuries before the emergence of the Cold War. Huntington can be criticized on many grounds. His definition of civilizations is essentialistic and to a certain extent ahistorical; his conclusion about the cultural consequences of economic integration can easily be disproved, his ideas about what constitutes 'the West' and 'the Islamic civilization' appear both one-sided and superficial. None the less, he has focused on a conflict which many people think is very important, and which will, no matter how scientifically useful the perspective is, influence the NGO arena for decades to come. Contrasted with the dogmas and myths that are being produced and reproduced continuously within the NGO channel about civil society and the role of NGOs, it may help to stimulate more rational and empirical analyses of NGO–state relations.

A donor state's NGO policy

Although the fundamental terms in NGO-speak have been common for the whole channel, it is thought useful to study the formulation of an NGO policy in detail in order to grasp how the state-NGO relationship has been concretely conceptualized and organized . The focus here will be on how the Norwegian Government has described these relations and what the government has advocated regarding this question in developing countries. Has the policy copied the Scandinavian model? To what extent has it reflected national political traditions? How has the role of NGOs in furthering democracy been conceptualized? It should be noted at the outset that none of the reports studied discussed the issue of civilizations. Such entities and such concepts were simply not included in Norwegian images of the developing world (see Tvedt 1990 and 1993). This analysis will be compared with NGO-state relations in Norway. The following is based on an analysis of the text of all Reports to the Storting about aid and NGOs from 1962 to 1992, as well as a reconstruction of the policy line inherent in NORAD guidelines for support to NGOs from 1962 to 1994.

The Storting debated support to Norwegian NGOs for the first time in 1962. Nobody talked then about a separate channel or the need to create separate public institutions to administer it. Norsk Utviklingshjelp, NORAD's forerunner, was at that time given a modest task: 'to establish contact and joint consultations between institutions, organizations and private persons in the field' (quoted in Tvedt, 1992:24). Co-ordination was regarded as neither necessary nor useful, since only a handful of organizations were seen at that time as potential actors. They were invited into the channel primarily to act as a force which could root the new development aid project in the Norwegian population and turn it into a national task. The first political-administrative guidelines for NGO support were finalized by Norsk Utviklingshjelp in August 1962. Change in political attitudes and the growth of the NGOs made it necessary for the state repeatedly to adapt the guidelines to new organizational circumstances. The political breakthrough for the NGO channel came with Report to the Storting No. 36 (1984–5), presented by the Christian-Conservative coalition government and the newly established Ministry of Development Co-operation. In this report support to NGOs was given a separate chapter, and their role and potential in development aid were described in very positive words. This report will be focused on here, partly because of its importance in the history of NGO development in Norway, and partly because it shows how this policy departed from what had been a traditional view of NGO-state relations in Norway and how different it was from the set-up of the Norwegian NGO channel.

NGOs and democracy in developing countries

The report put great emphasis on the role of organizations in creating democracy and economic development: Through the organization of small groups, society would be democratized, and their mobilization was described as a prerequisite for a sound and self-sustaining process of development. The state was necessary, but had to be pressured to implement good policies. Popular participation through the support of NGOs was, therefore, perceived as something more than just a method for the implementation of a project, although it represented that as well: it was underlined that the government would give priority to popular participation in development work and would choose 'forms of aid and implementing agencies that are' in accordance with this aim (Report to the Storting No. 36: 34). In addition, this aim was described as a main strategy for the furtherance of democratic development. It was by organizing such groups that internal structural changes could take place. The strategy was formulated as a general rule: 'If the groups organize in work for their rights, this will be an element of democratization in the internal affairs of a country' (ibid.:23).

This conceived role of organizations in furthering democracy was no copy of the plan for parliamentary, representative democracy in Norway, or of the Scandinavian model of closeness between state and organizations. The history of democracy in Norway was basically a struggle for participation in the governing of the state, and has been closely connected to the process of nation-building and the entry of the various classes to the national political arena. As a result, democracy has been associated with forms of central government, and its development with the citizens' struggle for the democratic right of influencing the state's decisions through negotiations inside and outside Parliament.

The Report's approach to democracy in developing countries was of a very different character. It was not concerned with state formations or national assemblies. This does not imply that it was unaffected by European experiences. The strategy's perception of democracy was in many ways similar to a pluralist participatory model, a doctrine tightly connected to the expansion of the industrial state in the early twentieth century. The demand for participation was a reaction to the increased power and presence of the state, and the aim was to defend various interest groups in society from the excessive use of that power. The underlying ideology was based on a belief that the groups were inherently representative, as opposed to the nature of the state. The model was to be applicable to organization-building and democracy-promotion in rural Africa where the state is often non-existent or very weak, although it was developed in Europe as a response to industrialization and a strong state. The Report did not discuss whether there was a material, political or cultural basis for its strategy of democratization.

Political institutions are not mere reflections of socio-economic conditions. However, experience indicates that in order to play a role in society in the long run, organizations must have some connection with the articulation of economic, political and social interests in the society itself. The question is whether the organizations that were mentioned as collaborating partners in this model of participation – 'agrarian- and fishery co-operatives, community councils, trade and enterprise organizations, womens' organizations, religious-, social- and human rights movements, etc.' (ibid.: 89) – had the necessary local basis, considering that they were usually established and/or kept alive by the financial and political support of the development aid organizations.

The target-oriented basic needs strategy, in its Norwegian version, assumed that the poor and the women in rural areas would establish not only social groups but formal groups of organized interests. Indirectly, it presupposed that the groups aimed at were participants in a conflict that more or less constituted not only the social system and the societal order, but also the groups' social and political consciousness. The strategy related to a different reality from that under which many of the targeted groups lived. Such groups do not primarily show affection to a social category, and they do not act as one either. The strategy did not reflect on the difference between organizing people whose primary solidarity is religion, ethnicity, or kinship and organizing those who have developed a consciousness about more universal social or economic interests.

The Report was uncritical of what were called 'popular organizations'. It did not distinguish between various phases of organizational development, such as mobilization, bureaucratization and demobilization. Since aid is a kind of gift economy, it manipulates local elite formations by projects and financial allocations. New elites emerge through these organizations on the basis of their control over the resources disbursed.

The NGO role and implicit images of developing countries

The principle of state sovereignty over competing domestic institutions, which emerged in European state theory and political practice in the eighteenth century, is not universally accepted. In many developing countries there is no consensus on what constitutes the national arena where political conflicts concerning state hegemony can take place. Influential groups in society may not only question a particular government's right to govern. They may also question the legitimacy of any government to rule, since the state formation itself is regarded as illegal or as an artificial construction. Implicitly the Storting Report presupposed that there is a state on which to make demands. But many states still fight to justify their supremacy over other institutions – especially ethnic groups and religious societies.

The model of participation in the Report did not limit itself to furtherance of the ideal of a balance between state and society through the modification of the state's power. 'Local participation', 'popular participation' and 'active mobilization' were presented as means for the establishment of counter-power for the 'furtherance of political and social demands'(Storting Report No 36: 89), to 'disclose decisions that compromise the interests of the poor', and to strengthen their 'ability to further their interests' (ibid.). Hence, the objective was counter-power against the elite and the state bureaucracy. Popular participation was not conceived of as being against the state as such, nor was it seen as historical stages in a process of national integration and consolidation. In the Report the 'people' was an entity with interests contrary to those of the existing states, and the organizations were inherently opposed to the existing state authorities. The popular organizations were also collectors of deviating attitudes and actions in relation to the state. The importance of creating national consensus concerning the basic rules of the game and its boundaries receded into the background, compared with the conflict and counter-power perspective. The Report emphasised popular participation rather than bureaucratic professionalization. There is no trace of the Weberian admiration for the national and state bureaucracies as institutions that can and should educate the self-interested people in 'moral behaviour' and act as potential negotiators and mediators between conflicting interests.

It was not a priority objective in the Report to support the development of representative parliamentarian democracy. On the contrary, it encouraged neglect of national assemblies and governments since this facilitated direct co-operation with organized interests. Thus organizations in society may be strengthened at the expense of representative democracy at the state level. As a general model, this vision of

democracy is incompatible with parliamentarianism, which is indirect and representative. The perspective in the strategy was, of course, not against parliamentarianism, but the difficult and important relation between direct and indirect
democracy was represented in such a way as to make direct democracy the most
important method to democraticize society. It was primary democracy, and not
committee democracy or representative democracy that at this time was presented as
the Norwegian state's ideal for developing countries.

The strategy disregarded the problem of accountability. It is generally acknowledged that a main problem in the democratic evolution of many developing countries
is to establish a political-administrative system and a political culture that make the
bureaucracy and administration accountable to the people. The direct co-operation
between the aid organizations and local NGOs will easily create structures that are
characterized by lack of accountability. This collaboration between aid experts and
bureaucrats that report to another country and local interest groups will make it
difficult to establish the accountability of various actors in policy articulation and
formation. The Report adopted a policy in which formal responsibility might deviate
radically from factual responsibility. The model did not consider that experts may
stand on the outside of the formal government of the state, but at the same time
govern.

Compared with international trends, Report to the Storting No. 51 (1991–2)
paid much more attention to support of the state and state institutions. This was
partly a reflection of research and debates in Norway since 1989. Only three and a
half pages in a document of 279 pages dealt specifically with NGO support, although
the channel was responsible for more than 25 per cent of Norwegian bilateral aid. In
many ways the Report represented a shift in orientation and emphasis in a more
'state-friendly' direction, apparently becoming closer to the ideology of the Scandinavian model. On the other hand, it argued that a challenge for the 1990s would be
to handle the ongoing redistribution of tasks between the public and the private
sectors. The government declared that, in this situation, the 'NGOs may enter an
even more important role' (Report to the Storting No. 51: 235). At the same time it
was of great importance for this new role to be 'integrated into the authorities'
administration'. The organizations in the co-operating countries are described as
'channels for support to increased pluralism, strengthened democracy and the defence
of human rights'. It was underlined that 'local and regional organizations will be
central in this respect'.

The Report further stated that the government wished 'to underline the important and positive role' played by Norwegian NGOs in Norwegian aid, and that it
would uphold 'an orderly and close relationship' with them. Co-operation with the
NGOs 'must build on their popular and voluntary character, at the same time as
their integrity and peculiarity must be respected'. The 'complementary' role that
NGOs could play in relation to state-to-state and multilateral aid was emphasized.
The Report also stressed that the competence requirements expected of Norwegian
aid in general should apply to the NGOs as well.

The work of the NGOs it was said, should be related to the total Norwegian aid
'to a singular country or a single region'. It was underlined as 'desirable' that it
should be aimed at 'priority groups and sectors' in the overall Norwegian aid
strategy. The government also welcomed the organizations as a 'more active part of

the Norwegian aid co-operation, and that the NGOs should be a part of the dialogue in the planning and follow-up of Norwegian aid'. The NGOs role as what were called 'listening posts' (this has nothing to do with espionage, the term notwithstanding). The word describes the NGOs' potential role as organizations that can inform the Norwegian public about living conditions in the South) was described as 'particularly valuable' when it comes to imparting knowledge, and in the promotion of positive attitudes among the Norwegian public concerning Norwegian development aid. The Report gave the organizations considerable credit for the fact that a large majority of Norwegians have a positive attitude to aid (ibid.:236). Their 'considerable experience' was also underlined, and the government invited them to put more emphasis on the transfer of experience and knowledge, and to get involved in co-operation with each other.

NGOs also represented another type of channel for state money, because of their 'well-developed network in important disaster- and conflict-ridden areas'. The government underlined that it saw as positive the fact that several organizations were 'developing strategies that entail a more integrated view of the two kinds of aid', because this would 'contribute in securing that acute emergency efforts are followed up by long-term development programmes, intended to prevent new catastrophes' (ibid.:239). The Norwegian NGOs were clearly not seen as adversaries in a zero-sum game, but as useful instruments in the donor state's policy, under-lining the need for 'complementarity' in aid efforts (ibid.: 235–6).

Implicitly the Report distanced itself from the new policy paradigm, although it had taken some crucial terms from it. Explicitly it rejected the general 'assault on the state' by focusing on the need for state building in developing countries, while at the same time employing a political language that borrowed some fundamental concepts advanced by the new paradigm. It underlinesd the importance of assessing the character of organizations. It argued that a 'rise in the tendency among the people to organize within society is a prerequisite for the evolution and consolidation of a democratic system. The indigenous NGOs in developing countries are particularly important in this respect.' But efforts should be geared towards 'strengthening a broad popular organizational activity' and support to NGOs was to be given 'on condition that the organizations have a broad and solid basis in the population'. The trade-union movement was described as particularly important in 'defending human rights and in the development of democracy'. The development of NGOs would happen 'through a process that emerges from 'below', i.e. through the population itself'. However, it was most 'important that the authorities in developing countries stimulate this process. Not only must the freedom of opinion and expression, and the freedom to organize, be secured, but the public administration must develop a system that incorporates properly the opinions of the organizations in civil society' (ibid.: 216).

On the other hand, the Norwegian Government underlined the importance of the state in the recipient countries. Relations with the recipient government 'are essential in any kind of development effort', and it 'has been an important principle for Norwegian aid that it shall be recipient-oriented. This means that such aid shall be included in the recipient country's plans and priorities' (this is historically questionable, but it underlines the change of direction). The Report criticized the fact that 'donors have in many cases started to operate alongside the national administration', because it is important that the countries themselves 'take responsi-bility for their own development, both when it comes to planning and implementa-tion. An integration of development efforts in the countries' own plans is the only way to secure that the recipient countries' authorities obtain control over their own development, and that they take responsibility for the choices that they make' (ibid.: 220–1).

Report to the Storting No. 51 distanced itself from the dichotomous perspective inherent in the new paradigm and underlined the importance of strengthening the state and the state's responsibility in strengthening the organizations in a society. The Report had few linkages to the zero-sum perspective inherent in the paradigm. The NGOs were described, not as the saviours or as a leading force in an associa-tional revolution, but as important actors within a country strategy formulated by the recipient government. At the same time a number of positive and general characteristics were attributed to them as if they, as a group, had important compara-tive advantages over other sectors or institutions in society.

The principle of 'recipient responsibility' for planning and implementation of development projects and initiatives should be gradually implemented. The Report argued in support of using the expertise and competence of the Norwegian NGOs in emergency situations, in disaster work and as channels for support to human rights issues and democratization. It did not discuss the possibilities of using local NGOs in this, or whether it is possible to find a balance between government and NGOs in recipient countries for such work. The Report did not consider the role of the NGOs as foreign policy actors in conflict situations, or the extent to which NGO actors should become involved in complicated foreign policy issues, nor whether important foreign policy issues, (perhaps not important to Norwegian public opinion, but important in the countries where Norwegian actors intervene) should be 'privatized' in a way which makes constitutional control less easy.

The aim of the above analysis has not been simply to put forward a critique of Norwegian policy. That policy is most probably no worse or better than other governments' policies in this respect. Rather, the analysis has shown how the NGO policy has been neither a conscious and consistent reflection of Norwegian historical experience, nor a policy based on factual experience in the developing countries. The content of the shifting policies should instead be interpreted as a reflection of how a donor country and a donor community, strongly influenced by international trends, conceptualize the world and what their notions of development, state and society are at a particular point in time. Since NGO language is so loaded with meaning about important questions like 'society', 'state', 'democracy' and 'develop-ment', parliamentary debates in Norway, as a small donor country with up to now relatively few strategic interests in this kind of aid, are more interesting as a mirror of donor communities' and politicians' way of thinking and their ideological history, than as a source of knowledge about the developing world. The policy has not given support to the new development paradigm, it has neither been concerned with building stronger states, nor has it ever discussed aid as an instrument in struggles or clashes between cultures or civilizations. The policy has been general and vague, very positive to NGOs, and has thus given the Norwegian NGO system (both NORAD and the NGOs) great freedom in pursuing their aims.

A case study:
Government and NGOs in a 'tug of war' in Bangladesh

To show how the impact and role of the NGO channel may be analysed in different contexts and how the state–NGO relationship has developed in different countries, two cases will be discussed in more detail. First, a study of the Bangladeshi NGO scene may demonstrate aspects of the NGOs' role in furthering pluralism and democracy, and also the relationship between NGOs and the state and how a civilization perspective influences attitudes to their work.

The relationship between the government of Bangladesh and the NGOs has often been uneasy. This study, which concentrates on the 'tug of war' in 1992, may be instructive in showing how these relations can be apprehended. The arguments are, of course, peculiar to Bangladesh, but the case contains issues and problems which are relevant for the NGO channel as an international system. NGOs in Bangladesh have played an important role in certain sectors such as education and rural credit, and have obtained quite a visible role in public life. They are a force here to a larger extent than in many other countries. It is therefore natural that their role is attracting public interest, which is also aroused because the majority of them are receiving funds from non-Islamic countries.

The NGO community developed into a comparatively strong social and political force during the 1980s. In Bangladesh the growth in the number of NGOs receiving foreign funding has been tremendous. The number of national NGOs increased by 1,040 per cent during the NGO decade, while international NGOs increased by 60 per cent. In 1981 there were 68 foreign NGOs registered, while in 1991 there were 109. In the same period the number of national NGOs supported by foreign funds increased from 45 to 513. The proportion of total foreign aid channelled through NGOs was about 1 per cent in 1972–3 (Abed *et al.*, 1984, quoted in Aminuzzaman, 1993). By the end of the fiscal year 1986–7 this had increased to 17.6 per cent (Alam 1988),[10] (from US$ 5m in 1972–3 to US$ 339m in 1986 (Aminuzzaman, 1993: 5). The number of projects undertaken by the registered NGOs rose from 162 in 1988–9 to 610 in 1991–2. Over 600 NGOs are now said to be supported by foreign funds, and not only from Western countries. Many Islamic NGOs have a direct liaison with Jamat-e-Islami, an Islamic fundamentalist party. One NGO, Rabeta Al-Alam Al-Islami, has its headquarters in Mecca and many of its top leaders in Bangladesh belong to the Islamic fundamentalist party.

The NGOs' importance has made it natural that they have also become an issue of public debate. One starting point for this short analysis is an interview published in *Courier*, 11–17 May 1990 with Mohammad Asafuddowlah, the then Secretary of the Ministry of Social Welfare in which he talked about the relationship between government and NGOs. 'There must be some motives behind offering such aid and in my opinion they are not always honest.' He said the people in Bangladesh would not give up their culture and religion, and he argued that 'some beliefs are purchased with money', thinking of the mission organizations in particular. 'Sale of religion is not social services, and conversion to another religion should not be a precondition to having social services. This sort of mentality has to be abandoned.' He also argued that when NGOs 'start accumulating wealth through their own projects then they are no different from multinational companies'. And what is the guarantee that the money generated by the project will be distributed among the distressed? Who will supervise it? Such NGOs should instead be registered by 'the Registrar of the Joint Stock Companies'. And he continued: 'Why should the laws be relaxed for the foreigners who work here? When the new ordinance will be introduced there will not be any confusion regarding this. The foreign organizations will have to work according to that law.' This interview mirrored opinion in important government circles.

The same year the NGO Affairs Bureau was established by the government. The NGOs immediately showed resentment, especially some of the big leading NGOs. The Bureau was criticized for delaying project approvals and for exercising control over NGO activities. The Bureau, on the other hand, alleged that NGOs had mushroomed during the Ershad regime, when, according to the new government, large-scale corruption and favouritism were the order of the day. This had made it possible for NGOs to work without any control from the authorities at the same time as they channelled enormous foreign funds. Some of the NGOs were blamed for being for-profit businesses and for being engaged in various forms of subversive activity.[11]

Open conflict between NGOs and the NGO Affairs Bureau

In July 1992 the conflict came into the open. The relationship between NGOs and the NGO Affairs Bureau had continuously deteriorated. ADAB, the NGO umbrella organization, submitted a memorandum to the Prime Minister's office with complaints against the Bureau, urging the office to facilitate NGO activities. It also urged the simplification of procedures for project approval, permission for the release of funds, renewal of registration, etc. The Prime Minister's office had also received written complaints against the Bureau from the US Ambassador.

These complaints prompted the Prime Minister to call for a report from the Bureau. The report, *NGOs Activities in Bangladesh*, alleged that the NGOs had received around Taka 1800 crore in the previous two years, 60 per cent of which was used for staff salaries and administrative costs. It recommended an evaluation of how the rest of the foreign assistance was used, and also mentioned that NGOs show unconditional loyalty and subjugation to the donor agencies. NGOs were said to make political statements from time to time, participate in local elections, publish news magazines with political propaganda, and carry out religious activities and proselytization by taking advantage of the illiterate and poor people. In addition they were said to be involved in embezzlement, irregularities, corruption and anti-state activities. In the absence of representative government during the previous regime, no action had been taken against their activities. As a result they raised huge sums in donations from the rich Western countries by exhibiting a poverty-stricken image of Bangladesh. The money thus collected was said to be used for luxury cars and lifestyles, fat salaries, wealth accumulation and at the instigation of foreign 'lords', the NGOs were said to be even engaged in politics (BK: 29 July 1992, DC: 14 August 1992, see note 11 for explanations of the acronyms).

The report contained allegations against 46 NGOs of receiving Taka 138 crore from foreign countries in the period 1988–91 without the approval of the government, and of spending it as they wished. Among them were BRAC, PROSHIKA, CARITAS and many others. The immediate action of the government in response to the report was to cancel ADAB's registration of foreign donations. It was not allowed to spend foreign assistance without prior government approval, or to engage in political activities. The government also cancelled the registration and operating licence of another NGO – the Society for Economic and Basic Advancement (SEBA). Further, a list of 52 NGOs alleged to be engaged in missionary work, especially in proselytization, was published. The Bureau also opened court cases against seven NGOs, and the Metropolitan Magistrate of Dhaka issued arrest warrants against three foreign nationals.

With 600 NGOs as members, ADAB was described as being 'beyond Government control' and 'NGOs defeating the Bureau?' (DC 28 August 1992). The article referred to ADAB's intimate relationship with big Western donor agencies, which also played a crucial role in pressurizing the government to withdraw its cancellation order of ADAB. Diplomats and aid officials from Western countries met the Prime Minister several times and complained that the Bureau was unnecessarily interfering in the activities of NGOs and obstructing their work. The charges against the NGO employees were withdrawn under the directions of the Prime Minister's office. Immediately afterwards, the Director-General of the NGO Affairs Bureau was placed under order of transfer while he was away on a foreign tour.

The Bureau also drew up some recommendations with the declared aim of making the NGOs more accountable to the government. These included: a) supervision of NGO activities by elected representatives of an area; b) the formation of a committee or a commission at the highest level to which the NGOs would be accountable; c) ensuring the application of legislation for regulating NGO activities; d) formulating laws to ensure punishment of defaulting NGOs; e) working out a salary structure for NGO employees; and f) ensuring that appointments of NGO personnel were made on the basis of competition. However, it was not yet made clear whether the government would go in for a new regulatory system for the NGOs (DC: 14 August 1992). The measures proposed were less relaxed, and the proposal to administer NGO activities at district level by the district administration was turned down. The suggestion of fixing the salaries of NGO executives at a maximum of Taka 20,000 and of limiting the number of foreign experts to ten in each NGO were, according to a left-wing newspaper (AK: 27 July 19.92), 'undermined'.

Most of the articles written on NGOs in 1992 in different newspapers, irrespective of their political colours, were negative in their attitude. The government was shown as an innocent victim of corrupt NGOs, which were generally accused of misappropriation of funds, administrative irregularities and anti-state activities. In September 1992 one of the NORAD-supported NGOs, Saptagram, was accused in the *Daily Sangram*, the organ of the Jamat Islami Party, of

carrying out persistent and systematic propaganda against the cultural and religious values of the people of Bangladesh ... They are also bringing in huge amounts of money from foreign sources and pocketing most of the finance ... Saptagram ... in the name of development is carrying on systematic propaganda among the poor women that purdah is standing in the way of their development. Through this propaganda they are bringing the women out of the house and encouraging them to become loose characters ... They are destroying and breaking down the discipline of family life. The lady who is the Project Director smokes cigarettes publicly...' (DS 2 September 1992)

The NGO responded critically to both the press articles and the Bureau's version of its work, and denied that its view of the government was that assigned to it. A common criticism levelled against government organizations was that they were not sensitive to local problems. An NGO source stated that the bureaucrats loved 'issuing edicts without a sense of urgency or a positive direction' and that 'approval of projects and registration are not given within the stipulated time, which is detrimental to programmes. The donor communities are backing out of their commitments and transferring their attention to other countries' (the *New Nation*: 19 November 92). Some NGO actors described the government as an authoritative, inefficient and reluctant partner, and stated that the NGOs emerged in the vacuum 'created as a result of an awful loss of sense of direction in the government' (DC: 20 August 1993). The government was considered inefficient and sloppy, while, for example, the Grameen Bank had come to be accepted as a model 'both at home and abroad' and BRAC's non-formal primary education project had recently attracted international attention (ibid.).

The media discussed the power relationship between the government and NGOs. In one article it was argued:

They [NGOs] have monstrous power. They are rich, have a huge network throughout the countryside and are not accountable to anybody. If this continues, they will be the main source of state power (K: 31 August 1992) .

The leader of BRAC replied:

NGOs are not an alternative government. NGOs work to complement the role of government. We are not thinking to become an alternative government. We are co-operating with government in its effort to alleviate poverty among the rural landless class. When everyone will be employed and become educated, the role of NGOs will come to cease (DB: 3 September 1992).

NGOs as Western agents

Two main arguments were used against NGOs in this context. First, they were held to be agents of imperialism, and secondly, they were said to be involved in proselytization of the poor to Christianity. The NGOs were proselytizing the poor to Christianity in the name of welfare services, the Islamic fundamentalist *Dainik Millat* argued (12 August 1992). Others argued that the NGOs were only imple-menting official government policy: developing systems and institutional structures for creating a sustainable health-care system at the community level through people's participation, and the delivery of those family planning and contraceptive services which had been approved by the government, measures which would improve the situation for women and then erode the power of the Islamists (TDS: 11 February 1993). Islamic forces also propagandized that, like the East India Company, the NGOs with foreign blessing were conspiring to occupy Bangladesh. BRAC was singled out for attack (in 1994 some of its schools were burnt down by Islamic fundamentalists): 'BRAC is now operating in 24 Zillas. BRAC, by purchasing land and constructing buildings in 24 Zillas, is establishing forts like the East India Company' (DM: 27 July 1992).

In aid politics Scandinavians were described and considered as benevolent imperialists, who were in subtle conflict with the 'American imperialists'. American imperialism had an institutional character and was thereby able to support industries like the garment industry. Because Scandinavian imperialism emerged much later than American imperialism, it was bound to be of a non-institutional character, it was argued. Therefore, a pro-establishment newspaper wrote in August 1987, instead of investing in the garment industry, the Scandinavian imperialists were more interested in supporting NGOs. The Scandinavians helped poor women to produce traditional quilts and paid them Taka 10 as a wage, whereas the quilt was being sold at US$10, which could be considered a vicious cycle of profit-making (DS: 31 August 1987).

Immediate consequences

In reaction to the Bureau report, the NGOs submitted written protests and issued rejoinders claiming that their goal was the well-being of the poor and that their activities were in accordance with the law of the country. They denied the allegation that they had received foreign donations without the knowledge of the government, and that they were engaged in communal politics and proselytization. BRAC denied that its executive director received a fat salary, and that its commercial ventures were established to make profits. PROSHIKA denied that it owned a printing press and a video library.

The July 1992 crisis led to an uneasy atmosphere and the relevant actors searched for an outlet to mitigate and normalize the tense situation. The crisis helped the government to assess its own position and attitudes towards NGOs. It began to examine the efficacy of the existing laws governing NGOs and set up a cabinet sub-committee to work on the formulation of a consolidated law that would authorize the government to look into NGO affairs. It also made an attempt to normalize its strained relationship with NGOs on the issue of allegations of their involvement in the country's politics. In the presence of the US Ambassador, the Finance Minister M. Saifur Rahman stated, 'We welcome the good NGOs for development, progress and prosperity' (TDS:14 August 1992), the good NGOs being defined as those who strictly followed an accountable, transparent and development-oriented system for national progress and prosperity. Thus, 'we want real NGOs and we do not want NGO business' (ibid.). The government set up a meeting attended by high officials of the Bureau, representatives of the Prime Minister's office, and the Chairman, Vice-Chairman and other officials of the ADAB. At the same time, the Bureau approved 35 projects submitted by NGOs. After the meeting, a leader of the NGO community stated that the government's attitude 'toward the problems faced by the voluntary organizations was positive' (TDS: 9 September 1992).

The July 1992 events created opportunities for both the government and the NGOs to make efforts to recognize and understand each other's roles. The political left gradually lessened its criticism, and the Communist Party came up with support for NGOs. The conflict became a conflict focusing on questions of culture and religion (Islam against the West and Christianity, with the NGOs as spearheads of Western-ization) and of accountability (to whom are the NGOs accountable and how should NGOs and government relate to each other) and about modernity and justice.

The trend of attacking NGOs, particularly by Islamic forces, has, by 1995, not weakened, but rather increased. BRAC, as the largest organization, has become the target of these Islamic forces. It is described as a Christian organization involved in proselytizing the poor with the Christian faith, but also as an atheist organization. 'BRAC is introducing atheism in its Non-Formal Primary Education (NFPE) programme. The NFPE programme of BRAC through 100 schools is teaching against Allah and spoiling innocent children' (DI: 22 November 1993). The immediate reaction of BRAC was to issue statements in various local dailies denying such allegations.

In 1994 BRAC's NFPE programme came under severe attack from Islamic fundamentalists in the rural areas. As a result, scores of schools run under the NFPE programme were burned down and hundreds of mulberry trees planted along the roadsides were uprooted (BK: 16 January 1994).

The government-NGO issue is, of course, perennial. A public statement by the US Ambassador can illustrate this: 'Our experience is that NGOs work best, and serve the society, when they are controlled the least'. They should neither be 'beholden to' or 'antagonistic' to the government (TDS, 28 April 1993). The same newspaper, some days before, had carried as its front-page lead: 'New policy to control NGOs' (TDS, 17 April 1993). ADAB sent an 'Urgent Memorandum from the NGOs of Bangladesh in the context of the proposed Act (draft) and the new circular' (it was referring to a cabinet sub-committee headed by the Commerce Minister which had drafted the report entitled 'Bangladesh Voluntary Social Welfare Organizations (Registration and Control Act)' the same month, which began: 'Deregulation of overly bureaucratic control is accepted as a principal means of the democratization of society and to bring more efficiency and productivity and to lessen the opportunity for corruption'. It warned that the NGOs' work would be 'crippled' (p.3), and stated that they wanted firmly to be 'recognized as part of the private sector in development, in this case the non-profit sector', referring to the deregulation of businesses.

NGO, society and state in the Southern Sudan

The Southern Sudan provides a setting in which the concepts of state, pluralism, democracy, civil society and accountability can be usefully studied.

The 1980s in Africa have been called the NGO decade when the NGOs 'entered the limelight' (Bratton, 1989: 569). In the Southern Sudan NGOs came to play a very important role as early as the 1970s.[12] The enormous task of socio-economic reconstruction of the whole region after the first civil war (1955–72), the emergency assistance to more than half a million Sudanese returnees and later to about 200,000 Ugandan refugees fleeing to the Southern Sudan between 1979 and 1983, and a new, weak state administration without enough money, people or experience to carry out these tasks on its own, made the region a natural location for extensive NGO involvement.[13] In Juba alone there were 38 foreign aid organizations in 1985.

There is no doubt that many of the NGOs were quite efficient development agents. The Norwegian Church Aid's Sudan Programme, which will be focused on in this chapter, definitely helped to raise living standards in its programme area on the east bank of the Nile in Equatoria Province. The area covered 86,000 km² and had an estimated population of around 500,000, comprising about 20 ethnic groups, approximately 90 per cent of them small farmers. Norwegian Church Aid built a number of new roads in the area and organized repair and maintenance on others. It helped establish 15 dispensaries and 40 primary health-care stations. It constructed 30 primary and 6 secondary schools and 16 schools which it helped to initiate on a self-help basis. It drilled hundreds of wells and installed Indian Pump II. Through its active support, Torit District Co-operative Union was able to organize 139 co-operatives at village level. Broadly speaking; NCA was an efficient aid organization, primarily concerned with doing a good humanitarian job while trying to stay out of local and regional politics. However, in this chapter the NGOs will be evaluated not in terms of their ability to reach their target groups and deliver the goods, because such impact assessments are rather uninteresting if they are not analytically linked to long-term macro-issues. Here their impact will be analyzed in relation to the dissolution of state administrative functions and institutions in the Southern Sudan, and to the whole underlying question of social integration and particularism versus universalism, or the impact of NGO-particularism.

The state–civil society dichotomy in the Southern Sudan

The relationship between governments and NGOs involves a fundamental question of the legitimacy of various types of institution exercising power and authority. This study will argue that in the Southern Sudan, the NGOs unintentionally contributed to the erosion of the authority of a very weak state. They did not organize civil society against the state, or consciously promote and strengthen it, as the current rhetoric supposes. Basically, they themselves became local substitutes for state administration. They assumed in a very efficient manner the welfare functions of an ordinary state (see Tvedt, 1994a for an analysis of the history of the state administration in the Southern Sudan). As the state was 'withering away' (though not in the way Karl Marx described), whole districts or sections of ordinary government departments' responsibilities were handed over to the NGOs to run. They set up their own authority and administrative systems, undermining the state institutions without establishing viable alternative structures, partly because there simply was no familiar civil society in which to root them. Project proliferation therefore imposed potential long-term burdens on the state administration and state finances. The NGOs represented different types of organizational behaviour, bureaucratic system and development philosophy. Their practices therefore came to express institutional and ideological opposition to the idea of region-wide, rule-oriented and universalistic state administration and bureaucracy.

These points will be substantiated mainly by a more detailed description of the programme of the biggest NGO in the region, Norwegian Church Aid. In important respects NCA was more concerned about developing good relations with the state and its administrative structures than many other NGOs. It continually emphasized the need for discussion and formal agreements with the state authorities. It warned against the danger of establishing institutions that the government could not take over and stressed the necessity for local participation as a way of rooting the projects locally.[14] Other agencies were apparently less concerned about the long-term sustainability of their projects. Its particular role makes NCA especially interesting, and the extensive documentation of its project activities, combined with its open-door attitude to external researchers, makes its history accessible and possible to reconstruct.

Both in Juba and in the rural areas, there were occasional open tensions between the state administration, which was trying to exert administrative control of all the different NGOs, and the NGOs' defence of their autonomy. In the first years after the 1972 Addis Ababa Agreement regular monthly meetings with the NGOs were co-ordinated by the Regional Ministry of Finance and Planning (Norwegian Church Relief, Sudan Programme, 1975:31). But these meetings gradually developed into empty rituals; the government representatives were formally in charge, but their words carried less and less authority, and their combination of officialdom and lack of knowledge of what was going on in the rural communities irritated the action-orientated agencies. There were NGOs which did not bother to register with the host government. Many had formal agreements approved by the central or regional government (some donor countries like Norway made this a requirement for financial support), while others looked upon this as unnecessary red tape. What is more interesting than these formal questions, however, and what will have far-reaching consequences in a longer historical perspective, is the imprint of the existence of different forms of authority and different types of organization and bureaucracy on the society.

In certain areas, the NGOs had strong infrastructural power compared with the state. NCA's total activities on the east bank of the Nile for the years up to 1986, including refugee aid, came to about US$75m, almost US$20m more than the regional government invested in the whole region. In a land-locked economy, and in a society where there were no regular newspapers, one local radio-station which was on the air for only a few hours a day, no inter-regional mail or functioning telegraph system, the NGOs and their employees in important areas monopolized the distribution of both information and goods, thanks to their well-developed, communication networks and superior means of transport. When petrol became very scarce in the mid-1980s, the few government cars often had to be supplied with fuel begged or bought from the NGOs or the UN.

Hilieu, just outside Torit, was NCA's administrative centre. It had excellent secretarial services, radio communication with Khartoum, Nairobi and most of the east bank of the Nile, and functioning mail and flight services. (For comparison: the regional government in Juba sometimes lacked even a functioning photocopying machine.) It also had about 200 vehicles and no fuel shortages. Until the evacuation in January 1985, NCA had about 50-60 expatriate personnel; the expatriate colony in Hilieu, including family members, came to about 200 people.

In one of NCA's six district centres, the Arapi Rural Development Centre (RDC) in Loa district, there were between five and ten expatriate experts until 1985. The centre's two administrative buildings were much better maintained and equipped than any house owned by the government or any other person in the area, and it had radio links to both Juba and Hilieu, plenty of cars, fuel, a workshop, etc. The local government, consisting of a Head Chief with only a cashier and one typist secretary, was housed in an old building badly in need of repair; the Chief had a bicycle, and when he had to get in touch with the government in Juba he often cycled to NCA's centre to ask if he could use its radio. The infrastructural weakness of the Sudanese state would have been the same whether or not the NCA had been there, but the existence of this efficient and successful programme demonstrated the state's weakness to the people and thus eroded its legitimacy.

NCA had become not only a state within a state, but 'the state'. It not only delivered services, it could also respond to local requests, take sick people to hospital, etc. The government's ordinary administrative authority was more or less confined to the radius of the old Chief's bicycle. (The police, the military or the coercive power of the state were of course another matter. This aspect is not included in the analysis.)

This situation led to what can be described as a process of local brain drain. The NGOs had relatively minor staffing problems as compared with the state. They did not necessarily pay higher wages, but salaries were regularly paid and there were certain fringe benefits, such as access to cars, motor-bikes, etc. In addition, to work for an agency generally brought higher work satisfaction because the organization functioned properly. The number of local Sudanese staff varied, but for years it was more than 2,000 people, which made NCA the biggest employer on the east bank of the Nile. It had a management staff of about 90 persons on 1 October 1985 (Norwegian Church Aid, Sudan, 1985:36–7), of whom 70 were Sudanese.

The NGOs' strong position reflected the fact that they could supply something which was much needed and which nobody else, and especially not the state, could deliver – social services. The state administration had very little money for development or social services projects. According to Madison, the expenditure of the Regional Ministry of Agricultural and Natural Resources up to 1981–2 totalled around Sudanese £7m (Madison, 1984:148). The Regional Ministry of Communication, Transport and Roads had spent about S£2.5m on projects. It did not even manage to pay all of the recurrent expenditures for teacher salaries causing government schools to close down temporarily, while agency-supported schools continued to function.

One might say that the big NGOs and the Khartoum Government had one thing in common: through the power of their purse they held the Southern Sudanese government machinery hostage. Most government-financed projects in the South failed to be implemented. Many of them were big, well-known projects, but, as the government admitted in 1977, 'though the list of projects is impressive, in fact the majority of them were not implemented' (*Peace and Progress*, 1977:38).

The local government on the east bank of the Nile naturally did not pay much heed to collecting unpopular social service taxes, since these services were provided anyway. By easing this burden of government, the NGO at the same time further alienated the state from society, and reduced its potential role as a meeting point for the compartmentalized components of society. By establishing what can be described as competing tax systems (in order to mobilize what was commonly called a 'sense of responsibility' among the local people and to raise the level of 'popular participation', the NGOs demanded that the local people should cover the costs of pump repairs, stationery, etc., paying the agency or some local committee established by it), the 'extraction/accountability cycle' was affected. Most normal functions of government became the domain of NCA, as in other areas they had become the domain of other NGOs.

In comparison with both the government administration and the institutional and organizational features of the local societies in which they worked, the NGOs represented, and in many areas introduced, different organizational modes and cultural values. They were goal-oriented (and value-sharing) organizations, in principle organized on a temporary basis. In the context of the surrounding society they were *ad hoc* problem-solvers rather than rule-oriented bureaucracies. Furthermore, they operated within geographically limited areas with limited objectives, and therefore did not have to develop more general, universalistic types of organization adapted to different types of activity and culture.

A local government bureaucracy was anathema to the NGO sector, as it had been to the British colonialists some decades before, though for different reasons. The NGOs' relationship to the state administration was often based on individual and personal contacts. These were important when it came to speeding up the removal of official stumbling blocks hindering efficient project implementation. The NGO-government relationship was therefore also personalized, and not rule-based, in many ways identical to the clientelist system which had been developed within the state administration itself. Their relations with the recipient society contrasted with cultural attitudes within the beneficiary groups, and they also played by different rules from those assumed by Western bureaucratic culture. From their expatriate compounds the aid workers made development excursions into the surrounding society. A relationship was established which had no traits of that reciprocity which has been said to be typical of local socio-cultural relations.

As a rule the NGOs did not try to establish anti-state structures or organizations. There was no deliberate policy of strengthening such organizations to counterbalance the state. The civil organizations which were established, like women's groups, co-operative societies, etc. were in line with government policies and priorities. Their fundamental basis, however, was money supplied from foreign sources. The kind of development institutions which were established through popular participation therefore had difficulties in growing roots in the local soil or in breaking down ethnically divided polities. Little consideration was given to the problem of organizational sustainability in this context, independent of aid injections. The NGOs created bases for alternative entities, but entities that did not possess the universalistic outlook of a regional or provincial administration and which ultimately depended on external money to survive.

The way in which services were provided was perhaps equally important. For some of the NGOs, money was not the decisive constraint on the scope of their activities. What affected project size and project components was usually not the purse, but arguments about what was morally right and most conducive to local development. Generally the NGOs acted within a culture of absolute affluence, in which goods and services were not costed. When NCA now and then tried to counter this unsustainable economic culture, as when they in January 1986 informed the UNHCR that if it needed NCA lorries for transport, it would have to pay for them, this was met by strong objections from the aid community, who characterized it as greed, although the charge did not cover the costs involved. It was difficult to question the principle that aid was free and in some mysterious way outside the realm of economic realities and the emergence of governmental systems.

The NGOs could also decide what kind of exchange relations should be subject to negotiations among the people, the state and the NGO. When a specialized agency worked in an area (education or health, for example), it delivered its specialities. An organization geared towards aid for education or the disabled could not or would not respond to proposals which, seen from a local or government perspective, were more important to society as a whole. On the east bank of the Nile, it was really in the NCA development centres and ultimately in Hilieu that decisions were taken as to where to drill bore-holes, where to assist self-help schools, which agricultural produce should be supported in what areas, which Primary Societies should receive most support. Through its control of the Co-operative Union NCA also fixed the prices of crucial agricultural components like seeds and ox-ploughs. The local people influenced the decisions, as did the government, but at the end of the day NCA made the decisions.

The prevailing development strategy of the NGOs, that of meeting the people's basic needs, had consequences both for how the agencies conceptualized NGO-government relationships and for the social, economic and political integration process. The NGOs had a particularistic strategy for development and a particularistic approach to the administrative system they tried to establish.

Most of the NGOs followed a target-oriented strategy that aimed to reach the poor people living in their villages. They had different approaches, and implemented different aspects of the basic needs strategy. Some worked only in the health sector and in small niches within it, such as combating blindness or helping the disabled. Others concentrated on educational services, while some NGOs, like NCA, implemented comprehensive, integrated, rural development projects. What was common to almost all these projects was that, in order to meet goals and to report success stories so as to maintain support from the home country or the UN family, the NGOs sought to circumvent inefficient state institutions and to work directly with the beneficiaries, and the better they did it, the more the authority and legitimacy of the local government structures were eroded. There was a contradiction between establishing programmes for costly social services and the state's potential for becoming a vehicle of economic transformation. The NGOs established social services which, although they differed in their level of ambition, had running and maintenance costs which could not be financed by local surpluses or local revenue, even in the foreseeable future.

The realization of people's basic needs was considered a right by the NGOs, by the local people and by the government's declarations and rhetoric. But their recurrent costs were bound to become, in the long run, a serious drain on the already strained budgets of the local councils. The legitimacy of the state institutions was undermined, and thus the chances of building institutions which could penetrate competing local institutions. The possibilities for local and state institutions to take a more active role regarding new investments, etc., simply were not there, no matter what might be the personal attitudes or wishes of the local administrators or government representatives. The NGOs were instrumental in relieving the government from would-be pressures by carrying out service-sector tasks. On the other hand, by letting others fulfil this role, the state, as a potential supra-ethnic and universalistic entity, could not point to its record as service provider to strengthen its position.

There was, therefore, a further contradiction between projects that aimed at realizing certain target groups' basic needs at the local level, and projects that aimed to strengthen the regional or national economy, or between a successful local project and a beneficial regional project. Since the aid input was so heavy and the local development councils and committees were so weak, this uneven relationship also created uneven development between people and areas defined as target areas and areas outside the spheres of development aid organizations. The ambitious programmes and projects and the lack of reflection on the administrative and financial situation in the Southern Region created a situation in which there was little correlation between development activities and implementation capacities in the would-be implementing institutions.

The NGOs were apportioned different parts of the region, in many ways similar to the way in which the British Government decades before had divided the region between different missionary societies. The NGOs tried to establish local institutions and local accountability by a policy of popular participation. They established formal administrative structures and informal authority networks independent of the state institutions and partly in competition with them. Bypassing local state institutions took different forms, unintentional in some cases and deliberate in others. The general impact of their activities, aimed at reaching the target groups with basic need projects, further marginalized the state in many areas and made local and provincial councils more or less redundant.

A type of development administration was created with very unusual traits. The aid handed out consisted mainly of grants, and the improvement of the lot of the people did not reflect an improvement in state finances. At least in important parts of Southern Sudan there were no 'tremendous setbacks' in meeting the basic needs of the rural people in the early 1980s, as the World Bank reported to be the general rule in Africa. On the contrary, there was an increase in living standards and without doubt an increase in collective services, at least in Equatoria. This development was mainly brought about by foreign donors and NGOs as implementing agencies. The aid helped the local people. But the aid mechanism and the asymmetric relationship between the weak infrastructural power of the state and the strong infrastructural power of the NGOs caused the state institutions to play an even more marginal role in large parts of the region. A system had been established whereby the people expected initiatives and development projects to come from individual foreign organizations rather than from a bankrupt, inefficient government. Social and economic conditions had improved, but due to the particular conditions of the region it is questionable whether this represented a strengthening of civil society. It weakened the possibility of building state institutions and a potentially universalistic, rule-oriented bureaucracy. A practice was established, however, whereby predominantly subsistence farmers started to talk to their government about their rights regarding education, clean water, health facilities, etc. A revolution had taken place in expectations, more profound than at any time in the region's history, without a parallel improvement in the state's ability to fulfil them or to guarantee these rights.

The success of the NCA programme and the consequential growth of its budgets and activities, created a 'state', an administrative machinery, which represented a 'revolution from outside' on the east bank as far as development administration was concerned. In the perspective of a local state-building process, however, this machinery represented a perpetuation of some of those processes which had helped to block a locally rooted state-building process in the past. Its actual and immediate role, however, was very different; it built and did not destroy, it gave and did not take away. Both in historical and contemporary perspectives this 'state administration' was a novelty. It was a state as a service institution, without functions of either suppression or extraction. The relative autonomy of this state in relation to the economic and social basis of society was complete, since its activities depended on money from abroad and on the moral-political judgements of the aid workers. These 'state officials' were social workers rather than rulers and parasites. New institutional structures and new normative models of state behaviour had been created, but based on structures and models which can hardly be implemented by any future Southern state. What had taken place was what can be termed a privatization and an externalization of the state, at the same time as the government continued its rhetoric about the state building socialism.

The NGOs also had conflicting and multiple loyalties and created an organizational system marked by a lack of accountability. Important ordinary state functions had been taken over by a Norwegian voluntary organization which was legally answerable first and foremost to Oslo, the capital of Norway, although morally to the local people. The lack of clear lines of administrative authority in the region in general was further blurred. From one point of view the NGO sector deepened the general problem of accountability. It was an in-built problem of the whole structure since the personnel and the organization were rewarded for implementing project targets within an alternative and fundamentally external reward system. What took place was downwards accountability to the people and upward accountability to the NGOs' headquarters, while local state institutions were often regarded as inefficient, time-wasting institutions that should preferably be circumvented.

NCA had established formal institutions and informal networks which were not only a counterweight to the state, but an alternative. In the same way as the British policy of 'indirect rule' created traditions and practices which influenced the framework for the administrative build-up of the Southern Region after 1972, the NCA programme and its operation will have a legacy for future state-building. NCA and the other NGOs were not important enough to bar the development of universalistic bureaucratic rule over the whole region, but by establishing their own localized bureaucracy with stronger infrastructural powers than the regular state in important sectors of the society, they represented one of many centrifugal forces. While the programme area was locally called 'Little Norway', the Sudanese administrative staff were called 'Black Norwegians'.

NGO mythology versus Southern Sudanese realities

The state administration in the Southern Sudan and its post-1972 history provide a dramatic contrast to most other state administrations, when compared not only with the industrialized world, but also with many other regions in Africa. Theoretical and universalistic concepts about the state, the 'Third World state', the 'African state', 'bureaucracy', 'African civil society' should not disregard the particular history of the Southern Sudan. Between 1972 and 1985 it is also an interesting area for studying the NGO-government relationship in a comparative perspective, because of the weakness of both the state and civil society and the relative strength of the international aid agencies.[15]

As is well known, the Southern Sudan, for a number of historical, geographical and economic reasons, was extremely structurally segmented and culturally diverse, and characterized by a lack of integration and complementarity between the various parts of the social system. There was virtually no value consensus, the relatively broad support for the Addis Ababa Agreement notwithstanding, and society was compartmentalized into relatively independent sub-systems, with only few points of contact. A great number of rural people and whole ethnic groups had only marginal participation in a common money economy. In Durkheimian terms such societies tend to be low on both 'mechanical' and 'organic' solidarity. The state-building efforts in the aftermath of the civil war could therefore be seen, from this point of view, as an effort at social integration. By subjugation of what were described as Southerners to a common body politic, a specific point of contact on a supra-tribal and supra-ethnic level could be established.

The focus here is on an empirical description and analysis of the state and the structure of the public bureaucracy and its characteristics and strength in the Southern Sudan. A study of the administrative structure of the state in the Southern Sudan should not reduce the state and its machinery to an arena for competing socio-economic interests, a locus of class struggle, an instrument of class rule or an expression of core values in the surrounding society. The state apparatus can be approached more fruitfully as a separate socio-spatial organization, which aimed at shaping social and political processes. The political and administrative elite possessed an unusual degree of autonomy in the Southern Sudanese agricultural and pastoral society. Financially and politically, however, it depended upon support from Khartoum, and the state therefore also became an object to be controlled for the purpose of supporting clients. Nevertheless it should not be conceived simply as a typical clientelistic state administration, since the same elite saw this very administrative system as a vehicle for reducing its dependence on Khartoum in the long run. The state administration is studied here as an entity in itself and as an actor by itself, but within this particular political and socio-economic setting.

The state administration 1972–81

To establish and build up regional and local state institutions was regarded as the main task for the regional government after the Addis Ababa Agreement in 1972. It was thought that the broader goal of reconstruction and development would come to nothing without such structures. The aim was to turn these instruments into motors of economic and social reconstruction and development and to secure a kind of semi-autonomy for the region, as embodied in the spirit of the agreement. The old institutions had been partly destroyed by the war, and a new bureaucracy was to be constructed: a) the civil service (the district and provincial administration) was Southernized completely and b) new political structures were created through the establishment of the Regional Government and the Sudanese Socialist Union Party. The Southern Provinces Regional Self-Government Act, 1972, meant that a new regional state apparatus was to be established in the South: a legislature, an executive, a regional administration, three provincial administrations and district-rural administrations were to be set up so as to initiate and implement the reconstruction and development of society. Khartoum was to keep control over matters of defence, foreign policy and trade, national economic planning, transport and communications, but the regional government was made responsible for the preservation of public order, internal security, administration and development in the cultural, economic and social fields. In April 1972, the Interim High Executive Council was set up, headed by Abel Alier.

For the Council and the political elite in the South, the top priority was the establishment of a new administrative structure manned by Southern staff which was to serve regional and Southern interests. For the first time Southerners were to govern Southerners, and in an institutionalized way. In fact an entirely new type of authority was to be established. Compared with the region's colonial administrative and cultural history the aim implied a far-reaching administrative revolution. This revolutionary drive was also influenced by a dominant ideology in the early 1970s in Africa in general, as well as in the Sudan after the 1969 revolution: the state and its administration was seen as the prime mover in societal transformation and development.

These overall aims for the legitimation of the new state structure soon faced competition from more practical matters, often mixed up with problems of a clientelist nature. Who were the Southerners to govern and who was to take command in the new state? There was a contradiction between Khartoum's strategy of appointing reliable and friendly staff and Southern aspirations of regional autonomy bringing hard-liners into the government institutions, but also between the Southern exiles and those Southerners who had remained in the South or in Khartoum, between soldiers and intellectuals, between people from different provinces and between people who could mobilize different ethnic constituencies. In addition, there were reportedly about 20,000 Anya Nya supporters returning from the bush and many thousands of refugees returning from neighbouring countries. When peace came, they all rushed to Juba and other regional centres competing for the new posts. It had important consequences that these posts were created in a period when free aid money poured (relatively speaking) into the region as part of the relief and resettlement programme. From the outset this state administration had very weak economic links with the region it was supposed to serve.

The contradiction between the two dominating leaders, Joseph Lagu and Abel Alier, was both related to and reflected differences and conflicts within Southern society. Lagu was part of a military bureaucratic hierarchy, and had won his position as a soldier during the war. Alier had practised as a barrister and was an elected politician before being made a minister by Nimeiri in 1969. Lagu was from a small Equatorian tribe, the Madi. Alier was from Bor and a Dinka. Lagu was appointed Major General in April 1972. The same month Alier was appointed President of the High Executive Council. The degree of conflict between the two men from 1972 to 1981, when Nimeiri dismissed Alier's administration, in important respects reflected the degree to which the Southern political elite and administration was unable to control centrifugal forces within itself, especially in a situation where these contradictions were fuelled by Khartoum's tactics.

The ethnic distribution of administrative posts had for decades been a central conflict in the South. The political struggle against Arab domination in the early 1950s had centred on Southernization of administrative posts. In the South the Sudanization of the British colonial administration was called Northernization. Since the elections of 1953 the political struggle had often centred on the staffing policy for the administration. The emergence of a Southern political consciousness was closely related to the fight for a greater role for Southerners in the administration of the

South. One might say that the preoccupation with this question had, by 1972, become part of the educated and political elite's 'common concern', of their political culture.

The competition among the returnees, the Anya Nya and the 'insiders' was, of course, fierce, not only for jobs but for the best jobs. After all, a high political or administrative position was an important foundation of wealth and also a basis for political support and clientelism. The political economy of similar state structures in Africa has been called 'the state as plunder capitalism' (Mamdani, 1986:46). In the Southern Sudan there was very little capitalism and not much to plunder, the most important exception being money given by foreign donors or by Khartoum. High official posts were also important to obtain regular business interests. In general, however, the jobs were less luxurious and the size of the administrative class smaller than in many other regions in Africa. In spite of this, the crux of the matter is that the difficult economic, social and infrastructural situation in 1972 rendered the state and its administration almost the only job alternative for many, and this naturally reinforced the political interest in who was appointed, where, by whom and why. Within the relatively small circles which made up the political-administrative elite, the question of distribution of positions soon became an obsessive game. From the very beginning of the administrative build-up, two sharply conflicting considerations influenced both the structure and the self-image of the employed administrators. Development and reconstruction of society were, on the one hand, regarded as being dependent upon a strong, efficient and rule-governed state machinery. At the same time, there was a need to handle the staffing problem with great care and with an eye to local, often particularistic and competing expectations.

When the Provisional Government was set up in Juba on 22 April 1972, it lacked almost everything a government usually takes for granted: qualified administrative personnel, office buildings and administrative experience.[16] By the end of 1973 the Regional Government had an estimated 30 per cent of the manpower required to run the Regional Civil Service and by 1976 still only about half of the required posts were filled (Alier, 1976: 38).

But perhaps as important was the quality of the new administrative staff at hand. The bureaucratic culture was very weak among the Southern administrators. The legacy of British colonialism had left few bureaucratic structures and institutions. The period of Condominium taken as a whole was basically a 'law and order' administration, with weak infrastructural power and limited functions. The overall strategy was 'to interfere as little as possible' and to work through tribal authorities. The policy was in general restricted to implementing the policy of 'care and maintenance', as it was called, and administrative expenses were cut to the bone. The result was an administrative apparatus which depended on the individual capabilities of British District Commissioners and the potential rapid deployment of technologically superior armed forces. The development of a centrally organized bureaucracy with ordinary political, administrative and economic institutions was thus discouraged. The British did not want to develop an educated elite of Southern administrators, since they feared a detribalized and discontented intelligentsia. The missionaries were allowed to start schools, but with other aims than creating bureaucrats or administrators. The colonial policy on religion barred a possible development of region-wide religious organizations. As part of its Nile Valley strategy and its Southern policy, Islam was suppressed. The expansion of the Christian Church did not lead to the establishment of an overarching ecclesiastical hierarchy nor serve the interest of building up a strong, region-wide state apparatus, partly because the South was partitioned between different Catholic and Protestant groups. The traditional religions were organized on a communal basis, often around a local cultic centre. They were therefore incapable of providing an ideological and organizational foundation for administrative centralization or broad regional bureaucratic organizations. The British aims created state institutions which were designed to be neither instruments of economic development or economic exploitation (as in Egypt, Uganda, Kenya or the northern riverain Sudan) nor efficient channels of Westernization or modernization, but to maintain peace at low cost. The imperial army's technological superiority and the role of the alien DCs, who from a purely local perspective could be seen as neutral arbiters in local conflicts, made success in this respect possible.

Educationally, the Southern Sudan was probably the least developed region in Africa. According to the 1973 census, 81 per cent of the population aged 7–24 had never attended school; of the workers employed in the modern sector 58 per cent had received no education at all. There was moreover, an imbalance in the distribution of educated people, not only between North and South, but also within the South between regions and ethnic groups. In 1978–9 fewer than ten out of some 1,000 students following degree-level agricultural courses at Khartoum University were from the South, a region where more than 90 per cent of the population were agriculturalists or pastoralists. The administrative language of the Southern bureaucracy was English, which only a few mastered better than they had mastered Arabic during the Khartoum-led administration in the 1950s and 1960s.

The character of the war, prior to the peace and the establishment of a state administration, was not conducive to the training of administrators. In contrast with other guerrilla movements elsewhere, the Anya Nya did not build up strong alternative administrative structures in the areas they controlled. Some chiefs and trained administrators defected to them and the Sudan Penal Code was used, but this did not create anything resembling a unified, bureaucratic system. Those who represented the Southern movement at Addis Ababa and who after the Agreement took up high posts in the Regional Government therefore had little administrative experience. The 'insiders' had more experience, but they were, on the other hand, generally less trusted by the people.

The Southern movement was very disunited. Legal instruments of conflict resolution or bureaucratic institutions for policy implementation had not been established within and between the different factions. This fluid situation came to the fore time and again. A period of three years from 1967 saw, for example, a number of different Southern governments, the Southern Sudan Provisional Government, the Nile Provisional Government, the Sue River Republic and the Anyidi Government. It was only when Joseph Lagu, in 1970, managed to establish a military leadership over both the Anya Nya and a new political wing, the Southern Sudan Liberation Movement, that one can say that the movement became united. Unity was imposed by a 'bush coup'. Lagu's authority was to a large extent derived from his ability to deliver the goods, i.e. military hardware and training (through the Israelis). This was a kind of authority which proved to be unstable and difficult to transfer to peaceful conditions.

In addition, two legal factors were important for the form the administrative build-up took. The Self-Government Act came into existence before the promulgation of the new national Constitution in 1973, and some of its articles contradicted articles later written into the Constitution. To have such fundamental legal instruments talking with two tongues, was not, of course, conducive to the establishment of a rule-oriented administrative system; on the contrary, it added to the uncertainty and confusion. The region, in line with Section 22 of the Act, was directly under the jurisdiction of the President, although the amending law was not enacted until July 1977 (Wieu, 1988:48). From the outset and during its formative years the build-up of a Southern public administration was *formally* guided by legal provisions and rule-oriented, i.e. a bureaucratic authority was to replace the traditional authority of the Native Administration. In reality, however, the administrative implementation of the Act was fundamentally personalized, since it depended to a large extent on Nimeiri's opinions and attitudes. What took place represented a 'centralized' decentralization, by which Nimeiri delegated some of his Khartoum-based authority to Juba.

Personalist polities are the very opposite of universalistic, rule-oriented administrations. The difference has been defined by the fact that, in the former, rulers themselves are the source of state norms (see Heper, 1987: 15). In the case of Nimeiri, the central norm became unpredictability (for examples and discussions, see Khalid, 1985; Woodward, 1991). In the South especially, due to the constitutional arrangements and Nimeiri's strong position among the regional politicians and in popular opinion, the fundamental arrangements were personalistic. Seen from the South, Nimeiri was the man who had given the Southerners peace and regional autonomy, or more precisely, he was the only leader in Khartoum who could safeguard that peace, and was given Southern support on that understanding. For the Southern elite in this context, with their multiplicity of local loyalties and the conflicting loyalties between supporting Nimeiri and pleasing the centre on the one hand,[17] and promoting the Southern cause more directly on the other, it was difficult to formulate and implement a consistent long-term policy on which the administration could work.

In addition, this initial build-up of an entirely new administration was guided by the regulations and instruments of the People's Local Government Act, 1971, the aim of which was to create a politicized administrative system in support of the May Revolution of 1969. This had important consequences in the South, because the new regional, provincial and local administration, both its core administrative system and administrative personnel, was given shape and identity by guidelines directly contradicting the idea of a neutral, bureaucratic administrative system. The highly politicized atmosphere in the South turned staff appointments into a tense struggle among competing interests, authorities and statuses. The core administrative personnel from the outset conceived their role as a political one, and were so regarded by the ruled. Many had obtained their bureaucratic posts in order to represent particular interests within the state administration rather than to promote universal regional, interests. Promotions were often too rapid, and many were given jobs for which they had no competence.

The Act, moreover, gave the People's Provincial Executive Councils responsibilities and functions that were self-contradictory. Their members were to be locally elected and appointed. Legally they were bodies which were to represent the local will and interests. They were to promote all kinds of development initiatives: primary and intermediate education, public health, agricultural development, village and town planning, recreational activities, etc. On the other hand, they were to mobilize public support behind government policies and maintain public security. Generally, they failed in both respects. In reality it was the Commissioner who was the strong man, also according to the 1971 Act. He was appointed by the President in Khartoum and answerable to him alone. He was chairman, treasurer and convener of the council sessions. He had supervisory and disciplinary powers over the staff, and was to report on the seconded staff to their respective ministers. He was at the same time SSU-secretary of his province. Due to his autocratic position *vis-à-vis* the rest of the civil service and the elected local politicians (Badal, 1984:90), his role eroded the possibilities for establishing a bureaucratized, rule-oriented system of government. If anything went wrong he was to blame. If no sugar, grain or petrol was available in the market, it was his fault. More often the Commissioner became a symbol of anti-institutionalism and anti-routinization; and he often used or misused the local councils haphazardly to boost personal political backing as he deemed fit (see Malik, 1984a:95).

The state administration was from the beginning an administration of a very special type, since it did not depend on the extraction of local resources or taxes for its existence. In this it resembled the British colonial state in the South. But contrary to the attitude and practice after 1972, the British had had as a main administrative interest the extraction of taxes, not primarily as a source of state income but as a symbol of local submission to an externally imposed administration. The government's taxation policy was therefore implemented in a rudimentary way and with an 'ear to the ground'. The chiefs were responsible for collection and were usually given a certain percentage of the taxes collected. The often personalized relationship between the DC and the local chiefs created a system of government based more on clientelism than on bureaucratic rules. Although taxation on a certain scale by a central authority in the South was started by the British, a 'coercion-extraction' cycle never seemed to have taken off. Finer (1975:95) describes general political mechanisms behind state formation as the 'extraction-coercion cycle'; extracting economic surpluses from the population makes it possible to maintain a state machinery, a permanent army, etc. which in turn serves to extract further surpluses and so on. It also makes the rulers accountable to the ruled. No such cycle ever existed in Southern Sudan.

The financial regulations of the new regional administration were chaotic. The basic rules were governed by Presidential Decree No. 39 of 1972 and the Self-Government Act, 1972 could be exploited both as a carrot and a stick *vis-à-vis* the South. The Provincial Executive Councils (PECs) were paid a 'deficiency grant' by Khartoum via the Regional Government, based on approved deficiency in the budgets submitted. This led the provinces to prepare their budgets more or less as 'bids' for the central grant. The gap between budget figures and actual disbursement widened every year. Moreover, the PECs were unable to collect more than about 50 per cent of their modest, budgeted local revenues (Malik, 1984b:6).

This affected the administrative system in two important ways. First, it became very vulnerable and the staff became continuously frustrated since their salaries depended on an uncertain and varying central grant. Planning problems in Khartoum were immediately felt in the South. In rural councils in remote areas, at the end of the disbursement chain, money never arrived in time, if it arrived at all. This helped create a work environment which diverted the civil service's attention away from administrative routine to personal matters. Secondly, since the personnel were in general paid by the North they did not have to cultivate relationships with local communities or to justify their work or lack of work to the local people. It became more important to be in the right office in Juba when money arrived from Khartoum, than to be in the villages to improve relationships and strengthen the administrative infrastructure. From the beginning there was no extraction-coercion cycle, or extraction-accountability cycle. It was a system for writing off responsibility. If no services were established locally the administrators could simply blame the 'centre'. At the same time these administrators depended upon this same 'centre'. For the 'centre' itself the system also functioned as a dumping ground for Southern grievances and criticism. When money was disbursed the payment of salaries was a first priority. These regulations therefore further alienated the administrator from the local societies, since they regularly diminished the money left for investment in local development. With the size and character of this financial base, the local administrations' power of penetrating Southern rural societies had to be very weak indeed. And not only that. As most of the Southern provinces established so-called Liaison Offices in Khartoum for follow-up of business with the bodies allocating resources, the South soon became governed directly from Khartoum. Even the High Executive Council was running the South from Khartoum. In the end, the 'minimalist' administration had to a large extent been transferred *de facto* to the centre. The South was gradually evacuated administratively.

In respect of development initiatives the Provincial Council was to combine its former revenue with local councils' sources of income and central government grants. The Provincial Council held the purse-strings and decided what to give to which Town or Rural Council and what to keep. The Province could form subordinate councils to perform development functions at district and sub-district levels. In 1973 there were no sub-provincial local councils in any of the provinces, but there were 35 Rural Councils (*Peace and Progress* 1973:11). In 1976 there were 24 Rural or Town Councils and in 1980, 53. A number of the reportedly established local councils existed only on paper, and the Development Committees at the various sub-levels did not function as a general rule. Legally the basic councils – the village and residential area councils – were to be elected first and were to send delegates to the higher councils. Local budgets were prepared as appendices to provincial budgets (Bior, 1984:61) and the commissioners continued to draw money from local councils' treasuries during the whole period. The policy of decentralization therefore became already at this early stage an activity resembling a symbolic ritual rather than effective devolution of power.

States and state administrative systems have generally tried to maintain their legitimacy and authority *vis-à-vis* those they govern by a claim to 'universalism'. When the state is seen to favour particularistic ties to kin, locality, ethnicity, etc., it has tended to lose its authority and legitimacy. The strength of tribalism in the South and the elite's political culture, obsessed with job distribution, caused the issue of Dinka domination to escalate by the end of the 1970s. It became fatal to later state-building. 'External' factors like the high floods in the 1960s caused conflicts over grazing and agricultural land, which contributed to the growth of ethnic animosity in the 1970s and 1980s. Whatever universalistic ideology about a 'Southern cause' had existed among administrators in the early years of regional autonomy, evaporated quickly in this inter-tribal conflict about control and jobs. The Jonglei Canal crisis of 1974 was the first open attack on the terms of the 1972 Agreement. The Akobo uprising in 1975 and the arrest of Benjamin Bol and Joseph Oduho on Alier's orders, because they called for a return to the bush (Alier, 1990), had already demonstrated a political split and sharpened the conflict between 'insiders' and 'outsiders'. In 1978 Lagu retired from the People's Armed Forces and was elected President of the High Executive Council. Alier was ousted. Two years later Lagu raised the issue of redivision in a petition to Nimeiri.

In his publication, *Decentralisation* (1980), Lagu warned against what he saw as Dinka domination and expansion. Taking the title of his pamphlet as a starting point, he could have focused on the deterioration of the regional and local economy and government structures, but such matters were peripheral to his assessment of the Southern problem. Giving figures and tables of the ethnic background of the politicians and administrators, he focused on the same job-distribution issue which had dominated election campaigns in the South since 1953, but in a different form and with different contenders. Redivision, for many, now meant 'anti-Dinka' sentiments. The tribal factor and the 'insider–outsider' dichotomy were also reflected in the different attitudes of the two main political rivals, Alier and Lagu. Alier was more concerned about building up bureaucratic structures and regulations. A lawyer by education, he tried to put the emphasis on regulations and rules, as evidenced by the *Peace and Progress Reports* published during his first period in office, the Southern Region Service Act, 1975, the Southern Region Public Service Pensions Act, 1976 and the Southern Region Employees Discipline Act, 1976. Lagu, in contrast, voiced more populist opinions. In his inauguration speech in 1978, he described the Southern citizen as the 'victim of officialdom', who must be liberated from 'institutional oppression'. The government was to work to cut 'the web of bureaucratic red-tape' (Lagu, 1978:7.).[18]

Alier and his High Executive Council had planned to establish an administrative structure based on Western models and replicating that of the North (see, for example, *Peace and Progress* and Alier's speeches of the 1970s). Seen from the perspective of the existing traditions, culture and organizational experience, this represented a bureaucratic revolution. Alier was trying to guarantee Southern access to these bureaucratic arms of the state, at the same time as Nimeiri was trying to subordinate the state to himself, partly through the SSU and partly through the 1973 Constitution.

The state administration 1981–3

In 1981 the regional administration suffered a mortal blow. In March, 12 Southern members of the National Assembly asked Nimeiri to dissolve the Southern government and decree the redivision of the South. On 5 October both the Regional Assembly and the High Executive Council were dissolved and Alier's administration was dismissed. The reactions in the South were mixed. The divisionists generally supported the dissolution; others saw it as part of a Northern strategy to fragment the South. The struggle between the two created a situation where the staffing of the administration again became a question of paramount importance.

The People's Local Government Act of 1981 abolished the PECs and devolved their power to Area Councils which were to be the central instruments of the government's decentralization policy and the rallying points for government support. In addition they were to be directly responsible for providing essential services to the population. But none of the fundamental problems had been solved. Rather they were magnified by the new Act. Local governments at different levels continued to inflate their budget estimates, hoping that the central government would fulfil its declared promise of meeting any deficits. But Khartoum was virtually bankrupt, and quite incapable of meeting all the demands, let alone its Southern strategy. As during the British period, the social service tax or the poll tax was the most important local tax, often forming more than half of the local revenues. The actual amount collected was, however, far from meeting the targets, due to the lack of co-operation from the people, the seasonal movements of pastoralists, the migration of young people to the towns, but, first and foremost, to lack of adminis-trative capability and will to levy and collect taxes. The machinery for the collection of taxes levied by the central government but collected by the regional government (personal income tax, land rental tax and business profit tax) was, however, strengthened over the years. It started as a one-man office but gradually the staff was increased to 33 officers and 119 tax collectors and base-level staff. But this system also faced great difficulties, especially in collecting the personal income tax.

The Area Councils' administrative, professional, technical and support staff were on secondment from the Regional Ministries. This made them a dumping ground on which to offload inefficient and incompetent staff from more central adminis-trative organs, since the Councils became responsible for their salaries. In spite of this, UNDP reported for 1981 that, for example, over 50 per cent of the provincial and local book-keeping and accountancy posts were vacant. However, the Act did not address the power vacuum created. Hence an additional unclear administrative structure was established.

Moreover, the training problem, which was highlighted already in 1972, remained a crucial issue. For example, not before 1982 was the *National Training Regulation 1976* translated into English and made available in the South; a Regional Civil Service Training Institute was never established; the Regional Institute of Public Administration was conceived, created by decree, but never materialized. A training centre offering courses in book-keeping and accounting, budgeting, auditing and tax administration was conceived in 1975, official approval was secured in 1978, and in July 1981 the Regional Accountancy Training Centre was officially started. The Training Advisory Board and the Steering Committee, established to provide policy and administrative guidance, never did manage to function (UNDP, 1984).

The state administration after redivision in 1983

Into this chaotic situation, marked by unclear management structures, serious shortages of trained staff, a weak *esprit de corps* among the administrators, and – first and foremost – no adequate finances to pay for administrative staff or development initiatives, came the redivision of June 1983 and the establishment by Presidential decree of three new regions in the South. With few educated people and money in short supply, the establishment of more administrative units added to the already unsolved staffing problems. The Speaker of one regional assembly was quoted as saying that the only surplus manpower was politicians, and they were the only ones who would benefit from the creation of new posts in the new regions (Arou, 1988: 171). The Area Councils came to depend entirely on grant-in-aid from the central government, but a regular formula for how this money should be allocated and disbursed was never established. In this transitional atmosphere regional and local politicians often tried to influence the posting of officers in such a manner that the 'right officer was not posted in the right place' (see Khamis, 1985:172).

The redivision made it impossible to generate both a rule-oriented and an efficient public administration. Before the redivision quite a few Area Councils had had their separate development budgets. Between June 1983 and October 1984 the situation deteriorated so fast that no money came to the Area Councils in Equatoria for development purposes, and the councils did not even bother to prepare any development budgets for 1983–4 and 1984–5. The ambiguity of the regulations continued. The relationship between the Chief Executive and the elected members of the Area Councils had not been settled. The legislature in every region should have been partly elected and partly appointed. Executive power in the region rested, however, with the Governor, appointed and solely responsible to the President in Khartoum. The administration did not have enough money to meet recurrent expenditure, and categories such as teachers were rarely paid; in 1984, for example, all the primary schools under government control were closed down for more than three-quarters of the year. Nor did it have the instruments to execute its tasks. Virtually none of the Area Councils, even in Equatoria, had vehicles; at best they had a few bicycles.

Nimeiri's decree of 1983 led to absurd situations. When, for example, the new Regional Executive Authority of Bahr el Ghazal came into being, no facilities had been provided, nor for the five new regional ministries. During this initial phase no work was done (Bahr el Ghazal Region Group, 1984:154). The problem of staffing the new ministries and councils was solved by 'applying speedy promotion' (ibid.:155). The Regional Ministry of Services, Department of Education upgraded the primary school teachers to intermediate school level overnight, and a great number of teachers were shifted to the Regional Ministry of Administration. Education suffered, and little administration was done. In Equatoria it led to further delays in the payment of salaries, and to transfer of office furniture from Juba to Wau and Malakal while 'personnel took extra long leave' (Directorate of Health and Social Service, 1983:37). Some departments became overstaffed, due to the 'influx of Equatoria Region personnel returning from the other Regions' (ibid.), while others experienced serious manpower shortages.

By 1985 development efforts undertaken by the government had almost been brought to a complete halt. Staff had gone on strike and in the schools there were neither teaching materials nor teachers. Many councils had stopped working during 1984 and 1985. Added to this was the staff-transfer policy. Senior administrators in the Western Area Council were changed three times during the three years 1981–4

(Pickering and Davies:54). Efforts at improving budget procedures and structures became almost impossible due to instabilities. In 1982 the government had appointed a number of technical committees to advise on regulations for the effective implementation of the systems as laid down in the 1981 Act. 'Unfortunately', as stated in a UN report, the new procedures were not pursued, due to further decentralization (Inter-regional Training Project, 1983:2). The redivision required new procedures and regulations; everything had to be done again, but now in three regions, by even fewer trained staff and with less money. The 1983 decision led to the fragmentation of an already weak administrative system, which it supplanted with new structures whose fragility and limited capacity were matched only by the paucity of financial and other resources at their disposal.

In the Southern Sudan, where ethnic groups have been more important as social categories than social class, a paramount problem in building up the administration has been one of 'ethnic arithmetic'. The difficulties in implementing universalistic bureaucratic principles in a context of ethnic rivalry and conflict were demonstrated again and again. Here we have analyzed the failure of the Southern Regional Government in a primarily Southern context. This focus does not relate the whole story, of course. It was a semi-autonomous state, to a large extent dependent upon the political will and decisions made in Khartoum and by Nimeiri.

NCA was in important respects more concerned about developing good relations with the state and its administrative structures than many other NGOs. It continually emphasized the need for mutual discussions and formal agreements with the state authorities. It warned against the danger of establishing institutions which the government could not take over, and stressed the necessity of local participation as a way to root projects locally. In 1986–7, when its long-lasting integrated rural development programme had been brought to a halt due to the civil war, NCA also reassessed its past policies and decided that in future development assistance programmes in the Southern Sudan more emphasis should be given to institution-building, including support to local state institutions.

Conclusion

The characters of, and relations between, state and society vary considerably between countries, reflecting historical developments, economic situation, the degree of social integration and compartmentalization, etc. A productive relationship between NGOs and the host government's administrative system must therefore adapt to NGOs' different roles and potentials. NGO interventions may be counter-productive in strengthening the state, creating development or building up society. One problem with the new development paradigm is that its strong position has led to lack of attention to a dominant aspect of many African countries: that of vanishing structures of statehood. Some have virtually collapsed, while others are mutating into local power centres. In the case of the Southern Sudan a kind of conceptual dogmatism played an important role; the prevailing perspective underestimated the weakness of the state institutions and overestimated the degree of social integration and value consensus in society.

In recent years a dominant perspective in much research on NGO-government relationships has focused on the contrasts between the political role and characteristics of states and those of voluntary organizations. This theory allocates NGOs a crucial role in the democratization of countries: they are to strengthen what is commonly called 'civil society'. The NGOs are conceived of as instruments for organizing local initiatives and promoting local participation and diversity as opposed to the state, whose approach is seen as *dirigiste* and top-down, and expressing the interests of a bureaucratized, alienated elite in search of illegitimate control. Irrespective of time and place, the emergence of NGOs has been analysed as an organizational expression of particular interests or objectives within the body politic, which are not adequately represented within the political system. They are therefore seen as implicitly expressing democratic interests on behalf of civil society.

The power of this concept has given birth to a mythology which has tended to disregard the differences in state–society relationships under industrial and post-industrial capitalism and in societies where 90 per cent of the population are subsistence farmers. When dogmatically applied in prescriptions about NGOs' contributions to development, the term has also failed to distinguish between societies with a long and internally rooted state tradition and those in which the state is a very recent phenomenon, introduced from above and partly maintained by external sources. Moreover, the actual and potential roles of the third sector (if the term is at all applicable) vary according to its homogeneity, organizational history, exchange relationships with the state sector, etc. Analytical perspectives which study NGO-government relations within frameworks based on general assumptions about a bureaucratized and parasitic state, on the one hand, and a civil society with supra-ethnic or supra-tribal organizations fighting to curb the role of the state and supported by NGOs as agents of micro-developments, on the other, may, of course, be fruitful. But it has been shown that neither in the case of the Southern Sudan nor of Bangladesh was such a perspective very illuminating. The impact of NGOs must be analysed concretely. Their role depends on the specific character of the state system and the civil society in which they operate.

The rolled-back state of the new paradigm implies erosion of universalism in welfare provisions. 'Particularism' has often been highlighted as one of the historical and institutional weaknesses of the voluntary sector. As J. S. Mill said in the last century: 'Charity almost always does too much or too little; it lavishes bounty in one place, and leaves people to starve in another' (Mill, 1891:585). Indeed, one of the prominent features of development NGOs is their particularistic, group-oriented approach and strategy. The very character of their power and role prevents them from guaranteeing the rights of the target group. The demand for guaranteed rights can only be addressed to the state, and recognition of such rights can only be the responsibility of the state. It is therefore appropriate to speak of 'philanthropic particularism' (see Salamon, 1986) when discussing development NGOs in relation to the state and civil society. Development NGOs are only a small, often a very small, section of the organizational landscape in a society. They can therefore never aspire to talk on behalf of society or of the people, or of popular organizations. They always talk on behalf of some particular group interests, no matter how broad and altruistically formulated their demands are.

NGOs' roles *vis-à-vis* a civil society may be different in societies where there is some kind of common identity and where the rules of the game are basically accepted, and in societies where they may become vehicles for ethnic chauvinism or localism or for forces questioning not only the boundaries of the state but also of civil society. Comparative research in European history has shown that a multiplicity of voluntary or private organizations in itself is not a vehicle for achieving a democratic society or a sign of democratic improvement. It can be, but it does not have to be. Research in developing countries has not substantiated this theory either (Smith, 1990). More important than the number of NGOs are their character, strength and mobilizing capacities – and not least, their legitimacy, roots and value-orientation in the society. What is important is that the differences between, and the multiplicity of institutional arrangements in, countries like Ethiopia, Bangladesh, Nicaragua or the Sudan make it necessary to distinguish different patterns of co-operation and conflict which operate jointly or separately in different countries at different times. In some countries there might be a contradiction between nation-building and the proliferation of NGOs, while in others such a growth may strengthen both the state and society. In a state where the citizens feel attached to the existing state borders, the consequences will be other than in multi-ethnic societies where the legitimacy of the state is fundamentally questioned, or where politics basically reflect ethnic or particularistic interests. To support diversity or a proliferation of organizations in a society where the issue is not who are the legitimate rulers of the state but whether the state itself has a right to exist, is a very different intervention with different implications from supporting diversity in a society with a bureaucratic and monolithic state structure which has undisputed or a relatively strong legitimacy. One of the characteristics of the NGO channel is that external funding from a foreign state might become a liability and a serious Achilles heel, precisely because it questions the sustainability and support of the organizations in a given society. It might increase the number of organizations, without strengthening a people's capacity to organize itself.

Within the perspective of the prevailing NGO language, the NGOs are generally regarded as being above ordinary social constraints and developments. The 'iron law' of organizations may be wrong, but within the NGO discourse it is as if the theory had never been formulated. It is also important to analyse how the NGOs role in civil society is affected by the NGO leaders, who in some areas form a new and very influential social group, in general belonging to the middle class but representing an elite in society as compared with the marginalized areas and the poor. This new elite represents an organization, often run in a paternalistic way; it is often on good terms with the leadership of the state and, not least, with the international donor community. Besides which, it is of course proficient in English and in the global jargon of the international NGO channel. But whereas historians of colonialism have grappled with the crucial question – how did colonialism affect the post-independence leadership of these states? – the NGO discourse is mute on a similar issue: will the NGO channel create *laissez-faire* entrepreneurs, citizens with community responsibility or strong men with a particularistic outlook – in the long run?

In parts of the NGO community it is common to equate NGOs with popular forces, the poor, etc. Another view holds that they represent elite interests (Arnove, 1980; Cockson and Persell, 1985), i.e. that the people-centred ideology is a sort of rhetorical camouflage. In this perspective charity is seen as a form of regressive redistribution, where the rich exchange domination for prestigious charity activities, an exchange which enhances their social status and thus maintains and legitimizes existing power structures. Far from representing democratic ideals and the interests of the poor, development NGOs can be fronts for seeking personal gain. It is possible to interpret foreign and national NGO communities as representing elite interests, exchanging riches for legitimacy in a chain of interlinked dependencies, with the role and impact of basically maintaining the *status quo*. Some argue that the multi-level NGO network contributes to the paralysis of social and political action. This has been a criticism of the successful service-providing NGOs in Bangladesh. Lowi (1969) and Olson (1982) argue that private associations have this effect in Western welfare states. In analyses of the 'crisis of the welfare state' it is said that states maintain legitimacy by delegating more and more functions to the non-profit voluntary sector. It is thus also possible to regard its growth and mushrooming as a sign of the crisis in legitimacy of the state. Since in developing countries it is not the state, but often the donors, who delegate services and therefore power to the NGOs, the state's legitimacy might in some cases be maintained, but in other cases it will be undermined without a parallel strengthening of civil society.

The whole issue of state–society relations and the actual role of NGOs has become highly ideologized – especially in the wake of the political and ideological triumph of liberal democracies in the West. To assess the role of NGOs and the potentials of civil society etc., will require both in-depth case studies and broad comparative studies, not only examining formal aspects of organizations, but also focusing on structural features of the NGO channel and on empirical and actual state-society relations. There is a gap between the talk of an 'associational revolution' and the fact that most of the organizations in the development aid channel which have been instrumental in the global growth of organizations, are getting most of their money from states, and while ideologically often engaged in a zero-sum game with the state, are, in reality, accountable to it for financial resources, policies and administrative routines. There is a problem with a definition of civil society which turns it into a place where 'progressive, compatible' ideas are produced and fought for, while researchers and politicians warn against a clash between civilizations and between religions, organized among other things in different NGOs, which might antagonize different groups both in society and in the channel itself.

Notes

1 The following quotation is one of the most clearly formulated arguments in support of directional history, ending in a liberal capitalist democracy, with a strong civil society and strong associations: 'Rather than a thousand shoots blossoming into as many different flowering plants, mankind will come to seem like a long wagon train strung out along a road. Some wagons will be pulling into town sharply and crisply, while others will be bivouacked back in the desert, or else stuck in ruts in the final pass over the mountains. Several wagons, attacked by Indians, will have been set aflame and abandoned along the way. There will be a few wagoneers who, stunned by the battle, will have lost their sense of direction and are temporarily heading in the wrong direction, while one or two wagons will get tired of the journey and decide to set up

permanent camps at particular points back along the road. Others will have found alternative routes to the main road, though they will discover that to get through the final mountain range they all must use the same pass. But the great majority of wagons will be making the slow journey into town, and most will eventually arrive there. The wagons are all similar to one another: while they are painted different colours and are constructed of varied materials, each has four wheels and is drawn by horses, while inside sits a family hoping and praying that their journey will be a safe one. The apparent differences in the situations of the wagons will not be seen as reflecting permanent and necessary differences between the people riding in the wagons, but simply a product of their different positions along the road' (Fukuyama, 1992: 338–9).

2 The concern of what often is called the new development paradigm echoes some of the problems envisaged by Hobbes and Adam Smith. When the public domain inaugurated by the social contract had been established, a problem arose: how could public power be controlled? Hobbes (in his *Leviathan* 1651), asked how the drive of self-interest (existing in a state of nature) could be harnessed for the common good, argued that to overcome the aggressiveness of self-interest it was necessary to submit to an absolute authority. But if this absolute power was necessary, how could one control the ruler or the government or the administration? As is well known, the British economist Adam Smith suggested a political and economic response to this problem: the market and its invisible hand (*Wealth of Nations*, 1776). The market represented the counterweight to the authoritarian tendencies of the political system. Establishment of NGOs is seen as a political and institutional response to the same problem. The state must be restricted in scope and constrained in practice to ensure the maximum possible freedom for its citizens.

3 If history had provided such clear-cut lessons and this summary of African state formation and the implicit assumptions about the history of democracy in the West had not been highly questionable, then the new paradigm could stand secure – on the shoulders of history. But it is doubtful whether there is such a clear causal link between the number and diversity of NGOs and democratic institutions in a society. The.expansion of social welfare services in the West required in general the active involvement of the state. An NGO-dominant paradigm might therefore be consistent with a high level of welfare provision or strengthened democracy, but this is no universal historical law. This view of civil society has a corollary: NGOs will be described as sources of diversity and innovation, and characterized as a group as a contribution to democracy, pluralism or people's empowerment by establishing centres of influence and institutions outside the state, and as a set of institutions that provide instruments which deprived or disenfranchised groups may use.

4 This quotation is taken from Pelczynski 1984:1. The literature on Hegel, Marx, Gramsci, Etzioni and many other social theorists' views on the relation between state and civil society is voluminous. The reasoning is often very complex, and in this overview it is impossible to do these theories justice. Here the point is not to give a history of these ideas, but to draw up a comparative background for the analysis of present conceptualizations.

5 Hegel's view on the state was quite clear: 'The march of God in the world, that is what the state is', or 'It is the way of God in the world, that there should be the state' (addition to paragraph 258 of the *Philosophy of Right*). In his *Philosophy of History*, Hegel, in his search for the ultimate design of the world (Hegel, 1956:16), argues that 'Truth is the Unity of the universal and subjective Will; and the Universal is to be found in the State, in its laws, its universal and rational arrangements. The State is the Divine Idea as it exists on Earth' (ibid.:39). Fukuyama reinterprets Hegel to boost his argument and says that Hegel makes rather similar arguments to Tocqueville in support of 'mediating institutions', that is to say, he thought the modern state was too large and impersonal to serve as a meaningful source of identity, and therefore argued that society ought to be organized into *Stände*. The 'corporations' favoured by Hegel, he says, were neither closed medieval guilds nor the mobilizing tools of the fascist state, but rather associations organized spontaneously by civil society that served as a focus for community and virtue (Fukuyama, 1992: 323).

6 Kuhnle and Selle (1990: 170) have characterized this with the term '*avhengig samordning eller binding*' ('integrated dependency').

7 Saul (1974) called these states state nations rather than nation states.

8 This situation has of course been noted by many scholars. Clapham (1985) described the states as both 'powerful' and 'weak', while Jackson and Rosberg (1982) discussed to what extent

African states existed as empirical realities in many societies. Migdal's state-centred theory analyses the state more as an autonomous product or reflection of social forces, and based on a viewpoint that regards the state as fundamentally a weak actor to a different extent from that of Clapham and Jackson and Rosberg.

9 From an empirical point of view it is highly questionable to describe states in general in the so-called Third World as weak. There are obvious exceptions to such generalizations, such as, for example, Egypt and China. This does not make Migdal's theory less relevant in our connection, however. It captures important aspects of state–society relations in many countries, and more importantly here, it puts forward an alternative to current hegemonic perspectives and can thus make the content of this paradigm easier to identify.

10 These figures are used by NORAD, while UNDP give the figure as less than 10% (see UNDP, 1993a).

11 The following is primarily based on information published in the press in 1992 and 1993 which widely covered the issue of the government–NGO relationship in Bangladesh. It represents a cross-section of daily and weekly newspapers (numbering 18), both in the vernacular and in English. The newspapers can be categorized into a) pro-establishment (*Dainik Bangla* (DB), *Dainik Sangbad* (DS), *Shaptahik Bichitra* (SB), the *Daily Star* (TDS), the *Bangladesh Observer* (TBO), *Dhaka Courier* (DC), b) Islamic (*Dainik Millat* (DM), *Dainik Inquilab* (DI), *Jago Mujahid* (JM) and c) left-wing *Bhorer Kagoj* (BK), *Ajker Kagaj* (AK), *Kagaz* (K) and *Shaptahik Khoborer Kagaj* (SKK). The information is based on a report (see Jamil and Manam, 1994) and also on the author's interviews with leaders of the NGO Affairs Bureau, November 1993, ADAB, November 1993 and discussions with central actors on the Bangladeshi NGO scene, and on press clippings at NORAD, Dhaka.

12 At the Relief and Resettlement Conference on Southern Region in 1972, 38 representatives of different foreign NGOs participated (Democratic Republic of the Sudan, 1972: 51-2).

13 Some of the Western NGOs operating in the Southern Sudan during the period of study were Action Committee for Relief of Southern Sudan (ACROSS), African Interior Mission, African Medical and Research Foundation (AMREF), Catholic Relief Service, Euro-Accord, German Volunteer Service (GTZ), German Leprosy Relief Association, International Volunteer Service, International Summer School of Linguistics, Lutheran World Federation, Missionary Aviation Fellowship, Norwegian Council for the Prevention of Blindness, Norwegian Association for Disabled, Norwegian Church Aid, Sudan Programme, Oxford Committee for Famine Relief (OXFAM), Save the Children Fund, Seventh-Day Adventists, Sudan Interior Mission, Swedish Free Mission, Voluntary Service Group, Swiss Interchurch Aid, Voluntary Service Overseas and World Vision. This list of NGOs is compiled from Madison, 1984, 174–91, and personal notes of implementing agencies for UNHCR, Juba. (The author worked in 1985–6 as a Programme Officer for UNHCR in Juba, being responsible for social services for all the Ugandan refugees in the South and for the rural settlement programme for about 40,000 refugees on the east bank of the Nile).

14 In 1986/7, when its long-standing integrated rural development programme had been brought to a halt due to the civil war, NCA also reassessed past policies and decided that in future development assistance programmes in the Southern Sudan should give more emphasis to institution building, including support to local state institutions.

15 The empirical parts of this chapter are based on a fairly extensive collection of reports produced by government officials and regional government departments, NGOs, UN organizations, the World Bank and a number of consultants working in the 'South' during this period.

16 See Alier, 1976 for his description of the government 'infrastructure' in 1972 (Alier, 1976:7-8).

17 It is important to remember the strong support Nimeiri had in the South through the 1970s because of the May Revolution, the Peace Accord and the fact that Nimeiri, because of the role in the region as his 'Southern constituency' for some years, responded positively to Southern aspirations. Malwal wrote in 1981: 'Second, the South has come to trust President Nimeiri personally very much, so much so that they do not question the basis of his decisions, even if those decisions could adversely affect the South' (Malwal, 1981: 217).

18 In the South, most ministries never established a proper archival system, and the red tape of the administration was not based on organized institutional memory, but more on particularism and clientelism.

8

NGOs: Angels of Mercy or State-Financed Development Diplomats?

In the old Norwegian saga about Torstein Vikingson there is a story about a drinking horn that brought joy, happiness and good health when one sipped from it, but also brought sorrow, unhappiness and sickness when it was emptied. Perhaps the NGO channel can be equated with this horn. Influential representatives have exaggerated its potential role – the NGOs not only reduce the undesirable effects of development processes, they also tackle the causes of poverty – and emphasized the 'comparative advantage'. Some NGOs have propagated a kind of universal altruism 'we are always reaching the poorest' or 'we help where the need is most severe' – while some at the same time are apparently happy with their image as modern angels of mercy (especially in disaster situations). Many outside the NGO community have rejected this declared universalism and it has also been confronted with a growing aid fatigue. The development NGOs have been unable to deliver their promises. Should their aim be to try to improve the standard of living of the poor on a permanent basis, or should they rather, or in addition, seek to develop a global 'community of interests' and try to mobilize these groups in improving living standards as well as to further pluralist values?

This chapter addresses challenges common to the NGO channel as a whole. Based on analysis of the systems mechanisms, to what extent will NGOs be able to organize a form of development co-operation and international relationships that other institutions (like states, the UN system, etc.) cannot do to the same extent or in the same way? This question is especially relevant in a situation where traditional official development assistance has been called into question across the political spectrum. Can NGOs develop other or better relations between the rich and the poor and between countries, cultures and civilizations? We shall discuss how options available to different NGOs are affected by structural constraints and opportunities inherent in this international social system, and also by particular forms of integration and context in different national sub-systems. DiMaggio and Powell (1993) argue that 'the more ambiguous the goals of an organization, the greater the extent to which the organization will model itself after organizations that it perceives to be successful'. The focus on project replicability in much of NGO literature implicitly rests on the idea that all NGOs can learn from good projects. The popularity of rural credit projects (especially in the wake of the projects of the Grameen Bank and

BRAC in Bangladesh) has caused NGOs all over the world to start up similar projects, irrespective of their value orientation, local conditions, competence, etc. There can be no doubt that the ambiguousness of many organizations' development aid policy must be one explanation of the speed with which aid slogans and project models are copied. This ambiguousness is natural in view of the complexity of aid relations, but it may also express a way of handling what is a permanent contradiction between conflicting agendas in the organizations' work (we shall discuss below how, for example, mission organizations have adapted to the prevailing aid rhetoric concerning aims and profiles, while simultaneously, within their own organisations, employing the old mission terminology and aims for more or less the same activities.) There is, it is argued here, a contradiction between an apparent galloping isomorphism and the actual pluralism in value orientations within the NGO community, and the way this contradiction is handled will be important for the future role of the channel

NGOs and the state

The NGO aid channel has led to an integration process between states and organizations all over the world and especially between donor states and the development NGOs they are funding. Organizations have become more like each other both in donor and in developing countries (most importantly, they share more or less the same rhetoric and have become accountable to donor states or international institutions), and they have in general accommodated the requirements or the integrative instruments employed by donor states (see Tvedt, 1995c). The character of this integration process varies among different types of organization and is not the same in donor and recipient countries; moreover, it has features that embody opportunities for affecting this trend of organizational isomorphism. This section will analyse the question of NGO-state relations with an emphasis on the organizations' situation.

Salamon (1987 and 1990) has put forward a theory to explain what is seen as a general process of integration. He argues that voluntary solutions are the 'natural solution' to social problems. Therefore, what needs explanation is the state's intrusion into what was originally the domain of organizations. It was made possible, it is argued, by what are called four types of voluntary failure: philanthropic insufficiency, philanthropic particularism, philanthropic paternalism and philanthropic amateurism. This theory does not fit very well in the development aid field, since the historical sequence was the other way round: Western states invited NGOs to supplement part of their work and to increase public support for official aid in non-Western countries. The whole integration process and its impact on NGO options, therefore, have to be analysed in a different perspective. The NGOs have come closer to the donor states, and donor states have become, to a certain extent, dependent on NGOs, during a period when both parties have basically shared the same rhetoric and underlined the great potentials and comparative advantages of NGOs.

DiMaggio and Powell (1993) have put forward a theory of 'institutional isomorphism', which aims at a general explanation of the development of institutional similarities. Isomorphism is defined as 'a constraining process that forces one unit in a population to resemble other units that face the same set of environmental conditions' (DiMaggio and Powell 1983:148). They argue that bureaucratization and professionalization are not necessarily the product of strategic plans for more rational organizations, but may reflect, or be caused by, dependency and closeness to other organizations: Organizations with common interests, tasks and value orientations will come closer together over time . So long as they constitute a field of their own, they will be influenced by forces which will eventually make them more alike. They suggest that a general mechanism is at work: 'The greater the dependence of an organization on another organization, the more similar it will become to that organization in structure, climate and behavioral focus' They also formulate their thesis in the following way: 'the greater the centralization of organization A's resource supply, the greater the extent to which organization A will change isomorphically to resemble the organization on which it depends for resources' (ibid.). This book, particularly chapter 4 on NGOs as an international social system, gives support to the above perspective, although the reason behind this development at the global level is not so much mechanical laws as Western economic and political power and discursive hegemony. As shown above, the financial dependence also of Northern NGOs on state funds has increased dramatically in most countries since the field was established in the early 1960s. By adapting to the donor states' requirements regarding aid profile, professionalism and reporting systems, organizations have been reshaped in the ways they operate and conceive of themselves.

The NGO aid channel has important distinguishable characteristics, however. Since integration processes are influenced by nearness, financial dependence and control relations with a particular state, a development NGO has possibilities of escaping the centralization of its resource supply by accessing different donors (its own government, the UN system, other governments). It can establish opportunities for counteracting integration with a particular state by becoming dependent on more donors for financial support. Some of the big NGOs in Bangladesh and Zimbabwe, for example, have employed this strategy; they are supported by different Western governments and different UN agencies as well as by different Northern NGOs. Similarly, some of the biggest Norwegian NGOs have in recent years received support not only from the Norwegian Government, but also from the UN system, other governments, different international institutions and networks, etc. DiMaggio and Powell argue that the greater the extent to which an organizational field is dependent 'upon a single (or several similar) source of support for vital resources, the higher the level of isomorphism'. By increasing the number of donors with whom they interact and transact, some NGOs are weakening the extent of isomorphism brought about by their relation with a particular state.

Two tendencies can be observed. On the global scale there is a high level of isomorphism. Organizations in different countries are much more similar within the NGO channel than was the case before the aid system was established. In remote rural districts in countries like Ethiopia and Bangladesh there are now local organizations employing the same language, attempting to follow the same reporting procedures and perhaps also succumbing to the mumbo-jumbo of the NGO channel, the Logical Framework Analysis, more or less in the same way as Northern

NGOs in most donor countries. On the other hand, there is a weaker counter-tendency, stimulated by the growth in the number of donors and, not least, in international networks for different types of organization.

To the extent that the literature on NGOs in aid has discussed the question of isomorphism at all, the focus has been on the issue of the 'NGO mission' and the dangers that can dilute it (an example can be found in a World Bank book on NGOs, edited by Paul and Israel in 1991). A common worry seems to be the pressure to take on increased project loads. Easily available funds may be a 'source of distraction'; and may create 'opportunistic' NGOs (Samuel and Israel, 1991:12), i.e. organizations for whom continued allocations of government funds become more important than working for their original aims. There is no doubt that examples can be found to show that rapid growth has turned value-oriented organizations into routine service-delivery institutions and over time also tended to produce organiza-tions that gradually have become more and more similar. But the above analysis is based on the untenable proposition that NGOs, as a group, are value-oriented organizations, and secondly, it implicitly argues that the main problem is the amount of funds, and not the structural relations between NGOs and their donors.

Paul and Israel (1991) do not discuss what the particular NGO mission has been or should be. By describing NGOs, as a group, as value-oriented, it de-emphasizes the wide and often conflicting 'missions' of NGOs. Many NGOs do not have any particular mission, except for one – they are in it for business. Or, put another way, some organizations are established with the clear intention of accomodating donor wishes in order to achieve organizational growth. Likeness is thus a product neither of relational mechanisms nor of overfunding, but of common or consciously ambiguous goals at the outset. Other NGOs have primary missions that to them are far more important than successful development projects, e.g. spreading the gospel of Christ or a particular vision about gender or man-nature relations, and for them aid is a means to this end. Some organizations therefore have good reason to appear less value-oriented than they in fact are, and they may be quite happy to be regarded as having diluted their original mission in certain aid contexts. Nor does Paul and Israel's book address what it is important not to downplay if the channel is to be one marked by pluralism and diversity: the potential political and ideological contradictions between donors and NGOs and between NGOs and other actors. These conflicts are often hidden by the consensual and shared NGO language of the social system as a whole, and this rhetorical situation will therefore tend more than anything else to further isomorphism in the long term.

A general tendency towards institutional isomorphism should not, however, be confused with actual NGO policies. How closely NGOs tend to work with the government in a particular country is also a reflection of their overall strategy, and not least, the concrete political situation in the country concerned and the organizations' coping strategies. A number of examples can show how the same NGO may follow very different policies *vis-à-vis* the state in different countries, while championing the same rhetoric about people-centered, grassroots-oriented development. Many NGO projects, when they started in the first half of the 1980s, were legitimized as a means not of strengthening civil society, but rather in the language of the day, of improving the target groups' standard of living. Although organizations may want to be always very up-to-date in how they describe their project profile, their history in a particular place may make this aim difficult to achieve. Other NGOs have operated as a conduit for government. Such a policy may have furthered their project aims, but how is it related to the aims now dominating the aid vocabulary, such as social mobilization and fundamentally changing social structures? The question of institutional isomorphism is affected by situations where NGOs in general face a balancing act between filling gaps which the government cannot handle on its own, on the one hand, and providing advocacy for democratic and social change, on the other. Answers to the problem will vary, and how the NGOs answer will be important not only for the development process at large, but also for future integration processes between donor states and NGOs.

Mission organizations in the NGO channel

The question of institutional isomorphism is especially interesting when it comes to the role of the mission organizations in aid, because of the important, high-profile role such organizations have played in the history of what today is called North-South relations. Many important NGOs, especially in certain regions in some countries, are mission organizations, both Christian and Muslim, although NGO literature tends to ignore this fact. Often mission organizations are simply defined out of the system, as not being proper NGOs – i.e. they are said to be primarily concerned with 'spiritual matters' as opposed to voluntary development organizations concerned with development construed in social and economic terms. Typologies of NGOs in aid often disregard the mission organizations without even bothering to discuss the matter. This not only reduces the complexity and heterogeneity of the system, it also takes away important parts of its history. The strategic dilemmas facing the mission organizations pose an interesting question, partly because of the missions' role in Western history and their central historical position in relations between 'us' and 'the others', but also because they may reveal in a more informative way some of the options that all real value-sharing organizations will face in co-operation with the state.

In the early 1990s religion entered centre stage in both discussions about development and processes of cross-cultural representation and communication. Social scientists and politicians have even started to talk of an era of clashes between civilizations, where the main conflict would be between the Islamic world and the Christian West. How will this situation affect the NGO channel as a system, and the official value orientation of the mission organizations? Will they talk about dialogue or religious struggle, and what is their actual policy likely to be? Can the expressed aim of dialogue be met at the same time as these organizations attain their own goals and further their own agenda, in this context of a clash between civilizations, i.e. between religions? Furthermore, the missions can no longer be seen as simply Northern NGOs or Northern influence in the South. Evangelization has become a global movement consisting of people in both North and South, united in a struggle against other beliefs. In this sense, religion is a truly cross-cultural institution or social movement. This potentially global and non-governmental network within which mission organizations may operate, can therefore demonstrate that the organizations in the NGO channel are less similar than they appear.

Research and empirical data on how these organizations function within the aid channel are hard to come by. The following is based on a) studies of two Norwegian mission organizations, the Norwegian Lutheran Mission and the Santal Mission in two countries, Ethiopia and Bangladesh, and of two of their longest-lasting projects there, in order to be able to assess changes over time. Searches of archival material, field visits and discussions with staff at field and headquarter level were conducted in both organizations. It is also based on b) collected data about project profiles, budgets and expatriates and missionaries in the mission field for all the 24 Norwegian mission and church organizations involved in aid in 1991, and similar data for the years 1981, 1986 and 1991 for two of the organizations. Finally these findings were compared with analysis in published studies of the same organizations before the development aid era and before they became attached to this aid channel. Only some general findings are presented here, but some of the same dilemmas and trends will most probably exist in other countries as well, since mission organizations will face some of the same constraints and possibilities owing to the international, systemic character of the NGO channel.

Two issues will be raised: the relationship between development aid and Christian mission and how it has been apprehended within the mission itself, and secondly, the importance of aid in influencing mission activities and creating conflicts between evangelization and development assistance within the mission organizations. Has the relative importance of diaconal work as compared with evangelization changed as a result of the organizations becoming members of a secular-oriented aid channel, and to what extent has the diaconal work itself become secularized in order to access and maintain governmental funds? Christian mission organizations that are involved in aid tend to downplay such value differences partly in order to get support from secular-oriented public donors, arguing that development aid is an integral part of the mission: It is the diaconal responsibility of the church and there is therefore no dilemma to be discussed. At the outset of this discussion it is important to underline that the grand era of Western missions in terms of activities and missionaries was not in the last century or during colonial times. It is now, during the era of development aid in the period after World War II.[1] Since religion has entered centre stage in world politics in many areas, it is important to find out what these organizations actually do, how they contribute to development, peace and dialogue and how they themselves are affected by the NGO channel.

The mission organizations studied face – and their leaders often seem to acknowledge this – a dilemma between being organizations formed to spread the gospel and at the same time being heavily funded by public institutions, like the Norwegian Government's development agency, NORAD, which since 1963 has adopted regulations clearly distinguishing between development work and mission. These regulations have brought integration and been instrumental in furthering institutional isomorphism, especially *vis-à-vis* the mission organizations. In fact, the so-called 'neutrality paragraph' (see Chapter 5) required likemindedness at the outset between donors and organizations and among organizations regarding fundamental policy and value issues. The regulations made it illegal to establish or implement state-funded projects motivated by religious or other 'partisan' ideas. In more than 25 years this paragraph was more or less untouchable, and the Christian-Conservative coalition government in the first half of the 1980s made no efforts to change it.

The mission organizations, although disagreeing on a number of religious issues and representing different traditions and working styles, reacted to the 1963 paragraph in more or less the same way. In general, they did abide by the rules. They downplayed evangelization in development projects co-financed by the state. Medical doctors working at hospitals partly funded by NORAD, but regarded by the organization as mission hospitals, were formally not allowed to do evangelical work in working hours. Discussions ran high: to what extent could they have prayers at such a hospital? At weekends only, after working hours or never? Self identity was at stake: a person might have been recruited as a missionary, but in budgets financed by NORAD he had to be described as a development aid worker. He had had a call from God to go out to the mission field, but ended up, formally, as an inexpensive development aid worker, because for years NORAD gave support to posts according to fixed wage levels. Since the missionaries were paid much lower salaries than the average expatriate, the difference could be rechannelled to the organization as a kind of hidden profit and used for evangelization. Contradictions emerged in most organizations between those who wanted to seek more state money for diaconal work, which they thought in the long run would benefit evangelization, and those who saw these funds as a danger to their real mission. But as organizations they all accepted that their traditional holistic approach to the spiritual and social needs of the human being had to be dropped in order to access donor money.

Seen over a longer period of time there can be no doubt that the mission organizations in the period under study (1963–93) became strongly influenced by secular development priorities and concerns. A main strategy was, and still is, to try to develop distinct departments or institutions within an organization: one working with aid where the language is the language of the NGO channel and where reports and budgets are produced to satisfy the donor, and one being traditionally mission-oriented. In many fields there have been only minor differences between a mission organization and other organizations. In the home country this separation of mission and development has functioned more or less as expected, but in the field it has often been regarded as irrelevant, difficult to maintain or as a combination of stupidity and dishonesty. Development aid workers paid by NORAD have been involved in evangelization, and missionaries have been involved in development aid work, and it is only in the reports to the donor that a clear distinction has been upheld. In some project areas mission organizations as mission organizations are now facing problems caused by NORAD's generosity in the past: buildings, schools and even hospitals, established with NORAD support, have become a burden to manage and maintain in the competition for staff, attention and time. The financial and political-administrative dependence on public funding has clearly influenced how fundamental questions in a mission strategy like nationalization and the balance between mission and diaconal work have been addressed.[2] In a longer time perspective it might be possible to regard this close relation to the secular state as a watershed in mission history. Evangelization has in some cases become subjugated to secular development concerns, because being a member of the NGO channel has robbed it of time, attention and resources. In Norway, the establishment of Bistands-nemda as an umbrella organization for the mission organizations (in Sweden the same type of organization has been established between the state and the individual mission organizations) has improved their ability to conform with state demands, while increasing the potential for maintaining their mission identity in the field. It has created distance at an organizational level and acts as a buffer or a two-way transmission belt between the missions and the state. What was initiated by the state as a solution to their administrative burdens, has furthered isomorphism at a rhetorical level (the staff of Bistandsnemda are experts in conveying the mission organizations' projects in the language of the aid community), while the mission organizations in the field have obtained increased freedom to nurture and further their own values.

As value-sharing organizations, the mission organizations, have experienced the conflict between their own and the state agendas as a bigger problem than it is for organizations with less focus on value promotion. This has been linked to the ongoing discussion within the missions about the relationship between religious, cultural and social change. There is a great difference between regarding 'sin' as a main reason for underdevelopment and the embracing of Christianity as a sufficient cause of real development, and giving emphasis to historical, economic and social conditions. In the former perspective the world's history is regarded as a religious drama, where development is a by-product of the right religious conviction. There has been disagreement on the relation between saving individual souls and building up local congregations and churches, and there have been different opinions about the role of the missionary as an agent for social and cultural change. The main aim of the organizations has, of course, been salvation, achieved only through Jesus Christ. Social responsibility is important and development is regarded as necessary, but not as identical with, or as important as, evangelization. Freedom and prosperity are not synonymous with salvation. So long as these are their convictions, should Christian missionaries, rather than becoming bogged down in project work and report-writing to the donor state, work as teachers and doctors in ordinary public or international projects, so that they can at least devote their free time to missionary activities? Mission NGOs have pointed to the temptation of becoming entrepre-neurs for public development work (see, for example, the Santal Mission:76-77). Public donor links give access to more funds, but steal time and attention from what is more important.

In important respects, the mission organizations have become more similar to the state in structure and behavioural focus in aid activities, but at the same time, by skilfully employing the official aid language, they have maintained important value orientations and deliberately presented themselves as more similar than they are in reality. Their existence within the NGO channel may demonstrate a more general but less visible phenomenon right across the organizational landscape. Many NGOs are value-oriented NGOs, but these values have not always been allowed to surface partly because of the organizations' coping strategies. The donor states' need for control, professionalism, efficiency and religious neutrality has had an impact on this integration process in particularly interesting ways, and in processes that so far are not much studied.

Ethics 'without frontiers' and the question of humanitarianism

Another issue which has been, and will continue to be, a dividing line among organizations and which also affects relationships with states, is the question of advocacy versus traditional humanitarianism.

NGOs have promoted themselves as being involved in both neutral humanitarianism and partisan activities. In fact, most organizations have taken on both roles in different circumstances. Organizations do not choose their profile on a purely political or theoretical basis; history and political traditions, image management and market considerations intervene. In Britain, for example, charities are not legally allowed to be politically partisan or involved in political advocacy (this has, for example, prevented Amnesty International from being registered as a charity), while no such laws exist in, for example, Norway (where Amnesty International and solidarity organizations, often critical of government policies, have been succesful in applying for government support over the NGO chapter). The option of becoming advocacy organizations will partly reflect national conditions (in Britain it has been argued that NGOs have tended to mute their criticism of official aid policies, partly because of the fear of coming into conflict with the charity laws (see Robinson, 1991:176), but also the funding possibilities enjoyed by different organizations and activity profiles. What organizations usually do and can do, is therefore influenced by different political contexts and situations, as has been recently demonstrated again in the wars in the Balkans and in Rwanda.

The general dilemma between humanitarian aid and 'speaking out' is not a new one. The International Red Cross is still dogged by its decision to say nothing about the conditions in German concentration camps during World War II. Médicins sans Frontiéres, led by Bernard Kouchner, later French Humanitarian Minister, was established after Kouchner and some other doctors denounced the genocide they had seen in Biafra while working for what they regarded as the tight-lipped International Red Cross. The conflict in Bosnia, as in Somalia and Eritrea earlier, has again presented traditional humanitarian NGOs with a moral dilemma: speaking out means taking sides. Some NGOs working in Bosnia, for example, ended up calling for war against Serbia. Humanitarian organizations have in general stood for bringing aid to anybody at any time, regardless of political or religious affiliations. Historically speaking, most NGOs have at least publicly tried to follow this principle.

In reality, of course, television has been a driving force in the last few years behind deciding who gets humanitarian assistance and who does not. The focus of CNN and other TV channels has decided where aid has gone. Moreover, humanitarian assistance has always been politically influenced. It is well known that the Reagan administration aimed at using food aid as a weapon against Mengistu, as the US Government used food aid as an instrument in the 1960s to persuade the Indian Government to implement the Green Revolution. Humanitarian aid has also helped to cover up the incapacity of politics to attack the evil at its roots, demonstrated in the recent Balkan wars.

The question, however, is one not only of morals but also of organizational strategy. The eventual choices reflect values, as well as questions of publicity, legal standing and market shares. A former Director of Christian Aid in Britain overlooked these structural features when he moralized about a 'curious, one might say almost pathological, discontinuity between an intense emotional commitment to a particularly dramatic symptom', such as famine in Ethiopia, 'and a continuing neglect of the chronic disease of which the symptom is part' (quoted in Burnell, 1991:11). This discontinuity is not so much pathological as both understandable and practical, given these structures and the media context. Médicins sans Frontières split after Kouchner chartered a hospital ship to rescue some 2,500 Vietnamese boat people drifting in the China Sea. Some thought he was pulling the organization into one publicity stunt too many, and Kouchner and some of his colleagues formed Médicins du Monde instead. After the discovery of the Serbian camps in Bosnia, they ran a poster campaign comparing Serbian President Milosevic to Hitler. In general, most NGOs seem to be less activist, and more geared towards humanitarian aid or towards long-term project implementation. This at least is the situation in Norway, although the most influential and the biggest organizations are thriving on publicity stunts in relation to emergencies. In many conflict situations the NGO communities appear as a humanitarian monolith, with some few exceptions. Solidarity organizations established in the heyday of Third Worldism have tended to emphasize that they have developed into ordinary aid organizations, etc., while mission organizations describe themselves in the secular language of development. When over 100 NGOs are working in Rwandan refugee camps, with all the politics and co-ordination problems involved, without raising great debates on policy or aid issues, this may partly reflect the fact that they have tacitly agreed not to criticize each other's policies in public, because this might turn out to be a Pandora's box, which would be dangerous for all as a coping strategy in a shrinking aid market. With thousands of NGOs working all over the world, many of them in the same countries, it is astonishing that they apparently disagree very seldom on fundamental policy issues or aid strategies or how the contradiction between 'speaking out' and neutral humanitarian aid should be solved. This may reflect what can be called the internal solidarity within the international social system. Although the issue of advocacy versus traditional humanitarianism will continue to be (as it has been from the beginning) a dividing line, it will most probably have marginal effects on the system as such, although it will be another counterweight to institutional isomorphism.

Operational or non-operational?

One dilemma which is likely in the near future to be even more important in deciding how different types of resources are transferred within the channel and how integration processes develop, is whether Northern NGOs will continue to be operational or whether they should change themselves into 'partnership' organizations. The problem is coming to the fore because of fundamental historical changes outside the channel itself. But it also embodies unavoidable internal value questions related to equity, transparency and partnership.

Northern NGOs have traditionally been implementing NGOs in their home countries (running hospitals, schools, etc.) and also in developing countries. Overseas this dates back to the start of mission activities. Northern organizations (including the mission organizations) became operational on a much larger scale and with much more weight in the development aid epoch. The 1970s and the 1980s in international aid were decades of integrated rural development programmes, which often were led by a great number of Northern NGOs. At no other time did so many Westerners work as administrators, development diplomats or expatriates in Africa and many other developing countries.[3]

The main point here is not to try to assess the overall impact of this aid profile, because the question of which model will prevail in the future will be not so much a question of what works in a development perspective, as it will be a political and ideological question. To have large projects implemented by foreign NGOs – a *modus operandi* which belongs to a period when developing countries lacked sufficient qualified manpower – is becoming less and less politically acceptable to governments, organizations and peoples in developing countries. Temporarily, some recipient countries are forced to accept anything, but as soon as they develop, experience shows, this situation will cease. Moreover, the competition from private firms in aid and emergencies will most probably increase. Operational Northern NGOs have been facing increasing criticism from the developing countries and also from within the NGO channel itself. There is no reason to believe that this is a fad. The political and ideological development in developing countries and between North and South, and the emergence of Southern NGOs wanting access to the same resources as Northern NGOs, will render obsolete the 'old' (1980s) model of Northern expatriates staying in an area for years on expatriate salaries. The organizations already face problems in recruiting sufficiently qualified personnel (accepted as qualified in the South) without losing their NGO identity, because demands will rise. (Mission organizations will be better able to tackle this challenge because of their great asset – the missionaries' willingness to live on low salaries.) The issue here is not therefore how effective operational organizations are (although this is often the only question asked in many impact assessment studies), but how different types of organization will adapt to the new political situation in the future. Some Northern NGOs are continuing as if the global, historical context has not changed. One available strategy of multi-functional organizations for organizational survival is obviously to become heavily involved in emergency aid, since that is still an area more or less monopolized by operational organizations from the North. But such a strategy will be available only to a minority of organizations, and it will be a strategy resting on feeble grounds, since the number and size of emergencies vary.

Some NGOs have built up a large organization, heavily operational and working hard to become what is seen as a more professional development agency (better planning tools, routines, organization, etc.). They are developing a wide range of activities (disaster relief, development education in the home country, refugee assistance both in the home and in Third World countries, advocacy, lobbying, campaigning and even policy research). They have also tried to enhance their impact by expanding projects or programmes that are judged to be successful. Others, especially those with a small staff of their own based in the country of operation, have chosen to work mainly by supporting various local groups, including co-operative endeavours, *ad hoc* women's organizations, Young Farmers'

Clubs, etc. and a number of newly established NGOs. The potential of finding good partners will also vary between organizational types. It is obvious that Northern church organizations will have a better chance of establishing a viable partnership, because there are already strong church organizations in many developing countries with a need both for additional funds and for advice on institution-building, than organizations with fewer established local NGOs as natural partners. As discussed earlier, over time such differences and such partnerships may counteract the process of isomorphy, and produce organizational difference rather than similarity. Some NGOs have profiled themselves as some kind of 'jack of all trades' in development aid. Others have lost some of their specific profile partly because of difficulties in deciding what are the root causes of the problems they want to solve (this is the case, at least in some countries, for Save the Children, US and UK as well as Redd Barna, Norway and Rädda Barnen, Sweden which have been involved in broad rural development projects with no focus on children's improvement), and partly because of changes in donor priorities. Very broad and ambitious aims create NGOs that are good at adapting to such trends, while other, mostly smaller, NGOs have managed, or have had very few alternative choices than to maintain their profile and restrict their activities within their special area of competence. The established project portfolio sets the NGOs' room for maneouvre, and many of them are stuck with projects that they cannot terminate or find local institutions willing or able to take over. The emerging question of 'partnership' and 'equity' cannot therefore be viewed in isolation from the problem of existing project commitments and past relations. Data from a questionnaire sent to all organizations receiving support from Norway showed that the great majority of the projects and even the NGOs themselves could not be sustained without external funds.

The NGO project honeymoon will, most probably, soon be over. This outcome will affect the balance between Northern and Southern NGOs and between different types of NGOs within the NGO channel. In this altered context to focus on communication and cross-cultural contact between people outside state apparatuses as much as on efficiency in promotion of economic, social or demo-cratic development in developing countries, will give space and legitimacy to the continued existence of a heterogeneous Northern NGO channel. It will also affect how the relationships between NGOs and governments, among Northern NGOs and between Northern and Southern NGOs are conceptualized and handled. This is a historical situation where the question of partners becomes crucial. The rush for good partners has already started internationally. Some organizations will have advantages, since they are part of a more or less global 'community of common interests', i.e. church-related organizations, trade unions, organizations for the disabled, etc. But organizations that have taken up new issues, like the Save the Children organizations, will face bigger challenges than those concerned with traditional issues in North-South relations.

NGOs, Partnership and Dialogue

The challenges of the NGO channel and developments in relations between NGOs and states cannot be discussed in isolation from the political-ideological trends framing them. What has been described as the present 'crisis of development theory' affects all social engineers. Aid is further questioned because the break-up of the Soviet bloc has made aid politically less important, since it was originally institutionalized as a weapon in the Cold War. In all the major donor countries the presence overseas, and not least for development aid, is losing the budget game.[4] Groups traditionally supportive of aid have started to question the realism of development aid and, privately, NGO actors also may express doubts about its usefulness. Moreover, governments, media and important groups in developing countries are often critical of the NGO channel, regarded as a channel of 'alien' Western influence and a transmission-belt of corruption, particularistic solutions to what are regarded as general societal problems, etc. Is there a supplement or an alternative to the way NGO aid has traditionally been carried out?

The issue of equity and partnership has been addressed by, among others, USAID, 1982, UNDP, 1989, Pact 1989 and Fowler, 1991:

> NGO partnerships are one link in a system of civic affiliations that urgently need to be forged in this decade in order to increase our hope for more equitable and sustainable development in the next century. Viewing partnership as one part of a broader strategy in the development of a value-driven sector of society may help persuade NGOs to temper self-interest in their negotiations in order to achieve fundamental realignments in society for the common good (Fowler 1991:16).

What could be the distinctive feature of this kind of partnership, what sense of mutuality and equality could be developed, taking into consideration the general processes of isomorphism and integration? How can it be established, since the parties to this partnership are so different when it comes to historical background, resources and conceptual and financial power? The question has been discussed for quite a few years, and there are clear signs that no simple approach can turn histori-cally shaped and continually reproduced unequal aid relationships into partnerships. Fowler put forward four preconditions: a mutually understood product, trust, development legitimacy and partnership as projection (ibid.:12–13). To what extent are these preconditions sufficient and how will they be influenced by the system's mechanisms?

Some of the mechanisms of power distribution affecting the NGO channel have already been discussed in this book. The donors in general call the tune, because of financial resources, conceptual dominance and the unequal distribution of sanction-ary instruments. NGO aid, like other donor channels, always produces unequal donor-recipient relations. A change in vocabulary – to 'equal partnership' or a 'global civil society' as it has recently been termed in UN documents – will not alter this reality. To prioritize partnership, not only rhetorically but in reality, will require a) attempts at bringing down deep-seated conceptual and cultural barriers between individuals and peoples and b) a change in the project focus of the past. By overemphasizing efficiency and goal achievement in project work, the overriding concern for the organization becomes what it achieves, not what it represents, namely, how human relations are built and identity negotiated, be it 'ours' or 'theirs'. Traditional project approaches tend to erect such barriers, instead of making them easier to overcome.

Slogans like 'partnership' and 'equality in dialogue' cannot be fully realized within existing system structures and language, even if trust and partnership as projection are achieved. It will also require, among other things, a *philosophical* acceptance of pluralism in a way that has been rare in most civilizations, not least within the Western and Islamic traditions. 'The other' which one wants to help cannot, within a truly pluralist perspective, be seen or conceptualized as identical to 'us' or 'me'. On the contrary, an acceptance of this pluralism requires that 'the other' is seen as being different from 'me' and one who lives within his own context with his own life projects. Can NGOs with strong missions, with a belief that their ideas represent the only path to 'heaven' or to 'development', use these slogans at all and at the same time be transparent? We are not here discussing NGO aid which imposes itself upon the receiver. Sometimes, without having been asked, NGO actors have arrived in hundreds to implement projects directed at some pre-conceived target group. NGOs have imposed both paternalism and forms of relative equity, without discussing how to strike a careful balance, or what paternalism is justifiable and what is illegal. There is no clear-cut answer as to how one should care for 'the other' without invading him, or how to advise without attempting to govern. This discussion is, however, different from the one raised here.

Authentic help, as it is often described in NGO-speak, is aid which should help the 'other's' projects; its aim is that the beneficiaries should succeed in achieving what they want. The question therefore becomes: do NGOs want a value to be realized, not because it is 'theirs' or because it is a value, but because it is a value for those who ask for help? And if they do not, how can the present NGO rhetoric be justified? NGOs with strongly felt shared values, in particular, will, if they are operational NGOs, face difficulties in implementing their own rhetoric about equity and dialogue. This is because gifts have everything to do with haves and have nots – and therefore with power – while the aid relationship officially aims at equality and partnership. NGOs have to some extent accepted this inherent contra-diction in aid, and instead attempted to solve it by image management. If the declared aim of equity and partnership is to be realized, they will have to ask how the question of generosity can become linked not only to the issue of altruism, but also to the question of freedom, not only for those who receive, but also for those who give. To what extent can the act of giving become an act of real reciprocity? Can aid, without the attitude and appearance of the helpers and without important hidden political-ideological agendas, be realized in NGO assistance? The actors are unable to form this channel by intention alone. The channel develops as a process, produced and reproduced by repetitive and continuous interaction between the actors, through a power struggle between donor and recipient NGOs or between official donors and NGOs, often taking the form of consensus-seeking negotiations about how it should develop. This continuous 'creation' of the channel has, in the past, mainly revolved around the project cycle of Northern NGOs, making talk about equity little more than an empty slogan.

To what extent will system structures hinder the channel in establishing relations where human beings can in reciprocity recognize and confirm each other's projects, and can it house activities where through praxis one can recognize oneself in the reality of the other? In spite of the institutional set-up of the channel, and its routine, repetitive and reifying service delivery, can the NGO channel initiate activities and relations that can help the actors to change not only the world, but the way people think about the world, themselves and the others? The obstacles have been many.

The shift away from development to emergency aid during the past few years has encouraged the reproduction of misery images and established new frames for foreign policy debates. A growing number of NGO employees are living on disasters and misery management. This creates and recreates all the time a social basis for a special type of image-production, both of 'the others' and of 'us'. Organizations use or exploit poverty for raising funds. Campaigns have been started where organizational survival and manifestation in the aid market have overshadowed the concern for lives in other countries. In the same way as the mission activities of the past depended on support from the home country, drawing on an image of 'dark, wild and uncivilized Africa' or the 'fatalistic Orient', this modern version of Western humanitarianism rests on an image of permanent emergencies and people's inability to help themselves.[5] This might have important impacts on donor communities' images and ways of thinking about the world, which in the long run may be as important in a global development perspective as what is currently achieved by the same NGOs in developing countries. These domestic ideological and political impacts have seldom been considered as integral parts of the way the NGO channel functions, and in particular the consequences it will have on equity and partnership.

If the NGO channel is to achieve its stated aim of improving understanding and empathy, which are also important justifications for the state support given to the channel, the question remains: how to increase the knowledge and solidarity of Northern populations as part of development aid, and how to establish methods for genuine partnership and cross-cultural communication and institutionalize an international network with fewer of the North-South power relations generally attached to it?

Some solutions have proved to be dead ends. In the international progressive NGO milieu, it has been very common to act as if there is somebody 'out there' who represents 'the other': the local people, the farmers, the South, etc. Meetings have been held where one or two Africans or Asians have been introduced to speak, not on their own behalf, or for a particular government or pressure group, but on behalf of 'women in the South', or 'the South', etc. The idea that such collectivities can be represented by individuals, makes communication, discussion and the re-enactment of others' thought, perspectives and understanding, less important or almost irrelevant. 'The South' – more than 100 countries, and billions of people – represented by one person is absurd. By inventing 'the others' as opposed to 'us', the complexity of the world becomes manageable, but in a way which may act as a barrier towards reaching the NGOs' goal: equity in communication. The channel, contrary to widespread rhetoric, is not involved in a dialogue between North and South, it has never been and will never be. The prevailing idea that NGO people communicate with 'the poor', 'the oppressed', 'the South' or 'the women', can be seen as a way of handling the need for conceptual control and action. But since dialogue is always between or among particular perspectives, interests and value orientations, only by liberating themselves from such ideas of representation, can the NGOs develop the dialogue they describe as the aim of NGO communication.

This tendency is linked to another feature of the prevailing NGO perspectives and NGO-speak: humanity is often described as 'one'. Consequently consensus on fundamental values is not only possible but also preferable. By continuous enlightenment (or cultural imperialism, others will say) and hard work (more projects and more donor money) they, i.e. the 'others', could be persuaded to agree with 'us', regarding either the gender or the equality question, pluralism or the only true religion. In this regard the practical side of NGO thinking has been in line with – and is certainly influenced by – a fundamental trait in Western thinking. This view has created a conceptual barrier against comprehending and acting on the growth of fundamentalism or the upsurge of ethnic chauvinism. NGO literature in general has seldom discussed or taken up such themes, mainly because this was a less important issue during the NGO decade and it was not naturally captured by the perspective of the so-called new development paradigm or the NGOs' 'articles of faith'. It is easier to acknowledge in the 1990s, with the upsurge of irrationalism, religious fanaticism and ethnic barbarism, than it was in the 'stable' Cold War situation, that conditions for communicative consensus, which has been a fundamental premise for most aid projects, have simply not existed in many cases. It has also reduced the importance of NGOs taking sides in the struggles between moralities and values, since existing differences have tended to be regarded as the results of the level of historical development, etc.

The challenge is to establish not only meeting points but arenas of cultural communication other than those created by the so-called Global Village, which tend to be a one-way communication from Hollywood to the African 'tukul'. The NGO channel, with its external constraints and possibilities, its characteristics and declared aims, may initiate more equality in these relations. Some of the NGOs attempted to distance themselves from mainstream aid in the past, because it was unequal and tended to reinforce the donor's belief in the universalism of his values. The channel may resolve the contradiction between aims and praxis by establishing zones of communication which utilize, and grow on the dialectical relationship between knowledge of oneself and knowledge of 'the other'. Cultural meetings do not have to be primarily a form of self-confirmation of one's own identity. Partnership requires the build-up of a societal consciousness in these zones, where people from different cultures become conversational subjects.

Partnership does not imply that the channel creates arenas or relations where people are 'nicer' to each other than they are generally, or more 'tolerant' and 'relativistic'. Their ability to 'let the grassroots speak' has been put forward as a particular feature, or an important comparative advantages, of NGOs. Not all studies of NGO achievements in the past will confirm this assertion. The point here is not to focus on the grassroots, because they cannot speak, just as nobody can speak on their behalf. The notion of the grassroots speaking has often acted as a camouflage for NGO project leaders to do what *they* (or the donors) regarded as most important. As a general concept the grassroots are manipulative within this system of inequality between NGOs and those assessed and of distance between donor and project implementation, because they have no institutionalized expression or voice, and they may therefore continuously enlarge and intensify differences between the giver and the recipient. Due to its very diversity in value orientations, aims and profile, the NGO channel has a potential for realizing its aims of dialogue if it accepts an understanding of pluralism which the notion of the 'collective grassroots' negates.

NGOs cannot meaningfully use the terms 'equal partnership', 'dialogue', 'advocacy' on behalf of 'the other' without rejecting the idea that the true answers are known to somebody, be it Adam in paradise or Muhammad in the desert. One has to accept that existing different moralities are incompatible, that there is no overarching criterion available whereby people are enabled to decide the right life for humankind, and, finally, that there is no path which leads to the discovery of such truths. In the aid context it is important to be aware of the fact that when such 'true answers' are found, they are not necessarily compatible with other true answers (for example, the best way to achieve economic development for the poor will not always be compatible with the best way to promote democracy). Mission organizations will not accept, and have not accepted this. They, and other types of organization that have 'discovered the true path', use such terms only rhetorically. To argue that the ideas the NGOs are carrying, or the mission they may have, is simply universal or belongs to the 'common pool of mankind', downplays the fact that some organizations are exporting their own notion of what is universal and also the unequal power relations inherent in the channel. Moreover, it gives strong support to integration and isomorphy, since everybody is fighting for the same universal ideas. NGOs have the potential, however, to enter into relationships where they have to argue in support of their project, without linking the enforcement of their will to the much stronger power available to states.

The multiplicity of NGOs indicates that there will always be conflict between true ends and between true answers to the central development problems. Many NGOs are religiously motivated. To understand religion is an efficient way of acquiring knowledge about cultures. In a world of religious, ethnic and national conflicts it can be argued that it is more important to establish such zones of contact, not because consensus is possible, but because arenas for cross-cultural meetings are necessary. This is so – because the world, for example, of the poor herder in Turkana, Kenya is different from that of the NGO bureaucrat, the world of the Muslim or Christian fundamentalist is not that of the liberal atheist, and the world of those who think and speak in Swahili is not that of the Norwegian-speaking expert. Each world is composed of everything its members do and think and feel – expressed and embodied in the kinds of words and forms of language that they use, in their images and forms of worship, in the institutions that they generate, all conveying their image of reality and of their place in it. Members of the same organization – for example, a man as compared to a woman, a married person compared to an unmarried, a field worker as compared to the home staff – will have different conceptions of the world. The conflict between true ends is therefore not culture-bound, but universal. The existence of fundamentalist NGOs, of women's-lib NGOs and leftist and rightist NGOs – all altruistically motivated – is an indication of this plurality of ends. Human life can be interpreted as a battle of perpetually new and ceaselessly conflicting wills, individual or collective. In our time this is empirically reflected by the heterogeneity of NGOs, at the same time as the existence of the NGO channel also reflects that there is culture-transcending knowledge.

To argue that there are no true answers, and that the NGO channel may be an expression of this idea, does not imply the institutionalizing of cultural relativism as the hegemonic ideology. Northern and Southern NGOs are not as a rule relativists. But these NGO actors can, by means of imaginative insight and face-to-face relations, better understand the values, ideals, and forms of life of each other's societies. They may find these values unacceptable, and they often do (that is not the problem), but they are still a starting point for communication. What is important is that the NGO channel can develop relations where one might learn and experience that 'the other' may well be a full human being, with whom one can communicate, although he lives in the light of values widely different from one's own. These values can nevertheless be seen as values, ends of life, ends which NGOs fight for and by which human life could be fulfilled. The channel itself may, therefore, be an argument against equating one tradition with the human condition as a whole.

Social or political collisions will take place in such meeting places, and that is unavoidable if value-oriented NGOs take part. The conflict of positive values alone makes it unavoidable. At the same time international NGO-speak is an important sign that one style of language, although born of Western history, is being adopted by the whole world. NGOs, and especially the proliferation of like-minded NGOs in almost all countries during the last few decades, are a sign of how fast this channel helps to transform the world. It has been created – and all who have taken part in NGO work will have experienced this – by a culture transcending knowledge. Although traditions differ, people do not live in cocoons and NGOs create one among many meeting places where people can argue for universal values and the rejection of cultural relativism. At the same time this international NGO system may create barriers against one culture allowing itself to pose as if it knows everything or has the final authority. Or at least these zones of cross-cultural communication may promote and preserve a kind of uneasy equilibrium, constantly threatened and in constant need of repair. Through these meeting points the organizations can be a channel for the idea that the notion of a single, perfect society of all mankind is internally self-contradictory. They can learn by praxis that the paradise of the Muslims is not that of Jews or Christians, the good life of a Nuer is not that of a social worker from Oslo, the society preferred by a Zulu is not the good society envisaged by a fishery expert from Troms, and the beliefs of an African rainmaker are not those of an umbrella-carrying researcher at the University of Bergen. Each will have his ideal constellation of virtues. The notion that a single perfect society is possible is incoherent.

NGOs can be mediators in this mid-way position between cultural relativism and aggressive uniformism. The channel as a social system and the organizations working in it are founded on the expectation and knowledge of the fact that there is a knowledge beyond culture. They are planning development projects and reporting systems that are not determined by the internal characteristics of different cultures. The whole discourse on NGOs and their profiles and activities within the social system itself – from Sylhet in Bangladesh to Awash in Ethiopia and Glasgow in Scotland, and involving poor farmers, illiterate women and medical doctors – is a clear sign that a 'universal' language has developed. In fact, seen from the remote villages in many parts of the world, the NGO decade and the proliferation of NGOs have been efficient vehicles for producing a knowledge valid for all. This creates the ground for an open and potentially just struggle among ideas and convictions about what constitutes a 'good society' and a 'good life'. On the other side, NGOs are, according to their aims, value-oriented organizations which justify their work with moral, altruistic arguments. They might be relatively big and powerful compared with weak peasant associations in Nicaragua or women's groups in Zimbabwe, but also junior partners when compared with the authority and standing of REST in

Eritrea and the Orthodox Church in Ethiopia. And compared with the state and the multilateral systems, NGOs – at least Norwegian NGOs – are relatively powerless. The fundamental structural relationship is therefore, compared with other channels, more conducive to dialogue rather than conditionality, openness rather than posing as having found the true path or the true answer, curiosity about the world rather than using aid as a means to reconfirm past outlooks.

If the NGO channel is based on this idea of pluralism and an acknowledgment of the infinite number of ways lives can take, and is without strong sanctionary powers, it will not suppress too many varieties of positive action or frustrate too many equally valid human goals. In a period when the world is marked by religious and ethnic strife and conflicts between and within states, the NGOs may play an important role in this respect. Since the channel was established in the early 1960s the prevailing understanding of history and development has changed. Most importantly, forces have emerged which were not predicted by those who established aid as a political and administrative project in the 1950s and 1960s, and which most modernization theories thought belonged to the dustbin of history: namely, the resurgence of religion and especially of ethnic chauvinism. Disregard of the strength of totalitarian or authoritarian nationalist or religious movements, and their triumph, was inherent in precisely those ideologies which at the same time helped to frame the whole idea and strategy of development aid. In this situation the NGO channel may have a role in affecting how solutions are arrived at when interests conflict. It might influence how information is brought to bear on entrenched values and beliefs, not necessarily to 'uproot' them but to transform behaviour which may be acceptable to the individual and small groups but is harmful to society. Some of these problems seem difficult to solve by technocratic improvements in government and political systems, and perhaps require alternative, although not necessarily better or more democratic, systems of international co-operation.

A pluralist channel outside the state system?

The principle of state sovereignty is coming under increasing pressure with the globalization of the economy and of information systems, and also because of problems of the environment and poverty. Many matters require indivisible and global solutions, and cannot be efficiently handled within the size and shape of sovereign states created by the historical processes of the past. One might argue that this 'state failure' at the international level creates niches for international NGOs, since they are organizations that cross national boundaries and should therefore be capable of mediating long-term, rational policies in the above-mentioned fields. In general, however, these tasks will mainly be the responsibility of supra-state or supra-national institutions like regional economic or political institutions, or international associations of states like the UN. The UNDP's 1993 *Human Development Report* noted (p.1) that, 'because future conflicts may well be between people rather than between states, national and international institutions will need to accommodate much more diversity and difference, and to open many more avenues for constructive participation'. Let us assume that the report is right: Can the international NGO system establish such avenues for constructive participation?

Whatever the future potential of NGOs in this regard, people in the NGOs have created a number of quite new types of cultural and economic network across national borders and outside the state system. These constitute, historically speaking, a new force in the international arena, and, significantly, a force which is engaged in global development issues and provides an arena for an ongoing international discourse on development where researchers, practitioners and beneficiaries alike can take part. This has been manifested at global conferences like the UN Conference on the Environment and Development in Rio de Janeiro in 1992, and more informally, but perhaps more significantly, in day-to-day contacts. The point here is not that these networks have proved to be better than public or official networks, but that they are different and involve other actors (the actual role and influence of such networks are not yet known, and more research needs to be carried out). The NGOs run the risk of becoming marginalized because they are formally outside the state system, but precisely because of these same structural features, they also have the possibility to establish unique face-to-face relations between people. Since equal partnership and real responsibility presuppose opportunities for physical co-existence in some form or other, the NGO channel as a 'meeting place' provides such opportunities.

The heterogeneity of NGOs represents alternative networks with different interests and kinds of people attached to them. There is no evidence to suggest that these networks are in general more marked by equality, dialogue and self-control than are state-to-state relations. Like the rest of this international NGO system, they are marked by social, political and cultural forms which are not replicable or sustainable over time. But most importantly in this connection the NGOs do not have the same possibilities of exploiting the tremendous power that interstate relationships in aid make available to the donor state, and their loyalty and frame of reference are not restricted to their own country. They therefore represent a force which may help to counteract regionalization and ethnification of the world economy and world politics. There are reasons to believe that some of the international networks and partnerships recruit, train and promote a network of 'ordinary people' who are more loyal to the world community and more sensitive to social and political issues. In this area also there is a need for more research. Some surveys give support to the above assumption, but there are no conclusive data about the relationship between NGO membership and such attitudes. Seen in a long historical perspective it is possible to suggest that the rules, procedures, norms, evaluations as well as organizations which have emerged within the channel have supplemented an international regime of dominance and dependency with one of pluralism and more equality. This system cannot be regarded as being separated from the constraints that define the overall global, strategic setting in which the organizations interact. But new institutions affect the forms of co-operation that emerge over time. In this sense institutions matter. These institutions reflect the distribution of power between international and local NGOs, but the power differences are less than in similar relations between the respective state institutions.

Most NGOs and donors would say that there is a need for institutional innovation in international relations. The NGO channel, comprising networks of organizations from different countries, cultures and civilizations but sharing a 'community of interest' (trade unions, business organizations, women's organizations, scouts' organizations, religious organizations, etc.), involved in both project work and advocacy, and with the aim of mobilizing new and less privileged people into the network, can represent such an innovation.

Notes

1 State support for Norwegian missions is not a new phenomenon. Both Thomas von Westen (1682–1727) and Hans Egede (1686–1768), who initiated mission among Inuits and the Sami people, were supported by the state by means of the establishment of the Misjonskollegiet in 1714. From the state's point of view this was primarily seen as a way of securing political authority in the periphery of the kingdom. Since 1963 the Norwegian state has supported mission organizations with funds earmarked for development assistance. Over the years an estimated NOK 1 billion of NORAD support has enabled a rapid growth in the number of missionaries. The mission organizations are now working in more mission fields than ever before.

2 The debate was initiated in March 1989 by Bistandsnemda, an umbrella organization for the mission organizations co-operating with NORAD, now under the heading: 'Sustainable co-operation'. The word nationalization was avoided, perhaps because they did not want to dramatize the impact of a process that has put strong pressure on former mission priorities, and has to a large extent been discussed within the secular NGO-speak. The Norwegian Missionary Council in 1991 supported a project called 'Nationalization and the development projects of the mission organizations' (in Norwegian), which was finalized in August 1994.

3 The growing importance of NGOs as compared to state-to-state aid in this respect can be illustrated by figures from Norway: NORAD and the Peace Corps in 1994 employed only 130 and 116 expatriates respectively, while the Norwegian NGOs had close to 1,000 in 1991 (see Tvedt, 1993). The figures are based on a questionnaire sent to all Norwegian NGOs. At the start of the 1980s NORAD had more expatriate personnel than all the NGOs combined.

4 In the US even the number of diplomats stationed abroad to track political affairs and monitor trade agreements is shrinking fast. The pressure that began in the mid-1980s, and accelerated with the Clinton Administration's plan to reduce the budget deficits, had led to the closing of consulates, libraries and aid missions. The Republican-controlled Congress has reduced the support for aid to such an extent that USAID has been forced to close 23 overseas missions since 1993. In some smaller donor countries, like Denmark and Norway, the development aid budgets have not been seriously reduced, but part of the aid is channelled to Eastern Europe and to fund assistance to asylum seekers in the donor countries.

5 For an analysis of Norwegian images of 'developing countries' in the era of development aid, see Tvedt, 1990.

References

Abed, F.H. *et al.*, 1984, 'NGO Effects and Planning: Development as an Experimental Process'. Paper presented at a seminar on Focus of 50 million: Poverty in Bangladesh, organized by ADAB, Dhaka, quoted in Aminuzzaman, 1993.

ADAB, (Association of Development Agencies in Bangladesh), 1993, *Directory of NGOs in Bangladesh 1993*, Dhaka: ADAB, Information and Support Services.

ADAB: *Bangladesh Private Voluntary Development Organisations (PVDOs). Definition, Statement and Code of Ethics* (no date)

Alam, M.,1988, 'Special Employment Programmes in Bangladesh: An Evaluation of Major Schemes' in M. Muqtada (ed.) *The Illusive Target: An Evaluation of Target Group Approach to Employment Generation in Rural Asia*, Geneva: International Labour Organization.

Al-Terafi, Al-Agub Ahmed, 1986, 'The Civil Service: Principles and Practice', in Muddathir Abd al-Rahim, Raphael Badal, Adlan Hardallo and Peter Woodward (eds), *Sudan since Independence*, London: Gower.

Alier, A., 1976, *Peace and Development in the Southern Region. A Statement*. Juba: Ministry of Culture and Information, The Democratic Republic of the Sudan.

Alier, A., 1990, *Southern Sudan; too many Agreements Dishonoured*, London: Ithaca Press.

Aminuzzaman, S., 1993, *Role of NGOs in the Socio-Economic Development of Bangladesh*, Dhaka, Bangladesh: Dept. of Public Administration, University of Dhaka.

Anheier, H.K., 1990, 'Private Voluntary Organizations and the Third World: The Case of Africa', in Anheier and Seibel, 1990: 361–376.

Anheier, H.K. and W. Seibel (eds), 1990, *The Third Sector: Compartive Studies of Nonprofit Organizations*, Berlin and New York: Walter de Gruyter.

Arén, G., 1978, *Evangelical Pioneers in Ethiopia*, Stockholm: Fosterlandsstiftelsen.

Arnove, R.F.,1980, *Philanthropy and Cultural Imperialism. The Foundations at Home and Abroad*, Boston, MA: G.K. Hall and Co.

Arou, M.K.N., 1988, 'Devolution: Decentralisation and the Division of the Southern Region into Three Regions in 1983', in Arou and Yongo-Bure, 1988: 166–88.

Arou M.K.N. and B. Yongo-Bure (eds), 1988, *North-South Relations in the Sudan since the Addis Ababa Agreement*, Khartoum: Khartoum University Press.

Asian Development Bank, 1989, *Cooperation with NGOs in Agriculture and Rural Development in Bangladesh*, Manila: National Support Services, Asian Development Bank.

Badal, R.K., 1984, 'The Role of the Commissioner under the People's Local Government Act', 1981, in Inter-Regional Training Project, 1984a.

Badal, R.K., 1988, 'The Addis Ababa Agreement Ten Years After', in Arou and Yongo-Bure, 1988: 12–40.

Bahr el Ghazal Region Group, 1984a, 'Decentralization Issues in Bahr el Ghazal', in Inter-Regional Training Project, 984: 153–159.

233

Bakke, J., 1987, *Christian Ministry Patterns and Functions within the Ethiopian Evangelical Church Mekane Yesus*, Oslo: Solum.

Bebbington, A. and D. Rivera, 1994, *Strengthening the Partnership. Evaluation of the Finnish Support Programme*, Country Case Study, Nicaragua, Helsinki: FINNIDA.

Bebbington, A., and R. Riddell, 1994, *New Agendas and Old Problems: Issues, Options and Challenges in Direct Funding of Southern NGOs*, London: Overseas Development Institute.

Bebbington, A. and G. Thiele with P. Davies, M. Prager and H. Riveros, 1993, *Non-governmental Organizations and the State in Latin America*, London and New York: Routledge.

Bior, Ajang, 1984, 'Evolution of Local Government in the Sudan', in Inter-Regional Training Project, 1984: 56–63.

Bjørnøy, H., 1988, *Undersøkelser om norsk utviklingshjelp utført av Statistisk Sentralbyrå i 1972, 1974, 1977, 1980, 1983, 1986, NSD Rapporter nr. 75*, Bergen: Norsk Sarnfunnsvitenskapelig Datatjeneste.

Bozeman, B., 1987, *All Organizations are Public. Bridging Public and Private Organizational Theories*, London/San Francisco: Jossey-Bass publishers.

Bratton, Michael, 1989, 'The Politics of Government-NGO Relations in Africa', *World Development*, 17 (4): 569–7.

Brons, M., W. Elisa, M. Tegegn and M.A.M. Salih, 1993. 'War and the Somali Refugees in Eastern Hararghe, Ethiopia', in Tvedt, 1993a: 46–68.

Brown. L. David and David C. Korten, 1991, 'Working More Effectively with Nongovernmental Organisations', in Paul and Israel, 1991.

Carroll, T., 1992, *Intermediary NGOs: The Supporting Link in Grassroots Development*, West Hartford, CT: Kumarian Press.

Chinemana, F., 1991, 'Review of NORAD Support to NGOs in Zimbabwe, Prepared for NORAD-Zimbabwe', Harare, January.

Christian Relief and Development Association, 1993, *Directory of Members*, Addis Ababa: CRDA.

CIDA (Canadian International Development Agency), 1986, *Corporate Evaluation of CIDAs Non-Governmental Organizations Program (Integrated Report)*, Ottawa: CIDA.

Clapham, C., 1985, *Third World Politics. An Introduction*, London: Croom Helm.

Clark, J. 1991, *Democratizing Development: The Role of Voluntary Organizations*, London: Earthscan.

CMI, 1986, *Bangladesh – Country Study and Norwegian Aid Review*, Bergen: The Chr. Michelsen Institute.

Cockson. P.W and C.H. Persell, 1985, *Preparing for Power*, New York: Basic Books.

Cohen, J.I. and A. Arato, 1992, *Civil Society and Political Theory*. Cambridge, MA: MIT Press.

COWI Consulting Engineers and Planners AS, 1992, *The Sahel-Sudan-Ethiopia Programme Evaluation Report* 2, 92, Oslo: Royal Ministry of Foreign Affairs.

Dalseng, T. 1993, *Statlige utbetalinger til private organisasjoner*, in Tvedt, 1993a.

DANIDA/CASA (Centre for Alternative Social Analysis),1989, *Evaluation Report: Danish NGOs, Report 1, Synthesis*, Copenhagen: DANIDA, November.

de Coninck, J., 1992, 'Evaluating the Impact of NGOs in Rural Poverty Alleviation – Uganda Country Study', *Overseas Development Institute*, Working Paper no. 51, London.

de Graaf, M., S. Moyo, and T. Dietz, 1991, *Non-Governmental Organisations in Zimbabwe*, NGO Landenstudie Zimbabwe/Impactsstudie Medefinancieringsprogramma, June.

Democratic Republic of the Sudan, 1972, *Proceedings of Relief & Resettlement Conference on Southern Region 21–23 February 1972 (Khartoum)*, Khartoum: Ministry of State for Southern Affairs.

DiMaggio, P.J. and H.K. Anheier, 1990, 'The Sociology of Nonprofit Organizations and Sectors', Annua.Rev.Sociol, 16: 137–59.

DiMaggio, P.J. and W.W. Powell, 1993, 'The Iron Cage Revisited: Institutional Isomorphism and Collective Rationality in Organizational Fields', *American Sociological Review*, 48, 147–60.

Directorate of Health and Social Welfare, Regional Ministry of Services, Equatoria Region, Juba, 1983, *Proceedings of the Firsr Regional Conference on Health and Social Welfare in Equatoria Region, Southern Sudan*, Nairobi: AMREF.

Douglas, J. 1987. 'Political Theories of Non-profit Organisations', in W.W. Powell (ed.), *The Nonprofit Sector: A Research Handbook*. New Haven, CT: Yale University Press.

Duffield, M and J. Prendergast, 1993, *Neutrality and Humanitarian Assistance: The Emergency Relief*

Desk and the Cross-Border Operation into Eritrea and Tigray, Washington, DC: Center of Concern and Birmingham: University of Birmingham. This report has been published as Duffield, M.R. and J. Prendergast, 1994, *Without Troops & Tanks: the Emergency Relief Desk and the Cross Border Operation into Eritrea and Tigray*, Lawrenceville, N.J.: Red Sea Press.

Edwards, M. and D. Hulme, 1996, *Beyond the Magic Bullet: NGO Performance and Accountability in the Post-Cold War World*, West Hartford, CT: Kumarian Press.

Egeland, J., 1988, *Impotent Superpower – Potent Small State*, Oslo: Universitetsforlaget.

Emmerich, H., 1969, *A Handbook of Public Administration: Current Concepts and Practices with Special References to Developing Countries*, New York: United Nations.

Eprile, C., 1974, *War and Peace in the Sudan, 1955–72*, Newton Abbot: David & Charles.

ERRA (Eritrean Relief and Rehabilitation Agency), 1992, 'General Guidelines for Indigenous and International NGOs Working in Eritrea', Asmara, May.

Esman, M. and N. Uphoff, 1984, *Local Organizations: Intermediaries in Rural Development*, Ithaca, NY: Cornell University Press.

Ethiopian Orthodox Church, 1990, *Ethiopian Orthodox Church*. Addis Ababa.

Etzioni, A., 1978, *Moderne organisasjoner*, Oslo: Tanum-Norli.

Etzioni. A., 1993, *The Spirit of Community. Rights, Responsibilities and the Communitarian Agenda*, New York: Crown Publishers Inc.

Etzioni, A., 1988, *The Moral Dimension. Towards a New Economics*, New York: The Free Press.

Eurobarometer 36, 1991, survey carried out by Norges Markedsdata and INRA (Europe), Oslo: Norwegian Social Science Data Service and Brussels: The Commission of the European Communities.

Farrington, J. and A. Bebbington with K. Wellard and D. J. Lewis,1993, *Reluctant Partners. Non-governmental Organizations, the State and Sustainable Development*, London: Routledge.

Finer, S., 1975, 'State and Nation-building in Europe', in C. Tilly (ed.), *The Formation of Nation States in Western Europe*, Princeton, NJ: Princeton University Press.

Fowler, A., 1988, *Non-governmental Organisations in Africa: Achieving Comparative Advantage in Relief and Micro-development*, Discussion Paper, 249, Brighton: Institute of Development Studies, Sussex University.

Fowler, A., 1990, 'Doing it better? Where and how NGOs have a Comparative Advantage in Facilitating Development', University of Reading: *AAERDD Bulletin* 28, February.

Fowler, A., 1991, 'Building Partnerships between Northern and Southern Development NGOs: Issues for the 1990s', *Development in Practice*, 1 (1).

Fowler, Alan, 1993, 'Non-governmental Organizations as Agents of Democratization: an African Perspective', *Journal of International Development* 5(3): 325–9.

Fukuyama, F., 1992, *The End of History and the Last Man*, New York: Free Press. .

Gellner, E., 1988, *Plough, Sword and Book: The Structure of Human History*, London: Collins Harvill.

Gidron, B., R. M. Kramer and L. M. Salamon (eds), 1992, *Government and the Third Sector. Emerging Relationships in Welfare States*, San Francisco: Jossey-Bass Publishers.

Hansmann, H., 1980. 'The Role of the Non-Profit Enterprise': *Yale Law Journal* 89 (April): 835–98. Reprinted in S. Rose-Ackerman (ed.), 1986, *The Economics of Nonprofit Institutions: Studies in Structure and Policy*, New York, Oxford University Press.

Harden, B., 1992, *Africa – Dispatches from a Fragile Continent*, London: Fontana Books.

Harir, S. and T. Tvedt (eds), 1994, *Short-cut to Decay. The Case of the Sudan*, Uppsala: Nordiska Afrikainstitutet.

Hegel, G.W.H., 1956, *The Philosophy of History* (tr. J.Sibree), New York: Dover Publications.

Hegel, G.W.H., 1942, *The Philosophy of Right* (tr. T.M.Knox), Oxford: Oxford University Press.

Heper, M.,1987, *The State and Public Bureaucracies. A Comparative Perspective*, London, Greenwood Press.

Hoedneboe, K., 1993, 'Guidelines of the Norwegian Government in Working with Private Organisations' (in Norwegian), in Tvedt (ed.) 1993a.

Hoedneboe, K. *et al.*, 1993, *Grace Period for a New Deal*, Report submitted to Norwegian Church Aid, Oslo: Norwegian Church Aid.

Hood, C. C., 1986, *Administrative Analysis. An Introduction to Rules, Enforcement and Organization*, Brighton: Wheatsheaf.

Hood, G. and F. Schuppert, 1990. 'Para-government Organizations in the Provision of Public Services: Three Explanations', in Anheier and Seibel, 1990: 93-106.

Huntington, S.P., 1993, 'The Clash of Civilizations?', *Foreign Affairs*, 72, 3, 22-49.

Inter-regional Training Project, 1984a. *Selected Papers from Seminars Organized during the Years 1981 to 1984*, edited and compiled by UNDP/DTCD Project SUD/83/002. Juba.

Inter-regional Training Project, 1984, *Decentralization. Tasks Ahead. Report on the Colloquium held on the 27 and 28 October 1983, the Council Room, University of Juba*, Juba: UNDPIDTCD Project SUD/83/002, ODA project AMTP.

Inter-regional Training Project, 1983, *Guidelines for Annual Budget and Monthly Financial Statements of the Area Councils. Compiled under the Supervision of the UNDP/DTCD/PROJECT SUD/83/002*, Juba: The Democratic Republic of the Sudan, Bahr el Ghazal Region, Equatoria Region. Upper Nile Region.

International Bank for Reconstruction and Development, 1981, *Project Performance Audit Report. Sudan Southern Region Agricultural Rehabilitation Project* (Credit 476-SU), IBRD: Washington, DC.

International Bank for Reconstruction and Development, International Development Association, 1973, Report of a Special Mission on the Economic Development of Southern Sudan, Country Programme Department, Eastern Africa, No 119a-SU, IBRD: Washington, DC.

Jackson, R.H. and C.G. Rosberg, 1982, 'Why Africa's Weak States Persist: The Empirical and the Juridical in Statehood', *World Politics*, XXXV (1).

James, E., 1990. 'Economic Theories of the Nonprofit Sector', in Anheier and Seibel, 1990: 21–31.

Jamil, L. and M. Mannam, 1994, 'A Study of Government-NGO Relations in Bangladesh in the Period 1992–1993: Collaboration or Confrontations', in Tvedt, 1996.

Johannesen, B. and G.M.Sørbø, 1996, 'NGOs at the Crossroads: Norwegian People's Aid and Save the Children, Norway in Zimbabwe', in Tvedt.

Johannessen, B., 1990, 'Foreign Aid to Bangladesh: the Norwegian Experience', in CHI 1986: pp. 283–93.

Karadawi, A., 1996, 'The NGO Scene in Ethiopia', in Tvedt, 1996.

Keen, D.A., 1996, 'A Comparative Study of Some Donor Countries' Experience', in Tvedt.

Khalid, M., 1985, *Nimeiri and the Revolution of Dis-May*, London: KPI.

Khamis, C., 1985, 'Decentralisation Issues in Equatoria Region', in Inter-Regional Training Project, 1984: 170–174.

Kjosavik, T.D., 1992, 'Ethiopia', in T. Jørgensen. (ed.), *I tro og tjeneste. Det Norske Misjonsselskap 1842–1992* II: 213–159, Stavanger: Misjonshøgskolen.

Korten, D.C., 1987, 'Third Generation NGO Strategies: A Key to People-centered Development', *World Development*, 15, Supplement, 145–60.

Korten, D.C., 1990, *Getting to the 21st Century – Voluntary Action and the Global Agenda*, Hartford, CT: Kumarian Press.

Kramer, R.M., 1992, 'The Roles of Voluntary Social Service Organizations in Four European States: Policies and Trends in England, the Netherlands, Italy and Norway', in Kuhnle and Selle, 1992: 34–52.

Kramer, R.M., 1981, *Voluntary Agencies in the Welfare State*, Berkeley, Los Angeles and London: University of California Press.

Kuhnle S., 1989, 'Den skandinaviske velferdsmodellen – skandinavisk? velferd? modell?', in Kuhnle S. and Stokke, L. (eds), *Visjoner om velferdssamfunnet*, Bergen: Alma Mater.

Kuhnle, S. and P. Selle (eds), 1990, *Frivillig organisert velferd – alternativ til offentlig?*, Bergen: Alma Mater.

Kuhnle, S. and P. Selle (eds), 1992, *Government and Voluntary Organizations. A Relational Perspective*, Aldershot, Avebury.

Kuhnle, S., 1992, 'Das Skandinavische Wohlfartstaatliche Modell im Zeitalter der europaischen Einigung', *Zeitschrift für Sozialreform* 10: 606–19.

Kuhnle. S. and P. Selle, 1992, 'Governmental Understanding of Voluntary Organizations: Policy Implications of Conceptual Change in the Post-World War II-period', Bergen: LOS-Senter Notat 92/1.

Lagu, J., 1980 *Decentralization. A Necessity for the Southern Provinces of the Sudan*: Juba: Juba University.

Lagu, J., 1978, 'Policy statement given by the President of the High Executive Council to the 2nd People's Regional Assembly' Juba: The Regional Ministry of Information and Culture, March.

Leat, D., 1990, 'Voluntary Organizations and Accountability. Theory and Practice', in Anheier and Seibel, 1990: 141–54.

Lorentzen, H., 1989, '"Voluntarism" and "Non-profit". A Discussion of two Central Concepts within the Third Sector' (in Norwegian), paper presented at 6th. Nordic Seminar on Social Politics, 1989, Oslo: Institutt for samfunnsforskning.

Lorentzen, H., 1993, *The Integration of Voluntarism. The State and the Voluntary Organizations* (in Norwegian), Oslo: Institutt for samfunnsforskning.

Lowe, R., 1993, *The Welfare State in Britain since 1945*, Basingstoke: Macmillan.

Lowi, T.J., 1969, *The End of Liberalism*, New York: Norton.

Madison, B.B., 1984, *The Addis Ababa Agreement on the Problem of Southern Sudan: A Study to Evaluate the Distribution of Benefits and Social Groups in the Southern Sudan and to Determine the Impact of this Distribution on the Region's Political Stability*, Ph.D. thesis, University of Denver, CO.

Malik, J.R, 1983, 'Decentralization of Powers to the Councils' in Inter-regional Training Project, 1984.

Malik, J.R., 1984, 'Issues of Local Finance in the Southern Region' in Inter-regional Training Project, 1984a.

Malwal, B., 1981, *People and Power in the Sudan – the Struggle for National Stability*, London: Ithaca Press.

Mamdani, M., 1986, 'Peasants and Democracy in Africa', *New Left Review*, 156, March-April: 37–51.

Migdal, J.S., 1988, *Strong States and Weak Societies. State-society Relations and State Capabilities in the Third World*, Princeton, NJ: Princeton University Press.

Mill, J.S., 1865, *Principles of Political Economy*. London: Longman, Green & Co.

Mills, R.L., 1977, *Population and Manpower in Southern Sudan*, Geneva: International Labour Organization.

Mishra, R., 1989, *The Welfare State in Capitalist Society*, Toronto: University of Toronto Press.

Moyo, S. and Y. Katerere, 1991, *NGOs in Transition. An Asessment of Regional NGOs in the Development Process*, ZERO Publications Working Paper, 6, Harare: ZERO.

Moyo, S., 1996, 'Development and Change in Zimbabwe's NGO Sector', in Tvedt, 1996.

Muir, A, 1992, *Evaluating the Impact of NGOs in Rural Poverty Alleviation – Zimbabwe Country Study* (with additional material by Roger Riddell), Working Paper 52, London: Overseas Development Institute.

Myklebust, T., 1989, *Åndelig utviklingshjelp? Kritisk søkelys på kristen misjon*, Oslo: Human-etisk forbund.

NANGO, (Zimbabwean National Association of Nongovernmental organizations), 1992, *Directory of NGOs in Zimbabwe 1992*, Harare: NANGO.

Nelson, R. and M. Krashinsk, 1973. 'Two Major Issues of Policy: Public Subsidy and Organization of supply', in D. Young and R. Nelson (eds) *Public Policy for Day Care of Young Children*, Lexington, MA: D.C. Heath.

NGO Affairs Bureau, 1990, *Guide to NGOs in Bangladesh*, Dhaka.

Nisbet, R.A., 1962, *Power and Community*, New York: Oxford University Press.

NORAD, 1993, *Handbook for Voluntary Organisations* (in Norwegian), Oslo: NORAD (Compiled by the Centre for Development Studies).

Norwegian Church Aid/Sudan Programme, 1984, *Agricultural Extension, Processing and Marketing Study. East Bank Equatoria Final Report*, Hemel Hempstead: Hunting Technical Services Ltd.

Norwegian Church Aid/Sudan Programme (various years), *Annual Reports*, Oslo, NCA.

Norwegian Church Aid/Sudan Programme, 1986a, *Economic Development. Potential Study. East Bank, Eastern Equatoria. Sudan.* Herst (England), Hunting Technical Services Ltd., p.l3.

Norwegian Church Aid/Sudan Programme, 1986b, *Proposal for Norwegian Church Aid Sudan Programme 1987-90*, Torit: NCA.

Norwegian Church Relief/Sudan Programme (various years), *Progress Reports*, Torit: NCA.

Norwegian Lutheran Mission, 1991, *Statement on Mission. A Declaration on the Mission Strategy of*

Norwegian Lutheran Mission in the Nineties, Oslo: The Norwegian Lutheran Mission.

Norwegian Lutheran Mission, 1993, *Giverkontakten*, No. 1, Oslo: NLM.

NOU, 1988, *Voluntary Organisations* (in Norwegian), Norges Offentlige Utredninger, 17, Oslo: Forvaltningstjenestene. Statens trykningskontor.

OECD, 1983, *The Role of Non-Governmental Organizations in Development Cooperation*, No. 10 in New series, Liaison Bulletin between Development Research and Training Institutes, Paris: OECD.

OECD, 1987, *Voluntary Aid for Development: The Role of Non-Governmental Organisations*. Development Co-operation Directorate, Document DCD/87, II. Paris: OECD.

OECD 1988, *Voluntary Aid for Development. The Role of Non-Governmental Organisations*, Paris: OECD.

OECD, 1990, *Directory of Non-Governmental Development Organisations in OECD Member Countries*, Paris: OECD.

Olsen, J.P., 1988, *Political Science and Organization Theory. Parallel Agendas but Mutual Disregard*, Bergen: Norwegian Research Centre in Organization and Management, Paper 88/22.

Olson, M., 1982, *The Rise and Decline of Nations*, New Haven CT: Yale University Press.

Organski, A.F.K.,1965, *The Stages of Political Development*, New York: Knopf.

Padron, M., 1987, 'Non-governmental Development Organizations: From Development Aid to Development Cooperation', *World Development*, 15, Supplement: 69–77.

Pardon, M, 1987, 'Non Government Development Organizations, *World Development*, 15, Supplement: 69–77.

Paul, S., and A. Israel, 1991, *Nongovernmental Organizations and the World Bank, Cooperation for Development*, Washington, DC.: World Bank.

Peace and Progress, 1972–1976–7, 1977, Juba: Regional Ministry of Information and Culture.

Peace and Progress, 1974, Juba: Regional Ministry of Information and Culture, Southern Region.

Peace and Progress, 1972-1973, 1973, A Report of the Provisional High Executive Council of the Southern Region of Southern Sudan marking the first Anniversary of the Addis Ababa Agreement and the Establishment of Regional Self-Government in Southern Sudan, Juba: Regional Ministry of Information and Culture.

Pelczynski, Z.A. (ed.), 1984, *The State and Civil Society, Studies in Hegel's Political Philosophy*, Cambridge: Cambridge University Press.

Pickering, A.K. and C.J. Davies, (undated), *Decentralisation Policy and Practice in the Southern Sudan. The Case of the Western Area Council*, The Inter-regional Training Project, Development Administration Group, University of Birmingham and UNDP project SUD/831002.

Powell, W. and P.J. DiMaggio, 1991, *The New Institutionalism in Organizational Analysis*, Chicago: University of Chicago Press.

Raaum, J., 1988, 'De frivillige organisasjonenes framvekst og utvikling i Norge', *NOU* 17: 239–356.

Redd Barna, 1993, *Bi-Annual Report* No. 2/93, Appendix 1.12., 'The formation and operation of NGOs in Ethiopia', Addis Ababa: Redd Barna.

Report to the Storting 29 (1971–72), *About some Main Questions regarding Norway's Cooperation with the Developing Countries* (in Norwegian).

Report to the Storting no. 34 (1986–87), *Some Main Questions in Norwegian Development Aid* (in Norwegian), Tilleggsmelding til prinsippmeldingen St.meld. nr. 36, 1985-85.

Report to the Storting no. 36 (1984–85), *About Some Main Questions in Norwegian Developmental Aid* (in Norwegian).

Report to the Storting no. 51 (1991–92), *About Some Main Trends in North–South Relations and Norway's Co-operation with the Developing Cuontries* (in Norwegian).

Report to the Storting no. 94 (1974–75), *Norwegian Economic Relations with the Developing Countries*, (in Norwegian).

Riddell, R.C., A. Bebbington and L. Peck, 1995, *Promoting Development by Proxy. The Development Impact of Government Support to Swedish NGOs*, London: Overseas Development Institute.

Riddell, R.C., 1990, *Judging Success: Evaluating NGO Approaches to Alleviating Poverty in Developing Countries*, Working Paper, 37, London: Overseas Development Institute.

Riddell, R.C and A.J. Bebbington with assistance from D.J. Davis, 1995, *Developing Country NGOs and Donor Governments. Report to the Overseas Development Administration*, London: Overseas Development Institute.

Riddell, R. and M. Robinson, 1995, *Non-governmental Organizations and Rural Poverty Alleviation*, Oxford: Clarendon Press in association with the Overseas Development Institute.

Riddell *et al.*, *Strengthening the Partnership – Evaluation of the Finnish NGO Support Programme*, Report 1994: 1, London: Overseas Development Institute and Institute of Development Studies, University of Helsinki.

Robertson, J., 1974, *Transition in Africa: From Direct Rule to Independence*, London: C. Hurst.

Robinson, M., 1991, 'An Uncertain Partnership: the Overseas Development Administration and the Voluntary Sector in the 1980s', in A. Bose and P. Burnell, *Britain's Overseas Aid since 1979: Between Idealism and Self-interest*, Manchester: Manchester University Press.

Sæverås, O, 1974, *On Church-Mission Relations in Ethiopia 1944–1969 – with Special Reference to the Ethiopian Evangelical Church Mekane Yesus (EECMY) and the Lutheran Mission*, Oslo: Lunde.

Salamon, L.M., 1987, 'On Market Failure, Voluntary Failure and Third-Party Government: Toward a Theory of Government-Nonprofit Relations in the Modern Welfare State', *Journal of Voluntary Action Research*, 16 (1–2): 29–49.

Salamon, L.M., 1990, 'The Nonprofit Sector and Government: The American Experience in Theory and Practice', in Anheier and Seibel, 1990: 219–41.

Salamon, L.M., 1994, 'The Rise of the Nonprofit Sector', *Foreign Affairs*, July/August: 109–22.

Salamon, L.M., 1981, 'Rethinking Public Management: Third-Party Government and the Changing Forms of Government Action', *Public Policy*, 29: 255–75.

Salamon, L.M., 1986, 'Governmental and the Voluntary Sector in the Era of Retrenchment: The American Experiment', *Journal of Public Policy*, 6.

Salamon, L.M. and H.K. Anheier, 1992, 'In Search of the Non-profit Sector I: The Question of Definition', *Voluntas*, 3, 2: 125–153.

Salamon, L.M. and H.K Anheier, 1992, In Search of the Non-profit Sector II: The Problem of Classification', *Voluntas*, 3, 3: 267–309.

Salokoski, M., T. Varis and S. Gebre, 1994, *Strengthening the Partnership, Evaluation of the Finnish NGO Support Programme, Country Case Study Ethiopia*, Helsinki and Addis Ababa: FINNIDA.

Santal Mission, 1986, *Misjon, utviklingshjelp og diakoni*, Oslo: Santal Mission.

Sanyal, B., 1991, 'Antagonistic Cooperation: A Case Study of Nongovernmental Oganisations, Government and Donors' Relationships in Income-generating Projects in Bangladesh', *World Development* 19 (10): 1367–79.

Saul, J., 1974, 'The State in Post-Colonial Society: Tanzania', *Socialist Register*, 1976.

Saxon-Harrold, S.KE., 1990, 'Competition. Resources and Strategy in the British Nonprofit Sector' in Anheier and Seibel, 1990: 123–40.

Seibel, W., 1989, 'The Function of Mellow Weakness. Non-Profit Organizations as Problem Nonsolvers in Germany', in E. James (ed.), *The Non-Profit Sector in International Perspective. Studies in Comparative Culture and Policy*, New York and Oxford: Oxford University Press.

Seibel, W., 1990, 'Organizational Behaviour and Organizational Function. Toward a Micro-macro Theory of the Third Sector', in Anheier and Seibel, 1990: 107–23.

Seip, A.L., 1984, *Veien lil velferdsstaten. Norsk sosialpolitikk 1920–75*, Oslo: Gyldendal.

Skar, Harald O., 1987, 'Norwegian Aia and the 3rd System. Norwegian Organizations in the Development Process: Future Directions', *NUPI-notat* 376, Oslo: NUPI.

Skar, H.O. (ed.), A. Haug and C. Littlejohn, 1996c, 'NGOs in the Nicaraguan Changing Reality. An Evaluation', in Tvedt, 1996.

Smillie, I. and H. Helmich (eds), 1993, *Non-Governmental Organisations and Governments: Stakeholders for Development*, Paris: OECD.

Smith, B., 1990, *More than Altruism. The Politics of Private Foreign Aid*, Princeton, NJ: Princeton University Press.

Smith, B.L.R. and D.C. Hague (eds), 1971, *The Dilemma in Accountability of Modern Government*, London: Macmillan.

Sodhi, P.S., 1981, 'Financial Issues – a Perspective', in Inter-regional Training Project, 1984.

Smith, S. and M. Lipsky, 1993, *Nonprofits for Hire. The Welfare State in the Age of Contracting*, Cambridge, MA: Harvard University Press.

Starkey, P., 1987, *Animal-drawn Wheeled Tool Carriers: Perfected Yet Rejected*, Berlin: GTZ.

Steen, O.I., 1988, 'Mål og milder i norske private organisasjoners utviklingshjelp. En undersøkelse av 11 organisasjoners prosjektvirksomhet i den 3. verden', *NUPI Report* 119, Oslo: NUPI.

Steen, O.I., 1989, 'Norwegian Nongovernmental Involvement in Zimbabwe', *NUPI Report 138*, Oslo: NUPI.

Steen, S., 1948, 'The Voluntary Organisations and Norwegian Democracy (in Norwegian). *Historisk Tidsskrift*, 34: 581–600.

Sudanow and Ministry of Guidance and National Information, 1983, *Perspectives on the South. An Analysis of Trends and Events Leading to the Final Decree of Regionalisation of the former Southern Region of the Sudan*, Khartoum.

TANGO (The Tanzanian National Association of Nongovernmental Organizations), 1994, *Directory of NGOs in Tanzania*, Dar es Salaam: TANGO.

Tendler, J., 1982, *Turning Private Voluntary Organisations Into Development Agencies: Questions for Evaluation*, Programme Evaluation Discussion Paper no. 12., Washington D.C.: USAID.

Tvedt, T., 1990, *Bilder av 'de andre'. Om utviklingslandene i bistandsepoken*, Oslo: Universitetsforlaget.

Tvedt, T., 1992, *The Nongovernmental Organisations as a Channel for Norwegian Aid. An Analysis of Historical Developments in the Relationsship between the Norwegian State and the Third Sector* (in Norwegian and written with assistance from E. Barkved, T. Dalseng, K. Hoedbneboe, K. Morvik and O.I. Steen), Evaluation Report 3, 92, Oslo: Royal Ministry of Foreign Affairs.

Tvedt, T. (ed.), 1993a, *An Analysis of Volunatry Organisations in Norwegian Development Cooperation* (in Norwegian), Bergen: Centre for Development Studies.

Tvedt, T. (ed.), 1993, *Conflicts in the Horn of Africa, Human and Ecological Consequences of Warfare*, Uppsala: EPOS.

Tvedt, T., 1994a, 'The Collapse of the State in the Southern Sudan after the Addis Ababa Agreement. Internal Causes and the Role of the NGOs', in Harir and Tvedt, 69–105.

Tvedt, T, 1994b, NGOs' Role at the End of History: Norwegian Policy and the New Paradigm', *Forum for Development Studies*, 1-2: 139–67.

Tvedt, T., 1995a, 'Voluntary Organizations and Norwegian Foreign Policy' (in Norwegian) in T.L. Knutsen, G.M. Sørbø and S. Gjerdåker, *Norwegian Foreign Policy*, Oslo: Cappelen: 238–260.

Tvedt, T., 1995b, *The Norwegian Samaritan: About Rituals, Self-images and Development Aid* (in Norwegian), Oslo: Gyldendal.

Tvedt, T., 1995c, *NGOs as a Channel in Development Aid. The Norwegian System*, Evaluation Report 3, 95, Oslo: Royal Ministry of Foreign Affairs.

Tvedt, T. (ed.), 1996, *Analyses of NGO Assistance in Some Selected Countries*, Bergen: Centre for Development Studies.

Tvedt *et al.* 1993 = Tvedt T., E. Barkved, L. Manger, and O.I. Steen, 1993, *Private Organisations as a Channel for Norwegian Aid. An Additional Study* (in Norwegian), Bergen: Centre for Development Studies.

UNDP, 1984, Sudan. *Accountancy and Financial Management Training in the Southern Region of Sudan. Report of the Evaluation Mission*, SUD/80/015, New York: UNDP.

United Nations. 1987. *Accountancy and Financial Management Training in the Southern Region of Sudan. Project Findings and Recommendations*. UNDPDP/UN/SUD-80-051/1, New York: UN Department of Technical Cooperation for Development.

United Nations, 1990. *International Standard Industrial Classification of all Economic Activities*, 3rd revised edition (Statistical Papers Series M, no.4, rev. 3), New York: United Nations.

United Nations, 1993, *Evaluation Bulletin*, New York: UN, Central Evaluation Unit, Spring.

UNDP, 1993a, *Human Development Report. 1993*, New York: Oxford University Press.

UNDP, 1993b, *UNDP and Organizations of Civil Society*, New York: Oxford University Press.

Uphoff, N., 1987, 'Relations between Governmental and Non-Governmental Organizations and the Promotion of Autonomous Development', Paper presented at the Experts' Consultation on Promotion of Autonomous Development, 27–30 October, Noordwijk.

USAID, 1982, 'A.I.D. Partnership in International Development with Private and Voluntary–Organizations', in *Aid Bureau for Programme and Policy Co-Ordination*, Washington DC: USAID.

van Heemst, J.P., 1989, *Size-Related Aspects of Donor NGOs: Some Findings for the Netherlands*, Working Series No. 55, The Hague: Institute of Social Studies.

Vaage, O.F., 1993, *Holdninger til norsk utviklingshjelp 1993*, Oslo: Statistisk Sentralbyrå.

Vivian, J and G. Maseko, 1994, *NGOs, Participation and Rural Development, Testing the Assumptions with Evidence from Zimbabwe*, Discussion Paper 49, Harare: United Nations Research Institute for Social Development.

Weisbrod, B., 1977, 'Towards a Theory of the Voluntary Nonprofit Sector in a Three-Sector Economy', in B. Weisbrod (ed.), 1977, *The Voluntary Nonprofit Sector, An Economic Analysis*, Lexington, MA: D.C.Heath, 51–76.

Weisbrod, B.A., 1988, *The Nonprofit Economy*. Cambridge, MA: Harvard University Press.

Wellard, K. and J.G. Copestake (eds), 1993, *Non-governmental Organizations and the State in Africa. Rethinking Roles in Sustainable Agricultural Development*, London: Routledge.

White, S. C., 1991, *Evaluating the Impact of NGOs in Rural Poverty Alleviation – Bangladesh Country Study*, Overseas Development Institute, Working Paper No 50, London: ODI.

Wieu, A.W.R., 1988. 'Southern Sudan Institutional Structure, Power and Inter-Governmental Relations Yesterday and Today', in Arou and Yongo-Bure, 1988: 40–57.

Williamson, O., 1985, *The Economic Institutions of Capitalism*, New York: Free Press.

Wils, F., 1991, *NGOs and Development in Brazil: An Overview and Analysis*, Co-financing Programme, Netherlands.

World Resources, 1988, *Report by World Resources Institute and the International Institute for Environment and Development*, New York: Basic Books.

Woodward, P., 1991, *Sudan 1898–1989. The Unstable State*, London: Lester Crook Academic Publishing.

Zimbabwe Country Study, 1989, Harare: Hifab International and Zimconsult.

Index

ACROSS 118
Addis Ababa Agreement 190, 196
Afar Relief and Development Association 28
African National Congress 46
al Manar Welfare Association 28
al-Barbara Relief and Rehabilitation
    Organization 28
al-Omimam Relief and Development Assosiation
    28
Alier, Abel 197
American Red Cross 56
Amnesty International 220
Analytical approaches: administrative dilemmas
    approach, 54; functionalist approach 57;
    global third sector 22; international social
    system approach 25, 64, 75-80; national-style
    approach 59, 60, 62, 63, 66, 75
Anya Nya 199
Armauer Hansen Institute 92
Asian Development Bank 27
Asociacíon para el Desarrollo de los Pueblos 66
    Asociacíon de Mujeres Frente à la
    Problematica Nacional 67
Association of Women's Clubs 29
Augusto C. Sandino Foundation 67
Australia 49
Austria 49

Bangladesh Northern Evangelical Lutheran
    Church 27
Bangladesh: classification of NGOs 27; code of
    conduct 159; Directory of NGOs 38; donor
    dependency 49, 72, 214; eligible for support
    77; evaluations of NGO activities 89; Foreign
    Donations (Volunatry agencies) Registration
    Ordinance 72; legal procedures 14; NGO
    Affairs Bureau 184, 185; Norwegian NGO
    support 100, 120-3; number of NGOs in aid
    49; Private Voluntary Development
    Organizations 16-17; proliferation of NGOs
    in aid 49, 72; registered non-governmental

organizations 22; state-NGO relations 183-
    188; Western pressure 127
Bani Shangoul Relief and Rehabilitation
    Association 28
BBC 52, 70, 91
Belgium 49
Blair, Tony 171
BRAC, Bangladesh 72, 83,138, 139, 150, 151,
    158, 185,186, 188
Brazil 22, 131

Canada 49, 90, 92
CARE 27, 47, 50, 56, 61
CARITAS 185
Caritas-Nicaragua 66
Catholic Church, Nicaragua 22, 73
Catholic Relief Service 56
Catholic Development Commission 29, 68
Central Evaluation Unit of the United Nations
    13
Centro de Educacíon y Promocíon Agraria 66
Centro Antonio Valdievieso 67
Chile 22, 131
China 44, 58
Christian Aid 93, 154, 156
Christian Relief Association 71
Christian Care 29, 68
Christian Committee in Solidarity with the
    People of Nicaragua 67
Christian Relief and Development Association
    28, 38
CIDA, Canada 69, 89
cvil society: activists 97; definitions 167-73; in
    Southern Sudan 189-96; in Bangladesh 183-
    88; in donor policies 179-83
Clinton, Hillary 171
communitarism 171ff
Consejo de Islesias Evangelicas Pro-Alianza
    Denominacional 20, 66
Cuba 113

243